U0146113

The Governance of China

I

XI JINPING

The Governance of China

I

FOREIGN LANGUAGES PRESS

First Edition 2014

Second Edition 2018

Sixth Printing 2019

ISBN 978-7-119-11394-4

© Foreign Languages Press Co. Ltd, Beijing, China, 2018

Published by Foreign Languages Press Co. Ltd

24 Baiwanzhuang Road, Beijing 100037, China

http://www.flp.com.cn

Email: flp@CIPG.org.cn

Distributed by China International Book Trading Corporation

35 Chegongzhuang Xilu, Beijing 100044, China

P.O. Box 399, Beijing, China

Printed in the People's Republic of China

Publisher's Note to the Second Edition

At the 19th National Congress, the Communist Party of China (CPC) recognized Xi Jinping Thought on Socialism with Chinese Characteristics for a New Era as the theoretical guidance that it will adhere to for a long period of time. This step forward provides a clear guide to action: first, in the decisive stage of completing a moderately prosperous society in all respects, second, on a new journey to fully build a modern socialist China, and third, in realizing the Chinese Dream of national rejuvenation. Xi Jinping is the principal proponent of this Thought.

Xi Jinping: The Governance of China was published in September 2014. It has been distributed in China and abroad in Chinese, English, French, Russian, Arabic, Spanish, Portuguese, German, Japanese, and many other languages. The book attracted widespread attention, and was highly acclaimed by readers. It has played a significant role in helping officials and the general public to study and understand Xi Jinping Thought on Socialism with Chinese Characteristics for a New Era. It is an important work that helps the international community to better understand China and the CPC. After the 19th CPC National Congress, a second volume of *Xi Jinping: The Governance of China* was published in November 2017, to help Chinese and foreign readers gain a systematic appreciation of the depth and innovative qualities of Xi Jinping Thought on Socialism with Chinese Characteristics for a New Era.

The two volumes are an integrated whole when studying Xi Jinping Thought on Socialism with Chinese Characteristics for a New Era. They present the developments and major contents of the Thought; record how the CPC Central Committee, with Xi Jinping as the core, has united and led the whole Party and the whole nation in developing socialism with Chinese characteristics in the new era; and embody the Chinese wisdom and Chinese solutions that the CPC has contributed to building a community of shared future for mankind and promoting peace and development. They will be an authoritative source through which readers can learn about Xi Jinping Thought on Socialism with Chinese Characteristics for a New Era and about the guiding principles of the 19th CPC National Congress.

This volume is thus republished.

January 2018

Publisher's Note

Since the 18th National Congress of the Communist Party of China (CPC) held in November 2012, the new central leadership with Xi Jinping as general secretary has led the whole Party and the people of China in confronting the problems and challenges they face: to drive reform and opening up to a deeper level, to modernize the national governance system, and to marshal their enormous strength behind the Chinese Dream of the great rejuvenation of the Chinese nation. Under the leadership of the CPC, the country is striving to build a bright future for socialism with Chinese characteristics.

China is attracting growing attention worldwide. The world wants to know what changes are in progress in China, and what impact they will have on the rest of the world.

As general secretary of the CPC Central Committee and president of the People's Republic of China, Xi Jinping has delivered many speeches on a broad range of issues. He has offered his thoughts, views and judgments, and answered a series of important theoretical and practical questions about the Party and the country in these changing times. His speeches embody the philosophy of the new central leadership.

To respond to rising international interest and to enhance the rest of the world's understanding of the Chinese government's philosophy and its domestic and foreign policies, the State Council Information Office, the Party Literature Research Office of the CPC Central Committee and the China International Publishing Group have worked together to produce this book – *The Governance of China*.

The book is a compilation of Xi Jinping's major works from November 15, 2012 to June 13, 2014. It includes speeches, talks, interviews, instructions, and correspondence. The 79 pieces are arranged in 18 chapters, and notes are added to help readers understand China's social system, history and culture.

The book also contains 45 pictures of Xi Jinping at work and in daily life, with focus on the period since the 18th CPC National Congress in 2012.

June 2014

CONTENTS

Socialism with Chinese Characteristics

The Chinese Dream

All-Round and Deeper-Level Reform

Economic Development

Rule of Law

Culturally Advanced China

Peaceful Development

New Model of Major-Country Relations

Neighborhood Diplomacy

Cooperation with Developing Countries

Multilateral Relations

Close Ties with the People

Combat Corruption

The CPC Leadership

Appendix

Index

This photo was taken in 1972 when he came back to Beijing to see his parents from a village in Shaanxi Province where he was working as an "educated youth."

This photo was taken in 1977 when he was a student at Tsinghua University (right).

This photo was taken in 1979 when he was serving at the General Office of the Central Military Commission.

In 1983, Xi Jinping, as Party secretary of Zhengding County, Hebei Province, set a table in the street to collect opinions of local residents.

This photo was taken during an overseas visit when he was deputy mayor of Xiamen City, Fujian Province.

Working together with locals during an inspection tour in 1989 when he was secretary of Ningde Prefectural Party Committee, Fujian Province.

Receiving people on the joint open day for officials of Fuzhou City and Taijiang District, August 1993. Xi Jinping was then secretary of Fuzhou Municipal Party Committee, Fujian Province.

Joining a team to reinforce the dyke to prevent flooding in the lower reaches of the Minjiang River in Minhou County, December 1995. He was then secretary of Fuzhou Municipal Party Committee, Fujian Province, and deputy secretary of Fujian Provincial Party Committee.

While visiting the Pingdu Township Nursing Home, Qingyuan County, Zhejiang Province, January 2007, he cooked for the elderly. He was then secretary of Zhejiang Provincial Party Committee.

Chatting with hearing-impaired children at Qiyin School in Minhang District, Shanghai, September 2007. He was then secretary of Shanghai Municipal Party Committee.

Visiting Tang Zhaowei and his family, who suffered a loss in a catastrophic snowstorm which hit the Dong ethnic people villages in Tongren Prefecture, Guizhou Province, January 2008.

With some of the American friends he made 27 years earlier, on a revisit to the State of Iowa, February 2012.

With his wife, Peng Liyuan, September 1989.

Cycling with his daughter Mingze in Fuzhou City, Fujian Province.

With his wife, daughter and father, Xi Zhongxun.

Taking a stroll with his mother, Qi Xin.

Socialism with Chinese Characteristics

The People's Wish for a Good Life
Is Our Goal*

November 15, 2012

Friends from the news media have extensively covered the 18th National Congress of the Communist Party of China (CPC), conveying to the world many voices from China. On behalf of the Secretariat of the Congress, I wish to express our sincere thanks to you.

We have just held the First Plenary Session of the 18th CPC Central Committee, and elected a new central leadership. I was elected general secretary of the Central Committee. On behalf of the members of the newly-elected leadership, I wish to express our thanks to all other members of the Party for their trust in us. We will do our utmost to be trustworthy and fulfill our mission.

We are deeply encouraged by both the trust from the Party members and the great expectations from the people of all ethnic groups in China, and we are keenly aware that this is also our important responsibility.

We are taking on this important responsibility for the nation. Ours is a great nation. Throughout 5,000 years of development, the Chinese nation has made a significant contribution to the progress of human civilization. Since the advent of modern times, our nation has gone through untold tribulations and faced its greatest perils. Countless people with lofty ideals rose up for the rejuvenation of the Chinese nation, but each time they failed. After it was founded in 1921 the CPC rallied and led the Chinese people in making great sacrifices, forging ahead against all odds, and transforming poor and backward

---

* Part of the speech at the press conference by members of the Standing Committee of the Political Bureau of the 18th CPC Central Committee.

China into an increasingly prosperous and strong nation, thus opening completely new horizons for national rejuvenation.

Our responsibility is to rally and lead the entire Party and the people of all China's ethnic groups in taking on this task and continuing to pursue the goal of the rejuvenation of the Chinese nation, so that China can stand firmer and stronger among the world's nations, and make a new and greater contribution to mankind.

We are taking on this important responsibility for the people. Our people are a great people. During the long history the Chinese people have worked with diligence, bravery and wisdom, creating a beautiful homeland where all ethnic groups live in harmony and developing a great and dynamic culture. Our people have an ardent love for life. They want to have better education, more stable jobs, more income, reliable social security, better medical and health care, improved housing conditions and a beautiful environment. They hope that their children will have sound growth, good jobs and more enjoyable lives. The people's wish for a happy life is our mission. A happy life comes from hard work. Our responsibility is to bring together and lead the whole Party and the people of all ethnic groups to free their minds, carry out reform and opening up, further unfetter and develop the productive forces, solve the people's problems in work and life, and resolutely pursue common prosperity.

We are taking on this important responsibility for the Party. Dedicated to serving the people, our Party has led them in making remarkable achievements, which we have every reason to be proud of. Nevertheless, we should never be complacent and rest on our laurels. In the new circumstances our Party faces many severe challenges as well as many pressing issues within the Party that need to be addressed, particularly corruption, being divorced from the people, and being satisfied merely with going through formalities and bureaucracy on the part of some Party officials. We must make every effort to solve such problems. The whole Party must stay on full alert. "A good blacksmith forges good tools." Our responsibility is to work with all Party members to uphold the principle that the Party should supervise its own conduct and run itself with strict discipline, effectively solve major problems within the Party, improve its work style, and maintain close ties with the people. By so doing, our Party will surely remain as the core of the leadership in advancing socialism with Chinese characteristics.

The people are the creators of history. They are the real heroes and the source of our strength. We are fully aware that the capability of any individual is limited, but as long as we unite as one like a fortress, there is no difficulty we cannot overcome. One can only work for a limited period of time, but there is no limit to serving the people with dedication. Our responsibility is weightier than mountains, our task arduous, and the road ahead long. We must always bear in mind what the people think and share weal and woe with them, and we must work together with them diligently for the public good and for the expectations of history and of the people.

China needs to learn more about the rest of the world, and the outside world needs to learn more about China. I hope our friends from the press will continue your efforts for mutual understanding between China and the rest of the world.

Study, Disseminate and Implement the Guiding Principles of the 18th CPC National Congress[*]

November 17, 2012

The political report to the 18th National Congress of the CPC has charted a grand blueprint for bringing about a moderately prosperous society in all respects,[2] accelerating socialist modernization, and achieving new victories for socialism with Chinese characteristics in the new historic circumstances. It is a political proclamation and action plan with which our Party will rally and lead the Chinese people of all ethnic groups in marching along the path of Chinese socialism and complete the building of a moderately prosperous society in all respects. It guides the work of the current central leadership. The CPC Central Committee has issued a notice on conscientiously studying, disseminating and implementing the guiding principles of the 18th National Congress, and Party committees at all levels should strictly comply with the notice.

It was emphasized at the 18th National Congress that we should uphold socialism with Chinese characteristics, that the socialist system with Chinese characteristics is the fundamental accomplishment made by the Party and the people during the arduous struggle over the past 90 years, and that we must cherish what has been accomplished and never deviate from it but rather continue to enrich it. The Congress has called on the whole Party to explore and master the laws of socialism with Chinese characteristics, ensure that the Party is always

---

* Speech at the first group study session[1] of the Political Bureau of the 18th CPC Central Committee which Xi presided over.

full of vigor and that China never lacks the driving force for development, and that we must strive for a bright future for developing China's socialism. In fact, adhering to and developing socialism with Chinese characteristics was the theme of the political report to the 18th National Congress. We must always stick to this theme, continue to develop socialism with Chinese characteristics, and work hard to reach the goal. This will enable us to study, understand and implement the guiding principles of the 18th National Congress more thoroughly, completely and conscientiously.

Why have I emphasized this? Because only socialism can save China, and only Chinese socialism can lead our country to development – a fact that has been fully proved through the long-term practice of the Party and the state. Only by upholding socialism with Chinese characteristics can we bring together and lead the whole Party, the whole nation and the people of all ethnic groups in realizing a moderately prosperous society by the centenary of the CPC in 2021 and in turning China into a prosperous, democratic, culturally advanced and harmonious modern socialist country by the centenary of the People's Republic of China in 2049, so as to ensure the people greater happiness and the nation a brighter future.

To study, disseminate and implement the guiding principles of the 18th National Congress with emphasis on adhering to and developing socialism with Chinese characteristics, in my opinion, it is important to pay particular attention to the following areas when applying theory to practice:

First, we must understand that socialism with Chinese characteristics is a fundamental accomplishment made by the Party and the people during long-term practice. China's socialist system was pioneered in the new era of reform and opening up, and it is an outcome of the Party's painstaking efforts. It was accomplished by the whole Party and whole people, under several generations of the Party's central collective leadership, through numerous trials and tenacious efforts at all costs. Relying closely on the people, our Party lowered the curtain, once and for all, on a poor and weak country that had suffered from both domestic turmoil and foreign aggression since the advent of modern times, and made an epic move towards the steady growth, development and renewal of the Chinese nation. It has thus enabled China, a country with a civilization of over 5,000 years, to stand firm among the nations of the world.

We must always remember the historic contribution made by the Party's three generations of central collective leadership and the Party Central Committee with Comrade Hu Jintao[3] as general secretary to the development of socialism with Chinese characteristics. The first generation of the central collective leadership with Mao Zedong[4] as the core provided invaluable experience as well as the theoretical and material basis for the great initiative of building socialism with Chinese characteristics in the new historic period. The second generation with Deng Xiaoping[5] as the core started the building of socialism with Chinese characteristics. The third generation with Jiang Zemin[6] as the core advanced socialism with Chinese characteristics into the 21st century, followed by Hu Jintao as general secretary of the Central Committee who adhered to and developed socialism with Chinese characteristics from a new historic starting point. It goes without saying that socialism with Chinese characteristics encapsulates the ideals and explorations of generations of Chinese Communists, embodies the aspirations of countless patriots and revolutionary martyrs, and crystallizes the struggles and sacrifices of the myriads of the Chinese people. It is a natural choice for the development of Chinese society in modern times, and it is the only way to bring about the country's development and stability.

Facts prove that Chinese socialism is a banner of unity, endeavor and victory for the CPC and the Chinese people as a whole. We must always uphold socialism with Chinese characteristics and firmly adhere to and develop Chinese socialism in order to bring about a moderately prosperous society in all respects, accelerate socialist modernization and achieve the great renewal of the Chinese nation. This is the very reason why the 18th National Congress has called on the whole Party to have full confidence in the path, theory and system of Chinese socialism.

Second, we must thoroughly understand that socialism with Chinese characteristics consists of a path, theory and system. The 18th National Congress expounded on the scientific meaning of the path, theory and system of socialism with Chinese characteristics, and the relationships between the three. The Congress stressed that the path of socialism with Chinese characteristics is a way to reach the goal, the theory offers a guide to action, and the system provides a fundamental guarantee. All three serve the great cause of building Chinese socialism. This is the most salient feature of socialism with Chinese characteristics.

This conclusion reveals that socialism with Chinese characteristics incorporates practice, theory and system. It synthesizes successful experience in practice into theories, uses these correct theories to guide new practices and incorporates effective principles and policies into Party and national systems. That is why socialism with Chinese characteristics is special – in its path, theory and system; in the intrinsic interaction between the way of realizing the goal, guide to action and fundamental guarantee; and in that all three serve the great practice of building Chinese socialism. In present-day China, adhering to and developing socialism with Chinese characteristics means upholding socialism in its true sense.

The path of Chinese socialism is the only way to achieve China's socialist modernization and create a better life. This path takes economic development as the central task, and brings along economic, political, cultural, social, ecological and other forms of progress. It adheres to both the Four Cardinal Principles[7] and the reform and opening-up policy. It entails further releasing and developing the productive forces, and achieving prosperity for all and the well-rounded development of everyone.

The theory of socialism with Chinese characteristics is the latest achievement in adapting Marxism[8] to China's conditions. It incorporates Deng Xiaoping Theory[9], the important thought of the Three

Represents[10] and the Scientific Outlook on Development[11]. It has inherited, continued and creatively developed Marxism-Leninism[12] and Mao Zedong Thought[13]. We should not abandon Marxism-Leninism and Mao Zedong Thought; otherwise, we would be deprived of our foundation. Moreover, we must focus our work on the practical problems in reform, opening up and modernization, and on our various endeavors, with a view to the application of Marxist theory, theoretical thinking on practical issues, and initiation of new practice for development. In contemporary China upholding the theory of socialism with Chinese characteristics means upholding Marxism in its true sense.

The socialist system with Chinese characteristics integrates the fundamental political system[14], the basic political systems[15], the basic economic system[16] and other systems and mechanisms. It combines national and local democratic systems, the Party's leadership, the position of the people as masters of the country, and law-based governance. This system conforms to the national conditions in China, showcases the special traits and strengths of socialism with Chinese characteristics, and provides a fundamental systemic guarantee for China's development.

The socialist system with Chinese characteristics is unique and effective. However, we should be aware that it is not perfect or fully functioning. The Chinese socialist system needs to improve to keep in step with the development of the socialist cause with Chinese characteristics. During his inspection tour of southern China in 1992 Deng Xiaoping pointed out, "It will probably take another thirty years for us to develop a more mature and well-defined system in every field."[17] It was emphasized at the 18th National Congress that it is imperative to give top priority to the building of systems while giving full play to the superiority of the socialist political system in China. We must improve current systems and promote institutional innovation with theoretical innovation based on practice. We must proceed from reality, formulate new systems in a timely fashion, and put in place a well-developed, systematically and rationally regulated, and effective framework of systems to ensure that all systems and institutions are working properly and functioning well, and thereby provide a more effective institutional guarantee for new victories.

Third, we must have an in-depth understanding of the basic foundation, overall planning and main mandate of building socialism with Chinese characteristics. It was emphasized at the 18th National Congress that the basic foundation for building socialism with Chinese characteristics is that China is in the primary stage of socialism[18], that its overall plan is to seek economic, political, cultural, social, and ecological progress, and that its main objective is to achieve socialist modernization and rejuvenation of the Chinese nation. The foundation, plan and objective are succinctly and pointedly defined. A better understanding and grasp of these new definitions will help us get to the essence and essentials of socialism with Chinese characteristics.

It is important to stress the basic foundation of China being in the primary stage of socialism. This is the paramount reality and the most important national condition in contemporary China. We must always bear it in mind and promote reform and development in all respects on the basis of this very reality. It is imperative not only in accelerating the economy, but also in speeding up political, cultural, social and ecological development; not only when our economy was small, but also when it is large; and not only when planning long-term development, but also during daily work. The Party's basic line for the primary stage of socialism is the lifeline of the Party and the state. In practice we must firmly adhere to "one central task, two basic points,"[19] neither deviating from the "one central task" nor neglecting the "two basic points." We must adopt a holistic approach to the realization of the common ideal of building Chinese socialism and the long-term goal of realizing communism, stand firm against various erroneous views aimed at abandoning socialism, and rectify all erroneous and unrealistic mindsets, policies and measures that go beyond the current primary stage of socialism. This will keep us from being either self-abased or over-confident, and enable us to achieve new victories for China's socialism.

We give top priority to overall planning, simply because we must achieve all-round development of socialism with Chinese characteristics. The most important thing for our Party is to govern the country well and rejuvenate the nation. The Party must always represent the requirements for developing the advanced productive forces. We must focus on economic development and promote coordinated political, cultural, social and ecological development on the basis of economic growth. As China steps forward socially and economically, it has become increasingly significant to pursue ecological progress. The 18th National Congress included ecological progress in its overall plan for building Chinese socialism, thus highlighting the strategic importance of ecological progress and making it possible to incorporate ecological efforts into those for economic, political, cultural and social progress in all respects and throughout the whole process. This is an important practical and theoretical achievement of our Party in our understanding of the law of building socialism. We must carry out the overall plan, pursue coordinated development in all areas of our modernization drive, and promote harmony between the relationships of production and the productive forces, and between the superstructure and the economic base.

We pay close attention to the main objective because the CPC has shouldered the historic mission of rejuvenating the Chinese nation ever since its founding. The very purpose of the Party in leading the Chinese people in revolution, development and reform is to make the people prosperous and the country strong, and rejuvenate the Chinese nation. According to the three-step strategic plan for modernization[20], it is the goal of our Party and state to build a prosperous, strong, democratic, culturally advanced and harmonious modern socialist country during the primary stage of socialism. The historic mission of our Party, the fundamental purpose of reform and opening up, and the goal of our country all converge in the main objective and are also derived from it. This is an objective for which we should never relax our efforts, nor should our future generations.

During different historical periods our Party has always been able to put forth inspirational goals in line with the will of the people and the needs of our development, and lead the people in achieving those goals. In response to both domestic and international changes and new economic and social developments in China, and living up to the new expectations of the people, the 18th National Congress revised the goal of building a moderately prosperous society in all respects, with a clearer policy guidance, greater inclination towards development problems, and better responses to the people's expectations. The updated goal is coherent with those set at the Party's 16th and 17th national congresses, and in line with the overall plan for the cause of socialism with Chinese characteristics. The whole Party and the country must act with one mind, work in a down-to-earth manner, be creative and pioneering, and forge ahead in realizing a moderately prosperous society in all respects, and continuing reform and opening up in all areas – the two goals set at the 18th National Congress.

Fourth, we must have a thorough knowledge of the basic requirements for achieving new victories for Chinese socialism, which the 18th National Congress identified and which we must fulfill with firm determination in the new historic circumstances. These requirements are based on six decades of our experience in building socialism, especially socialism with Chinese characteristics, and on the Party's basic theories, lines, platforms and experience. They are the essentials that reflect the laws of governance by the CPC, laws of building socialism, and laws of the development of human society. They are testimony to the new understanding by our Party of the laws of Chinese socialism.

The basic requirements set forth at the 18th National Congress answer the question of how to achieve new victories for Chinese socialism on the new historic journey. Socialism with Chinese characteristics is a cause for the people in their hundreds of millions – this is why we must give full play to the role of the people as the masters of the country. Freeing and developing the productive forces is a fundamental task of Chinese socialism – this is why we must focus on economic development and pursue a people-oriented, all-round,

coordinated, proper and sustainable development. Reform and opening up is the only way leading to Chinese socialism – this is why we
must always apply the spirit of reform and innovation to all aspects
of governance, and continuously promote the self-improvement
and development of China's socialist system. Fairness and justice are
inherent requirements of Chinese socialism – this is why we must,
relying on the concerted efforts of all the Chinese people and based
on economic and social development, double our efforts to develop institutions that are vital to ensuring social fairness and justice,
and establish in due course a system for guaranteeing social equity.
Common prosperity is the fundamental principle of Chinese socialism – this is why we must ensure that all the people share the fruits of
development in a fair way, and move steadily towards common prosperity. Social harmony is an inherent attribute of Chinese socialism
– this is why we must rally all the forces that can be rallied, maximize
the factors for harmony, stimulate the creative vitality of society, and
ensure that the people lead a happy, stable life and the country enjoys
enduring peace. Peaceful development is an inevitable prerequisite of
Chinese socialism – this is why we must pursue development through
opening up and cooperation to benefit all, expand areas of common
interests with all others and build a harmonious world of enduring
peace and common prosperity together with other countries. The
CPC is the core leadership for the cause of Chinese socialism – this is
why we must enhance and improve the Party's leadership and give full
play to its leading and core role in exercising overall leadership and
coordinating the efforts of all.

The basic requirements set forth at the 18th National Congress
positively responded to the need of addressing pressing issues in
China's economic and social development, the challenges in the difficult in-depth reforms and in speeding up the transformation of the
growth model, and the sensitive issues that officials and the general
public are especially concerned about. They have also given us good
guidance on how to pursue reform, development and stability, handle
national defense and domestic and foreign affairs, and run the Party, the

country and the military in this decisive stage at which China is striving to realize a moderately prosperous society in all respects. These basic requirements cover many areas – the productive forces and relations of production, the economic base and the superstructure, the great cause of Chinese socialism and the new undertaking of Party building, and a holistic approach to both the domestic and international situations. The 18th National Congress stuck close to and fully reflected these basic requirements in making plans and arrangements for actions in various areas. If we truly meet all the basic requirements we will be able to pool our strength more effectively, overcome all difficulties, pursue balanced, proper and coordinated development, promote social harmony and improve our people's lives. Then we can complete the glorious and arduous tasks bestowed by the times.

Fifth, we must fully understand why we need to ensure that the CPC is always the firm core leadership guiding the cause of Chinese socialism. It was emphasized at the 18th National Congress that the CPC shoulders the great responsibility for bringing together and leading the people in building a moderately prosperous society in all respects, in advancing socialist modernization and in achieving the great renewal of the Chinese nation. The Party's strength and its close ties with the people have ensured China prosperity and stability, and the Chinese people peace and happiness. The new developments, the need for progress in our cause and the people's expectations have all made it imperative for us to carry out the great new undertaking of Party building in the spirit of reform and innovation, and upgrade our efforts in all respects to a new level. To run the country well we must first run the Party well, and to run the Party well we must run it strictly. For this purpose, the 18th National Congress set forth the overall requirements for systematic Party building in the new circumstances, and spelled out the specific tasks involved. The whole Party must learn and understand them, and implement them to the letter.

The overall requirements for Party building set forth at the 18th National Congress are derived from the need to inherit and develop the fundamentals that have shored up the advanced nature of our

Party, a Marxist party, for over 90 years. They respond to changes in the world, in our country and within our Party. Over the years we have been pressing ahead with the new task of Party building in all respects. The Party has enhanced its governing capabilities, preserved and improved its pioneering nature and purity, and strengthened and improved its leadership. However, in view of the need to manage changes in domestic and international conditions, and to accomplish its historic mission, there is still considerable room for our Party to improve its art of leadership, governing capacity and organization, and the quality, competence, and practices of its members and officials. Party building in the new circumstances, in particular, faces "four tests"[21] and "four risks,"[22] which makes it more difficult and pressing to ensure that the Party properly manages its own affairs and strictly disciplines itself. All Party members must heighten their sense of urgency and responsibility, focus on the overall requirements of Party building, steadily improve the Party's art of leadership and governance, and enhance its ability to resist corruption, prevent degeneration and ward off corruption risks, so that our Party may always remain ahead of the times in its historic journey accompanied by profound changes worldwide, always act as the backbone of the Chinese people in its historic response to domestic and international risks and tests of all kinds, and always be the strong core leadership in the historic journey to adhere to and develop Chinese socialism.

It has always been the foundation for the lifeline and pursuit of all Communists to have full confidence in ideals and firm faith in communism. Belief in Marxism and faith in socialism and communism are the political soul of Communists, enabling them to withstand all tests. Put figuratively, the ideals and convictions of Communists are the marrow of their faith. Without, or with weak, ideals or convictions, they would be deprived of their marrow and suffer from "lack of backbone." This has been proved true by the cases of some Party members and officials who acted improperly due to lack of ideals and confused faith. All Party members, in accordance with the plans set at the 18th National Congress, must earnestly study and implement the system of socialist theories with Chinese characteristics, especially the Scientific Outlook on Development, reflect Party awareness in their actions, observe moral standards, set good examples and work hard for the common goal of realizing Chinese socialism.

Maintaining close ties between the Party and the people and between officials and individuals has always been the basis of our success. Facts prove that the future and destiny of a political party and government depend on popular support. If we stray from the people and lose their support we will end up in failure. We must bear in mind the new characteristics and requirements for public work in the new circumstances. We must organize our people, communicate with them, educate them, serve them, learn from them, and subject ourselves to their oversight. We should always be part of the people, work for their interests, and maintain close ties and share good and bad times with them. We should draw wisdom and strength from their great practice; deliver more concrete services to the people that meet their needs, relieve their burdens and benefit their lives; and put a stop to all acts that prejudice their interests. The 18th National Congress put forward the idea of carrying out an extensive program throughout the Party to heighten awareness of and implement the Party's mass line[23], with the focus on serving the people and staying pragmatic and honest. The CPC Central Committee will make specific arrangements for this program, and Party committees at all levels should implement them, solve pressing problems of major concern to the people and make the program a success.

It has always been the CPC's consistent and clear political position to combat corruption, promote political integrity and keep the Party healthy. Building a fine Party culture and a corruption-free Party is a major political issue of great concern to the people. "Worms can only grow in something rotten."[24] In recent years, long-pent-up problems in some countries have led to resentment among the people, unrest in society and the downfall of governments, with corruption being a major culprit. Facts prove that if corruption is allowed to spread, it will eventually lead to the destruction of a party and the fall of a government. We must keep up our vigilance. Serious violations of Party discipline and state laws that have occurred inside our Party during the past few years are of a vile nature and have produced shockingly harmful political consequences. Party committees at all levels must firmly oppose and combat corruption, and prevent and crack down on it more effectively to ensure that all officials are honest and upright, governments clean and incorruptible, and Communists of political integrity. Officials at all levels, especially high-ranking officials, must conscientiously observe the code of conduct. They should exercise strict self-discipline, strengthen education and restrain their family and immediate staff. It is absolutely impermissible to abuse one's power for personal gain or to seek privileges. All violations of Party discipline and state laws must be punished without exception, and we shall not be soft in dealing with them.

The 18th National Congress pointed out that developing Chinese socialism is a long-term arduous task of historic importance, and that we must be prepared for a great struggle with many new historic features. All Party members must make strenuous efforts with firm conviction and unswervingly develop socialism with Chinese characteristics in a pioneering spirit. We must keep improving the practice and theory of Chinese socialism in line with the national features in a timely fashion. We must bring together and lead the Chinese people of all ethnic groups in accomplishing goals and tasks for a moderately prosperous society in all respects. We must continue to work for the three historic missions of modernization, reunification of the motherland, and world peace and the common development of all nations. These are missions of historic importance that have been bestowed on our generation of Communists, and to which we must dedicate all our wisdom and strength.

Notes

[1] The Political Bureau of the CPC Central Committee holds regular study sessions. The sessions are presided over and addressed by the general secretary of the

Central Committee, and attended by all members of the Political Bureau. Leaders of relevant departments, experts and scholars are invited to lecture on economics, political science, history, culture, social affairs, science and technology, military and international affairs.

[2] The 18th National Congress of the CPC put forward the accomplishment of the goal of bringing about a moderately prosperous society in all respects by 2020. The main elements of the goal are healthy and sustainable economic development with both the GDP and per capita income for urban and rural residents doubling those of 2010; expanded people's democracy; significantly improved cultural soft power; substantially improved people's living standards; and major progress in building a resource-conserving and environmentally friendly society.

[3] Hu Jintao, born in 1942, was general secretary of the CPC Central Committee, president of the People's Republic of China, chairman of the Central Military Commission of the CPC, and chairman of the Central Military Commission of the People's Republic of China. He is the principal founder of the Scientific Outlook on Development.

[4] Mao Zedong (1893-1976) was a Marxist, Chinese proletarian revolutionary, military strategist and theorist. He was one of the main founders of the CPC, the Chinese People's Liberation Army and the People's Republic of China, and the leader of the Chinese people. He was also the progenitor of Mao Zedong Thought.

[5] Deng Xiaoping (1904-1997) was a Marxist, Chinese proletarian revolutionary, statesman, military strategist and great diplomat. He was an outstanding leader of the CPC, the Chinese People's Liberation Army and the People's Republic of China. He was the chief architect of China's socialist reform and opening up and modernization drive, and the main founder of Deng Xiaoping Theory.

[6] Jiang Zemin, born in 1926, was general secretary of the CPC Central Committee, president of the People's Republic of China, chairman of the Central Military Commission of the CPC, and chairman of the Central Military Commission of the People's Republic of China. He is the main founder of the important thought of the Three Represents.

[7] The Four Cardinal Principles refer to the principles of adhering to the socialist path, the people's democratic dictatorship, the leadership of the CPC, and Marxism-Leninism and Mao Zedong Thought. The Four Cardinal Principles are the foundation of the state, and the political cornerstone for the survival and development of the Party and the state.

[8] Marxism is a system of theories initiated by Karl Marx and Friedrich Engels, including the scientific worldview, the interpretation of social and historical development, the theory of proletarian revolution, and the theory of building socialism and communism. It is the theoretical basis and guiding thought of the working class and its political party. Initiated in the 1840s, it was the outcome of intensified capitalist

conflicts and growing workers' movements. It has three components, namely, Marxist philosophy, political economics and scientific socialism. In the late 19th century and the early 20th century, when capitalism entered the stage of monopoly which would be imperialism, Vladimir Lenin drew on the experience of the proletarian revolution and socialist construction in Russia, and creatively upgraded Marxism to a new stage – Leninism. Since its founding in 1921 the CPC has solemnly marked its banner with Marxism-Leninism, innovatively applied the basic principles of Marxism-Leninism to the practice of Chinese revolution, socialist construction and reform, enriched and developed Marxism-Leninism, and generated the theoretical fruits of sinicized Marxism – Mao Zedong Thought and the system of theories of Chinese socialism that both carry on Marxism-Leninism and advance with the times.

[9] Deng Xiaoping Theory is an important component of the system of theories of Chinese socialism, and the guiding thought of the CPC. For the first time, Deng Xiaoping Theory systematically answered a series of basic questions concerning the building of socialism in economically and culturally backward China, and the consolidation and development of socialism there. The principal proponent was Deng Xiaoping.

[10] The important thought of the Three Represents is a major component of the system of theories of Chinese socialism, and the guiding thought of the CPC. This theory emphasizes that the CPC must always represent the requirements for developing China's advanced productive forces, the orientation of China's advanced culture, and the fundamental interests of the overwhelming majority of the Chinese people. The principal proponent is Jiang Zemin.

[11] The Scientific Outlook on Development is an important component of the system of theories of Chinese socialism, and the guiding thought of the CPC. It gives top priority to development, puts people first and seeks all-around, balanced and sustainable development with a holistic approach. The principal proponent is Hu Jintao.

[12] See note 8, p. 19.

[13] Mao Zedong Thought has always been the fundamental guiding thought of the CPC. It is a series of theoretical summarizations and conclusions that Chinese Communists represented by Mao Zedong drew from their unique experiences in China's revolution and development in accordance with the basic tenets of Marxism. It includes correct theories, principles and systems of scientific thinking on China's revolution and development which have been attested by facts. It is the crystallization of the collective wisdom of the CPC, and the principal proponent is Mao Zedong.

[14] The fundamental political system refers to the system of people's congresses, which is the organizational form of the political power of the People's Republic of China. According to the system, the people elect deputies to the National People's

Congress (NPC) and local people's congresses that are the organs in which the people exercise state power. The NPC is the highest organ of state power, and has the right to amend the Constitution, enact laws and decide on major issues concerning the country. Local people's congresses at all levels are local organs of state power, which decide on major issues in their localities within the power bestowed on them by the Constitution and laws.

[15] The basic political systems include the system of CPC-led multiparty cooperation and political consultation, the system of regional ethnic autonomy and the system of community-level self-governance. The system of CPC-led multiparty cooperation and political consultation refers to the system of consultation on political matters among the CPC, other political parties and personages with no party affiliation. The system of regional ethnic autonomy refers to the exercise of regional autonomy in areas inhabited by minority ethnic groups in compact communities under unified state leadership, where autonomy is exercised by organs of self-government. The system of community-level self-governance is a form of people's participation in the management of state and social affairs. Neighborhood committees and village committees set up in urban and rural areas, respectively, are the self-governance organizations of the people in their own residential areas.

[16] The basic economic system refers to the economic system in which public ownership is dominant and diverse forms of ownership develop side by side.

[17] Deng Xiaoping: "Excerpts from Talks Given in Wuchang, Shenzhen, Zhuhai and Shanghai," *Selected Works of Deng Xiaoping,* Volume III, Eng. ed., Foreign Languages Press, Beijing, 1994, p. 360.

[18] The primary stage of socialism is a particular historical stage in the building of Chinese socialism. It refers to the historical stage in which China has gradually come out of under-development and will have by and large realized socialist modernization. It will take at least 100 years to take shape from the completion of the socialist transformation of the private ownership of the means of production in the 1950s to the completion of socialist modernization.

[19] "One central task, two basic points" is the main content of the CPC's basic guideline in the primary stage of socialism. The "one central task" refers to economic development, while the "two basic points" are the Four Cardinal Principles and the reform and opening-up policy.

[20] The three-step strategic plan for modernization refers to China's development strategy for realizing initial modernization in three steps. The 13th CPC National Congress in 1987 proposed doubling the 1980 GNP by the end of the 1980s and ensuring that the people would have adequate food and clothing as the first step; doubling the 1990 GNP by the end of the 20th century and ensuring the people a moderately prosperous life as the second step; and increasing the per capita GNP level to that of moderately developed countries, ensuring the people a relatively af-

fluent life, and realizing modernization by and large by the middle of the 21st century as the third step.

[21] The "four tests" refer to the tests of exercising governance, carrying out reform and opening up, developing the market economy and responding to external development.

[22] The "four risks" refer to the risks of inertia, incompetence, being divorced from the people, and corruption and other negative phenomena.

[23] The program to heighten awareness of and implement the Party's mass line has been carried out throughout the CPC since its 18th National Congress in order to maintain the CPC's advanced nature and purity. The program focuses on serving the people and building a clean government. Priorities are given to leading organs, leading groups and leading officials at and above the county level. It aims to enhance education of all Party members in the Marxist mass viewpoint and the Party's mass line, and solve such problems as going through the motions, excessive bureaucracy, self-indulgence, and extravagance that are of grave concern to the people. The campaign was launched in late 2013 and has been unfolded in two sessions from the top down.

[24] Su Shi: *On Xiang Yu and Fan Zeng.* Su Shi (1036-1101), also known as Su Dongpo, was a famed poet, calligrapher and painter in the Song Dynasty (960-1279).

Uphold and Develop Socialism with Chinese Characteristics[*]

January 5, 2013

Which path should we follow? This is the paramount question for the future of the Party and the success of its cause. Socialism with Chinese characteristics is the integration of the theory of scientific socialism[1] and social development theories of Chinese history. Socialism has taken root in China. It reflects the wishes of the people and meets the development needs of the country and the times. It is a sure route to success in building a moderately prosperous society in all respects, in the acceleration of socialist modernization, and in the great renewal of the Chinese nation.

All Party members must follow the guidance of Deng Xiaoping Theory, the important thought of the Three Represents and the Scientific Outlook on Development, be firm in their commitment to socialism with Chinese characteristics and to the Marxist view on development, treat practice as the sole criterion for testing truth, and apply their historic initiative and creativity.

We must be clearly aware what is changing and what remains constant in the international, national and Party situations. Never should we hesitate to blaze new trails, bridge rivers, forge ahead with determination, and audaciously explore new territory. We should have the courage and capability to address pressing issues in our work and remove doubts in people's minds, and come up with solutions. We should drive reform and opening up to a deeper level, make new

---

* Main points of the speech at the seminar of the members and alternate members of the newly-elected Central Committee of the CPC for implementing the guiding principles of the Party's 18th National Congress.

discoveries, create new ideas, achieve new progress, and promote innovation in our theories, practices and systems.

The guiding principles of the Party's 18th National Congress, in essence, boil down to upholding and developing socialism with Chinese characteristics. The year 2013 is the 31st year since Deng Xiaoping put forward the concept of building socialism with Chinese characteristics. He provided for the first time clear systematic answers to several basic questions about how to build, consolidate and develop socialism in China, an economically and culturally underdeveloped country. His answers brought a new perspective to Marxism, opened up new realms, and raised the understanding of socialism to a new scientific level.

Socialism with Chinese characteristics is socialism and nothing else. The basic principles of scientific socialism must not be abandoned; otherwise it is not socialism. What doctrine a country may choose is based on whether it can resolve the historical problems that confront that country. Both history and reality have shown us that only socialism can save China and only socialism with Chinese characteristics can bring development to China. This conclusion is the result of historical exploration, and the choice of the people.

As socialism progresses, our institutions will undoubtedly mature, the strengths of our system will become self-evident, and our development path will assuredly become wider. We must have confidence in our path, our theory and our system. We must be as tenacious as bamboo, as described by Zheng Xie: "In the face of all blows, not bending low, it still stands fast. Whether from east, west, south or north the wind doth blast."[2]

The process by which the people build socialism under the leadership of the Party can be divided into two historical phases – one that preceded the launch of reform and opening up in 1978, and a second that followed on from that event. The two phases – at once related to and distinct from each other – are both pragmatic explorations in building socialism conducted by the people under the leadership of the Party. Chinese socialism was initiated after the launch of reform and opening up and based on more than 20 years of development since the socialist system was established in the 1950s after the People's Republic of China (PRC) was founded. Although the two historical phases are very different in their guiding thoughts, principles, policies, and practical work, they are by no means separated from or opposed to each other. We should neither negate the pre-reform-and-opening-up phase in comparison with the post-reform-and-opening-up phase, nor the converse. We should adhere to the principles of seeking truth from facts and distinguishing the trunk from the branches. We should uphold truth, rectify our errors, draw on practical experience, and learn lessons. This is the foundation which facilitates further advance of the cause of the Party and the people.

Marxism will not remain stagnant. It will certainly keep up with the times, the progress of our practice and the advance of science. Socialism too always advances through practice. Developing Chinese socialism is a great cause. Deng Xiaoping clearly defined some basic thoughts and principles on the subject. The Central Committee headed by Jiang Zemin, and later by Hu Jintao also added some outstanding chapters to it. Now, the job of the Communists of our generation is to continue with this mission.

We must adhere to Marxism and socialism from a developmental perspective. With each step forward we will encounter new situations and unfamiliar problems, we will face greater risks and challenges, and we will be confronted by the unexpected. We must be prepared for adversity and danger, even in times of prosperity and peace.

We should not pretend to know what we do not know. We should try to put what we already know to use, and lose no time in learning what we do not know. We must not be muddle-headed.

Party members, particularly Party officials, should maintain a firm belief in lofty communist ideals, along with the common ideal of building socialism with Chinese characteristics, and pursue them with dedication.

We must be rigorous in implementing the Party's basic lines and programs in the primary stage of socialism, and do all our work well.

Our revolutionary ideals are of the greatest importance. A Party member devoid of ideals lacks an essential quality – as does one who engages in empty talk about lofty ideals without doing anything.

There are objective criteria to measure whether Party members or Party officials have these high communist ideals. Can they stick to the basic principle of serving the people heart and soul? Can they be the first to bear hardship and the last to enjoy comfort? Can they work hard and remain honest and dedicated? And can they make every possible effort and even lay their lives for the sake of their ideals?

Flawed thinking, hedonistic desires, corrupt behavior and passive attitudes – all are at odds with the communist ideals.

Notes

[1] Scientific socialism, also known as scientific communism, refers to the entire thought system of Marxism in a broad sense and to one of the three major components of Marxism in a narrow sense. The latter meaning is commonly used. Founded by Karl Marx and Friedrich Engels in the 1840s, scientific socialism is a science that examines the nature, conditions and general purpose of the proletariat liberation movement. It mainly proposes eliminating private ownership and embracing public ownership, vigorously enhancing productivity, generating abundant social material wealth, implementing planned economy, and getting rid of commercial production and exchanges involving money. It endorses the principle of "to each according to his contribution," and predicts that classes and class distinctions will disappear, the nation state will gradually vanish, and a community of free individuals will come into being.

[2] Zheng Xie: *Bamboos amid Rocks*. Zheng Xie (1693-1765), also known as Zheng Banqiao, was a calligrapher and writer in the Qing Dynasty (1644-1911).

Carry on the Enduring Spirit
of Mao Zedong Thought*

December 26, 2013

The enduring spirit of Mao Zedong Thought refers to the stand, viewpoint and method crystalized in the Thought, which features three basic tenets – seeking truth from facts, the mass line and independence. In the new conditions, we should uphold and apply the enduring spirit of Mao Zedong Thought in building our Party and advancing the great cause of socialism with Chinese characteristics.

As a fundamental tenet of Marxism, seeking truth from facts is a basic requirement for Chinese Communists to understand and transform the world. It is also our Party's basic thinking, working and leading approach. We have upheld and should continue to uphold the principle of proceeding from reality in everything we do, integrating theory with practice, and testing and developing truth in practice.

Mao Zedong once said, "'Facts' are all the things that exist objectively, 'truth' means their internal relations, that is, the laws governing them, and 'to seek' means to study."[1] He also used the metaphor "shooting the arrow at the target," that is, we should shoot the "arrow" of Marxism at the "target" of China's revolution, modernization drive and reform.

To seek truth from facts, we must acquire a deep understanding of a matter as it is, see through the surface into the heart of the matter, and discover the intricate link between matters amidst fragmented phenomena.

---

* Part of the speech at the symposium to commemorate the 120th anniversary of Mao Zedong's birth.

We should follow objective laws on the basis that we recognize the existence of a matter and its development laws. Upholding the principle of seeking truth from facts is not done once and for all. You may succeed by following the principle at a certain place and at a certain time, but that does not mean that you may succeed again by following the principle at another place and at another time. The conclusion or experience drawn at a certain place and at a certain time does not necessarily apply at another place and at another time. We should conscientiously strengthen our conviction in seeking truth from facts and enhance our ability to apply it. We should always bear it in mind and implement it in our work.

As we stand now, seeking truth from facts means that we should clearly understand our basic national condition, that is, our country is still in the primary stage of socialism, and will remain so for a long time to come. When advancing reform and development, and formulating guidelines and policies, we should do everything in line with this basic national condition. Any tendency to pursue quick success regardless of objective conditions and timing should be avoided, and any outdated or complacent ideas and actions which do not conform to reality, or which neglect fundamental changes of reality, should be corrected without exception.

While seeking truth from facts, we should always uphold the truth and correct mistakes for the sake of the people's interest. We should be frank, selfless and fearless, courageously speak out truth based on facts, discover and correct ideological deviations and mistakes in decision-making and work as soon as they arise, and discover and solve all kinds of conflicts and problems when they come up so as to make our thoughts and acts conform to objective laws, the requirement of the times and the wishes of the people.

In seeking truth from facts, we should promote theoretical innovation based on practice. The basic tenets of Marxism are universal truth with eternal ideological value. Nevertheless, the classical Marxist authors did not exhaust truth but blazed a trail to seek and develop truth. Today, new problems will arise while we adhere to and develop socialism with Chinese characteristics, drive reform to a deeper level, and deal effectively with foreseeable and unpredictable difficulties and risks on our way ahead. All these things are crying out for new and appropriate theoretical solutions. We should review the fresh experience gained by the people under the leadership of the Party, constantly adapt Marxism to Chinese conditions and make contemporary Marxism shine brighter in China.

The mass line is the Party's lifeline and fundamental work principle. It is a cherished tradition that enables our Party to maintain its vitality and combat capability. We have always been and will always be obligated to do everything in the interests of the people and rely on their strength, and carry out the principle of "from the people, to the people," translating the Party's policies into the people's conscientious action and implementing the mass line in all government activities.

The mass line in essence encapsulates the basic tenet of Marxism that the people are the creators of history. We must adhere to this principle in order to grasp the basic laws governing the advance of history. We must observe these laws so that we can be invincible. History has time and again proved that the people are the major force behind historical development and social progress. As Mao Zedong said, "Once China's destiny is in the hands of the people, China, like the sun rising in the east, will illuminate every corner of the land with a brilliant flame."[2]

Adhering to the mass line is recognizing that the people are the fundamental force in deciding our future and destiny. The strong foundation keeping the Party invincible lies in our adhering to the people's principal position in the country, and bringing their initiative into full play. Before the people, we are always students. Therefore we must seek advice from them. We must fully respect their wishes, experience, rights and role. We should cherish the power conferred on us by the people and exercise it discreetly, and welcome their supervision. We should rely closely on them to create historic achievements, so as to make the foundation of our Party rock-solid.

Adhering to the mass line means following the fundamental tenet of serving the people wholeheartedly.

"Decrees may be followed if they are in accordance with the aspirations of the people; they may be ineffective if they are against the aspirations of the people."[3] Serving the people wholeheartedly is the fundamental purpose and outcome of all the work of the Party, and a symbol that distinguishes our Party from all other parties. The supreme criterion for all Party actions is that it serves the interests of the great majority of the people. The effectiveness of all our work should ultimately be measured by the real benefits the people have reaped, by the improvement in their lives and by how well their rights and interests are protected. Their expectation for a better life does not allow us to be complacent or slack, but requires us to work harder to enable everyone to share more fruits of development in a fairer way and move steadily towards common prosperity.

Adhering to the mass line means maintaining close ties between the Party and the people. The supreme political advantage of our Party is its close ties with the people, and the biggest danger for a ruling party is for it to become divorced from the people. Mao Zedong said, "We Communists are like seeds, and the people are like the soil. Wherever we go, we must unite with the people, take root and blossom among them."[4] All Party members should bear in mind the concept of people first and the mass line, and put them into practice. We should do our utmost to solve problems within the Party and especially those the people are particularly dissatisfied with, so that our Party can always have their trust and support.

Adhering to the mass line means asking the people to judge our work. "It is the people who know whether a decree is good or not."[5] The future and destiny of any political party is determined by the popular support for it. Popular support is what we draw our strength from. The number of Party members is small compared to that of the people. The grand goal of our Party can never be realized without popular support. It is not up to us to judge our Party's governance capacity or performance; they must and can only be judged by the people, the supreme and ultimate judge of the Party's work. If we are pretentious and divorce ourselves from the people or put ourselves above them, we will surely be abandoned by them. This is the case for any party, and is an iron law which admits of no exception.

Independence is an inevitable conclusion drawn by our Party from China's reality, after going through the stages of revolution, development and reform by relying on the strength of the Party and the people. We should always rely on ourselves when seeking our national development and defending our national pride and confidence, and resolutely follow our own road now and in the future as we did in the past.

Independence is a fine tradition of the Chinese nation and an essential principle for building the Party and the PRC. The reality and the mission to carry out revolution and development in China, an Eastern country with a large population and backward economy, have determined that we have no other choice but to follow our own path.

Boasting a vast land of 9.6 million sq km, a rich cultural heritage and a strong bond among the 1.3 billion Chinese people, we are resolved to go our own way. We have a big stage to display our advantages on, a long and rich history to draw benefit from, and a powerful impetus to push us ahead. We Chinese people – every single one of us – should draw confidence from this.

Adhering to independence means that Chinese affairs must be dealt with and decided by the Chinese people themselves. There is no such thing in the world as a development model that can be applied universally, nor is there any development path that remains carved in stone. The diversity of historical conditions determines the diversity of the development paths chosen by various countries. In the whole history of mankind, no nation or state has ever been able to rise to power and rejuvenate itself by relying solely on external forces or blindly following others; doing so inevitably leads to failure or subservience.

Our Party has always independently explored its own development path while leading revolution, development and reform. This spirit of independent exploration and practice, and the confidence and determination to stick to its own road is the bedrock of all the theories and practice of our Party, and the guarantee that our Party and people will go from victory to victory.

Adhering to independence means that we will firmly take the socialist path with Chinese characteristics. We will not take the old path of a rigid closed-door policy, nor an erroneous path by abandoning socialism. We should enhance our political faith and our confidence in the path, theories and systems of Chinese socialism. We should expand this path, enrich these theories and improve these systems through comprehensive reform and in response to changing conditions and tasks. We should modestly draw on the achievements of all other cultures, but never forget our own origin. We must not blindly copy the development models of other countries nor accept their dictation.

Adhering to independence requires us to uphold our independent foreign policy of peace, and follow the path of peaceful development. We should hold high the banner of peace, development, cooperation and benefit for all, maintain friendly relations with other countries on the basis of the Five Principles of Peaceful Coexistence[6], conduct exchanges and cooperation with other countries on the basis of equality and mutual benefit, staunchly safeguard world peace, and promote common development. We should take our positions and make our policies on issues on their own merits, uphold fairness and justice, respect the right of each people in deciding its own development path independently, and never force our will upon others nor allow anyone to impose theirs upon us. We stand for peaceful resolutions to international disputes, oppose all forms of hegemony and power politics, and never seek hegemonism nor engage in expansion. We will resolutely defend our sovereignty, security and development interests. No country should assume that we will trade away our core interests, nor will we accept anything that harms our sovereignty, security or development interests.

Notes

[1] Mao Zedong: "Reform Our Study," *Selected Works of Mao Zedong*, Vol. III, Eng. ed., Foreign Languages Press, Beijing, 1965, p. 22.

[2] Mao Zedong: "Address to the Preparatory Meeting of the New Political Consultative Conference," *Selected Works of Mao Zedong*, Vol. IV, Eng. ed., Foreign Languages Press, Beijing, 1961, p. 408.

[3] *Guan Zi*, compiled by Liu Xiang, is a collection of writings by scholars of the Warring States Period (475-221 BC) in the name of Guan Zhong. Liu Xiang (c. 77-6 BC) was a Confucian scholar, bibliographer, and man of letters of the Western Han Dynasty (206 BC-AD 25). Guan Zhong (?-645 BC), also known as Guan Zi, was a statesman of the State of Qi in the early Spring and Autumn Period (770-476 BC).

[4] Mao Zedong: "On the Chongqing Negotiations," *Selected Works of Mao Zedong*, Vol. IV, Eng. ed., Foreign Languages Press, Beijing, 1961, p. 58.

[5] Wang Chong: *Discourses Weighed in the Balance* (*Lun Heng*), which drew extensively on Confucianism, Taoism and Mohism, and the achievements in the natural sciences in the Han Dynasty (206 BC-AD 220), and criticized the theology and divination popular in his time. Wang Chong (27-c. 97) was a philosopher, thinker and literary critic in the Eastern Han Dynasty (25-220).

[6] The Five Principles of Peaceful Coexistence are the principles of mutual respect for each other's territorial integrity and sovereignty, mutual non-aggression, mutual non-interference in each other's internal affairs, equality and cooperation for mutual benefit, and peaceful coexistence. From December 1953 to April 1954 delegates of the Chinese government and the Indian government held negotiations on China-India relations concerning the Tibet region of China. On December 31, 1953, the first day of the negotiations, Chinese Premier Zhou Enlai met the delegation from India, and first put forward the Five Principles of Peaceful Coexistence. Later, the five principles were officially written into the preamble to the Agreement on Trade and Intercourse Between the Tibet Region of China and India. During his visit to India and Burma (Myanmar) in June 1954, Zhou issued joint declarations with Indian Prime Minister Jawaharlal Nehru and Burmese Prime Minister U Nu successively, advocating the establishment of the Five Principles of Peaceful Coexistence as the basic norm governing relations between states.

The Chinese Dream

Achieving Rejuvenation
Is the Dream of the Chinese People[*]

November 29, 2012

The exhibition "The Road to Rejuvenation" is about the past, present and future of the Chinese nation, and it is a highly educational and inspiring one. In the old days, the Chinese people went through hardships as grueling as "storming an iron-wall pass."[1] Its sufferings and sacrifices in modern times were rarely seen in the history of the world. However, we Chinese never yielded. We waged indomitable struggles and succeeded in becoming masters of our own destiny. Imbued with the national spirit of patriotism, we have launched the great cause of building the country. Today, the Chinese nation is undergoing profound changes, like "seas becoming mulberry fields."[2] Having reviewed our historical experience and made painstaking efforts to probe our way forward in the past 30 years and more since the reform and opening-up process was started, we have finally embarked on the right path to achieve the rejuvenation of the Chinese nation and made impressive achievements in this pursuit. This path is one for building socialism with Chinese characteristics. In the future, the Chinese nation will "forge ahead like a gigantic ship breaking through strong winds and heavy waves."[3] Our struggles in the over 170 years since the Opium War[4] have created bright prospects for achieving the rejuvenation of the Chinese nation. We are now closer to this goal, and we are more confident and capable of achieving it than at any other time in history.

Reviewing the past, all Party members must bear in mind that backwardness left us vulnerable to attack, whereas only development makes us strong.

---

* Speech made when visiting the exhibition "The Road to Rejuvenation."

Looking at the present, all Party members must bear in mind that the path we take determines our destiny and that we must resolutely keep to the right path that we have found through great difficulties.

Looking ahead at the future, all Party members must bear in mind that we still have a long way to go and much hard work to do before we can turn our blueprint into reality.

Everyone has an ideal, ambition and dream. We are now all talking about the Chinese Dream. In my opinion, achieving the rejuvenation of the Chinese nation has been the greatest dream of the Chinese people since the advent of modern times. This dream embodies the long-cherished hope of several generations of the Chinese people, gives expression to the overall interests of the Chinese nation and the Chinese people, and represents the shared aspiration of all the sons and daughters of the Chinese nation.

History shows that the future and destiny of each and every one of us are closely linked to those of our country and nation. One can do well only when one's country and nation do well. Achieving the rejuvenation of the Chinese nation is both a glorious and arduous mission that requires the dedicated efforts of the Chinese people one generation after another. Empty talk harms the country, while hard work makes it flourish. Our generation of Communists should draw on past progress and chart a new course for the future. We should strengthen Party building, rally all the sons and daughters of the Chinese nation around us in a common effort to build our country and develop our nation, and continue to boldly advance towards the goal of the rejuvenation of the Chinese nation.

I firmly believe that the goal of bringing about a moderately prosperous society in all respects can be achieved by 2021, when the CPC celebrates its centenary; the goal of building China into a modern socialist country that is prosperous, strong, democratic, culturally advanced and harmonious can be achieved by 2049, when the PRC marks its centenary; and the dream of the rejuvenation of the Chinese nation will then be realized.

Notes

[1] Mao Zedong: "Loushan Pass," *Mao Zedong Poems*, Eng. ed., Foreign Languages Press, Beijing, 1998, p. 31.

[2] Mao Zedong: "The People's Liberation Army Captured Nanjing," *ibid.*, p. 49.

[3] Li Bai: *The Hard Road: Three Poems*. Li Bai (701-762) was a Tang Dynasty poet.

[4] The Opium War was a war of British aggression against China from 1840 to 1842. In 1840, in response to China's opposition to the import of opium from British traders, the British government sent troops to invade China on the excuse of protecting trade. The Chinese troops fought back under the leadership of Lin Zexu (1785-1850), governor of Guangdong and Guangxi provinces. People in Guangzhou organized armed groups to fight the invaders. Anti-British struggles were also seen in Fujian and Zhejiang provinces. In 1842 British troops invaded the Yangtze River area and forced the Qing government to sign the Treaty of Nanking, the first unequal treaty in the history of modern China.

Address to the First Session
of the 12th National People's Congress

March 17, 2013

Fellow deputies,

This session has elected me president of the People's Republic of China, and I wish to express my heartfelt thanks to you and the people of all ethnic groups for your trust in me.

I am keenly aware that the presidency entails both a glorious mission and important responsibilities. I will faithfully perform the duties vested in me by the Constitution, be loyal to the country and the people, fulfill all my duties, dedicate myself to public service, advance the interests of the people and the country, subject myself to public oversight, and live up to the trust you and the people of all ethnic groups in China have placed in me.

Fellow deputies,

The People's Republic of China has a splendid history. Led by the first generation of the Party's collective central leadership with Mao Zedong as the core, the second generation of collective central leadership with Deng Xiaoping as the core, the third generation of collective central leadership with Jiang Zemin as the core, and the CPC Central Committee with Hu Jintao as general secretary, the Chinese people of all ethnic groups have, making unremitting efforts one generation after another, surmounted all difficulties and obstacles on our way ahead, and made world-renowned achievements.

Today, our People's Republic stands proud and firm in the East.

With his rich political vision, outstanding leadership and dedication, Comrade Hu Jintao made remarkable achievements in upholding and building socialism with Chinese characteristics during his ten years in office as Chinese president, and he won the heartfelt love of the Chinese people of all ethnic groups and wide acclaim from all over the world. We express our sincere gratitude and great respect to him.

Fellow deputies,

The Chinese nation has an unbroken history of more than 5,000 years of civilization. It has created a rich and profound culture and has made an unforgettable contribution to the progress of human civilization. Over the course of several thousand years, what have closely bound us together, the 56 ethnic groups of China's 1.3-billion-plus people, are our indomitable struggles, the beautiful homeland we have built together and the national spirit we have nurtured together. Running through this history, most importantly, are the ideals and vision that we share and hold dear.

Realizing the goals of building a moderately prosperous society in all respects and a modern socialist country that is prosperous, strong, democratic, culturally advanced and harmonious, and achieving the Chinese Dream of the rejuvenation of the Chinese nation, means that we will make China prosperous and strong, rejuvenate the nation, and bring happiness to the Chinese people. They both embody the ideals of the Chinese people today and represent our forefathers' glorious tradition of untiring pursuit of progress.

Facing the mighty tide of the times and the great expectations of the people for a better life, we must not become complacent or slacken off in the slightest. We must redouble our efforts and forge ahead relentlessly to advance the cause of building Chinese socialism and endeavor to realize the Chinese Dream of the rejuvenation of the Chinese nation.

– To realize the Chinese Dream, we must take our own path, which is the path of building socialism with Chinese characteristics. It is not an easy path. We are able to embark on this path thanks to the great endeavors of reform and opening up made in the past 30 years and more, the continuous quest made in the 60-plus years of the PRC, a thorough review of the evolution of the Chinese nation in its 170-plus years of modern history, and carrying forward the 5,000-plus years of Chinese civilization. This path is deeply rooted in history and broadly based on China's present realities. The Chinese nation has extraordinary capabilities, with which it has built the great Chinese civilization and with which we can expand and stay on the development path suited to China's national conditions. The people of all ethnic groups in China should have full confidence in the path, theory and system of socialism with Chinese characteristics, and steadfastly forge ahead along the correct Chinese path.

– To realize the Chinese Dream, we must foster the Chinese spirit. It is the national spirit with patriotism at its core, and it is the spirit of the times with reform and innovation at its core. This spirit unites the people and pools their strength, and it is the source for rejuvenating and strengthening the country. Patriotism has always been the inner force that binds the Chinese nation together, and reform and innovation have always been the inner force that spurs us to keep abreast of the times in the course of reform and opening up. Our people of all ethnic groups must foster the great national spirit and follow the call of the times, strengthen our inner bond of unity and perseverance, and vigorously march towards the future.

– To realize the Chinese Dream, we must pool China's strength, that is, the strength of great unity among the people of all ethnic groups. The Chinese Dream is the dream of our nation and every Chinese. As long as we close ranks and pursue this common dream with great determination, we can create enormous strength to achieve it and enjoy vast space for each and every one of us to fulfill our own dreams. All the Chinese who live in our great country in this great age share the opportunity to pursue excellence, realize our dreams, and develop ourselves along with our country. With a dream, opportunities and efforts, all beautiful things can be created. We the people of all ethnic groups in China should bear our mission in mind and make concerted efforts to turn the wisdom and strength of our 1.3 billion people into an invincible force.

The Chinese Dream is, in the final analysis, the dream of the people; so we must rely firmly on them to realize it, and we must steadily deliver benefits to them.

We must uphold at the same time the leadership of the Party, the position of the people as masters of their own destiny, and the rule of law, maintain the principal position of the people, expand people's democracy, and promote law-based governance. We should uphold and improve the system of people's congresses as China's fundamental political system and the basic political systems of multi-party cooperation and political consultation under the leadership of the CPC, of regional ethnic autonomy, and of community-level self-governance. We should build a service-oriented, accountable, law-based and clean government, and fully motivate the people.

We should be guided by the strategic thinking that only development will make a difference, and steadfastly take economic development as the central task. We should comprehensively promote socialist economic, political, social and ecological advancement, further reform and opening up, boost balanced development, and continue to lay a solid material and cultural foundation for realizing the Chinese Dream.

We should always bear the people's aspirations in mind and be responsive to their expectations, ensure their equal rights to participate in governance and develop themselves, and uphold social fairness and justice. We should make steady progress in ensuring that all the people enjoy the rights to education, employment, medical and old-age care, and housing; and we should continue to fulfill, uphold and develop the fundamental interests of all the people. All these efforts will enable our people to share fully and fairly the benefits of development and move steadily towards shared prosperity on the basis of continued economic and social development.

We should consolidate and develop the broadest possible patriotic United Front, strengthen our Party's unity and cooperation with other political parties and personages without party affiliation, consolidate and develop socialist ethnic relations of equality, unity, mutual assistance and harmony, give full play to the positive role that religious figures and believers play in promoting economic and social development, and do our utmost to rally all the possible forces around us.

Fellow deputies,

"One must both have great ambition and make tireless efforts to achieve great exploits."[1] China is still in the primary stage of socialism and will remain so for a long time to come. There is still much to do and a long way to go before we can realize the Chinese Dream and create a better life for all our people, so every one of us should continue working towards this goal as hard as possible.

Workers, farmers and intellectuals throughout the country should give full rein to their talents, work diligently, and play a key role in promoting economic and social development. All functionaries should selflessly act in the public interest, be honest and industrious, show concern for problems encountered by the people, and deliver practical services to them. All officers and men of the People's Liberation Army and the People's Armed Police Force should strive to build powerful armed forces that follow the command of the Party, are able to win battles and have fine conduct. They should become better able to perform their mission, steadfastly uphold China's sovereignty, security and development interests, and resolutely protect the lives and property of the people. All the people working in the non-public sector of the economy and from new social groups should promote creativity and entrepreneurship through hard work, give back to society what they have gained from it, bring benefits to the people, and become actively involved in building socialism with Chinese characteristics. Young people should aim high, acquire more knowledge, temper their will, and make their formative years richly rewarding ones in an era of progress.

Our compatriots in the special administrative regions of Hong Kong and Macao should put the overall interests of the country and their regions first, and uphold and promote long-term prosperity and stability in Hong Kong and Macao. Our compatriots in Taiwan and on the mainland should join hands in supporting, maintaining and promoting the peaceful growth of cross-Straits relations, improving the people's lives on both sides of the Taiwan Straits, and creating a new future for the Chinese nation. Overseas Chinese should carry forward the Chinese nation's fine traditions of diligence and kindness, and contribute to the development of the country and friendship between the Chinese people and the people in their host countries.

We Chinese are peace-loving people. We will uphold the principle of peace, development, cooperation and mutual benefit, stay firm in pursuing peaceful development, resolutely follow a mutually beneficial strategy of opening up, and continue to promote friendship and cooperation with other countries. We will fulfill our international responsibilities and obligations, and continue to work with the peoples of all other countries to advance the lofty cause of peace and development of mankind.

Fellow deputies,

The CPC is the central force for leading and bringing together people of all ethnic groups in advancing the great cause of building Chinese socialism. It shoulders a historical mission and faces the tests of our times. We must uphold the principles that the Party was founded for the public good, that it exercises state power for the people, and that it should supervise its own conduct and operate under strict discipline. We must strengthen Party building in all respects, steadily improve the Party's art of leadership and governance, and make it better able to fight corruption, prevent degeneration and ward off risks. All our Party members, leading officials in particular, should be firm in our belief, always place the people above all else in our hearts and carry forward the Party's fine traditions and conduct. We should firmly oppose going through the motions, excessive bureaucracy, self-indulgence, and extravagance, resolutely combat corruption and other misconduct, preserve Communists' political integrity, and dedicate ourselves to the cause of the Party and the people.

Fellow deputies,

Achieving great goals requires perseverance. All political parties, organizations, ethnic groups, social groups and people from all walks of life in China should rally more closely around the CPC Central Committee, comprehensively implement the guiding principles of the Party's 18th National Congress, follow the guidance of Deng Xiaoping Theory, the important thought of the Three Represents and the Scientific Outlook on Development. We should remain modest and prudent, work hard, and forge ahead with determination to achieve new and bigger victories in realizing a moderately prosperous society in all respects and accelerating socialist modernization, and thus make new and bigger contribution to mankind.

Notes

[1] *The Book of History* (*Shang Shu*), a collection of documents and speeches by rulers of the Shang (c. 1600-1046 BC) and Zhou (1046-256 BC) dynasties.

Hard Work Makes Dreams Come True[*]

April 28, 2013

We have set the goals of completing the building of a moderately prosperous society in all respects by the centenary of the CPC in 2021 and building China into a modern socialist country that is prosperous, strong, democratic, culturally advanced, and harmonious by the centenary of the PRC in 2049 so as to realize the Chinese Dream of the rejuvenation of the Chinese nation.

Although the way ahead is rugged and the tasks of achieving reform, development and stability are arduous, we are confident in our future. The working class of our country must play an exemplary and leading role in taking the Chinese path, fostering the Chinese spirit and building up China's strength, and make concerted efforts to realize the Chinese Dream.

People make history, and work creates the future. Work is the fundamental force driving the progress of human society. Happiness does not fall from the sky, nor do dreams come true automatically. To achieve our goals and create a bright future we must rely closely on the people, always act in their interests, and work in an industrious, honest and creative way. We often say, "Empty talk harms the country, while hard work makes it flourish." This means we must first get down to work.

As we forge ahead, we must give full rein to the vital role of the working class and its historical initiative, and arouse its motivation for work and creation.

First, we must make sure that the working class is our main force. The working class is China's leading class; it represents China's

* Part of the speech at a discussion session with national model workers.

advanced productive forces and relations of production; it is our Party's most steadfast and reliable class foundation; and it is the main force for realizing a moderately prosperous society in all respects, and upholding and building socialism with Chinese characteristics.

Since the introduction of the reform and opening-up policy more than 30 years ago, our working class has been growing and improving, and its structure becoming better. It has taken on a new look, and its advanced nature has been strengthened. To uphold and build Chinese socialism in the future, we must rely wholeheartedly on the working class, enhance its position as China's leading class, and give full play to its role as our main force. Relying fully on the working class is not just a slogan or label; rather, we should rely on it in the whole process of formulating Party and government policies, and implement it in our work, as well as in all aspects of production and operation of enterprises.

Second, we must rely firmly on the working class to build socialism with Chinese characteristics. Chinese socialism is what we must pursue if we are to achieve development and make progress in contemporary China, realize the Chinese Dream and create a bright future for China's working class. Chinese workers should enhance their sense of historical mission and responsibility, do their jobs well, and keep the country's overall interests in mind. They should pursue their ideals of life and work for the wellbeing of their families while working to make the country prosperous and strong, and rejuvenate the nation. They should pursue both their personal aspirations and the Chinese Dream, and, as the masters of the country, contribute to upholding and building socialism with Chinese characteristics.

The working class should have a firm belief in the vision of socialism with Chinese characteristics, closely follow the Party, resolutely support the socialist system, reform and opening up, and be the mainstay of upholding the Chinese path. The working class should practice the core socialist values[1], give full play to its own great strengths, influence and lead the whole of society with its vision and exemplary actions, infuse new energy into the Chinese spirit and be a model of fostering the Chinese spirit. The Chinese working class should take it as its mission to rejuvenate the nation, unleash its great creativity, carry forward its glorious tradition of acting in the overall interests of the country, maintain political stability and unity, and remain the core force for building up China's strength.

Third, we must continue to respect work and make all those who work enjoy happiness. Work is the source of wealth and happiness. To realize beautiful dreams, solve difficulties hampering development, and be successful in life, one must do honest work. Work has shaped the Chinese nation and its glorious history, and it is work that will shape its bright future. "There is nothing that cannot be accomplished through hard work." We must be firm in the belief that work is what is most honorable, most sublime, most magnificent and most beautiful; and we should spur the enthusiasm for work of all the people and release their creative potential to create a better life through work.

The whole of society should follow the important policy of respecting work, knowledge, talent and creation, uphold and develop the interests of people who work, and protect their rights. We should uphold social fairness and justice, remove obstacles that prevent workers from participating in development and sharing in the benefits of development, and ensure that workers have decent working conditions and achieve all-round development. The whole of society should love work, be diligent and guard against indolence.

Fourth, we must emulate model workers. The power of a good example is enormous. Model workers are the cream of the country and role models for the people. Over the years, model workers have made extraordinary achievements out of ordinary work. They have nurtured the ethos of the model workers, namely, dedication to work, striving for excellence, working hard, being bold in innovating, not being lured by fame and wealth, and being ready to make sacrifices. This has enriched the ethos of our nation and the times, and become an invaluable source of inspiration.

To meet our development goals, we must enrich ourselves not only materially but culturally and ethically as well. The people of all ethnic groups in the country should learn from model workers, follow their examples and, with a sense of urgency, strive to realize the rejuvenation of the Chinese nation. Model workers and other role models should cherish the honor conferred upon them and deliver an even better performance. They should be dedicated to work and make selfless contribution, and become pacesetters, having firm vision and conviction, working hard and promoting unity. Workers in China today should have not only strength, but also vision, expertise, and the capability to invent and innovate, so that they can create with action a splendid China. Party committees, governments and trade unions at all levels should value the role of model workers, care for them, support them in playing their key role, help them solve all the difficulties they encounter in work and life, and widely publicize their exemplary deeds, so as to promote the ethos of model workers.

Both the Party and workers place high hopes on the trade unions. The Chinese trade unions are workers' organizations under the leadership of the CPC, and they serve as bridges through which the Party maintains contact with workers. They are an important social pillar supporting the government in our socialist country. The path for developing trade unions with Chinese characteristics is an important part of socialism with Chinese characteristics; it represents the nature and features of trade unions, and is an important guarantee for the trade unions to stay on the right track of development. We should keep to this path and steadily widen it.

Times keep changing, and innovation is a regular feature of our mission. Likewise, the trade unions should keep developing themselves and make innovations in their work. We should, adapting to the times and social changes, develop good and effective working methods to make workers feel that the trade unions are their "homes" and trade union officials are their "family members" whom they can turn to for help. We should make providing dedicated services to people as the starting point and goal of all the work of the trade unions, work for them heart and soul, heed their views, uphold the legitimate rights and interests of workers, including rural migrant workers, provide them with voluntary services, help solve problems they face in a down-to-earth manner, and promote harmonious socialist work relations. We need to pay close attention to the diversified demands of people who work, unleash the potential for their career development, and strive to train large numbers of high-caliber people who are knowledgeable, have a good command of technical expertise, and are innovative. Party committees and governments at all levels should strengthen and improve their leadership over the trade unions, support them in their work, and provide more resources and means to them so that they are better able to perform their functions.

A journey of one thousand miles begins with a single step. There is a bright future for our country, but reaching it will not be easy. We cannot accomplish our goal with one single effort, nor can we realize our dream overnight. Every accomplishment in the world is hard-won. The more beautiful the future, the harder we must work for it.

Hard work will overcome difficulties and make one's dream come true. We should endeavor to foster throughout society the work ethic of being down-to-earth and diligent. Leading officials at all levels should foster the ethos of model workers. They should pursue realistic policies, boost morale and handle things in a pragmatic way. They should not be pretentious or just pursue image-building accomplishments, and they should firmly oppose going through the motions, excessive bureaucracy, self-indulgence, and extravagance, which both government officials and the public detest. They should lead the people by example and deliver a good performance in all their work.

I firmly believe that under the leadership of the CPC Central Committee and with the concerted efforts of the Chinese working class and all other workers and the people of all ethnic groups in China, we can certainly create an even brighter future and realize the Chinese Dream of the rejuvenation of the Chinese nation.

Notes

[1] The core socialist values are prosperity, democracy, civility, harmony, freedom, equality, justice, the rule of law, patriotism, dedication, integrity and friendship. They first appeared in the political report delivered in November 2012 to the 18th CPC National Congress, titled "Firmly March on the Path of Socialism with Chinese Characteristics and Strive to Complete the Building of a Moderately Prosperous Society in All Respects."

Realize Youthful Dreams[*]

May 4, 2013

The 18th CPC National Congress put forward a master blueprint for completing the building of a moderately prosperous society in all respects and accelerating socialist modernization, and it issued a call for achieving the Two Centenary Goals[1]. We made clear our desire to realize the Chinese Dream of the rejuvenation of the Chinese nation in accordance with the guiding principles of the Congress. At present, all are discussing the Chinese Dream and thinking about how it relates to them and what they need to do to realize it.

– The Chinese Dream pertains to the past and the present, but also the future. It is the crystallization of the tireless efforts of countless people with lofty ideals, embraces the yearnings of all the sons and daughters of the Chinese nation, and reveals the prospect of a bright future, when our country will be prosperous and strong, the nation will be rejuvenated, and the people will enjoy a happy life.

– The Chinese Dream is the dream of the country and the nation, but also of every ordinary Chinese. One can do well only when one's country and nation do well. Only if everyone strives for a better tomorrow can our efforts be aggregated into a powerful force to realize the Chinese Dream.

– The Chinese Dream is ours, but also yours, the younger generation. The great renewal of the Chinese nation will eventually become a reality in the course of the successive efforts of the youth.

During all periods of revolution, construction and reform, the Party has always valued, cared about and trusted young people, and placed great expectations on the younger generations. The Party

---

* Part of the speech to outstanding young representatives from all walks of life.

believes that young people represent the future of our country and the hope of our nation, regards them as a vital contingent for the cause of the Party and the people, and always encourages them to realize their ideals in the great struggle of the people.

Today, we are closer than at any time in history to attaining the goal of the rejuvenation of the Chinese nation, and we have greater confidence in and capability for achieving this goal than ever before. "The last one tenth of the journey demands half the effort."[2] The closer we are to achieving the goal of the rejuvenation of the Chinese nation, the more we should redouble our efforts and not slacken our pace, and the more we must mobilize all young people to this end.

Looking ahead, we can see that our younger generation has a promising future, and will accomplish much. It is a law of history that "the waves of the Yangtze River from behind drive on those ahead," and it is the responsibility of young people to surpass their elders. Young people need to boldly assume the heavy responsibilities that the times impose on you, aim high, be practical and realistic, and put your youthful dreams into action in the course of realizing the Chinese Dream of the rejuvenation of the Chinese nation.

First, young people must be firm in your ideals and convictions. "One must both have great ambition and make tireless efforts to achieve great exploits."[3] Ideals provide direction in life, and convictions determine the success of a cause. Without ideals and convictions one's spirit becomes weak. The Chinese Dream is the common ideal of the people of all ethnic groups, and a lofty ideal that young people should harbor. Socialism with Chinese characteristics is the correct path for leading the people in realizing the Chinese Dream that the Party articulated after untold hardships, and all young people should firmly adopt it as a guideline for your lives.

Young people should guide your actions with Deng Xiaoping Theory, the important thought of the Three Represents and the Scientific Outlook on Development; base your ideals and convictions on the rational recognition and acceptance of scientific theories, on a correct understanding of the laws of history, and on an accurate understanding of the basic national conditions; keep enhancing your confidence in the Chinese path, theories and system; have more faith in the Party's leadership; and always follow the Party in upholding Chinese socialism.

Second, young people must have professional competence. Learning is necessary for growth and progress, while practice is the way to improve competence. The qualities and competence of young people will have a direct influence on the course of realizing the Chinese Dream. There is an ancient Chinese saying, "Learning is the bow, while competence is the arrow."[4] This means that the foundation of learning is like a bow, while competence is like an arrow; only with rich knowledge can one give full play to one's competence. Young people are in the prime time of learning. You should regard learning as a top priority, a responsibility, a moral support and a lifestyle. You should establish a conviction that dreams start from learning and career success depends on competence. You should make assiduous learning a driving force and competence building a resource for your youthful endeavors.

Young people must orient yourselves to modernization, the world and the future, have a sense of urgency in updating your knowledge, study with great eagerness, lay a good foundation of basic knowledge while updating it promptly, assiduously study theories while enthusiastically developing skills, and constantly enhance your competence and capabilities to meet the development needs of our times and the requirements of our undertaking. Young people must apply what you have learned, stay close to the grassroots and the populace, and, in the great furnace of the reform and opening up and socialist modernization, and in the great school of society, acquire true skills and genuine knowledge, improve competence, and make yourselves capable personnel who can shoulder important social responsibilities.

Third, young people must dare to innovate and create. Innovation is the soul driving a nation's progress and an inexhaustible source of a country's prosperity. It is also an essential part of the Chinese national character. This is what Confucius meant when he said, "If you can in one day renovate yourself, do so from day to day. Yea, let there be daily renovation."[5] Life never favors those who follow the beaten track and are satisfied with the *status quo*, and it never waits for the unambitious and those who sit idle and enjoy the fruits of others' work. Instead, it provides more opportunities for those who have the ability and courage to innovate. Young people are the most dynamic and most creative group of our society, and should stand in the forefront of innovation and creation.

Young people should dare to be the first, boldly free their minds and progress with the times, dare to seek high and low for a way to forge ahead, and be ambitious to learn from and then surpass the older generation. With your youthful energy, you can create a country of youth and a nation of youth. Young people should have the willpower to cut paths through mountains and build bridges over rivers, and be indomitable and advance bravely in bringing forth new ideas. You should have a pragmatic attitude that pursues truth, so you can constantly accumulate experience and achieve results in the course of bringing forth new ideas in your chosen occupations.

Fourth, young people must be devoted to hard work. "The sharpness of a sword results from repeated grinding, while the fragrance of plum blossoms comes from frigid weather." Human ideals are not easy to achieve, but need hard work. From poverty to prosperity, and from weakness to strength, China has been able to progress step by step over centuries thanks to the tenacity of one generation after another, and to the nation's spirit of constant self-improvement through hard work. Currently we are facing important opportunities for development, but we are also facing unprecedented difficulties and challenges. The dream stretches out before us and the road lies at our feet. Those who overcome their weaknesses are powerful, and those who keep improving themselves come out victors. If we are to achieve our development goals, young people must work long and hard without letup.

Young people must bear in mind that "empty talk harms the country, while hard work makes it flourish" and put this into practice.

You must work hard at your own posts, start from trivial things, and create your own splendid life with hard work, outstanding performances and remarkable achievements. Young people must never fear difficulties, but try to overcome them; you should go to the grassroots with tough conditions and the frontline for national construction and project development to temper yourselves and enhance your capabilities. Young people must have the courage and determination to start up businesses and do pioneering work, try to blaze new trails and start new endeavors in reform and opening up, and constantly create new prospects for their career development.

Fifth, young people must temper your character. Socialism with Chinese characteristics is a form of socialism in which material and cultural progresses go hand in hand. It is difficult for a nation without inner strength to be self-reliant, and a cause that lacks a cultural buttress cannot be sustained for long. Young people are a social force that leads the social ethos. The cultural attainment of a nation is represented mostly by the morality and mental outlook of the younger generation.

Young people must integrate correct moral cognition, conscious moral development and active moral practice, conscientiously establish and practice the core socialist values, and take the lead in advocating good social conduct. Young people must strengthen theoretical improvement and moral cultivation, take the initiative to carry forward patriotism, collectivism and socialism, and actively advocate social and professional ethics, and family virtues. Young people should bear in mind that "virtue uplifts, while vice debases"[6] and always be optimists and persons of integrity who have a healthy lifestyle. Young people should advocate new social trends, be the first in learning from Lei Feng[7], take an active part in voluntary work, shoulder social responsibilities, care for others, help the poor, the weak and the disabled, and do other good and practical deeds, so as to promote social progress with their actions.

The theme of the Chinese youth movement today is to strive to realize the Chinese Dream of the rejuvenation of the Chinese nation.

The Chinese Communist Youth League should carry out extensive educational and practical activities with the theme of "My Chinese Dream" for young Chinese. It should sow the seeds of and ignite the dreams of each youth so that more young people dare to dream and pursue their dreams. In this way all young people can increase their youthful energy to realize the Chinese Dream. The League should lay a solid intellectual basis for all young Chinese with the Chinese Dream, and educate and help them to establish a correct world view, outlook on life and sense of values, always love our country, our people and our nation, and firmly follow the Party along the Chinese path. The League should inspire young people's sense of historical responsibility through the Chinese Dream, carry forward the fine tradition of "the League taking action upon the Party's call," combine its work with Party and government work, and organize and mobilize young people to support reform, promote development and maintain stability. The League must actively offer services for young people in pursuing their dreams, effectively improve its practice, get close to young people at the primary level, address their concerns and pressing needs, represent and protect the common interests and needs of the young people, and try to build a favorable environment for their growth and development.

Role models from among the youngsters are good examples for young people to learn from; they shoulder more social responsibilities and public expectations, and play a strong exemplary and leading role among young people, and even in society as a whole. I hope these role models will make persistent efforts, be strict with themselves, be determined to go ahead, and set a good example to all young people with their personal development, moral pursuit and exemplary action.

A country prospers if its youth is thriving; a country is strong if its youth is robust. Ever since its founding in 1921 the Party has represented, drawn over and relied on young Chinese people. Party committees and governments at all levels must fully trust in, care for and be strict with young people; give a wider scope for their thoughts, build a larger stage for their practice and innovation, provide more opportunities for the pursuit of their life goals, and create more favorable conditions for their career development. Officials at all levels must pay attention to young people's aspirations, help them to grow, support them to start their own businesses, become their bosom friends, and show enthusiasm for youth work.

Everybody is young once in their life. Now is the time for you to make the most of your youth; and the future is a time for you to look back on it. The path of life is sometimes level, sometimes steep; sometimes smooth, sometimes rough; sometimes straight, sometimes crooked. Young people are faced with a wide range of choices. But what is important for you is to be guided by a correct world view, outlook on life and sense of values when you are making your choices. The life experiences of countless successful people suggest that young people who choose to endure hardships will be duly rewarded, and those who make contributions to society are the ones who deserve respect. Tribulations, setbacks and tests have proved to be good for young people in their later life. You need to have strength of character to be undaunted when confronting good or bad fortune, have a firm will to keep pressing forward in spite of repeated setbacks, remain optimistic in all circumstances, turn your failures into a driving force, and learn from your experiences, so that your life is raised to a higher plane. In short, the only way you can have fond memories of a well-spent, warm and lasting youth with no regrets is to work enthusiastically and energetically, tenaciously overcome all obstacles, and make a contribution to the people while you are still young.

I firmly believe that if the people of all ethnic groups unite under the Party's leadership, stand on solid ground and forge ahead with a pioneering spirit, we can certainly build a prosperous, strong, democratic, culturally advanced, and harmonious modern socialist country by the middle of this century. And all our young people will surely witness and share in the realization of the Chinese Dream along with the people of all ethnic groups.

Notes

[1] The Two Centenary Goals were put forth by the CPC at its 18th National Congress for building socialism with Chinese characteristics. The two goals are to complete the building of a moderately prosperous society in all respects by the centenary of the CPC (founded in 1921) and to build China into a modern socialist country that is prosperous, strong, democratic, culturally advanced, and harmonious by the centenary of the PRC (founded in 1949).

[2] *Strategies of the States (Zhan Guo Ce)*, a collection of stories of political strategists of the Warring States Period (475-221 BC).

[3] See note 1, p. 46.

[4] Yuan Mei: *Sequel to Discourses on Poetry (Xu Shi Pin)*. Yuan Mei (1716-1797) was a poet and critic of the Qing Dynasty.

[5] *The Great Learning (Da Xue)* is one of the "Four Classics of Confucianism," the other three being *The Analects of Confucius*, *The Mencius* and *The Doctrine of the Mean*.

[6] *The Discourses of the States (Guo Yu)* records important events taking place during the Western Zhou Dynasty (1046-771 BC) and the Spring and Autumn Period (770-476 BC). The book is believed to have been written by Zuoqiu Ming (556-451 BC), a noted historian of the State of Lu.

[7] Lei Feng (1940-1962) was a PLA soldier and a role model. He served the people wholeheartedly, was ready to help others, and loved whatever work he was assigned to. He died at his post in an accident. In 1963 Mao Zedong wrote "Learn from Comrade Lei Feng," starting a national campaign for people to copy his selfless deeds. March 5 is a national memorial day to learn from him.

The Chinese Dream Will Benefit Not Only the People of China, But Also of Other Countries[*]

May 2013

The Chinese nation has emerged resilient from trials and tribulations, and it never gave up the pursuit of its beautiful dreams. Realizing the Chinese Dream of the rejuvenation of the Chinese nation has been a long-cherished wish of the Chinese people since the advent of modern times.

In this new historical period, the essence of the Chinese Dream is to make our country prosperous and strong, revitalize the nation and make the people live better lives. Our objectives are to double the 2010 GDP and per capita income of urban and rural residents, and complete the building of a moderately prosperous society in all respects by 2020. By mid-century, we aim to build China into a modern socialist country that is prosperous, strong, democratic, culturally advanced and harmonious, and realize the Chinese Dream of the great renewal of the Chinese nation.

To realize the Chinese Dream, we must adhere to the path of socialism with Chinese characteristics. We have followed this path for over 30 years, and history has shown us that this is the correct path that suits China's national conditions, a path that makes the people wealthy and the country strong. We will firmly continue along this path.

To realize the Chinese Dream, we must carry forward the Chinese spirit. We need to use the national spirit of patriotism and spirit of the times centered on reform and innovation to bring forth the vigor and vitality of the whole nation.

---

* Part of the answers in a written interview with reporters from Trinidad and Tobago, Costa Rica and Mexico.

To realize the Chinese Dream, we must build up cohesive strength. Empty talk harms the country, while hard work makes it flourish. We need to use the wisdom and strength of our country's 1.3 billion people to build a strong China and a prosperous nation with the constant efforts of the Chinese people for generations to come.

To realize the Chinese Dream, we must pursue peaceful development. We will always follow the path of peaceful development and pursue an opening-up strategy that brings mutual benefits. We will concentrate both on China's development and on our responsibilities and contributions to the world as a whole. We will bring benefits to both the Chinese people and the people of the rest of the world. The realization of the Chinese Dream will bring the world peace, not turmoil, opportunities, not threats.

Although there is a vast ocean between China and Latin America, we are connected heart and soul. We are bound together not only by profound traditional friendship and close interests, but also by our common pursuit of beautiful dreams.

In recent years Latin American and Caribbean countries have made steady progress in achieving common development through joint efforts. The establishment of the Community of Latin American and Caribbean States fully testifies to the vigorous efforts made by Latin America and the countries of the Caribbean to realize the dream of unity, coordination and common development championed by the pioneers of the Latin American and Caribbean independence movements.

China is ready to work with Latin American and Caribbean countries hand in hand, supporting one another and cooperating sincerely on the path to realizing the great dream of development and prosperity.

Right Time to Innovate and
Make Dreams Come True*

October 21, 2013

Completing the building of a moderately prosperous society in all respects, accelerating socialist modernization and achieving China's great rejuvenation, this is a glorious cause with a bright and splendid future. All people who are dedicated to this worthy cause can expect to accomplish great deeds. With hundreds of millions of fellow Chinese marching in their ranks, the Chinese students and scholars studying abroad are deciding that this is the right time to innovate and make their life-long dreams come true. You are called upon to integrate your patriotic love, your aspiration to make the country strong and your actions to serve it, and link your dreams with the stupendous efforts of your fellow countrymen to turn the Chinese Dream into reality, and by doing so have your names recorded in the annals of China's great renewal.

Here I would like to propose four points as my hope for Chinese students and scholars studying abroad.

First, I hope you will adhere to patriotism. China's history stretches over thousands of years, and patriotism has always been a stirring theme and a powerful force inspiring the Chinese of all ethnic groups to carry on and excel. No matter how long the shadow it may cast, the tree strikes deep roots in soil forever. No matter where they are, Chinese students should always keep the home country and its people in their hearts. Qian Xuesen[2] once said, "As a Chinese scientist, I live

---

* Part of the speech at the centenary celebration of the Western Returned Scholars Association[1].

to serve the people. I hope the people are satisfied with the work I have done in my lifetime. Their approval will be my highest reward."

I hope that you will carry forward the glorious tradition of studying hard to serve the country and be defenders and messengers of patriotism, always bearing in mind the ideal of "being the first to worry about the affairs of the state and the last to enjoy oneself,"[3] always taking the wellbeing of the country, the nation and the people as the goal of your endeavors, and willingly associating the fruits of personal success with the evergreen tree of patriotism. The Party and the country respect the choice you make. If you decide to return, we will welcome you with open arms. If you decide to stay abroad, we will support you in serving the country in various ways. All of you should remember that wherever you are you are a member of the Chinese family; the country and the people back home always care about their sons and daughters, and your homeland is always a warm spiritual land for you.

Second, I hope you will study hard. Learning is a lasting theme for one to conduct oneself in life and society. It is also an important basis for one to serve one's country and people. A dream starts with learning, and careers with practice. In the world today, knowledge and information are quickly updated, and if one slackens even a little in study, one is likely to fall behind. Some say that the world is a circle for everyone, with the amount of knowledge as the radius. He who has a bigger radius has a broader scope to act within.

I hope that you will orient yourselves to modernization, to the whole world and to the future, and aim to broaden your knowledge in advanced knowhow, technologies and management expertise. You should keep the perseverance and diligence in reading as related in stories of Confucius[4], Sun Jing and Su Qin[5], Kuang Heng[6], and Che Yin and Sun Kang[7]. You should learn by reading and from other people's practical experiences with equal devotion, temper your moral character, and make yourselves competent and well-versed in genuine skills. Those who have completed their study programs need to broaden their horizon, renew their knowledge promptly, improve their knowledge structure, and make themselves outstanding talented people capable of assuming heavy responsibilities and accomplishing great deeds.

Third, I hope you will be more innovative and creative. Innovation is the soul of a nation's progress, the inexhaustible force enhancing a country's prosperity, and indeed the profound endowment of the Chinese nation. Against the backdrop of international competition, only those who innovate can make progress, grow stronger and prevail. Students and scholars studying abroad have a broad vision, and they ought to take the lead in making innovations. China's reform, opening-up and modernization drive provide all ambitious pioneers of innovation with a wide stage for success.

I hope you will throw yourselves into extensive efforts of innovation and creation, and dare to lead the way forward with vision, courage and stamina, so that you can succeed in making breakthroughs and achievements. Trying to accomplish something in China, one must set oneself firmly on the soil of the home country, keep in mind the expectations of the people, correctly identify the point where one's professional strength and the needs of social development converge and where advanced knowledge and China's conditions meet. Only in this way can innovation and creativity succeed and deliver real benefits.

Fourth, I hope you will work for dynamic exchanges with other countries. China cannot develop without the rest of the world; nor can the world as a whole prosper without China. We must open still wider to the outside world, strengthening our connectivity and interaction with it, and enhancing our understanding and friendship with other peoples. Growing up in China and living overseas extensively, you have been steeped in inter-personal relationships and cross-cultural communications. Many foreigners have got to know China through you while many Chinese have learned about the outside world also through you.

I hope you will make full use of your advantages to strengthen connections and exchanges between China and other countries, acting as unofficial ambassadors to promote people-to-people friendship, and explaining China's culture, history and points of view in such a way that the people from other countries can understand and identify with China, and be ready to give it greater appreciation and support.

Founded 100 years ago when the survival of the nation was at stake, the Western Returned Scholars Association practiced patriotism by organizing its members to participate in patriotic and democratic movements and join the cause for national salvation and people's liberation, thus becoming a famous patriotic association for democracy and science at that time. After the People's Republic was founded in 1949, the Association became a progressive association under the leadership of the Party and government by vigorously encouraging the return of Chinese students abroad. Since the beginning of China's reform and opening up, the Association has energetically carried out the "serve the country program," making itself a people's organization dedicated to socialism with Chinese characteristics. In 2003, with approval from the central authorities, the Association was given an additional name – the Chinese Overseas-educated Scholars Association – with its scope of operation expanded to cover the entire country and its members spreading all over the world. Its influence as a people's organization has thus become more extensive.

Facing a new situation and new tasks, the Western Returned Scholars Association and Chinese Overseas-educated Scholars Association must give full play to its advantages as a people's organization and part of the United Front with prominent intellectuals as its members, based in China while reaching out overseas to turn itself into a talent pool in the service of the country, a think tank of good ideas and proposals and a vital force in people-to-people diplomacy; and strive to become a bridge between the Party and the overseas students and scholars, an assistant in the work of the Party and government towards them, and a warm home to rally overseas students and scholars closely around the Party. The Association should care for the work, study and life of overseas Chinese students and scholars, reflect their wishes and views, protect their lawful rights and interests, and constantly enhance the Association's appeal and cohesion.

"Exaltation of the virtuous is fundamental to governance."[8] Party committees and governments at all levels must earnestly implement Party and government policies concerning students and scholars studying abroad, and train more effectively and on a larger scale all kinds of talented people badly needed by our reform, opening up and modernization. When the environment is sound, talented people will gather, and our cause will thrive; but when it is not, they will go their separate ways, and our cause will fail. We must improve our working mechanisms, and enhance the awareness of service, strengthen education and guidance, build more platforms of innovation, be good at finding, uniting with and using talented people, and help bring forth people of high caliber by creating an environment favorable for the students to return and serve China, and in general to realize their potential. We should support the Association in its work by strengthening its organization, improving its working apparatus and personnel, and providing the necessary conditions for its operation.

In the course of its development and opening up, China needs still more overseas talented people and welcomes their arrival with open arms. Empty talk harms the country, while hard work makes it flourish. We are convinced that as long as students and scholars studying abroad remember this and choose to stand and work with the people, they will surely write a brilliant page in the book of the Chinese Dream, a page that is worthy of our times, of our people and of history.

Notes

[1] The Western Returned Scholars Association was founded in October 1913. It is a voluntary group composed of Chinese scholars who have returned to China after studying overseas. In 2003 it was given the additional name of the Chinese Overseas-educated Scholars Association.

[2] Qian Xuesen (1911-2009) went to study in the United States in 1935, and returned to China in 1955. He was directly involved in the organization and guidance

of the research and development of China's carrier rockets, missiles and satellites, and made an outstanding contribution to China's space development.

[3] Fan Zhongyan: *The Yueyang Tower*. Fan Zhongyan (989-1052) was a statesman and literary scholar of the Northern Song Dynasty (960-1127).

[4] Confucius is said to have read *The Book of Changes* (*Yi Jing*) so many times that the leather strings binding the bamboo slips upon which the book was written broke several times.

[5] Sun Jing of the Han Dynasty (206 BC-AD 220) loved reading. He tied his hair to a roof beam to prevent himself from falling asleep when reading. Su Qin of the Warring States Period (475-221 BC) poked himself in the thigh with an awl to keep him from dropping off when studying at night. These stories are used to describe studious persons.

[6] Kuang Heng of the Han Dynasty studied hard when young, but he could not afford candles. So he bored a hole in a wall to make use of a neighbor's light to study by. This metaphor is used to describe a studious person.

[7] Che Yin of the Eastern Jin Dynasty (317-420) was too poor to afford lamp oil. He caught dozens of fireflies and placed them in a bag made of thin white cloth so that he could study by their light at night. Sun Kang of the Southern Dynasties (420-589) could not afford candles, so he had to read by the reflected light from snow on winter nights. These stories are used to describe studious persons.

[8] *Mo Zi*, a collection of works of the Mohist school of thought.

The Rejuvenation of the Chinese Nation
Is a Dream Shared by All Chinese*

June 6, 2014

For Chinese people both at home and abroad, a united Chinese nation is our shared root, the profound Chinese culture is our shared soul, and the rejuvenation of the Chinese nation is our shared dream. The shared root fosters eternal brotherhood, the shared soul links our hearts, and the shared dream holds us all together – we will go on to write a new chapter in the history of the Chinese nation.

We Chinese often say, "Your eyes brim with tears when you encounter a fellow townsman in a distant land." It makes me feel at home to meet you today. On behalf of the CPC and the State Council, I would like to extend my congratulations to the convening of the Seventh Conference of Friendship of Overseas Chinese Associations, my warm welcome to overseas Chinese attending the conference, and my sincere greetings to overseas Chinese all over the world.

The tens of millions of overseas Chinese across the world are all members of the Chinese family. In the best of Chinese traditions, generations of overseas Chinese never forget their home country, their origins, or the blood of the Chinese nation flowing in their veins. They have given their enthusiastic support to China's revolution, construction and reform. They have made a major contribution to the growth of the Chinese nation, to the peaceful reunification of the motherland, and to the friendly people-to-people cooperation

---

* Main points of the speech to representatives attending the Seventh Conference of Friendship of Overseas Chinese Associations.

between China and other countries. Their contribution will always be remembered.

At present, the Chinese people are striving to realize the Two Centenary Goals and the Chinese Dream of the rejuvenation of the Chinese nation. Overseas Chinese will play an essential role in this process. The Chinese Dream is a dream of the country, the nation as well as all Chinese individuals. With a strong sense of patriotism, economic strength, rich intellectual resources, and extensive business connections, overseas Chinese constitute a major force for realizing the Chinese Dream. As long as all Chinese both at home and abroad unite as one and contribute whatever they can, be it strength or intelligence, they can marshal great power for realizing this dream.

Chinese civilization, with a history going back more than 5,000 years, provides strong intellectual support for the country's ceaseless self-improvement and growth. No matter where a Chinese is, he always bears the distinctive brand of the Chinese culture, which is the common heritage of all the sons and daughters of China. I hope all Chinese will continue to carry forward Chinese culture and draw strength from it, while promoting exchanges between Chinese civilization and other civilizations. Let us tell the stories of China well, and make our voices heard; let us promote mutual understanding between the people of our own country and those of other lands, and create a better environment for achieving the Chinese Dream.

The Chinese Dream is a desire for happiness, similar to the dreams of the people of other countries. The people can attain happiness only when their country and nation thrive. China will thrive only when the world prospers. China provides positive energy for world prosperity and development by holding to the path of peaceful development. Overseas Chinese should take full advantage of their strengths and their circumstances to serve as a bridge for wide-ranging exchanges and cooperation between China and their new home countries. They should better integrate themselves into their local communities and contribute to world peace and development.

All-Round and
Deeper-Level Reform

Reform and Opening Up
Is Always Ongoing and Will Never End[*]

December 31, 2012

Reform and opening up is a long-term and arduous cause, and people need to work on it generation after generation. We should carry out reform to improve the socialist market economy of China, and adhere to the basic state policy of opening up to the outside world. We must further reform in key sectors with greater political courage and vision, and forge ahead steadily in the direction determined by the Party's 18th National Congress.

The past, the present, and the future are all interconnected. History is about the past, while the present is the history of the future. To implement the major propositions on reform and opening up raised at the 18th National Congress, we need to review reform and opening up, better understand its historical necessity, conscientiously master its laws, and firmly assume the responsibility of extending it.

We must review and apply the useful experience we have gained in reform and opening up.

First, reform and opening up is an in-depth revolution, and we must follow the correct direction and stay on the correct path. Regarding the issue of direction, we must keep a cool head. Our direction is to continuously promote the self-improvement and development of the socialist system, and stride forward with resolve on the path of socialism with Chinese characteristics.

Second, reform and opening up is a cause that has never before been pursued. We must adopt the right methods and advance this

---

* Main points of the speech at the second group study session of the Political Bureau of the 18th CPC Central Committee which Xi presided over.

cause through continuous exploration and practice. Wading across the river by feeling for the stones is a reform method with Chinese characteristics and in line with the prevailing conditions in China. Wading across the river by feeling for the stones, we can identify the laws that apply, and acquire knowledge in practice. Wading across the river by feeling for the stones and top-level design are two component factors for our reform effort. Reform and opening up in a region at a certain stage should be subject to top-level design; top-level design should be strengthened on the basis of progressive reform and opening up in the region at a certain stage. To continue reform and opening up, we need to strengthen our macroscopic thinking and top-level design, and make sure that reform is systematic, integrated and coordinated. At the same time, we must still encourage bold experiments and breakthroughs.

Third, reform and opening up is a systematic project, which should be pushed forward in an all-round way with all kinds of reforms well coordinated. Reform and opening up is an in-depth and all-round social transformation. Every reform will have great impact on other reforms, and all reforms support each other and interact positively. We will promote both all-round progress and breakthroughs at key points, and form a strong force for the further advance of reform and opening up.

Fourth, stability is a prerequisite for reform and development. We must make sure that reform, development and stability proceed in tandem. Social stability makes it possible for us to carry out reform and development which in turn provide a solid foundation for social stability. We should take into full consideration the momentum of reform, the speed of development, and the capacity of the general public to sustain change. And improvement of the people's wellbeing should be regarded as an important link in balancing reform, development and stability.

Fifth, reform and opening up is a cause of the Chinese people. We must respect the people's pioneering spirit and advance this cause under the leadership of the Party. Every breakthrough and step forward in theory and practice that we make in this cause comes from the experience and wisdom of the people, so does every new thing we bring into being and develop, and every experience we gain. The more arduous the task of balancing reform, development and stability, the more we need to strengthen and improve the Party's leadership and maintain close ties between the Party and the people. We should be adept in formulating and implementing sound guidelines and policies and use them to direct the people forward, and be good at improving our policies through the work and experience of the people and their demands for development. We must ensure that more fruits of reform and development are shared by the people in a fairer way, and secure solid popular support for continuing reform and opening up.

Reform and opening up is always an ongoing task and will never end. Without reform and opening up, China would not be what it is today, nor would it have the prospects for a brighter future. Problems occurring in reform and opening up can only be solved through reform and opening up. To advance reform and opening up, we must carry out the guidelines of the 18th National Congress, and follow the guidance of Deng Xiaoping Theory, the important thought of the Three Represents and the Scientific Outlook on Development. In response to the call of the people and their expectations for further reform and opening up, we should build a social consensus, and promote reforms in all sectors in a coordinated way.

Explanatory Notes to the "Decision of the Central Committee of the Communist Party of China on Some Major Issues Concerning Comprehensively Continuing the Reform"*

November 9, 2013

On behalf of the Political Bureau of the Party Central Committee, I will now explain to the plenary session the "Decision of the Central Committee of the Communist Party of China on Some Major Issues Concerning Comprehensively Continuing the Reform."

I. The Drafting Process of the Decision

Since the reform and opening-up initiative was introduced in 1978 the third plenary sessions of past CPC central committees have provided the public with important information for judging the governance policy and focus of the new generations of Party leadership. The discussion topics, decisions made, measures to take, and signals released bore great significance for the Party's work in the five to ten years following the plenary sessions.

After the Party's 18th National Congress, the Central Committee set out to determine the topics for discussion at the Third Plenary Session of the 18th CPC Central Committee. The 18th National Congress set the goal of completing the building of a moderately prosperous society in all respects and continuing reform and opening up, and emphasized that the Party must, with greater political courage

---

* Explanatory notes made to the Third Plenary Session of the 18th CPC Central Committee.

and wisdom, lose no time in continuing the reform in key sectors, and resolutely discard all notions and systems that hinder efforts to pursue sustainable development. It also pointed out that the Party should set up a well-developed, standardized and effective framework of systems, and ensure that operating institutions in all sectors are fully functioning. To achieve the strategic goals and carry out the plans set at the 18th National Congress, we must lose no time in promoting reform comprehensively.

Thirty-five years have passed since the Party made the historic decision of shifting the focus of the work of the Party and state to economic development and initiating the reform and opening-up drive at the Third Plenary Session of the 11th CPC Central Committee[1]. The propelling force behind the improvement of the Chinese people's life, the advancement of our socialist country, the progress of our Party, and the fact that China has gained important international status is no other than our perseverance in carrying forward the reform and opening-up drive.

During his inspection tour of the South in 1992, Deng Xiaoping said, "If we did not adhere to socialism, implement the policy of reform and opening to the outside world, develop the economy and raise living standards, we would find ourselves in a blind alley."[2] Today, in retrospect, we have a better understanding of his remarks. This is why, as we are well aware, only socialism can save China, and only reform and opening up can develop China, socialism and Marxism.

In light of the historical lessons we have learned and the needs of the current times, the Party Central Committee has been repeatedly stressing since its 18th National Congress that reform and opening up plays the decisive role in determining the destiny of contemporary China. It is also the key to realizing the Two Centenary Goals and the great rejuvenation of the Chinese nation. There are no bounds to practice and development, to freeing the people's minds, or to the reform and opening-up effort. We will reach an impasse if we stall or go into reverse on our path; reform and opening up is always ongoing and will never end. Facing the new situation and new tasks, we must continue the reform comprehensively to strive for solutions to the major problems challenging China's development, and work tirelessly to promote the improvement and progress of socialism with Chinese characteristics.

As extensive and profound changes are taking place domestically and internationally, China's development faces a series of prominent dilemmas and challenges, and there are quite a number of problems and difficulties on its path of development: Unbalanced, uncoordinated and unsustainable development remains a big problem. We are weak in scientific and technological innovation. The industrial structure is unbalanced and the growth mode remains inefficient. The development gap between urban and rural areas and between regions is still large, and so are income disparities. Social problems are markedly on the rise. There are many problems affecting the people's immediate interests in education, employment, social security, health care, housing, the ecological environment, food and drug safety, workplace safety, public security, law enforcement, administration of justice, etc. Some people still lead hard lives. Going through the motions, excessive bureaucracy, self-indulgence, and extravagance are serious problems. Some sectors are prone to corruption and other types of misconduct, and the fight against corruption remains a serious challenge for us. To solve these problems, the key lies in continuing the reform.

In April this year, after deep thinking and research, and after soliciting opinions extensively both inside and outside the Party, the CPC Central Committee's Political Bureau decided that continuing the reform comprehensively would be the central topic for discussion at the Third Plenary Session of the 18th CPC Central Committee and that the session would come up with a decision.

On April 20 the CPC Central Committee issued the "Notice on Soliciting Opinions on Continuing the Reform Comprehensively for Discussion at the Third Plenary Session of the 18th CPC Central Committee." It was unanimously agreed by all regions and departments that by selecting this topic for discussion at the session, the Party answered the calls of the Party members, officials and common people in an effort to address the issues that are of most concern to the whole of society. The public showed widespread support for the decision.

All the third plenary sessions of the CPC Central Committees convened since the reform and opening-up initiative was introduced in 1978 have focused on the discussion of how to continue the reform, sending an important signal that our Party will unswervingly uphold reform and opening up, and firmly adhere to the theories, guidelines and policies put forth since the Third Plenary Session of the 11th Party Central Committee. In a word, it is to answer the question of what banner to hold and what path to take in the new historical conditions.

Continuing the reform comprehensively as the central topic at the Third Plenary Session of the 18th CPC Central Committee was an important proclamation made by our Party, which well reflects the CPC's adherence to the guidance of Deng Xiaoping Theory, the important thought of the Three Represents and the Scientific Outlook on Development. In the new conditions, the Party is unswervingly implementing its basic guidelines and political program, learning from its past experiences and meeting its fundamental requirements, and firmly upholding reform and opening up.

After the topic was decided upon, the Political Bureau of the CPC Central Committee set up a drafting group for the Decision of the plenary session. I served as the head of the group, with Liu Yunshan[3] and Zhang Gaoli[4] as deputy heads. Persons in charge of related departments and leaders of some provinces and municipalities also took part. The drafting work was overseen by the Standing Committee of the Political Bureau of the CPC Central Committee.

Over a period of about seven months following its founding, the drafting group extensively solicited opinions, carried out appraisals of important topics, conducted investigations and researches, and held discussions and revised the document many times. During this period, three meetings of the Standing Committee of the Political Bureau and two meetings of the Political Bureau were held to review the draft

Decision. The draft was also circulated among a certain number of Party members and retired Party officials for their suggestions. Opinions were also heard from the central committees of other political parties, heads of the All-China Federation of Industry and Commerce and prominent individuals without any party affiliation.

The feedback showed that all consulted groups and individuals had reached the consensus that the Decision offers an in-depth analysis of the key issues challenging China's reform, development and stability both in theory and practice, and expounds on the significance of continuing the reform comprehensively and the future of our reform. It sets forth the guidelines for continuing the reform comprehensively, as well as the goals, tasks and underlying principles; it delineates a new blueprint for the reform effort, and envisions the new targets with vigor; it includes the new thoughts, judgments and measures for continuing the reform comprehensively, and reflects the calls, appeals and aspirations of society; and it epitomizes the Party's and the general public's political consensus and wisdom in action to continue the reform comprehensively.

A consensus was reached among all groups and individuals that the Decision lays out a balanced plan for the strategic key areas in continuing the reform comprehensively, with prioritized goals and focal points. It also introduces the working mechanism, methods of implementation, and the timetable and road map for the reform plan, making a series of major breakthroughs in the theories and policies guiding the reform effort. It once again makes overall plans for continuing the reform comprehensively, serving as a general mobilization for the nation to take action. The Decision is bound to exert a significant and far-reaching influence on the development of the socialist cause with Chinese characteristics.

In the course of soliciting opinions, people from all sides offered many valuable ideas and suggestions. With careful study and discussion of these ideas and suggestions within the drafting group, as instructed by the Party Central Committee, important revisions were made to the Decision.

II. The General Framework and Key Issues of the Decision

The Political Bureau of the Party Central Committee believes that, facing the new situation with new tasks and new requirements, China must take comprehensive measures to continue its reform. To do this, the key lies in further developing an environment for fair competition, further invigorating economic and social growth, further enhancing the efficiency of the government, further achieving social equality and justice, further promoting social harmony and stability, and further improving the Party's leadership and governance.

To carry out these resolutions, it must be stressed that we should be fully aware of our problems, focus on the key issues for further study and research, and strive to solve the major dilemmas and problems challenging our development. As the CPC has fought its way through revolution, construction and reform, its sole aim has always been to solve the problems of China. It is fair to say that existing problems force us to reform, and reforms are going deeper while problems being tackled and solved.

In the past 35 years we have overcome many problems hindering the development of the Party and the state through reform. But new problems always replace old ones during our course of exploration and transformation. This is why our system needs to be constantly improved, why reform cannot be accomplished in one stroke and why we cannot rest on our laurels indefinitely once existing problems are solved.

The draft Decision stressed five major considerations. One, it had to meet the new requirements for the development of the Party and state, and carry out the strategic task of continuing the reform comprehensively, as set forth at the Party's 18th National Congress. Two, it had to center on reform and foreground the new measures for continuing it comprehensively, leaving out general and repetitive measures and measures solely for enhancing development. Three, it had to address the key issues, properly deal with the pressing concerns of the people, respond to their calls and aspirations, focus on important areas and crucial segments, and highlight the leading role of the reform of the economic system in promoting development. Four, it had to take an active yet discreet attitude when designing the reform measures. Five, it had to plan the tasks according to the timetable, which set forth that by 2020 decisive results would have been achieved in the reform of important areas and crucial segments.

The plenary session set as the framework of the Decision the important issues that China needs to deal with, and arranged the Decision according to its various points. In addition to the Foreword and Conclusion, there are 16 parts divided into three main sections. The first part is also the first section and the General Remarks, which mainly elaborates on the significance, guiding thoughts and overall direction of continuing the reform comprehensively. Section two consists of Parts 2-15, introducing the arrangement of the main tasks and important measures for continuing the reform in six aspects – the economy, politics, culture, society, ecology and national defense/armed forces. The different aspects are arranged as follows: The economy from Part 2 to Part 7, politics from Part 8 to Part 10, culture in Part 11, society from Part 12 to Part 13, ecology in Part 14, and national defense/armed forces in Part 15. Part 16 composes the third section, Organizational Leadership, which mainly elaborates on strengthening and improving the Party's leadership in the course of continuing the reform comprehensively.

Here, I would like to explain the considerations of the CPC Central Committee on the major issues and key measures mentioned in the Decision of the Third Plenary Session of the 18th CPC Central Committee.

First, allowing the market to play the decisive role in allocating resources and letting the government perform its functions better. This is a major theoretical proposition in the Decision, because the reform of the economic system is still the focus of continuing the reform comprehensively, and the appropriate handling of the relationship between the government and the market is still the core issue of the reform of the economic system.

In 1992 the Party's 14th National Congress stipulated that China's economic reform aimed at establishing a socialist market economy, allowing the market to play a basic role in allocating resources under state macro control. This key breakthrough in theory played an extremely important role in guiding China's reform and opening-up effort, and its economic and social development. It also illustrated that theoretical innovation paves the way for innovation in practice. To comprehensively continue the reform we must renew our theory first.

After 20 years of practice a socialist market economy has been basically established in China. But there are still many problems. The market lacks order, and many people seek economic benefits through unjustified means; the market for factors of production lags behind in development, unable to allocate the factors of production to meet the effective demand; the lack of unified market rules has resulted in rampant protectionism initiated by departments or local governments; and market competition is not good enough to select the superior and eliminate the inferior, and thus slows down economic restructuring. If left unsolved, these problems will hinder the development of a sound socialist market economy.

Over the past two decades since the Party's 14th National Congress we have kept searching for a new positioning for the relationship between the government and the market through practice and theoretical research. The Party's 15th National Congress proposed that "the market plays a basic role in allocating resources under state macro control," the Party's 16th National Congress proposed to "give fuller play to the basic role of the market in allocating resources," the Party's 17th National Congress sought to "introduce institutions to give better play to the basic role of the market in allocating resources," and the Party's 18th National Congress stipulated that the Party should "leverage to a greater extent and in a wider scope the basic role of the market in allocating resources." From the above progression it can be seen that we have been constantly deepening our understanding of the government-market relationship.

During the discussion and consultation sessions regarding the Decision, many people suggested that the Party should further define the government-market relationship from a theoretical perspective, which would have great significance for continuing the reform comprehensively. With due consideration to these opinions and the current circumstances, and after much discussion and research, the Party Central Committee agreed that it was time to introduce a new theoretical expression concerning this matter, and that the "basic role" of the market in allocating resources should be revised to a "decisive role."

We have now basically established a socialist market economy in our country, with considerable improvement in the degree of marketization. We have gained better knowledge of the market rules and enhanced our capacity to use it to our benefit, and have improved the macro-control system. With both the subjective and objective conditions in place, we should take a new step forward to improve our socialist market economy.

To further balance the relationship between the government and the market we need to decide which of the two is to play the decisive role in allocating resources. To boost the economy we must enhance the efficiency of the allocation of resources, especially that of scarce resources, so that we can use fewer resources to make more products and gain more benefits. Both theory and practice have proved that the allocation of resources by the market is the most effective means to this end. It is a general rule of the market economy that the market decides the allocation of resources, and a market economy in essence is one in which the market determines resource allocation. We have to follow this rule when we improve the socialist market economy. We should work harder to address the problems of market imperfection, too much government interference and lack of oversight. Positioning the market as playing a "decisive role" in resource allocation is conducive to establishing the correct notion of the government-market relationship in the whole Party and the whole of society, and conducive to transforming the economic growth pattern and government functions, as well as reining in corruption and other forms of misconduct.

Our market economy is socialist, of course. We need to give leverage to the superiority of our socialist system, and let the Party and government perform their positive functions. The market plays a decisive role in allocating resources, but is not the sole actor in this regard.

To develop the socialist market economy, leverage should be given to both the market and the government, with differentiated functions. The Decision put forth clear requirements for improving the functions of the government, emphasizing that scientific macro control and effective governance are the intrinsic requirements for giving more leverage to the advantages of the socialist market economy. The Decision also makes plans for improving macro control, correctly performing government functions in all areas, and improving the organization of government. It stresses that the main responsibility and role of the government is to maintain the stability of the macro economy, strengthen and improve public services, ensure fair competition, strengthen market oversight, maintain market order, promote sustainable development and common prosperity, and intervene in situations where market failure occurs.

Second, adhering to and improving the basic economic system. The basic economic system with public ownership playing a leading role and all forms of ownership growing side by side is an important pillar of the socialist system with Chinese characteristics.

Since the introduction of the reform and opening-up policy in 1978 the structure of ownership has undergone gradual adjustment, with the weights of the public and non-public sectors changing in their contribution to the economy and employment. The economy and society have grown more vigorous during this process. In such conditions, how to better recognize the leading role of public ownership and stick to this position and how to further explore the effective forms for materializing the basic economic system have become major topics for us.

It is emphasized in the Decision that we must unswervingly consolidate and develop the public economy, persist in the leading role of public ownership, give full play to the leading role of the state-owned economy, and incessantly increase its vitality, leveraging power and impact.

Adhering to and furthering the relevant deliberations made since the Party's 15th National Congress, the Decision proposes to vigorously develop the mixed-ownership economy. It stresses that such an economy, with cross-shareholding by and integration of state-owned capital, collective capital and non-public capital, is important to materialize the basic economic system of China. It will help to improve the functions of state-owned capital, maintain and increase its value and raise its competitiveness. It is an effective channel and inevitable choice for us to adhere to the leading role of public ownership and improve the vitality, leveraging power and impact of the state-owned economy in the new conditions.

The Decision states that China will improve the state assets management system, strengthen state assets oversight with capital management at the core, and reform the authorized operation mechanism for state capital. State-owned capital investment operations must serve the strategic goals of the state, invest more in key industries and areas that are vital to national security and are the lifeblood of the economy, focus on offering public services, develop important and future-oriented strategic industries, protect the ecological environment, support scientific and technological progress, and guarantee national security. The government will transfer part of the state-owned capital to social security funds. We will increase the proportion of state-owned capital gains that are turned over to the public finance, to be used to ensure and improve the people's livelihood.

State-owned enterprises (SOEs) constitute an important force for advancing modernization and protecting the common interests of the people. Through many years of reform SOEs have by and large assimilated themselves into the market economy. At the same time, however, they have also found problems and drawbacks in their system, which call for further reform. The Decision proposes a series of targeted reform measures: We must ensure that state-owned capital increases its input into public-service-oriented enterprises; in natural monopoly industries in which state-owned capital continues to hold controlling interests, carry out a reform focusing on separation of government administration from enterprise management, separation of government administration from state assets management, franchise operation, and government oversight, separate network ownership from operation, and deregulate control over competitive businesses in light of the conditions of different industries; improve the corporate governance structure to ensure smooth operation and effective checks and balances; establish a system of professional managers, and give better play to the role of business executives; establish a long-term incentive-and-restraint mechanism, and strengthen investigations into the accountability of SOE operations and investment; and explore ways to publicize important information, including SOE financial budgets. Moreover, SOEs should appropriately increase the proportion of market-based recruitment, and properly determine and strictly regulate the salary level, post-related benefits and expenses as well as business spending of SOE managerial personnel. These measures will stimulate SOEs to improve the modern corporate system, enhance their operating efficiency, better fulfill their social obligations and play a better role in the economy.

We must adhere to the "two unswervinglys"[5] in order to continue and improve our basic economic system. The Decision proposes reform measures on multiple levels to encourage, support and guide the development of the non-public sector of the economy, and to stimulate its vigor and creativity. On functional positioning, the Decision points out that both the public and non-public sectors are important components of the socialist market economy, and an important basis for China's economic and social development. On the protection of property rights, the Decision points out that the property rights of both the public and non-public sectors are inviolable. On policy treatment, the Decision stresses equal rights, equal opportunities and identical rules, and a unified market access system. The Decision encourages non-public enterprises to participate in the reform of SOEs, encourages development of mixed-ownership enterprises in which private capital holds majority shares, and encourages qualified private enterprises to establish a modern corporate system. All these will contribute to the healthy development of the non-public sector of the economy.

Third, continuing the reform of the fiscal and taxation systems. Finance is the foundation and an important pillar of national governance. Good fiscal and taxation systems are the institutional guarantee for improving resource allocation, maintaining market unity, promoting social equity, and realizing enduring peace and stability. Developed on the basis of the tax distribution system[6] reform initiated in 1994, the current fiscal and taxation systems have played an important role in increasing the government's financial strength and promoting the rapid growth of the economy.

As the situation changes, the current fiscal and taxation systems cannot effectively respond to the requirements for dividing powers between the central and local governments to improve national governance. They have lagged behind our effort to transform the economic growth pattern and promote the sustained and healthy development of the economy and society, and are causing problems that hinder economic and social development.

Reform of the fiscal and taxation systems is one of the key points in continuing the reform comprehensively. The reform mainly includes improvement of the budgeting and taxation systems, and establishment of a system in which authority of office matches responsibility for expenditure.

The Decision stipulates that we will adopt a complete, standardized, open and transparent budget system, and appropriately increase the authority of office and responsibility of expenditure of the central government, including those concerning national defense, foreign affairs, national security, and unified national market rules and management. The authority of office over some social security programs, and the construction and maintenance of major trans-regional projects will be shared by the central and local governments, and the authority of office will be gradually clarified in this regard. The central government can delegate some expenditure responsibilities to local governments through transfer payments. In terms of trans-regional public services with great impacts on other regions, the central government will shoulder some of the expenditure responsibilities of local governments through transfer payments.

The main aim of the reform is to clearly define authority of office, reform the taxation system, make tax burdens stable and budgets transparent, and increase efficiency. It also aims to accelerate the development of a modern fiscal system that is conducive to the transformation of the economic growth pattern, the establishment of a fair market under unified rules, and the promotion of equal access to basic public services; develop fiscal and taxation systems that are compatible with the financial resources and authority of office of the central and local governments; and mobilize the initiative of both the central and local governments.

Reform of the fiscal and taxation systems is a step-by-step process, and will take some time to complete. The Party Central Committee has clearly stated that we must maintain the stability of the current financial patterns of the central and local governments, and further rationalize the division of revenues between them.

Fourth, improving mechanisms and institutions for the integrated development of urban and rural areas. The unbalanced development between urban and rural areas is a serious problem hindering the development of our economy and society, a major problem we must solve in order to complete the building of a moderately prosperous society in all respects and accelerate socialist modernization. Tremendous changes have taken place in China's rural areas since the reform and opening-up policy was introduced in late 1978. However, the separate urban-rural structures have not changed fundamentally, and the widening gap between urban and rural development has not been reversed. To solve these problems, we must push forward the integrated development of urban and rural areas.

The Decision states that we must improve the mechanisms and institutions to form new relations between industry and agriculture and between urban and rural areas in which industry promotes agriculture, urban areas support rural development, agriculture and industry benefit each other, and there is integrated urban and rural development, so that the overwhelming majority of farmers can participate in the modernization process on an equal basis and share the fruits of modernization.

The Decision proposes reform measures to improve the mechanisms and institutions for the integrated development of urban and rural areas: One, accelerating the building of a new type of agricultural operation system. We will maintain the fundamental status of family operation in agriculture; encourage the transfer of contracted land-use right to big, specialized operators, family farms, farmers' cooperatives and agrobusinesses; encourage rural areas to develop cooperative economies; encourage and guide industrial and commercial capital to invest in rural areas to develop modern planting and breeding industries suited to commercialized management; and allow farmers to develop industrialized operation of agriculture by becoming shareholders using their contracted land-use right, among other measures. Two, endowing farmers with more property rights. We will protect farmers' contracted land-use right by law, safeguard the rights and interests of farmers as members of collective economic organizations, ensure rural households' usufruct of their homesteads, and select several pilot areas to steadily and prudently push forward the mortgage, guarantee and transfer of farmers' residential property rights. Three, promoting equal exchanges of factors of production and balanced allocation of public resources between urban and rural areas. We will ensure migrant workers receive equal pay for equal work, and ensure farmers equally share the gains from added value of land; improve the agricultural insurance system; encourage investment in rural development, and permit enterprises and social organizations to start all kinds of undertakings in rural areas; make a balanced allocation of compulsory education resources between urban and rural areas, integrate the basic old-age insurance and healthcare insurance systems of urban and rural residents, and improve the balanced development of the minimum living allowance system in both urban and rural areas; and steadily make basic urban public services available to all permanent residents in cities, and incorporate farmers who have settled down in urban areas into the urban housing and social security network.

Fifth, promoting wide, multi-tiered and institutionalized consultative democracy. Consultative democracy is a unique form and distinctive advantage of China's socialist democracy, and an important embodiment of the Party's mass line in the political field. Promoting consultative democracy is conducive to improving the people's orderly participation in political affairs, strengthening the ties between the Party and the people, and promoting scientific and democratic decision-making.

Promoting wide, multi-tiered and institutionalized consultative democracy is an important issue of political restructuring as stipulated in the Decision. The Decision stresses that, under the leadership of the Party, China will promote consultation throughout society with regard to major issues of economic and social development, and practical issues closely related to the interests of the people, and adhere to the principle of consultation before policy-making and during policy implementation. We will build a consultative democracy featuring appropriate procedures and complete segments to expand the consultation channels covering organs of state power, committees of the Chinese People's Political Consultative Conference (CPPCC), political parties, and community-level and social organizations; conduct intensive consultations on issues relating to legislation, administration, democracy, political participation and social problems; give full play to the important role of the United Front[7] in consultative democracy, make the CPPCC serve as a major channel for conducting consultative democracy, improve the system of the CPPCC, specify the contents and procedures for consultation, diversify forms of consultative democracy, and more actively carry out orderly consultations on particular issues with those working on these issues, with representatives from all sectors of society, and with the relevant government departments on the handling of proposals, and increase the frequency of consultations to improve their effectiveness.

Sixth, reforming the judiciary and its operation mechanism. The judiciary is an important component of the political system. Miscarriage of justice has been a major concern of the people in recent years, and the judiciary suffers a lack of credibility largely due to its current defective system and operation mechanism, which need improvement.

Judicial reform is one of the key points in continuing the reform comprehensively. The Decision puts forward a series of new and related measures in the following aspects: reform of the judicial management system, unification of the management of staff, funds and properties of courts and procuratorates at and below the provincial level and exploration of ways to establish a judicial jurisdiction system that is appropriately separated from the administrative divisions; improvement of the mechanism for the use of judicial power; improvement of the responsibility system for handling cases by the presiding judge and the collegiate bench, by which the judges hand down verdicts and the collegiate bench is responsible for carrying them out; strict regulation of the procedures of sentence commutation, release on parole and medical parole; improvement of the mechanism for preventing and correcting wrong cases and the accountability system, and strict implementation of the rule banning illegal evidence; establishment of a system for settling complaints involving law violations and lawsuits made in the form of letters and visits in accordance with the law; and abolition of the re-education through labor system, and improvement of laws for the punishment and correction of unlawful and criminal acts.

These measures are of vital significance for ensuring that judicial departments independently exercise their judicial and procuratorial powers according to law, improving the judicial power operation mechanism in which rights and responsibilities are clear, improving judicial transparency and credibility, and safeguarding human rights.

Seventh, improving leading and working mechanisms for anti-corruption efforts. Fighting corruption has always been a widely discussed topic inside and outside the Party. We are now mainly challenged by the following problems: Anti-corruption forces performing functions separately makes it difficult to build up synergy; some cases are not dealt with resolutely; and the accountability system is too lax to handle reoccurring corruption cases.

The Decision lays out plans for promoting innovation in the anti-corruption mechanisms and institutions, and strengthening institutional guarantees. The main points are: strengthening the Party's unified leadership to build a clean and honest government and combat corruption; ensuring that Party committees bear primary responsibility and the commissions for discipline inspection take the responsibility for oversight, and working out and implementing a feasible accountability system; improving the leading and working mechanisms for anti-corruption efforts, reforming and improving the functions of anti-corruption coordination groups at all levels, and leaving the investigation of corruption cases mainly to commissions for discipline inspection of higher levels; strengthening the leadership role of the higher levels over the lower levels of the discipline inspection commissions, and the simultaneous reporting of the related investigation process to the Party committee at the same level and the commission for discipline inspection at the next-higher level; and fully ensuring that the Central Commission for Discipline Inspection dispatches resident discipline inspection agencies to the central-level departments of the Party and the government, and improving the discipline inspection system at both the central and local levels, so that it covers all regions, all sectors, all enterprises and all public institutions.

All these measures are based on past experience and the suggestions of various groups and individuals.

Eighth, accelerating the improvement of the leadership for the management of the Internet. Cyber security and information security bear on national security and social stability, and pose new challenges for us in many aspects.

Falling behind the rapid development of Internet technology and applications, our current management of the Internet is seriously flawed and cannot function properly. Different administrative bodies engaged in multi-channel management of the Internet, overlapping functions and mismatch between powers and responsibilities – all these have led to inefficient management. Also, as the Internet grows into a new form of the media, the management of this online medium and the industry is lagging far behind the development of the business. With fast growth in the number of the users of micro-blogs, WeChat and other social network services and instant communication tools, which spread information quickly over wide areas and can mobilize large numbers of users, how to strengthen oversight within a legal framework and guide public opinion and how to ensure the orderly dissemination of online information, while at the same time safeguarding national security and social stability, have become pressing problems for us.

The Decision stipulates that we must adhere to the principles of proactive usage, well-planned development, management in accordance with the law and ensuring safety in strengthening management of the Internet in accordance with the law, and accelerating the improvement of the leadership for the management of the Internet. The aim of this is to integrate the functions of the related departments and form joint forces in the management of the Internet covering both technology and contents, and ranging from daily security to combating crimes, to ensure correct and safe Internet usage.

Ninth, establishing the National Security Commission. National security and social stability form the basis for further reform and progress. Currently we are challenged by pressure from two sources: Internationally we must safeguard state sovereignty, national security and our development interests, and domestically we need to maintain political and social stability. All kinds of foreseeable and unforeseeable risks are increasing significantly, but our security system is not good enough to meet the demands of ensuring national security. We need to establish a strong platform to coordinate our national security work. For this purpose, establishing the National Security Commission to strengthen unified leadership of national security at the central level has become an urgent matter.

The main responsibilities of the National Security Commission are to formulate and implement national security strategy, promote national security legislation, design principles and policies for national security work, and discuss and resolve key issues concerning national security.

Tenth, improving the country's natural resource management and oversight systems. Improving the country's natural resource management system is an important reform for developing the property right system for natural resources. It is also the intrinsic requirement for building an ecologically friendly country with complete support systems.

Some of our major frustrations in ecological protection are caused by problems in the ecological management system. One problem lies in the vague concept of ownership of natural resources by the whole people, which leads to problems in the identification of the rights and interests of the owners. To solve this problem, the Decision puts forth measures for improving the natural resource management system. The guiding thoughts are: ensuring people's property rights to natural resources in accordance with the principle of separation between ownership and management, one issue belonging to one department, and establishing a unified responsibility mechanism for people who act on behalf of the public to manage public natural resource assets.

There is a difference between the state's exercise of power and management over the natural resource assets owned by the whole people and the state's supervision and management of the natural resources within its territory. The former is the owner's right, while the latter is the manager's right. This requires us to improve the system of oversight of natural resources, and fulfill our duties as the managers of our territorial space. The owners of state-owned natural resource assets and the managers of state natural resources must act independently, while cooperating with and supervising each other.

We need to realize that our mountains, waters, forests, farmlands and lakes form a living community. The lifeline of the people comes from the farmland, that of the farmland comes from the water, that of the water comes from the mountain, that of the mountain comes from the earth, and that of the earth comes from the tree. To control the exploitation of natural resources and restore the ecosystem, we must follow the laws of nature. If people only tend to their own responsibilities, for example, growing trees, regulating rivers or protecting farmland in isolation, they are prone to gaining in one area and losing in another, which eventually leads to systemic destruction of the ecology. Therefore, it is of the utmost importance to put one department in charge of the usage of the entire territory of a country, and carry out unified protection and restoration programs for its natural resources.

Eleventh, establishing the Leading Group for Further Reform under the CPC Central Committee. Continuing the reform comprehensively is a complicated system engineering project, which requires more than one or several departments to carry out. Therefore, leadership at a higher level should be established for this purpose.

The Decision stipulates that the Party Central Committee will set up the Leading Group for Further Reform. This is to give better play to the Party's core function as leader having a picture of the whole situation and as chief coordinator of different aspects, so as to ensure the reform progresses smoothly and the assigned tasks are implemented as planned. The main responsibilities of this leading group are planning key national reforms, promoting coordinated reforms in various fields, coordinating various forces into a joint force for reform, strengthening supervision and oversight, and promoting full implementation of the reform's aim and tasks.

III. Several Matters That Require Attention in Discussion

The task of this plenary session is to discuss the guiding thought and plans for continuing the reform comprehensively as proposed in the Decision. For the discussion, please bear the following in mind:

First, we must be more confident and courageous in pushing forward reform. Reform and opening up is a new great revolution of the Chinese people led by our Party in the new era. It is the most outstanding characteristic of contemporary China, and the distinctive feature of our Party. What has helped our Party inspire the people, unify them and pull their strength together over the past 35 years? What have we been relying on to stimulate the creativity and vitality of our people, realize rapid economic and social development and win a competitive advantage over capitalism? The answer has always been reform and opening up.

Looking to the future, there is no alternative to continuing reform and opening up if we are to solve all sorts of difficult problems hindering our development, defuse risks and meet challenges in all aspects, give better play to the advantages of socialism with Chinese characteristics, and promote the steady and healthy development of the economy and society.

At the current stage, close attention to our reform and opening-up drive comes from inside and outside the Party and inside and outside the country as well. The entire Party and all sectors of society have high expectations for us. Our reform has come to a critical juncture. We must not waver in the slightest degree in carrying out reform and opening up, and we must continue to uphold and firmly adhere to the correct path of socialism with Chinese characteristics. The whole Party must reaffirm our conviction to push forward reform with greater political courage and wisdom, and stronger measures and methods.

Second, we must continue to free our minds and seek truth from facts. To keep our banner of reform and opening up flying high, we must also take pragmatic measures once we have a strong conviction. Actions speak louder than words. It is a strategic choice of the CPC Central Committee to make overall plans for continuing the reform comprehensively at the Third Plenary Session of the 18th CPC Central Committee. We must take this opportunity to make new breakthroughs in our reform. For this to happen, we need to further free our minds.

To break down the barriers of old notions and the fences of interest groups, freeing the mind is the first and most important step. Often, the roadblocks in our minds that hinder reform do not come from outside the system, but from within. If the mind is not freed we can hardly see the crux of our problems with the interest groups, or pinpoint the direction of our effort to break down the barriers. We will also find it difficult to come up with innovative reform measures. Therefore, we must have the courage and breadth of vision to seek self-improvement. We need to throw off the trammels of outdated ideas and overcome the constraints put in place by various departments for their own interests, and proactively conduct research and propose reform measures.

Before putting forth a reform measure, we must research and discuss it carefully, but this does not mean being overcautious or hesitant to try anything new. It is not possible to carry out reforms while keeping our current work pattern and operation system intact, nor is it possible to do it in a rock-steady or risk-free manner. As long as we have done thorough research and appraisal, and know what we are going to do agrees with the actual conditions and needs to be done, we will go ahead without looking back.

Third, we must put the interests of the state first when making deliberations. Continuing the reform comprehensively is a major strategic plan concerning the overall development of the Party and the state, rather than a single program to reform a certain aspect of a sector. "One who fails to plan for the whole situation is incapable of planning for a partial area."[8] You come from different departments and units, and you need to see things from a wider perspective. For major decisions, first we should judge whether a proposed reform measure meets the needs of the country, and whether it is condu-cive to the long-term development of the cause of the Party and the state. We must strive to look forward into the future, think beyond the times, and proactively draw up plans. This will enable us to put through reform measures that will genuinely promote the cause of the Party and the people.

To continue the reform comprehensively, we should strengthen planning at the top level and adopt a holistic approach in doing so. We should study more intensively the connectedness, consistency and feasibility of our reform measures. As we say, "We must push reform forward boldly and steadily." Here "steadily" means adopting a holis-tic approach in planning, doing overall research and making deci-sions scientifically. Reforms in the economy, politics, culture, society and ecology are closely connected to and integrated in the reform of Party building. Reform in one sector will always affect other sectors and require other sectors to reform accordingly. If reforms in differ-ent areas do not support each other, and the measures taken in some sectors turn out to check the progress of other sectors, we will find it difficult to continue the reform comprehensively; we will get into a muddle with the reform if we disregard these factors.

Notes

[1] The Third Plenary Session of the 11th CPC Central Committee was convened in Beijing from December 18 to 22, 1978. At this plenary session, Marxism was reestablished as the guideline for the Party's ideological, political and organizational work. This plenary session also made the historic decision to shift the focus of the Party and state to economic development and to introduce the reform and opening-up initiative, which marked a great transition of far-reaching significance in the his-tory of the CPC since the founding of the People's Republic in 1949, and thereby ushering in a new period of reform and opening up in China.

[2] Deng Xiaoping: "Excerpts from Talks Given in Wuchang, Shenzhen, Zhuhai and Shanghai," *Selected Works of Deng Xiaoping*, Vol. III, Eng. ed., Foreign Languages Press, Beijing, 1994, p. 358.

[3] Liu Yunshan, born in 1947 and a native of Xinzhou City, Shanxi Province, was then a member of the Standing Committee of the Political Bureau of the Party Central Committee, a member of the Secretariat of the Party Central Committee and president of the Central Party School.

[4] Zhang Gaoli, born in 1946 and a native of Jinjiang, Fujian Province, was then a member of the Standing Committee of the Political Bureau of the Party Central Committee and vice premier of the State Council.

[5] The "two unswervinglys" are: We will unswervingly consolidate and develop the public sector of the economy, and at the same time unswervingly encourage, support and guide the development of the non-public sector of the economy.

[6] The tax distribution system is a model fiscal management system. It divides the distribution of all taxation items of the country between the central and local governments, so as to define the ranges of their respective revenues. Its nature is to specify the financial power of the central and local governments according to their authority of office, and to form the respective revenue systems of the central and local governments through the distribution of taxation items between them. China adopted the tax distribution system on January 1, 1994.

[7] The United Front refers to the political union formed by various social and political forces, including social classes and strata, political parties and groups, and even ethnic groups and nations, based on their common interests, to achieve a common goal under certain historical conditions. The United Front under the leadership of the CPC is the broadest revolutionary, socialist and patriotic United Front formed by all ethnic groups, all political parties, all social strata and people of all circles in China during the New Democratic Revolution (1919-1949), socialist construction and reform, to achieve national independence, democracy and prosperity and the rejuvenation of the Chinese nation.

[8] Chen Danran: "Proposals on Moving the Capital and Establishing Feudatories," *Enlightening Speeches* (*Wu Yan*). Chen Danran (1859-1930) was a litterateur in the Qing Dynasty.

Align Our Thinking with the Guidelines of the Third Plenary Session of the 18th CPC Central Committee[*]

November 12, 2013

We have to unify the thinking and will of the whole Party first in order to unify the thinking and will of the people of all China's ethnic groups so that everyone works together to advance our reform.

Here, I need to make a few points on how we should implement the guidelines of the plenary session, with the focus on the guiding principles, overall plans, objectives and tasks it has set forth.

First, we must take improving and developing the socialist system with Chinese characteristics and modernizing our national governance system and capacity as the general goal of continuing the reform comprehensively. Deng Xiaoping said in 1992 that it would probably take another 30 years for us to develop a more mature and well-defined system in every field. Based on his strategic thought, the plenary session proposed modernizing our national governance system and capacity. This is something that must be done to improve and develop the socialist system and to achieve socialist modernization. We decided to focus on the question of continuing the reform comprehensively at the plenary session – not the reform of one or several fields, but of all areas. We made this decision out of the overall consideration of improving our national governance system and capacity.

The national governance system and capacity of a country epitomize not only its many systems but also how well it can enforce them. Our national governance system is a system of institutions within

* Part of the speech at the second full assembly of the Third Plenary Session of the 18th CPC Central Committee.

which the country is governed with the leadership of the Party. It comprises economic, political, cultural, social and ecological as well as Party-building systems and mechanisms, laws and regulations. This is a complete set of closely connected and coordinated systems of the state. Our national governance capacity is the ability to use these systems to manage social affairs, including reform, development and stability, domestic and foreign affairs, national defense, and the running of the Party, state and military. Our national governance system and capacity complement each other and form an organic whole. An effective governance system will lead to greater governance capacity, while greater governance capacity can make the governance system more effective.

Actually, how to govern a socialist society, a completely new society, has not been clearly addressed by world socialism so far. Karl Marx and Friedrich Engels had no practical experience in the comprehensive governance of a socialist country, as their theories about a future society were mostly predictive. Vladimir Lenin, who passed away a few years after the October Revolution (1917) in Russia, was thus unable to explore this question in depth. The Soviet Union tackled this question and gained some experience, but it made serious mistakes and failed to resolve the problem. Our Party has worked on the same question steadily ever since it came to national power, and, in spite of serious setbacks, has accumulated rich experience and achieved great success in improving our governance system and enhancing our governance capacity. The success has been particularly resounding since we adopted the policy of reform and opening up. Enjoying political stability, economic growth, social harmony and ethnic unity, today's China poses a striking contrast to many regions and countries that suffer constant chaos. This shows that our national governance system and capacity are on the whole quite sound and suited to our national conditions and development needs.

At the same time, we should also realize that, compared with China's needs for social and economic development and our people's expectations, and compared with today's increasingly intense international competition, and the need to ensure prolonged stability at home, we still have many shortcomings to overcome in improving our national governance system and capacity. To realize genuine social harmony and stability, and lasting peace and security, we must rely on our effective institutions, our high capacity in governance and our high-caliber personnel. To give free rein to the advantages of Chinese socialism, we must promote the modernization of our national governance system and capacity in all fields.

To modernize our national governance system and capacity we should adapt properly to the changing times, and reform outdated systems, mechanisms, laws and regulations, while building new ones to make our institutions in all respects more appropriate and complete and the governance of Party, state and social affairs more institutionalized, standardized and procedure-based. We should pay more attention to building our governance capacity, enhancing our awareness of the need to act in accordance with institutions and the law, and our skills in running the country with institutions and the law, transforming our institutional advantages into greater governance effectiveness, and enhancing the Party's capacity to govern in an effective and democratic way, and in accordance with the law.

Second, we must further free our mind, further release and develop the productive forces, and further stimulate and strengthen the vigor of society. The "three furthers" put forward at the plenary session are both objectives and conditions of our reform. Freeing our mind is a prerequisite or the ultimate switch for releasing and developing the productive forces, and strengthening the vigor of our society. Without freeing our mind, our Party would not have been able to make the historic decision to shift the focus of the work of the Party and the country to economic development and launch reform and opening up shortly after the ten-year turmoil of the Cultural Revolution, ushering in a new era in China's development. Without freeing our mind, our Party would not have been able to promote theoretical and practical innovation, remove risks and challenges effectively to advance reform and opening up steadily, and remain at the forefront of the times. Releasing and developing the productive forces, and stimulating and strengthening the vigor of our society are an inevitable outcome as well as an important basis for freeing the mind.

To complete the building of a moderately prosperous society in all respects, achieve socialist modernization and the great renewal of the Chinese nation, the most essential and urgent task is to further release and develop the productive forces. The purpose of freeing our minds, and stimulating and strengthening the vigor of society is to better release and develop the productive forces. Deng Xiaoping said, "Revolution means the emancipation of the productive forces, and so does reform. After the basic socialist system has been established it will be necessary to fundamentally change the economic structure that has hampered the development of the productive forces and to establish a vigorous socialist economic structure that will promote their development."[1] By continuing reform, we will unleash the vitality of work, knowledge, technology, management, capital and other factors to open an abundance of social wealth. In addition, we must keep vitality and order in proper balance, as society needs vitality to progress, but such vitality should be accompanied by order. Neither a pool of stagnant water nor a surging undercurrent is what we want.

We stress the need to have confidence in our path, in our theories and in our system. In other words, we need to have strong will power and faith. At the same time, we also need a strong material power that bolsters such will power and faith. This requires constant reforms and innovations to ensure that Chinese socialism is more efficient than capitalism in releasing and developing the productive forces, stimulating and strengthening the vigor of society and promoting a well-rounded development of the person, and the arousing of greater enthusiasm, initiative and creativity among the people, create more favorable conditions for social development, and show a better edge in competition, thus fully displaying its advantages.

Third, we must keep our focus on economic reforms, and give full play to their catalytic role. The plenary session presented a road map for furthering reform comprehensively, with "six centering-ons,"[2] stressing the need to focus on economic reforms and their leading role. The basic fact that China is still in the primary stage of socialism and will long remain so has not changed; nor has the principal problem in our society, namely, inadequacy in meeting the ever-growing material and cultural needs of the people, because of backward social production; and nor has China's international position as the world's largest developing country. All this dictates that economic development will remain the focus of the work of the whole Party.

Currently, most structural and institutional barriers hindering China's proper development are found in the economy. Our economic reforms have not been completed, nor has the potential of such reforms been fully released. To keep economic development as our central task we must continue to focus on economic reforms without the slightest hesitation.

The economic base determines the superstructure. Economic reforms have a significant and pervasive bearing on the reform of other fields. And the tempo of progress in major economic reforms determines that of a host of other reforms, playing a critical part in the overall situation. In the "Preface to *A Contribution to the Critique of Political Economy*," Karl Marx observed that "In the social production of their existence, men inevitably enter into definite relations, which are independent of their will, namely, relations of production appropriate to a given stage in the development of their material forces of production. The totality of these relations of production constitutes the economic structure of society, the real foundation, on which arises a legal and political superstructure and to which correspond definite forms of social consciousness."[3] As we continue to reform comprehensively, we should keep our focus on economic reforms, and strive to make breakthroughs in the reform of key fields, so that such breakthroughs will drive and stimulate reforms in other areas, and ensure that these reforms can work together and progress in concert. We should not take a fragmented and uncoordinated approach in this regard.

Fourth, we must uphold the direction of reform towards a socialist market economy. Identifying our reform as aiming to establish a socialist market economy is a significant theoretical and practical innovation our Party made in the course of building socialism with Chinese characteristics. This resolved a major problem that other socialist countries had long failed to resolve.

Over the past two decades or so we have advanced economic and other reforms centering on the goal of establishing a socialist market economy, and realized a great historic transition from a highly centralized planned economy to a robust socialist market economy, from seclusion and semi-seclusion to all-dimensional opening up, and from a life of subsistence to one of initial prosperity. The historic leap forward by which China's economy rose to the second place in the world has greatly increased the enthusiasm of the Chinese people, greatly boosted the development of China's productive forces, and added great vigor to the Party and the country.

At the same time, we should also be aware that although our socialist market economy has taken shape initially, it is not complete as a system, and it is not yet mature. In particular, a balance between the role of the government and that of the market in effectively and unrestrictedly allocating resources is yet to be established. So we have to make strenuous efforts to fulfill the strategic task of quickly improving our socialist market economy set by the 18th Party Congress.

The key to establishing a sound socialist market economy lies in striking a proper balance between the role of the government and that of the market, so that the market can play a decisive role in allocating resources and the government can play its own role more effectively. This represents another major step forward in our Party's theoretical and practical exploration.

Establishing a sound socialist market economy is not only the basic need for the economic reforms, but also the core requirement for comprehensively continuing our reform. Letting the market play a decisive role in allocating resources will mainly require economic reforms, but it will also inevitably affect politics, culture, society, ecological progress and Party building. Institutional reforms of all areas should be promoted in concert with establishing a sound socialist market economy, while ensuring that their related links better meet the demands of a growing socialist market economy.

Fifth, we must make the promotion of social fairness and justice and the improvement of wellbeing both the starting point and ultimate goal. Since the beginning of reform and opening up, China has made remarkable achievements in economic and social development, which provide a solid material foundation and favorable conditions for social fairness and justice. Nevertheless, given the current level of development, injustice and inequality are still quite common in our society. As China develops further and the people's living standards improve, public awareness of equality and democracy, and of rights and interests has been steadily enhanced, and hence people's resentment at injustice becomes more pronounced.

After comprehensively reviewing and analyzing China's current social and economic development, the CPC Central Committee has concluded that this problem, if not resolved in good time, will reduce public confidence in our reform and opening up, and undermine social harmony and stability. As the 18th Party Congress pointed out, fairness and justice are inherent requirements of socialism with Chinese characteristics. We must, relying on the concerted efforts of all the Chinese people and based on economic and social development, step up efforts to develop institutions that are vital to ensuring social fairness and justice; establish in due course a system for ensuring fairness in society featuring, among other things, equal rights, equal opportunities and fair rules for all; and foster a fair social environment and ensure the people's equal right to participation in governance and to development.

This plenary session stressed that to comprehensively continue reform we must make the promotion of social fairness and justice, and improvement of the people's lives both the starting point and ultimate goal. This is a necessary requirement of the fundamental purpose of our Party, which is to serve the people wholeheartedly.

Comprehensively furthering the reform must be the guarantee of building a more equitable and just social environment, addressing breaches of equity and justice, and bringing more of the benefits of development to all the people in a fairer fashion. If we cannot deliver tangible benefits to the people, and create a fairer social environment, and, worse still, if we cause more inequality, then our reform will lose its meaning and cannot be sustained.

Realizing social fairness and justice requires multiple factors, a higher level of social and economic development being the most crucial one. Understanding of and desires for social fairness and justice may differ when there are differences in development levels and historical periods, and people's outlook and social background. When we speak of social fairness and justice, we mean to proceed from the fundamental interests of the overwhelming majority of the people, and view and address this problem from the larger picture of social development, social harmony and the people as a whole. The violations of social fairness and justice in the country are mainly fundamental problems in the course of development, which can be resolved by institutional, legal and policy arrangements in tandem with continued development. We must take economic development as the central task, promote sustained and sound growth, and "make the cake bigger," thereby laying a more solid material foundation for greater social fairness and justice.

This does not mean that we should wait to address the problem of social fairness and justice until the economy is developed. The nature of the problems may differ from period to period, bearing the features of society – developed or not so developed – in which they are found. Even when the "cake" has indeed become bigger, we must cut it fairly. The Chinese people have always had a perception that "inequality rather than want is the cause of trouble."[4] Based on continued development, we should do a better job of promoting fairness and justice, trying our best while being mindful of our limitations so that we can keep making progress in ensuring people's access to education, remunerable employment, health care, old-age care and housing.

No matter what development level a society is at, institutions are always an indispensable guarantee of social fairness and justice. We should strive to overcome injustice and inequality caused by man-made factors through innovative institutional arrangements, and ensure our people's rights to equal participation and development. We should take social fairness and justice and the living standards of the people as a mirror to examine our systems, mechanisms, policies and regulations in all respects, and introduce reforms accordingly by focusing on areas where the problems of injustice and inequality are most prevalent. As for problems caused by unsound institutional arrangements, timely measures should be taken to reflect better the principle of fairness and justice in our socialist society and better realize, maintain and develop the fundamental interests of our people.

Sixth, we must rely on the people to promote reform. The people are the creators of history and the source of our strength. The fundamental reason why our reform and opening up has won the people's wholehearted support and vigorous participation all along lies in the fact that from the very beginning we let the cause strike deep roots among the people. The Decision of this plenary session reviewed the valuable experiences of our reform and opening up, one of which highlighted the importance of putting people first, respecting their principal position in the country, giving free rein to their creativity, and promoting reform with the close support of the people. In the absence of the people's support and participation, no reform can possibly succeed. No matter what difficulties and challenges we may encounter, we will prevail as long as we have the people's support and participation. We must implement the Party's mass line and rally closely with the people, sharing weal and woe with them, and working vigorously by their side.

To push forward any key reform we must have the major issues concerning the reform examined and addressed from the people's standpoint, while formulating guidelines and measures based on the people's interests. Wang Fu of the Eastern Han Dynasty (25-220) said, "The roc soars lithely not merely because of the lightness of one of its feathers; the steed runs fast not merely because of the strength of one of its legs."[5] If China wants to fly high and run fast, it must rely on the strength of its 1.3 billion people.

When we encounter complicated problems hard to weigh and balance in the course of comprehensively promoting reform, we should think of the actual conditions of the people. What are they expecting? How can their interests be safeguarded? Are they satisfied with our reform? To make our decisions on reform more appropriate, the most important thing is to listen extensively to the opinions and proposals of the people, promptly review their fresh experience, fully mobilize their enthusiasm, initiative and creativity, bring their wisdom and strength to the cause of reform, and work with them to move the cause forward.

Notes

[1] Deng Xiaoping: "Excerpts from Talks Given in Wuchang, Shenzhen, Zhuhai and Shanghai," *Selected Works of Deng Xiaoping*, Vol. III, Eng. ed., Foreign Languages Press, Beijing, 1994, p. 358.

[2] The "six centering-ons" is a road map for continuing the reform comprehensively contained in the "Decision of the Central Committee of the Communist Party of China on Some Major Issues Concerning Comprehensively Continuing the Reform" adopted at the Third Plenary Session of the 18th Central Committee of the CPC: We must continue economic system reform by centering on the decisive role of the market in allocating resources; we must continue political system reform by centering on the unity of upholding the leadership of the Party, the people being the masters of the country, and governing the country according to rule of law; we must continue cultural system reform by centering on building the core socialist value system and developing a strong socialist culture in China; we must continue social structural reform by centering on safeguarding and improving the people's wellbeing and promoting social fairness and justice; we must continue ecological environment management reform by centering on building a beautiful China; we must continue the reform of the Party-building system by centering on enhancing the Party's capacity to govern in a scientific and democratic way and in accordance with the law.

[3] Karl Marx: "Preface to *A Contribution to the Critique of Political Economy*," *Karl Marx and Friedrich Engels: Collected Works*, Vol. 29, Eng. ed., Progress Publishers, Moscow, 1987, p. 263.

[4] *The Analects of Confucius* (*Lun Yu*) is one of the Confucian classics. Written by the disciples of Confucius, it records the words and deeds of Confucius, and also comprises dialogues between Confucius and his disciples. *The Analects of Confucius* (*Lun Yu*), *The Great Learning* (*Da Xue*), *The Doctrine of the Mean* (*Zhong Yong*) and *The Mencius* (*Meng Zi*) are collectively known as the "Four Classics of Confucianism."

[5] Wang Fu: *Comments of a Recluse* (*Qian Fu Lun*). Wang Fu (c. 85-c. 163) was a philosopher and political commentator in the Eastern Han Dynasty (25-220).

Push Ahead with Reform Despite More Difficulties[*]

February 7, 2014

Sergei Brilyov[1]: The Third Plenary Session of the 18th CPC Central Committee adopted the "Decision of the Central Committee of the Communist Party of China on Some Major Issues Concerning Comprehensively Continuing the Reform," and you have been made head of the Central Leading Group for Comprehensively Continuing the Reform. What I want to know is how you will govern. What will China's reform focus on next? What do you think of the prospects for China's development?

Xi Jinping: These are important questions concerning China's development. It has been more than 35 years since the Third Plenary Session of the 11th CPC Central Committee launched China's reform and opening up in 1978. We have made remarkable achievements, but we should continue to make progress. We have set the Two Centenary Goals. At present economic globalization is progressing rapidly, intense competition in overall national strength is intensifying between countries, and the international situation is complicated and volatile. We have concluded from this that fundamentally speaking, caught in fierce international competition, we are like a boat traveling upstream: We must press ahead or we will fall behind.

China's reform has been greatly furthered in both breadth and depth. Top-level design is needed to advance reform. Last November the Third Plenary Session of the 18th CPC Central Committee made overall planning for advancing reform comprehensively, and formulated the road map and schedule for reform. The plan includes over 330 reform measures for 15 areas, such as the economy, politics, culture,

---

* Part of an exclusive interview with the Russia Television.

society, ecological progress and Party building. So we have sounded the bugle to advance reform. Our general objective is to improve and develop the socialist system with Chinese characteristics, and modernize our national governance system and capacity.

To concentrate on advancing reform, we founded the Central Leading Group for Comprehensively Continuing the Reform with me as the head. The group is designed to make overall planning and coordination for major issues, and share out the tasks to be implemented. Now that we have a plan, it is most important to implement it.

It is no easy job to advance reform in China, which has a population of over 1.3 billion. Having been pushed ahead for more than 30 years, China's reform has entered a deep-water zone. It can be said that the easy part of the job has been done to the satisfaction of all. What is left are tough bones that are hard to chew. This requires us to act boldly and progress steadily. To act boldly means to advance reform despite difficulties and be eager to take on challenges, chew tough bones, and wade through dangerous shoals. To progress steadily means to stay on course and proceed in safety, and, more importantly, make no fatal mistakes.

I have full confidence in the prospects for China's development. Why? The underlying reason is that after long-term exploration we have found a correct development path suited to China's actual conditions. As long as we rely closely on the 1.3 billion Chinese people and firmly stay on our own path we will overcome all difficulties and obstacles, make new achievements, and finally reach our goal.

The CPC exercises state power for the people. The people's aspiration for a better life is our goal. To put it briefly, I will govern by serving the people and fulfilling all my responsibilities.

Brilyov: You have been the president of China for almost a year. How do you feel as the leader of such a big country? What hobbies do you have? What are your favorite sports?

Xi: China covers a land of 9.6 million sq km and has 56 ethnic groups and a population of over 1.3 billion. China's social and economic development level and its people's living standards are not high. It is not easy to govern such a country, so I must ascend a height to enjoy a distant view while planting my feet on solid ground. I worked in different regions in China for a long time, so I am fully aware that the differences are great between the country's east and west, between the central and local governments, between different localities and between different levels of local governments. Therefore, as a Chinese leader, I must take all factors into consideration based on a correct understanding of China's conditions, maintain an overall balance, and concentrate on priorities to promote the overall situation. I alternate my attention between major and minor issues, and, to put it figuratively, it is like playing the piano with all ten fingers.

Since the people have put me in the position of head of state, I must put them above everything else, bear in mind my responsibilities that are as weighty as Mount Tai, always worry about the people's security and wellbeing, and work conscientiously day and night; share the same feelings with the people, share both good and bad times with them, and work in concerted efforts with them.

Speaking of hobbies, I like reading, watching movies, traveling and strolling. As you know, I almost have no private time in the position I am in. A song titled, "Where Did the Time Go" became popular in China during this Spring Festival. For me, the question is where my private time goes. I spend all of it on my work. Now, the only thing I have managed to keep as a hobby is reading, which has become my way of life. Reading invigorates my mind, gives me inspiration and cultivates my moral force. I have read many works by Russian writers, including Ivan Krylov, Alexander Pushkin, Nikolai Gogol, Mikhail Lermontov, Ivan Turgenev, Fyodor Dostoyevsky, Nikolay Nekrasov, Nikolay Chernyshevsky, Leo Tolstoy, Anton Chekhov and Mikhail Sholokhov. I remember clearly many of their excellent chapters and stories.

Speaking of sports, I like swimming and mountaineering. I learned to swim at the age of four or five. I also like football, volleyball, basketball, tennis and martial arts. Among snow and ice sports, I like to watch ice hockey, speed skating, figure skating and freestyle skiing. Ice hockey is my favorite. It requires not only individual strength and skill but also teamwork and collaboration. It is indeed a good sport.

Notes

[1] Sergei Brilyov is a host of the Russia Television.

Improve Governance Capacity Through
the Socialist System with Chinese Characteristics*

February 17, 2014

To keep up with the overall progress in the national modernization process, we must improve the CPC's capability for scientific, democratic and law-based governance, and enhance the efficiency of government departments. We must improve the general public's ability to manage state, social, economic and cultural affairs in accordance with the law. In this way, Party, state and social affairs will be administered in accordance with rules, standards and procedures, and we will become better able to govern the country through the socialist system with Chinese characteristics.

The Third Plenary Session of the 18th CPC Central Committee pointed out that the overall goal of continuing the reform to a deeper level is to develop the socialist system with Chinese characteristics, and modernize our national governance system and capacity. This is a prerequisite for adhering to and developing socialism with Chinese characteristics and for realizing socialist modernization.

Since the introduction of the reform and opening-up policy some three decades ago, our Party has begun to ponder the issue of national governance system from a new perspective, and come to the conclusion that the issues of leadership and organizational systems are fundamental, comprehensive, stable and permanent ones.

---

* Main points of the speech at a provincial-level officials' seminar on studying and implementing the decisions of the Third Plenary Session of the 18th CPC Central Committee on continuing reform.

Today, we are tasked with an important historic mission, that is to make our socialist system with Chinese characteristics more mature and better established, and provide a set of more complete, more stable and more effective systems for the development of the Party and the nation, the wellbeing of the people, social harmony and stability, and the enduring prosperity and stability of the country.

This is a grand project. It entails carrying out all-round and systematic reform, and integrating reform in various fields to promote the overall modernization of our national governance system and capacity.

A country's governance system and capacity are the major barometers of its system and that system's governing efficiency. The two are complementary. Our governance system and capacity are good overall and have unique advantages. Moreover, they suit our national conditions and development needs.

Nevertheless, our national governance system and capacity still have much room for improvement, and we should exert greater efforts to enhance our national governance capacity. Our governance system will become more efficient as long as we focus on improving the Party's governance capacity while raising the moral and political standards, scientific and cultural levels, and professional abilities of officials at all levels and administrators of all areas, and as long as we make Party and government agencies, enterprises, public institutions, and social organizations more efficient.

We must understand that the overall goal of continuing the reform to a deeper level consists of two aspects, that is, to improve and develop the socialist system with Chinese characteristics, and to modernize our national governance system and capacity. To accelerate the modernization of the national governance system and capacity, we must follow the socialist path with Chinese characteristics.

The kind of governance system best suited for a country is determined by that country's historical heritage and cultural traditions, and its level of social and economic development, and it is ultimately decided by that country's people. Our current national governance system has been developed and gradually improved over a long period of time on the basis of our historical heritage, cultural traditions, and social and economic development.

Our national governance system needs to be improved, but we should have our own opinion on what improvements are necessary. The Chinese nation is open-minded. Over centuries, we have been continuously drawing on others' strengths and shaping the character of our own nation. Without unwavering confidence in our system we cannot have the courage to further reform, and without continuous reform our confidence in the system cannot possibly be full and long-lasting.

Continuing our reform to a deeper level involves improving our socialist system with Chinese characteristics. When we say boosting our confidence in the system, we do not mean to be complacent. Instead, we should continue to eradicate drawbacks in the system, and make it more mature and more enduring.

To modernize our national governance system and capacity, we should foster and promote the core socialist values and the relevant system,[1] and accelerate the building of a value system that fully reflects the characteristics of China, the Chinese nation and the times. To safeguard our value system and core values, we must let culture play its due role.

A nation's culture is a unique feature that distinguishes that nation from others. We should delve deeper into and better elucidate China's excellent traditional culture, and make greater efforts to creatively transform and develop traditional Chinese virtues, promoting a cultural spirit that transcends time and national boundaries, and has eternal attraction and contemporary value.

We should also present to the world China's contemporary creative cultural products that carry both our excellent traditional culture and contemporary spirit, and that are based in China and oriented towards the outside world.

As long as the Chinese people pursue lofty virtues generation after generation our nation will be forever filled with hope.

Producing a good document is only the first step in the long march of thousands of miles. The key is to implement the document. We should meticulously and strenuously study and promote the guiding principles of the Third Plenary Session of the 18th CPC Central Committee, and gain a solid understanding of continued reform. While studying the document, we should not stop at the surface, quote it out of context, copy it mechanically or apply it blindly. We should straighten out the relationship between the general policy arrangement and a particular policy, between a policy chain and a link, between top-level policy design and policy interfaces at different levels, between policy consistency and diversity, and between long- and short-term policies. We cannot replace the whole with any part, nor can we compromise principles for the sake of flexibility, or vice versa.

While implementing the document we should avoid empty talk, hesitation or seeking quick success, and instant benefits. We should implement it with a very strong sense of urgency and responsibility.

Reform is a gradual process. We should make bold breakthroughs while advancing step by step, so as to ensure the realization of the reform goals.

Continuing all-round reform to a deeper level is aimed at serving the overall, basic and long-term interests of the country. We should avoid picking reform areas according to personal preferences, and should get rid of reform-hindering mindsets. We must firmly carry out reform that benefits the Party and the people, and contributes to prosperity and long-term stability. Doing this will enable us to fulfill our historic mission and our responsibilities to the people, the country and the nation.

Notes

¹ The system of the core socialist values was introduced in the "Resolutions of the CPC Central Committee on Major Issues Regarding the Building of a Harmonious Socialist Society," which was adopted at the Sixth Plenary Session of the 16th CPC Central Committee in October 2006. The system includes the guiding thoughts of Marxism, the common ideal of socialism with Chinese characteristics, the national spirit centering on patriotism and the spirit of the times highlighted by reform and innovation, as well as the socialist maxims of eight honors and eight disgraces.

Economic Development

Economic Growth Must Be Genuine and Not Inflated[*]

November 30, 2012

Since the beginning of this year, China has been confronted with a complex international economic situation, as well as the demanding tasks of reform, development and stability. By taking a balanced and coordinated approach to development, we have focused on transforming our economic growth model. Following the general guideline of making steady progress, we have acted promptly to improve macro control and placed more emphasis on sustainable development. So far, we have seen positive results in many areas, including steady economic growth, adjustment of the economic structure, reform to a deeper level, and improvement of the people's wellbeing.

Although we have a generally positive analysis of China's economic and social development, we must not underestimate the risks and challenges facing us now and in the near future. We must be aware that the pace of world economic growth will continue to be slow, the problem between sluggish demand and overcapacity continues to grow, and domestic companies are troubled by rising costs and weaknesses in their capacity to innovate. The conflicts between the environment, natural resources and economic growth are becoming more serious.

Every coin has two sides. We must see both the advantages and disadvantages in the international and domestic situations, make full preparations for adversity, and strive to get the best possible results.

---

* Main points of the speech at a symposium with non-Party members held by the CPC Central Committee.

Next year will be the first full year to see the implementation of the decisions made by the Party's 18th National Congress. It is very important to do a good job of our social and economic development. We should focus on improving the quality and efficiency of economic growth, make steady progress, encourage innovation, lay a solid foundation for future development, press forward with reform and opening up, and realize sustainable and healthy economic development together with social stability and harmony.

First, we must maintain reasonable economic growth by continuing with our proactive fiscal and prudent monetary policies, and increase the natural vitality and motive force that drive economic growth. We must pursue real rather than inflated economic growth. In other words, we want efficient, high-quality and sustainable growth.

Second, we must consolidate the position of agriculture as the foundation of the economy, increase support for agriculture, improve our policies that benefit farmers and bring prosperity to them, accelerate modernized operation of agriculture, and ensure the supply of grain and other important agricultural products.

Third, we must make substantial progress in economic restructuring, expand domestic demand while stabilizing external demand, intensify our industrial restructuring and upgrading, and promote well-planned and healthy urbanization.

Fourth, we must carry out reform to improve the socialist market economy, have a good top-level design, carry out timely and targeted reform measures, combine steady progress in overall reform with breakthroughs in specific areas, experiment boldly, and pursue substantial results.

Fifth, we must improve the people's standard of living, with a particular focus on low-income groups, provide subsidies to poor students in colleges and universities, keep the employment market steady while doing all we can to expand it, and improve the urban and rural social security system. We will encourage the people to achieve prosperity through hard work, thereby combining the aim of the Party and the government's work with the goals that ordinary people strive for.

Open Wider to the Outside World[*]

April 8, 2013

The prospects for China's economic development are bright. China will make greater contributions to the world as it pushes forward reform and opening up, accelerates the transformation of the growth model, implements the opening-up policy, and provides a better economic environment and favorable conditions for foreign enterprises.

Entrepreneurs, who are also the main participants of this forum, are an important force in creating jobs and wealth and in promoting development and cooperation. Your decisions will have a major impact on the Asian economy as well as the wider world. I would like to take this opportunity to listen to your views and exchange ideas with you.

The world economy is still in a phase of instability and uncertainty, and recovery will be a lengthy process of advances and setbacks. In contrast, economic growth in Asia is relatively robust. In this context, China's economic prospects have become an issue of universal interest. I would like to share with you my views on this topic.

China has maintained sound overall economic development. Its growth will continue in the foreseeable future as industrialization, IT application, urbanization and agricultural modernization greatly expand the domestic market. The basics of our social productive forces remain solid, our advantages in productive factors are obvious, and our management and control systems and mechanisms continue to improve.

---

* Main points of the speech at a discussion of representatives of Chinese and foreign entrepreneurs during the Boao Forum for Asia Annual Conference 2013[1].

125

At the 18th CPC National Congress we set the Two Centenary Goals as our objectives, and committed ourselves to the Chinese Dream of the rejuvenation of the Chinese nation. We will continue to inject new energy into the Chinese economy as we strive to realize these objectives and the Chinese Dream. As a result of our endeavors, we can be very optimistic that the Chinese economy will maintain a relatively high growth rate. China will shift its development focus to improving the quality and efficiency of growth, and make every effort to promote a green, circular, and low-carbon economy.

The Chinese market operates fairly. Every company registered in China is an important component of the country's economy. Our commitment to the socialist market economy will remain resolute. We will continue to enhance the rule of law and actively improve our investment environment so that all enterprises can enjoy equal access to the factors of production, market competition and legal protection, and the Chinese market can become fairer and even more attractive. Our policies of utilizing foreign investment and protecting the legitimate rights and interests of foreign enterprises in accordance with law will not change.

China will never close its door to the outside world. Over the past ten years it has fulfilled its promises to the WTO by creating a more open and standardized business environment. We will open up new areas and enable deeper access. Our economy will remain open to foreign investors, and we hope that other countries will extend the same access to Chinese investors. We firmly oppose protectionism in any form, and we are willing and ready to solve economic and trade differences with other countries through consultation. We actively promote the establishment of a multilateral trade system characterized by balanced and mutually beneficial development.

China's domestic development benefits the rest of the world, and first of all its neighbors. In 2012 almost 16 million Chinese people traveled to our neighboring countries in east and southeast Asia. China has made a substantial contribution to Asia's economic development. In the next five years China's imports will reach US$ 10 trillion-worth and its outbound investment is expected to grow rapidly. China is making great efforts to increase its connections with its neighbors, to the advantage of both the regional and the world economy.

China remains committed to reform and opening up, and we will improve the relevant policies. We will continue to improve the capacity and quality of our services, and provide a better environment for foreign entrepreneurs to invest and launch ventures in China. We hope that foreign enterprises will seize these opportunities to achieve further development.

Notes

[1] The Boao Forum for Asia (BFA) is a non-governmental and non-profit international organization with a fixed conference date and a fixed address. It was founded in Boao, Hainan Province, China, on February 27, 2001. With equality, mutual benefit and cooperation as its themes, the BFA bases itself in Asia and aims to expand economic exchanges, coordination and cooperation among Asian countries while enhancing dialogue and economic ties between Asia and the rest of the world.

The "Invisible Hand" and the "Visible Hand"*

May 26, 2014

We should let the market play the decisive role in allocating resources, while allowing the government to better perform its functions. This is a theoretical and practical issue of great importance. A correct and precise understanding of this issue is very important to further the reform and promote the sound and orderly development of the socialist market economy. We should make good use of the roles of both the market, the "invisible" hand, and the government, the "visible" hand. The market and the government should complement and coordinate with each other to promote sustained and sound social and economic development.

The Third Plenary Session of the 18th CPC Central Committee pointed out that economic structural reform is the focus of continuing the reform comprehensively. The underlying issue is how to strike a balance between the functions of the government and the role of the market, and let the market play the decisive role in allocating resources and the government better perform its functions.

The proposal to let the market play the decisive role in allocating resources is a breakthrough in our Party's understanding of the laws governing the development of socialism with Chinese characteristics as well as a new achievement in the sinicization of Marxism. It symbolizes that the socialist market economy has entered a new stage.

To let the market play the decisive role in allocating resources and the government better perform its functions we must have a good understanding of the relationship between the role of the market and

* Main points of the speech at the 15th group study session of the Political Bureau of the 18th CPC Central Committee which Xi presided over.

that of the government, which represents a core issue in our economic structural reform.

The Third Plenary Session of the 18th CPC Central Committee changed the market's role in allocating resources from "basic" to "decisive." Although only one word was altered, the market's role was redefined. "Decisive role" is a continuation and extension of "basic role."

Letting the market play the decisive role in allocating resources and letting the government better perform its functions are not contradictory. It does not mean that the market can replace the government's functions, nor vice versa.

Actually this is an effort to keep our economic reform targeted at existing problems. For more than two decades our socialist market economy has been developing, yet there are still quite a number of problems and drawbacks that inhibit the vitality of market entities and prevent the laws of the market and value from fully playing their roles.

If these problems are not solved properly it will be difficult to establish a well-developed socialist market economy, further transform the development model and adjust the economic structure.

We should remain committed to the reform to establish and improve the socialist market economy and bring the reform to a deeper and wider level. We should reduce the government's direct involvement in resource allocation and its direct interference in micro-economic activities. We should step up efforts to develop a uniform market system characterized by openness and orderly competition, and set fair, open and transparent market rules. The government should refrain from getting involved in the economic activities that the market can regulate effectively, and let the market do what the government is not supposed to do, so that the market can play its role of maximizing the effectiveness and efficiency of resource allocation, and enterprises and individuals can have more room to develop the economy and create wealth with vigor and vitality.

Balanced macro control and effective governance are the intrinsic requirements for giving full play to the strength of the socialist market economy. To ensure that the government better performs its functions, we should transform government functions, further the reform of the administrative system, use new administrative methods, improve the macro-control system and enhance the monitoring of market activities. We should strengthen and improve public services, and promote social fairness, justice and stability, as well as common prosperity.

Governments at all levels should exercise administration strictly in accordance with the law, and conscientiously fulfill their responsibilities. The government should manage well all matters that fall within its purview, and appropriately delegate powers that should be delegated. The government should make resolute efforts to avoid overstepping its bounds or failing to play its due role.

We should uphold the Party's leadership and let the Party play its role as the leadership core in exercising overall leadership and coordinating all efforts. This is an important feature of our socialist market economy. Over the last three decades since the introduction of the reform and opening-up policy, we have made marked achievements in our social and economic development, and the people's living standards have improved noticeably. These successes are attributable to the fact that we have firmly upheld the Party's leadership, and given full play to the roles of Party organizations at all levels and of all Party members. In China, the Party's strong leadership is the basic guarantee for the government to play its due role.

While comprehensively continuing the reform, we should uphold and develop our political advantages, and use them to guide and push forward the reform. We should motivate all the people to make constant efforts for a better socialist market economy.

Today, officials at all levels, especially leading officials, should continue to learn through practice, and put what they have learned into practice, study new problems and draw on new experiences. They should learn to correctly use both the "invisible hand" and the "visible hand," and become experts in balancing the relationship between the government and the market.

Transition to Innovation-Driven Growth[*]

June 9, 2014

Currently, all Party members and people of all ethnic groups are striving for the completion of the building of a moderately prosperous society in all respects and the realization of the Chinese Dream. The 18th CPC National Congress put forward an important plan for the implementation of an innovation-driven strategy, and emphasized that scientific and technological innovation is pivotal to improving social productivity and the comprehensive national strength, so it must be put in a core position in our overall national development. This is an important strategy made by the CPC Central Committee, following a general analysis of the domestic and international situations, and of the overall picture of our development.

The 21st century heralds a new round of scientific, technological and industrial revolution. Global scientific and technological innovation has exhibited new trends and features. Cross-disciplinary integration is accelerating, new disciplines continue to emerge, and scientific frontiers keep spreading. Significant breakthroughs are being made or expected in basic scientific fields such as the structure of matter, the evolution of the universe, the origin of life and the nature of consciousness. Widespread diffusion of information, biological, new-material and alternative-energy technologies has brought about a green, intelligent and ubiquitous technological revolution.

The boundaries between research into basic and applied sciences, technological development and industrialization in the traditional

---

* Part of the speech at the 17th General Assembly of the Members of the Chinese Academy of Sciences and the 12th General Assembly of the Members of the Chinese Academy of Engineering.

sense are becoming increasingly blurred. The chain of scientific and technological innovation has become more flexible, technology upgrading and conversion have become quicker, and industry upgrading continues to speed up.

Scientific and technological innovation is constantly transcending geological, organizational and technological limitations. It intensifies the competition between innovation systems and makes innovative strategic competition more important in the competition for comprehensive national strength. Scientific and technological innovations, like a fulcrum which is said to be able to lever the earth, always create miracles. This has been proved in the development of contemporary science and technology.

In face of the new trends of scientific and technological innovation, the world's major countries are seeking to make new scientific and technological breakthroughs and gain competitive edges in future economic as well as scientific and technological development. We cannot afford to lag behind in this important race. We must catch up and then try to surpass others.

Since the introduction of the reform and opening-up policy some three decades ago, China has made remarkable achievements in social and economic development. Its economy has leapt to No. 2 in the world, and many of its major economic indices rank high on the world's list.

Nevertheless we must be clear that our economy, though large in size, is not strong. Its growth, though fast, is not of high quality. The extensive development model featured by economic growth mainly driven by factor inputs such as natural resources is not sustainable.

Now, the total population of well-off countries in the world is about 1 billion, while China has more than 1.3 billion people. If we are all to become modernized, the well-off population must more than double. If we are to consume as much energy in production and daily lives as the present well-off people do, all the existing resources in the world would be far from enough for us! The old path seems to be a dead end. Where is the new road? It lies in scientific and technological innovation, and in the accelerated transition from factor-driven and investment-driven growth to innovation-driven growth.

A few days ago, I read an article which argued that the Third Industrial Revolution would be a Robot Revolution. It asserted that robots would change the pattern of the global manufacturing industry, and China would become the world's largest robot market. The International Federation of Robotics predicted that the Robot Revolution would create a market value of trillions of US dollars.

Hardware and software for producing robots are becoming increasingly mature, the production cost keeps dropping and the functions robots can perform are more diversified thanks to the integration between robot technology and the new generation of information technology, such as big data, cloud computing and the mobile Internet, and the rapid development of 3D printing and artificial intelligence. Military unmanned aerial vehicles, self-driving cars and home-service robots have been put into application. Some artificially intelligent robots have pretty sturdy self-thinking and learning ability.

Robots are dubbed "pearls on the crown of the manufacturing industry." A country's achievement in robotics research, development, manufacturing and application is an important yardstick with which to measure its level of scientific and technological innovation and high-end manufacturing. Major robot-producing companies and countries have stepped up their efforts to gain advantages in terms of technology and markets.

I couldn't help wondering: China will be the largest robot market in the world, yet can its technology and manufacturing capability sustain it through the competition? We should make better robots and seize bigger market shares. There are many such new technologies and new fields. We should size up the situation, take the overall picture into account, and make plans as soon as possible and implement them solidly.

To carry out the innovation-driven strategy, the basic thing for us is to enhance our independent innovation ability, and the most urgent thing in this regard is to remove institutional barriers so as to unleash to the greatest extent the huge potential of science and technology as the primary productive force. Most importantly, we should unswervingly follow an independent innovation path featuring Chinese characteristics, stick to the guiding principles of independent innovation, leap-frogging development in key sectors, and development supported by science and technology and oriented towards the future, and speed up the pace of building an innovative country.

Years of painstaking efforts have resulted in great progress for China in science and technology, and China has entered the advanced ranks in the world in some important fields. In certain fields, it has become a "forerunner" or "parallel runner" instead of a "follower." China has entered a vital period, when new industrialization, application of information technology, urbanization and agricultural modernization are forging ahead simultaneously, in parallel or interactively. This has created ample space and an unprecedentedly strong momentum for independent innovation.

I have repeatedly said that the great rejuvenation of the Chinese nation can in no way be realized easily. In fact, the stronger we become, the greater resistance and pressure we will encounter. That's why we say that timing and resolution are vital, as historical opportunities are often ephemeral. Now we have an important historical opportunity to promote scientific and technological innovation. We must not miss it, but seize it tightly.

We are blessed with a solid material foundation laid over the 30-plus years of reform and opening up, and the fruits of persistent innovation, which are favorable for the innovation-driven strategy. Hence, we should take the initiative and adopt a proactive strategy. As to scientific and technological policies of great strategic value to our country and nation, we should make up our minds and act without any hesitation. Otherwise, we will let slip the historical opportunity, and may even have to pay a higher price.

In March 2013 I talked about scientific and technological innovation at a group discussion with scientists during the First Session of the 12th National Committee of the Chinese People's Political Consultative Conference. Generally speaking, the foundation of our scientific and technological innovation is not solid enough; our independent innovation ability, especially in the area of original creativity, is not strong. We still have to depend on others for core technology in key fields. Only by holding key technology in our own hands can we really take the initiative in competition and development, and ensure our economic security, national security and security in other areas.

We cannot always decorate our tomorrows with others' yesterdays. We cannot always rely on others' scientific and technological achievements for our own progress. Moreover, we cannot always trail behind others. We have no choice but to innovate independently.

Facts prove that it is self-sufficiency that has enabled the Chinese nation to stand among the world's independent nations, and independent innovation is the only path to the summit of science and technology. With this understanding, we should waste no time in making a difference. We cannot keep on talking year in and year out but do nothing about making a drastic change.

Of course, we don't mean to make independent innovation behind closed doors or all by ourselves. We shall never reject good experiences from others, from any part of the world. We should engage in international scientific and technological exchanges and cooperation more proactively, and make good use of both domestic and international resources.

Science and technology are global and time-sensitive, so we must have a global vision when we move forward. Currently, important scientific and technological breakthroughs and their accelerated application are highly likely to reshape the global economic pattern, and change the nature of industry and economic competition.

In traditional international playgrounds, the rules are set by others, and we play games by the established rules. Seizing the important opportunities made available by the new scientific, technological and industrial revolution means that we should be part of the games, and yet we can play a major role in the construction of the playgrounds, even at the beginning, so that we can make rules for new games. We will not have a chance if we are not capable enough to be part, indeed a major part, of the construction team. Opportunities are always for those who are fully prepared, and for those who are independent-minded, aspiring and persevering. We cannot move forward by leaps and bounds unless we do so with innovation.

Geo-scientist Li Siguang[1] said, "Science exists because of new discoveries made by it. It would die without new discoveries."[2] French writer Victor Hugo said, "Things created are insignificant when compared with things to be created."[3] The direction of our scientific and technological development is innovation, innovation and more innovation. We should attach great importance to breakthroughs in basic theories, step up the construction of scientific infrastructure, continue to push ahead with basic, systematic and cutting-edge research and development, and provide more resources for independent innovation. We should actively integrate and make good use of global innovation resources. In response to our current and future needs, we should selectively participate in the construction and use of the world's major scientific appliances, and research and development bases and centers.

We should seize strategic opportunities in key scientific and technological realms, select strategically important segments and priority areas relevant to overall and long-term development, and promote collaborated innovation and open innovation through effective and rational resource allocation. We should build an efficient and strong supply system of key generic technology, work hard to make great breakthroughs in key technology and hold key technology in our own hands.

"A person with sharp ears can hear sounds others cannot, and a person with keen vision can see things others cannot."[4] There is no end to scientific and technological innovation. Scientific and technological competition is like short-track speed skating. When we speed up, so will others. Those who can skate faster and maintain a high speed longer will win the title. Xun Zi[5] asserted, "If a gallant steed leaps only once, it can cover a distance of no more than ten steps; if an inferior horse travels for ten days, it can go a long way because of perseverance. If a sculptor stops chipping halfway, he cannot even cut dead wood, but if he keeps chipping, he can engrave metal and stone."[6]

Our scientists and engineers should bravely shoulder their responsibilities, overtake others, and find the right direction, to which they should stick. They should have the courage and confidence to blaze new trails, overcome difficulties and seek excellence, and audaciously make world-leading scientific and technological achievements.

The implementation of an innovation-driven development strategy is a systematic project. Scientific and technological achievements can generate real value and pay off only if they meet the needs of the country, the people and the market, and only after they have gone through the stages of research, development and application.

I have been wondering about the reason why our science and technology gradually lagged behind from the late Ming (1368-1644) and early Qing (1644-1911) dynasties. Studies show that Qing Emperor Kangxi[7] was very interested in Western science and technology. He invited Western missionaries to give him lectures on astronomy, mathematics, geography, zoology, anatomy, music and even philosophy. More than 100 books on astronomy were introduced to him. When did he study these subjects, and for how long? He continuously studied them for two years and five months sometime between 1670 and 1682.

He began his study quite early, and learned quite a lot. The problem was that, at that time, although some people were interested in Western learning and learned quite a lot of it, they did not apply what they had learned to social and economic development. Rather, they simply talked, without taking any action.

In 1708 the Qing government asked some foreign missionaries to draw a map of China. It took them ten years to complete *The Map of Imperial China* – the first of its kind at that time. However, this important work was confined to the imperial storehouse as a top-secret document, away from the public eye. Therefore, it had no impact on social or economic development. But the Western missionaries who had drawn the map took the data back to the West and had it published. Hence, for quite a long time the West knew China's geography better than the Chinese people did.

What can we learn from this story? It means that science and technology must be combined with social development. No matter how much one has learned, it cannot possibly have any impact on society if the knowledge is merely put aside as a novelty, refined interest, clever trick or doubtful craft.

For years, our scientific and technological achievements could not be smoothly converted to productivity. Why? Because there were institutional bottlenecks in the scientific and technological innovation chain and loose connections between the various links in the innovation and conversion process. It is like a relay race: The second baton carrier is not there or has no idea of where to head when the first arrives.

To solve this problem, we must further scientific and technological system reform, change mindsets and remove institutional barriers hindering scientific and technological innovation, properly handle the relationship between government and market, and better integrate science and technology with social and economic development. We must open a channel through which science and technology can boost industrial, economic and national development. We must spur innovation with reform, accelerate the construction and improvement of a national innovation system, and let the well water of innovation gush out fully.

If we compare scientific and technological innovation to a new engine driving our development, reform is an indispensible ignition system with which to start the engine. We should take more effective measures to improve the ignition system, and let the new engine run at full speed.

While carrying out the reform of the scientific and technological system we should prepare ourselves to solve difficult problems, and implement the relevant decisions made at the Third Plenary Session of the 18th CPC Central Committee. We should put scientific and technological innovation in the center of our overall national development, speed up the preparations for the innovation-driven development strategy, and draw road maps and timetables for important tasks in this regard.

The reform of the scientific and technological system should be carried out at the same time as social and economic reform. We should reform the planning and resource allocation mechanism for the national scientific and technological innovation strategy, improve the performance evaluation system and incentive policies for officials, further cooperation between industries, universities and research institutes, and solve key problems obstructing the conversion of scientific and technological achievements as soon as possible.

We should vigorously improve coordination in scientific and technological innovation so as to avoid fragmentation and isolation, as well as overlapping and repetition in campaigns launched by departments in various fields. We should set up a national innovation system within which experts in all fields can interact and collaborate to achieve high efficiency.

We should improve the basic system of scientific and technological innovation, build and improve the national scientific and technological reporting system, and make innovations in the survey system, and national scientific and technological management information system as soon as possible, so as to maximize resource sharing. We should deploy the innovation setup around the industrial setup as well as the capital setup around the innovation setup. We should focus on national strategic goals and pool resources to tackle key scientific and technological problems pertaining to the national economy and the people's livelihood.

We should move faster to improve the basic research system, with the focus on cutting-edge basic research, key common technology, and high-tech for public welfare and that of strategic importance. We should double our efforts in completing important national scientific projects, and race to the front of international scientific research. While centering on scientific and technological innovation, we should also accelerate innovation in product, brand, industrial structure and business model. We should carry out the innovation-driven strategy throughout the modernization process.

While furthering the reform of scientific and technological systems, we should pay attention to a magic wand vital to our success – our socialist system. We have made many noticeable achievements in science and technology this way. This practice must not be given up! We should let the market play a decisive role in allocating resources and the government play its role better. We should step up planning and coordination as well as collaborative innovation. We should pool our efforts to accomplish big tasks, and focus on important, cutting-edge and basic research.

"To accomplish extraordinary feats, we must wait for extraordinary persons."[8] Competent personnel are the most crucial factor for scientific and technological innovation. Respecting them has long been a fine Chinese tradition. As described in *The Book of Songs*[9], King Wen of the Zhou Dynasty[10] respected competent people, who hence flocked to him, so his country became strong and prosperous. They are the most important factors for a country's long-term development. We need them for our great national rejuvenation. The more talented, the better; the more knowledgeable, the better.

China is a country rich in manpower and brainpower. The wisdom of our 1.3 billion people is our most precious possession. Knowledge is power, and competent personnel shape the future. If we want to get to the forefront of global scientific and technological innovation we must discover, nurture and retain such people throughout the whole process of innovation. We must train a large number of high-caliber, creative scientists and engineers.

We are proud of having the greatest number of scientists and engineers in the world. Nonetheless, we face a serious structural deficiency of innovative scientists and engineers, particularly world-class and other leading and high-caliber ones. The education and training that our engineers have received so far are not geared towards production and innovation.

"If you want one year of prosperity, then grow grain; if you want ten years of prosperity, then grow trees; if you want one hundred years of prosperity, then you cultivate people."[11] We should make human resource development a top priority for scientific and technological innovation. We should improve the mechanism for training, recruiting and using competent personnel. We should work hard to foster a contingent of world-class scientists and engineers and other leading and high-caliber ones, as well as high-level innovation teams. We should focus on training young innovative scientists and engineers for the front lines.

We should perfect our competence-nurturing mechanism according to personnel development laws. "We should respect a tree's nature, and let it grow freely."[12] We should not seek quick success and instant benefits, or try to help young shoots grow by dragging them up. We should encourage both competition and cooperation, and promote a rational and orderly flow of competent personnel. We should attract outstanding experts and scholars from overseas for our scientific and technological innovation. We should create a social environment that encourages innovation and values success while tolerating well-intentioned failure. We should improve the competent-personnel evaluation system and create ample space for such people to give full play to their talents.

The future belongs to the young. Innovative young people are the source of our creativity and the best hope for our scientific and technological development. "I beg Old Man Heaven to bestir himself, and send down talented people of more kinds than one."[13] Academicians should not only be pioneers in scientific and technological innovation, but also guides for young people. I hope that they will shoulder their responsibility in nurturing young scientists and engineers, instruct them through words and actions, and continuously discover, train and recommend competent personnel, so that innovative people can stand out from the crowd. Young scientists and engineers should be dedicated to science, develop innovative thinking, tap innovative potential and enhance innovative ability. They should continue to push ahead while learning from previous generations.

Notes

[1] Li Siguang (1889-1971) was a famous Chinese geologist and one of the founders of China's geomechanics.

[2] Li Siguang: "What Have Geologists Done in the Scientific Frontline?", *The Complete Works of Li Siguang*, Vol. 8, Chinese ed., Hubei People's Publishing House, 1996, p. 243.

[3] Victor Hugo: *On William Shakespeare.*

[4] Sima Qian: *Records of the Historian (Shi Ji)*. Sima Qian (c. 145 or 135-? BC) was a historian and writer in the Western Han Dynasty. The book, China's first biographical-style historical and literary masterpiece, covers more than 3,000 years from the legendary Yellow Emperor to Emperor Wu of the Han Dynasty.

[5] Xun Zi (c. 325-238 BC) was a philosopher, thinker and educator of the late Warring States Period. He believed that man could conquer nature, and that human nature was evil. His book *Xun Zi* summarizes and develops the philosophical thoughts of Confucianism, Taoism and Mohism in the pre-Qin Dynasty period.

[6] *Xun Zi.*

[7] Emperor Kangxi (1654-1722) ruled the Qing empire from 1661 to 1722.

[8] Ban Gu: *The Book of the Han Dynasty (Han Shu)*, also known as *The Book of the Western Han Dynasty (Qian Han Shu)*. This was the first chronological dynastic history of China. Ban Gu was a historian in the Eastern Han Dynasty (25-220).

[9] *The Book of Songs (Shi Jing)* was the earliest collection of poems in China. It contains 305 poems collected over some 500 years from the early Western Zhou Dynasty (c. 11th century-771 BC) to the middle of the Spring and Autumn Period (770-476 BC).

[10] King Wen of Zhou (dates unknown), also known as Ji Chang, was the founder of the Zhou Dynasty.

[11] *Guan Zi.* Guan Zi (c. 720-645 BC), also known as Guan Zhong, was a reform-minded official of the State of Qi during the Spring and Autumn Period.

[12] Liu Zongyuan: *Tree Planter Hunchback Guo.* Liu Zongyuan (773-819) was a writer and philosopher in the Tang Dynasty (618-907).

[13] Gong Zizhen: *Miscellaneous Poems of 1839 (Ji Hai Za Shi)*. Gong Zizhen (1792-1841) was a thinker, historian and poet in the Qing Dynasty (1644-1911).

Revolutionize Energy Production
and Consumption[*]

June 13, 2014

Energy security is an issue of general and strategic significance in the economic and social development of a country. It is crucial to driving national development and prosperity, improving standards of living, and ensuring lasting social peace and stability. In the face of changes in energy demand and supply and new developments in the international energy landscape, China must ensure national energy security by increasing energy production and creating a revolution in consumption. This is a long-term strategy, but it must be supported by key tasks and major steps that require immediate action.

After years of development, China has become the world's largest energy producer and consumer, with an energy supply structure that includes coal, electricity, petroleum, natural gas, new energy, and renewable energy. Remarkable improvements have been made in technology and equipment, and in the efficiency of both domestic and industrial energy use. Although China has achieved great success in energy development, it still faces a range of challenges, including huge pressure on the demand side, a number of supply limitations, serious environmental damage caused by energy production and consumption, and outdated technology. We must develop a strategic overview of national development and security to assess the situation, and then define a sound energy blueprint for the future.

First, we must revolutionize energy consumption, and rein in irrational energy use. We need to impose strict controls on overall energy

---

* Main points of the speech at the sixth meeting of the Central Leading Group on Financial and Economic Affairs.

use, effectively implement a policy in which energy conservation is the top priority, and save energy across the board in all spheres of economic and social activity. We should also adjust the structure of the energy industry, make energy conservation a priority in urbanization, and encourage an attitude to consumption characterized by diligence and thrift. We must build an energy-conserving society.

Second, we must revolutionize energy supply. To ensure energy security we must set up a supply system reliant on diversified energy sources, promote the clean and efficient use of coal, and develop non-coal energy sources, thereby creating an energy supply system driven by coal, petroleum, natural gas, nuclear energy, new energy and renewable energy. At the same time, we should upgrade our transmission and distribution network, and build more storage facilities.

Third, we must revolutionize energy technology, and upgrade the related industrial structure. We should encourage innovation in technology, in industry, and in business models, and pursue green and low-carbon energy development suited to our national conditions and adapted to positive international trends in the energy technology revolution. We will combine such innovation with new and high technology in other fields, and transform our energy technology and related industries into a new powerhouse to drive the overall industrial upgrading of our country.

Fourth, we must revolutionize the energy market. We will proceed with reform, restore energy's status as a commodity, build a system of workable competition, and put in place a mechanism in which energy prices are largely driven by the market. In addition, we will change the way that the government supervises the energy industry, and establish and improve the legal framework for energy development.

Fifth, we must enhance international cooperation in all sectors, and ensure that opening up supports energy security. While relying mainly on domestic energy sources, we will strengthen international cooperation in all sectors related to energy production and consumption, and make effective use of resources from other countries.

We need to study the 13th Five-year Plan for energy development, and work out a strategy to revolutionize energy production and consumption by 2030. We will move faster in revising energy efficiency standards. All outdated regulations must be revised, updated on a regular basis and implemented. We will continue to build large coal-fueled electricity generating power bases each with a capacity of ten million kw. We will tighten the criteria for coal-burning power stations, upgrading all those that do not meet energy conservation and emission reduction standards within a specified time, and continue to develop long-distance, high-capacity power transmission technology. New nuclear projects on the coast will be launched as soon as possible, and they will be subject to the world's highest safety standards.

In addition, China will encourage energy cooperation through the Belt and Road Initiative,[1] and expand oil and gas cooperation with countries in Central Asia, the Middle East, the Americas and Africa. We will also intensify our efforts in energy exploration and extraction, and build more oil and gas pipelines and storage facilities. We will improve our emergency response, enhance capacity building, improve systems providing energy statistics, and launch initiatives to create, revise and abrogate laws and regulations in the energy sector.

Notes

[1] The Belt and Road refer to the Silk Road Economic Belt and the 21st-century Maritime Silk Road.

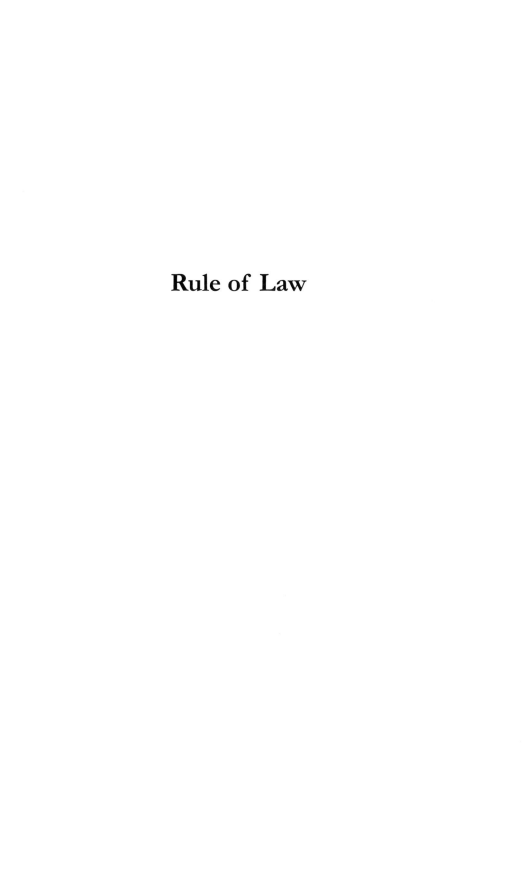

Rule of Law

Commemorate the 30th Anniversary
of the Promulgation and Implementation
of the Current Constitution*

December 4, 2012

Comrades and friends:

On December 4, 1982 the Fifth Session of the Fifth National People's Congress (NPC) adopted the Constitution of the People's Republic of China. It has been 30 years since the Constitution was promulgated and implemented. Today, we are gathered here to solemnly commemorate this event of great historical and practical significance in order to ensure the comprehensive and effective implementation of the Constitution and carry out the guidelines of the 18th CPC National Congress.

History is always inspiring. Looking back on the progress of the Chinese constitutional system, we are deeply aware that it is closely connected with the arduous struggle and splendid achievements of the Party and the people, and with the trail we have blazed and the valuable experience we have gained.

The current Constitution can be traced back to the Common Program of the Chinese People's Political Consultative Conference (CPPCC), which was promulgated in 1949 to serve as the provisional Constitution, and the Constitution of the People's Republic of China adopted at the First Session of the First NPC in 1954. These documents affirmed the heroic struggle of the Chinese people

---

* Speech at the Meeting of the People from All Walks of Life in Beijing to Commemorate the 30th Anniversary of the Promulgation and Implementation of the Current Constitution.

against domestic and foreign enemies and their striving for national independence and people's freedom and happiness over the previous 100 years in modern China, and affirmed the history in which the CPC led the Chinese people in winning victory in the New Democratic Revolution[1] and in acquiring state power.

In 1978 the CPC convened the Third Plenary Session of the 11th Central Committee, which was of great historical significance, ushering in a new historical period of reform and opening up. Developing socialist democracy and improving the socialist legal system became the unalterable basic principle of the Party and the state. It was at this meeting that Deng Xiaoping pointed out profoundly: "To ensure people's democracy we must strengthen our legal system. Democracy has to be institutionalized and written into law, so as to make sure that institutions and laws do not change whenever the leadership changes, or whenever the leaders change their views or shift the focus of their attention."[2] In accordance with the guidelines, principles and policies set forth at the Third Plenary Session, we reviewed China's positive and negative experience in building socialism, drew the hard lessons from the ten-year Cultural Revolution[3] (1966-1976), learned from the gains and losses of world socialism, and adapted to the new requirements of reform and opening up and socialist modernization, and the new demands of socialist democracy and the legal system in China, whereby we promulgated the current Constitution. However, the Constitution must adjust to new circumstances, draw on new experiences and affirm new achievements, so as to maintain ever-lasting vitality. In 1988, 1993, 1999 and 2004, respectively, the NPC made necessary and important amendments to the Constitution, so as to ensure that it kept up with the times while maintaining its consistency and authority.

As the fundamental law of the state, the Constitution verifies the developments concerning the path, theories and system of socialism with Chinese characteristics, demonstrates the common will and fundamental interests of the Chinese people of all ethnic groups, and has become the supreme expression of the central work, basic principles, major guidelines and important policies of the Party and the state in the national legal system.

Over the past 30 years the Constitution, relying on its supreme legal status and powerful legal force, has convincingly ensured that the Chinese people are the masters of the country, vigorously promoted reform and opening up and socialist modernization, advanced the building of a law-based socialist country, facilitated the cause of human rights, safeguarded national reunification, ethnic unity and social stability, and exerted a profound influence on the political, economic, cultural and social life of China.

The Constitution has fully proved over the past 30 years that it is a good Constitution that suits China's national conditions and reality, and the requirements of the times; that it is a cogent Constitution that demonstrates the common will of the people, safeguards their right to democracy, and protects their fundamental interests; that it is a vigorous Constitution that promotes national development and progress, guarantees a happy life for the people, and ensures that the Chinese nation achieves its great rejuvenation; and that it is the fundamental legal guarantee enabling our country and people to pass through all difficulties, risks and tests and to forge ahead along the socialist path with Chinese characteristics.

From the implementation of the Constitution over the past 60-plus years since the founding of the People's Republic in 1949, we can see that the Constitution is closely bound up with the future of the country and the destiny of the people. Safeguarding the authority of the Constitution is safeguarding the authority of the common will of the Party and the people. Upholding the dignity of the Constitution is upholding the dignity of the common will of the Party and the people. Ensuring the implementation of the Constitution is ensuring the people's fundamental interests. As long as we respect and implement the Constitution the people will be able to be masters of the country, and the cause of the Party and the state will be able to progress smoothly. If the Constitution is disregarded, weakened or even sabotaged, the people's rights and freedoms cannot be guaranteed, and the cause of the Party and the state will suffer. Therefore, precious inspirations from long-term practice must be cherished. We should be more active in taking the initiative in abiding by the principles prescribed by the Constitution, carrying forward its essence and fulfilling the duties it prescribes.

While fully affirming our achievements, we should also be aware of our shortcomings: The oversight mechanisms and pertinent systems to ensure the implementation of the Constitution are not yet complete; laws are not properly observed or strictly enforced, and lawbreakers are not prosecuted by some local regions and government agencies; problems concerning the people's direct interests remain prominent in law enforcement and jurisdiction; abuse of power, malfeasance and dereliction of duty by government employees, and lawbreaking by law-enforcement personnel for personal gain have seriously damaged the authority of the national legal system; and awareness of the need to observe the Constitution among citizens and some officials needs to be further enhanced. We must pay close attention to and earnestly solve these problems.

Comrades and friends,

The 18th CPC National Congress stressed: The rule of law is a fundamental principle by which the Party leads the people in running the country; the rule of law is the basic way to run the country; we should give greater scope to the important role the rule of law plays in the country's governance and social management; and we should promote law-based governance of the country in an all-round way, and accelerate the building of a socialist country based on the rule of law. To achieve this objective, we must comprehensively implement the Constitution.

Comprehensively implementing the Constitution is the primary task and groundwork for building a law-based socialist country. The Constitution is the fundamental law of the state and the general program for managing state affairs; enjoying supreme legal status, legal authority and legal validity, it is fundamental and consistent, and is of overall and long-term importance. The people of all ethnic groups, all government agencies, the armed forces, all political parties and public organizations, and all enterprises and public institutions in the country must take the Constitution as the basic standard of conduct and regard it as a duty to uphold the dignity of the Constitution and ensure its implementation. No organization or individual is privileged to act beyond the Constitution or the law. All acts in violation of the Constitution or the law must be investigated.

The life of the Constitution is in its implementation, and so is its authority. We must persistently ensure the implementation of the Constitution, and raise the comprehensive implementation of the Constitution to a new level.

First, we should uphold the correct political direction, and keep to the socialist path of making political progress with Chinese characteristics. Since the reform and opening-up policy was introduced in 1978 our Party, rallying and leading the people, has made major progress in developing socialist democracy, and successfully opened up and kept to the socialist path of making political advance with Chinese characteristics, thus charting the correct course for achieving the most-extensive-possible people's democracy in China. The core thought, underlying component and basic requirement of this political path are all affirmed in the Constitution, their theoretical essence being closely related, integrated and mutually reinforcing. We must uphold, implement and develop the systems and principles set forth in the Constitution, namely, the basic system and basic tasks of the state, the core leadership and theoretical guidance of the state, the state system which is a socialist state under the people's democratic dictatorship led by the working class and based on the alliance of workers and farmers, the system of people's congresses as the system of government, the system of multiparty cooperation and political consultation under the leadership of the CPC, the system of regional ethnic autonomy, the system of community-level self-governance, the patriotic United Front, the socialist legal system, the principle of democratic centralism, and the principle of respecting and safeguarding human rights.

The key to keeping to the socialist path of making political progress with Chinese characteristics is to ensure the unity of the leadership of the Party, the position of the people as masters of the country and law-based governance, so as to guarantee the fundamental position of the people, to reach the goal of enhancing the vitality of the Party and the country and keeping the people fully motivated, to expand socialist democracy and to promote socialist political progress. We must uphold the idea prescribed in the Constitution that all power of the state belongs to the people; extensively mobilize and organize the people to exercise state power through people's congresses at all levels, and to manage state and social affairs and economic and cultural programs by various means and in various forms; and ensure that the people jointly participate in national development, share the benefits of progress, accomplish the common cause, and become the masters of the country, of society and of themselves. Adhering to the principle of democratic centralism, the system of state power and the standards of actions defined in the Constitution, we should exercise state power through the people's congresses, ensure that decision-making power, executive power and oversight power function independently but are coordinated with each other, ensure that government agencies exercise their power and perform their duties in accordance with statutory mandates and procedures, and ensure that government agencies organize all undertakings concertedly and effectively. Abiding by the systems and principles established by the Constitution, we should correctly handle the relationship between the central and local governments, between all ethnic groups and between the interests of all parties, and mobilize all positive efforts to consolidate the political situation and make it more democratic, unified, stable and harmonious. We should adapt ourselves to the needs of expanding people's democracy and promoting social and economic development, proactively and steadily advance political reforms, make people's democracy more extensive, adequate and complete, give full play to the strength of our socialist political system, and constantly push forward the self-improvement and development of the socialist political system.

Second, we should implement the rule of law as the basic strategy, and accelerate the building of a law-based socialist country. The Constitution establishes the fundamental principle of our socialist legal system, explicitly stipulates that the People's Republic of China practices the rule of law and builds a law-based socialist country, and the state upholds the uniformity and dignity of the socialist legal system. To implement the rule of law as the basic strategy, and accelerate the building of a law-based socialist country we should make laws through proper procedures, enforce them strictly, administer justice impartially, and ensure that everyone abides by the law.

We must take the Constitution as the supreme legal norm, continue to improve our socialist system of laws with Chinese characteristics underpinned by the Constitution, bring all state undertakings and work onto the track of the legal system, ensure that there are laws to abide by, that laws are observed and strictly enforced, and that lawbreakers are prosecuted, safeguard social fairness and justice, and make state and social life more institutionalized and law-based. The NPC and its Standing Committee must enhance legislation in key fields, expand the channels for the people's orderly participation in legislation, promote the implementation of the Constitution through well-established laws, and ensure the implementation of the systems and principles established by the Constitution. The State Council and local people's congresses along with their standing committees with legislative power must formulate and amend administrative and local regulations in accordance with current laws, so as to ensure the effective implementation of the Constitution and laws. State administrative, judicial and procuratorial bodies at all levels must exercise government administration in accordance with the law, administer justice impartially, accelerate the building of law-based government, and constantly increase judicial credibility. The State Council and local people's governments at all levels are the executive and administrative bodies of state power, and bear the major responsibility of strictly implementing the Constitution and laws, and so must promote procedure-based government conduct and conscientiously ensure strict, impartial and civilized law enforcement. We should continue the reform of the judicial structure to a deeper level, and ensure the independent and impartial exercise of judicial and procuratorial powers pursuant to law. The NPC and its Standing Committee and related state oversight bodies should fulfill their oversight duties, enhance oversight and inspection for the implementation of the Constitution and laws, improve oversight mechanisms and procedures, and resolutely correct breaches of the Constitution and laws. Local people's congresses at all levels and their standing committees must exercise their powers in accordance with the law, and make sure that the Constitution and laws are observed and enforced in their respective administrative regions.

Third, we must maintain the people's dominant position in the country, and ensure that all citizens enjoy their rights and perform their duties. The fundamental rights and duties of citizens are the core of the Constitution, which in turn serves as the fundamental guarantee for every citizen to enjoy his rights and perform his duties. The underpinning of the Constitution is the people's heartfelt support, and the power of the Constitution lies in the people's sincere faith. Only by ensuring that all citizens are equal before the law, by respecting and protecting human rights and by ensuring that the people enjoy extensive rights and freedoms as prescribed by law, can the Constitution take root in the people's minds, can it be well received by the people, and can all the people take the initiative in implementing the Constitution.

We must ensure that all citizens enjoy extensive rights in accordance with the law, that their right of the person and property and basic political rights are inviolable, and that their economic, cultural and social rights are exercised. We must safeguard the fundamental interests of the overwhelming majority of the people, and fulfill their aspirations for and pursuit of a better life. We should address public demands impartially and in accordance with the law, enable the people to feel that justice is served in every case before the courts, and eradicate elements that hurt their sentiments or damage their interests.

We should enhance publicity and education about the Constitution widely in society, improve the awareness of the need to abide by the Constitution and legal system among all the people, especially among officials at all levels and government employees, carry forward the socialist rule of law, cultivate a law-based socialist culture, make the Constitution known to every household, and create a good social atmosphere of studying, observing and applying the law. We should make unremitting efforts to firmly establish the authority of the Constitution and laws, get the people to fully trust the law, consciously apply the law and be aware that the Constitution is not only the code of conduct that all citizens must abide by but also a legal weapon to safeguard their rights and interests. We should take education about the Constitution as a major element of Party officials' training, ensure that officials at all levels and government employees master the basic knowledge of the Constitution, and cultivate the consciousness to be loyal to, abide by and uphold the Constitution. Law is written morality, while morality is conscious law. We should integrate the rule of law with rule by virtue, pay more attention to the rule of virtue in citizens' conduct, and encourage citizens to protect their legitimate rights and interests in accordance with the law while conscientiously fulfilling their duties prescribed by law, which means enjoying rights while performing duties.

Fourth, we should uphold the Party's leadership, and lay greater emphasis on improving the way it exercises leadership and governance. In essence, the rule of law is rule by the Constitution; the key to law-based governance is Constitution-based governance. In the new circumstances, to perform its duty properly in state governance and national rejuvenation, our Party should exercise strict discipline, and govern the country in accordance with the Constitution. As it leads the people in formulating and implementing the Constitution and laws, the Party must act within the limits prescribed by the Constitution and laws, and ensure that it exercises leadership in legislation, guarantees law enforcement and takes the lead in observing the law.

We must ensure that the Party plays its proper role as the leadership core in exercising overall leadership and coordinating the efforts of all, upholds the rule of law as the fundamental strategy and administration in accordance with the law as the basic way, turns the Party's views into the will of the state through legal procedures, trains candidates recommended by Party organizations to become leaders of agencies of state power, exercises the Party's leadership over the country and society through the agencies of state power, and supports the agencies of state power along with the administrative, judicial and procuratorial bodies to carry out their work separately yet concertedly in accordance with the Constitution and laws. Party organizations and officials at all levels should set an example in promoting the rule of law, constantly improve their law-based governance capacity and level, and persistently push ahead institutionalized and law-based management of state affairs. Officials at all levels should upgrade their ability in both thinking and action to further the reform to a deeper level, promote development, resolve problems and maintain stability, form a law-based approach to administering affairs, dealing with difficulties, handling problems and resolving conflicts, and advance all undertakings along the path of the rule of law. We should improve the mechanism for conducting checks and oversight on the exercise of power, through linking power with responsibility, supervising the exercise of power, enforcing accountability for dereliction of duty, and prosecuting breaches of the law, so that the power granted by the people can always be exercised in their interests.

Comrades and friends,

The whole Party and the people of all ethnic groups must rally closely around the Party Central Committee, uphold socialism with Chinese characteristics, follow the guidance of Deng Xiaoping Theory, the important thought of the Three Represents and the Scientific Outlook on Development, promote the rule of law and law-based governance and administration, build a law-based country, government and society, and conscientiously implement the guiding principles of the 18th CPC National Congress in all their work for the goals of building a moderately prosperous society in all respects and ushering in a new stage of socialism with Chinese characteristics.

Notes

[1] The New Democratic Revolution (1919-1949) is a bourgeois democratic revolution against imperialism and feudal dictatorship under the leadership of the proletariat. It did not aim at founding a republic ruled by the bourgeoisie, but a people's republic led by the proletariat, based on the worker-peasant alliance, and ruled by all the revolutionary classes. Spanning three decades from 1919, when the May 4th Movement began, to 1949, when the People's Republic of China was founded, the revolution waged by the CPC against imperialism, feudalism and bureaucrat-capitalism is dubbed the New Democratic Revolution.

[2] Deng Xiaoping: "Emancipate the Mind, Seek Truth from Facts and Unite as One in Looking to the Future," *Selected Works of Deng Xiaoping*, Vol. II, Eng. ed., Foreign Languages Press, Beijing, 1994, p. 156.

[3] The Great Proletarian Cultural Revolution, or Cultural Revolution for short, refers to the political movement wrongly launched by Mao Zedong that lasted from May 1966 to October 1976 and was participated in by the general public. Manipulated by Lin Biao and the counter-revolutionary group represented by Jiang Qing, it caused grave disasters to the CPC, the country and the people of all ethnic groups.

Develop a Law-Based Country, Government and Society[*]

February 23, 2013

Our efforts to complete the building of a moderately prosperous society in all respects presuppose a higher demand for the rule of law. We should comprehensively implement the guiding principles of the 18th CPC National Congress, and follow the guidance of Deng Xiaoping Theory, the important thought of the Three Represents and the Scientific Outlook on Development. We should take a well-designed approach to legislation, enforce the law strictly, administer justice impartially, and ensure that everyone abides by the law. We should exercise governance and administration in accordance with the law, develop a law-based country, government and society simultaneously, and thereby bring the rule of law to a new stage.

A system of socialist laws with Chinese characteristics, with the Constitution to the fore, has been formed in China, so overall we have laws to abide by in all aspects of state and social life. This is a great achievement. The laws, based on practice, should develop as the situation changes. We will improve legislation plans, concentrate on priorities, attach equal importance to making new laws and revising and repealing existing ones, make legislation more appropriate and democratic, and make laws more targeted, timely and systematic. We should improve the working mechanism and procedures of legislation, expand the scale of orderly public participation, and give full consideration to the opinions of all parties involved, so as to make

---

* Main points of the speech at the fourth group study session of the Political Bureau of the 18th CPC Central Committee which Xi presided over.

160

the laws properly reflect the needs of economic and social development, better coordinate interests, and give full play to the leading and motivational role of legislation.

We should strengthen the enforcement of the Constitution and the law, and uphold the unity, dignity and authority of the socialist legal system, so that people neither want, nor are able, nor dare to break the law. We will make sure that laws are abided by and strictly enforced, and lawbreakers are prosecuted. Administrative bodies are important in implementing laws and regulations, so they should take the lead in enforcing laws and safeguarding public interests, the people's rights and public order. Law executors should be faithful to the law. Leading bodies and officials at all levels should become better able to think and act based on law, and work to reach consensus on reform, promote procedure-based development, resolve conflicts, and safeguard social harmony in accordance with the law. We will strengthen the oversight of law enforcement, make sure that there is no illegal interference in law enforcement, and prevent and overcome regional and departmental protectionism. We will fight corruption, and make sure that those who have power take responsibility, the exercise of power is subject to oversight and lawbreakers are prosecuted.

We will make every effort to ensure that the people feel that justice is served in every court case. Bearing this in mind, all judicial bodies should improve their work, focusing on resolving the deep-seated problems that affect judicial justice and constrain our judicial capacity. We should ensure justice for the people and improve our judicial working practices. We should provide good services to help people overcome barriers to justice, particularly by increasing legal aid for people in difficulties to safeguard their legitimate rights. Judicial workers need to maintain close ties with the people, carry out procedure-based judicial activities, increase judicial transparency, and respond to the people's concern and expectations for judicial justice and transparency. We will ensure that judicial and procuratorial bodies exercise their power independently and impartially in accordance with the law.

All organizations and individuals should act within the scope prescribed by the Constitution and the law. All citizens, social organizations and government agencies should act and exercise their rights and powers, and fulfill their obligations and duties in accordance with the Constitution and the law. We will make sure that the laws are well received by the people, foster socialist rule of law throughout society, encourage all the people to observe the law and solve their problems by the law, and form a favorable environment in which it is held to be honorable to observe the law. We will combine education in the legal system with law-based governance, and promote social administration under the rule of law. We should integrate the rule of law with rule by virtue and legal enforcement with ethical progress, encourage both regulation by laws and by self-discipline, and ensure that the rule of law and rule by virtue complement and reinforce each other.

The CPC is the ruling party in China. The Party's law-based governance is of great significance for ensuring the rule of law. We must ensure the unity of the Party's leadership, the position of the people as masters of the country and law-based governance, and follow the Party's leadership in the entire process of ruling the country by law. Party organizations at all levels should act within the scope prescribed by the Constitution and the law. Officials at all levels should perform their duties in accordance with the law and take the lead in abiding by the law. Organization departments of the Party at all levels should make the performance of officials in accordance with the law an important criterion for their assessment.

Promote Social Fairness and Justice, Ensure a Happy Life for the People[*]

January 7, 2014

We should make safeguarding social stability our basic task, promote social fairness and justice as core values, and ensure a happy life for the people as our fundamental target. We should enforce the law strictly, administer justice impartially, further promote reform, strengthen and improve judicial, procuratorial and public security work, and safeguard the vital interests of the people. In so doing, we will ensure the realization of the Two Centenary Goals and the Chinese Dream of the nation's great renewal.

Judicial, procuratorial and public security departments should take a clear stand in upholding the leadership of the Party. This means upholding the people's status as the masters of the country and implementing law-based governance, the Party's basic strategy of leading the people in governing the country. We should unswervingly adhere to the Party's leadership over judicial, procuratorial and public security work, and at the same time strengthen and improve its leadership.

We should correctly balance the Party's policies and the state's laws. Both reflect the fundamental will of the people, and share the same nature. The Party leads the people in enacting and enforcing the Constitution and laws. It guarantees the enforcement of the laws enacted under its leadership and takes the lead in observing them. Judicial, procuratorial and public security officers should conscientiously safeguard the authority of the Party's policies and the state's laws, and make sure that both are executed properly. We should properly

---

[*] Main points of the speech at a central conference on judicial, procuratorial and public security work.

balance the need to uphold the Party's leadership and the need for judicial, procuratorial and public security organs to exercise their power independently and impartially in accordance with the law. Party organizations and officials at all levels should support these organs in taking responsibility independently in accordance with the Constitution and laws, and carrying out their work in a concerted and coordinated way. Commissions for judicial, procuratorial and public security affairs under the Party committees should have clearly defined functions. They should apply the rule of law to their leadership over judicial, procuratorial and public security work and play a key role in modernizing the governance system and capacity of the state.

It is a basic task for judicial, procuratorial and public security organs to maintain social stability. We should keep a careful balance between maintaining social stability and safeguarding the people's legitimate rights and interests. We should address the people's proper and lawful demands on matters affecting their interests, and improve the institutions that are important for safeguarding their vital interests. We should assert the authority of the law in solving conflicts, so that people are convinced that their rights and interests are protected impartially and effectively. In addition, we should identify a balance between enlivening development and maintaining public order. We need to deal with social conflicts systematically and comprehensively at the source and in accordance with the law, as well as to mobilize the whole of society to safeguard social stability.

Judicial, procuratorial and public security work is aimed at achieving social fairness and justice as core values. In a sense, promoting fairness and justice is the lifeblood of this work, and judicial, procuratorial and public security organs are the last line in defense of social justice and fairness. Judicial, procuratorial and public security officers should use the scales of fairness and the sword of justice to guarantee a fair and just society with concrete actions, and ensure access to fairness and justice for every individual. We should focus on addressing serious violations of people's rights and interests. We should never turn down people who ask us for help, never refuse to accept their cases because they cannot pay, never abuse power to violate people's legitimate rights and interests, or violate the law to create injustices and wrongly decided cases.

It is the fundamental purpose of judicial, procuratorial and public security work to ensure that the people lead a happy life. Judicial, procuratorial and public security organs and officers should address the people's problems the way they do their own, and work on the people's small problems the way they do their own big problems. We will work for the satisfaction of the people and correct any of our practices they are not happy about. We will provide effective legal protection for the people's happy life. We should strengthen the comprehensive maintenance of public order, and resolutely reverse the rising incidence of serious crimes to protect the people's lives and property.

To accomplish their noble mission entrusted by the Party and people, judicial, procuratorial and public security organs must enforce the law strictly and administer justice impartially. Justice breeds trust, and honesty fosters credibility. We should uphold our professional conscience and enforce the law for the good of the people. We should guide judicial, procuratorial and public security officers to act within the bounds of their professional code of conduct, never tolerate what the people detest, act quickly if the people so require, and strictly administer justice with awe-inspiring integrity. We should believe in and implement the rule of law, acquire a good knowledge and profound understanding of the law, and abide by and defend the law. We should hold our position firm, uphold righteousness, and respect only facts and the law in law enforcement.

Impartial law enforcement should be guaranteed by institutions. We will apply institutions to every aspect of law enforcement as a "wall" wired with "high-tension electricity line." Violators will be subject to the severest possible penalties, or be prosecuted for criminal liability if the circumstances constitute a crime. Open trials promote justice, and transparency ensures impartiality. We should take the initiative in making trials open and inviting oversight to render manipulation and judicial corruption impossible.

Officials at all levels should take the lead in acting in accordance with the law, and make sure that they do not do anything that violates the law. They should not exercise power that is not allowed for them by law or, even worse, override the law by fiat or bend the law. We should establish a sound registration, filing and reporting mechanism, as well as an accountability mechanism for officials' intervention in judicial affairs in violation of statutory procedures.

On the whole, our judicial, procuratorial and public security officers are good. They are loyal to the Party, serve our people, are able to take on tough challenges, and brave death. They are highly competent functionaries the Party and the people can absolutely trust. Party committees and governments at all levels should implement preferential policies and measures for these officers, and help them with their practical problems. We should build a contingent of judicial, procuratorial and public security officers who have firm political beliefs, strong professional expertise, a good sense of responsibility and discipline, and good moral character, are firm in their faith, enforce the law for the people, are not afraid to take on responsibilities, and are upright and honest.

It is essential for our judicial, procuratorial and public security officers to have firm ideals and convictions. We should give top priority to education in this regard for these officers. We should make sure that they uphold socialism with Chinese characteristics, faithfully follow the orders of the Party, and remain true to their mission. We should see to it that they put the Party's cause, the people's interests and the Constitution and laws above everything else, and remain politically loyal to the Party, nation, people and law.

Judicial, procuratorial and public security officers should fully shoulder their responsibility to fight crimes instead of turning a blind eye to them. When facing dangerous, urgent or intractable tasks, they should go all out and complete them without hesitation. We should strengthen education in discipline and improve the mechanism that maintains discipline, and use iron discipline to train a strong contingent of judicial, procuratorial and public security officers. We should improve their professional expertise to make sure that they complete their tasks. We should wipe out corruption in the judicial, procuratorial and public security fields with the strongest will and the most resolute actions, and remove the bad apples from them.

Judicial reform is a major part of our political reforms, and greatly helps modernize the state's governance system and capacity. We should provide stronger leadership and better coordination, and focus on real results in the process of building a just, efficient and authoritative socialist judicial system in order to better uphold the Party's leadership, give full play to the special features of China's judicial system, and promote social fairness and justice.

Meeting Chinese and foreign journalists at the Great Hall of the People in Beijing on November 15, 2012, soon after he was elected general secretary of the CPC Central Committee at the First Plenary Session of the 18th CPC Central Committee, along with other newly-elected members of the Standing Committee of the Political Bureau: Li Keqiang (3rd from right), Zhang Dejiang (3rd from left), Yu Zhengsheng (2nd from right), Liu Yunshan (2nd from left), Wang Qishan (1st from right) and Zhang Gaoli (1st from left).

Shaking hands with Hu Jintao, his predecessor, when meeting with specially-invited deputies and non-voting deputies to the 18th CPC National Congress, at the Great Hall of the People in Beijing, November 15, 2012.

Visiting "The Road to Rejuvenation" exhibition at the National Museum of China, along with other leaders, namely Li Keqiang, Zhang Dejiang, Yu Zhengsheng, Liu Yunshan, Wang Qishan and Zhang Gaoli, November 29, 2012, when he for the first time put forward the idea of the Chinese Dream of national rejuvenation.

Talking with marines on the navy vessel Haikou, *December 8, 2012.*

Chatting with farmer Tang Rongbin and his family in Luotuowan Village, Longquanguan Township, December 30, 2012, during a visit to people experiencing financial difficulties in Fuping County, Hebei Province.

Giving a keynote speech at the closing ceremony of the 12th National People's Congress, March 17, 2013. He was elected president of the People's Republic of China at the First Session of the Congress three days earlier.

Putting on a bamboo hat given to him by local Li ethnic people at Lande Rose Cultural Park on Yalong Bay, during an inspection tour of Hainan Province, April 9, 2013.

With children during a Young Pioneers activity themed "Happy Childhood with Dreams" at Beijing Children's Palace, May 29, 2013.

Greeting astronauts Nie Haisheng, Zhang Xiaoguang and Wang Yaping prior to the launching of the Shenzhou 10 manned spacecraft at the Jiuquan Satellite Launching Center in Gansu Province, June 11, 2013.

Visiting Yangluo Container Harbor in Wuhan, during his inspection of reform and economic development in Hubei Province, July 21, 2013.

Reviewing the marine guard of honor on the Liaoning, *China's first aircraft carrier, August 28, 2013.*

Chatting with farmers of Shibadong Village, Huayuan County, Xiangxi Tujia and Miao Autonomous Prefecture, during an inspection of Hunan Province, November 3, 2013.

Holding the hand of 83-year-old Wang Kechang, a war veteran, when visiting Zhucun Village, Linshu County, an old revolutionary base area in Shandong Province, November 25, 2013.

With a soldier on a patrol along the border in Arxan area of the Inner Mongolia Autonomous Region, January 26, 2014. The local temperature was below -30°C.

Checking the growth of wheat in Zhangshi Township, Weishi County, on an inspection tour in Henan Province, May 9, 2014.

Speaking to sci-tech personnel of the Design, Research and Development Center, May 23, 2014, while visiting Commercial Aircraft Corporation of China, Ltd.

Culturally Advanced China

Enhance Publicity and Theoretical Work[*]

August 19, 2013

Our publicity and theoretical work must help us accomplish the central task of economic development and serve the overall interests of the country. Therefore, we must bear the big picture in mind and keep in line with the trends. We should map out plans with focus on priorities and carry them out in accordance with the situation.

Economic development is the Party's central task, and ideological progress is one of its top priorities.

Since the convocation of the Third Plenary Session of the 11th CPC Central Committee in 1978 the Party has made economic development its central task, devoting itself to accelerating the economy and improving the people's lives. This central task will not and should not change as long as the domestic or international situation does not change dramatically. It is a basic requirement for the Party to adhere to its basic line for 100 years and to solve all the problems of contemporary China.

Moreover, to enhance the cause of Chinese socialism we must promote material, cultural and ethical progress, strengthen the nation materially, culturally and ethically, and improve the material, cultural and ethical lives of the people of all ethnic groups.

Our publicity and theoretical work aims to consolidate Marxism as the guiding ideology in China, and cement the shared ideological basis of the whole Party and the people. Both Party members and officials must hold a firm belief in Marxism and communism, make unremitting and pragmatic efforts to realize the Party's basic program at the

---

* Main points of the speech at a national meeting on publicity and theoretical work.

present stage, take every step needed for progress and pass the baton dutifully to our successors.

Officials, especially high-ranking ones, should master the basic theories of Marxism as their special skill and diligently study Marxism-Leninism and Mao Zedong Thought, and especially Deng Xiaoping Theory, the important thought of the Three Represents and the Scientific Outlook on Development.

Marxism must be a required course in Party schools, executive leadership academies, academies of social sciences, institutes of higher learning and groups for theoretical studies. These places should serve as the centers for studying, researching and disseminating Marxism.

New and young officials in particular should work hard to study Marxist theory, learn to observe and solve problems from the Marxist stand, viewpoint and method, and become firm in their ideals and convictions.

More efforts should be made to enhance the awareness of socialism with Chinese characteristics among the people of all ethnic groups, so as to inspire the people to strive for Chinese socialism.

We should intensify the recognition of the core socialist values, foster and practice these values, improve civic morality, and cultivate the social trends of recognizing honor and disgrace, practicing integrity, encouraging dedication and promoting harmony.

Party spirit and the idea of serving the people have long been interrelated. Preserving Party spirit means keeping a correct political direction, taking a committed political stand and disseminating the Party's theories, lines, principles and policies, in addition to the major work plans of the CPC Central Committee and its major analyses and judgments on the country's situation. It also means maintaining a high degree of unity with the Party Central Committee and upholding its authority. All departments, institutions and all Party members and officials specializing in publicity and theoretical work must preserve their Party spirit without fail.

Serving the people means putting the people first and making realizing, safeguarding and developing the fundamental interests of the overwhelming majority of the people our starting point and goal. Our work should focus on serving the people. We should serve the people while educating and guiding them, satisfy their demands while upgrading their personal quality, disseminate and report more on their great endeavors and vigorous lives, role models and their moving stories. This way, we can enrich the people culturally and ethically, enhance their moral strength, and meet their cultural and intellectual demands.

An important platform for publicity and theoretical work is the stressing of unity, stability and encouragement, and putting the focus on positive publicity. We are new to a battle with many new historic features. We are facing unprecedented challenges and difficulties. Therefore, we must continue to enhance and intensify the underlying trend of thought in our country, advocate the themes of the times, popularize positive energy, and encourage the whole country to strive as one for progress.

The key to success lies in raising the quality and level of our publicity and theoretical work. We should have the proper timing, tempo and efficiency, make this work more attractive and influential, inform the people about what they love to hear, read and watch, and let positive publicity play its role in encouraging and inspiring the people.

When it comes to major issues, including those of political principle, we must take the initiative in helping officials and the people draw a line between right and wrong and acquire a clear understanding in this regard.

Over the years, our Party has accumulated abundant experience in publicity and theoretical work. Hard-earned and extremely precious, this experience serves as major guidance for our future work, and should be thoroughly reviewed and carried forward on a long-term basis, and continuously enriched and developed.

As an old Chinese saying goes, "A wise man changes his way as circumstances change; a knowledgeable person alters his means as times evolve."[1] As for publicity and theoretical work today, we should pay close attention to innovation in the fields of ideas, methodologies and grassroots work, and move forward with new ideas to tackle difficulties, with emphasis on work in local communities. We should step up cultural reforms, push forward the culture industry, and build China into a country with a strong socialist culture.

At this time when China is opening its door wider to the outside world, it has become an important task for those engaged in publicity and theoretical work to help guide the people to a better understanding of present-day China while learning about the rest of the world more comprehensively and objectively.

To explain and publicize the special characteristics of modern China, we need to make it clear that 1) because different countries and nations have different historical traditions, cultural accomplishments and basic conditions, their development paths are different; 2) Chinese culture encompasses the deepest cultural and ethical pursuits of the Chinese nation, nourishing the people for generations; 3) fine traditional Chinese culture is a great strength of the Chinese nation and its most profound cultural soft power; 4) rooted in Chinese culture, socialism with Chinese characteristics represents the Chinese people's aspirations, suits the times and facilitates the development of the country, and is based on a long history and solid reality. The time-honored Chinese culture is capable of adding glory to it today and in the days to come.

It is inevitable for China, a country with a unique culture, history and basic conditions, to choose a development path featuring its own characteristics. As for traditional Chinese culture and foreign things, we should make the past serve the present and foreign things serve China; discard the dross and select the essential; eliminate the false and retain the true, and adopt traditional Chinese culture and foreign things after a thorough and well-considered review of both.

We should intensify our publicity of and report on the changes and developments worldwide, and the new thoughts, ideas and discoveries in other countries, so as to help draw on the achievements of other civilizations.

We should enhance our foreign-oriented publicity work through trying methods with new concepts, domains and expressions that are understood by both China and the rest of the world, telling the true story of our country and making our voice heard.

The departments concerned with publicity and theoretical work have an extremely important task to shoulder. They should play their part well and try their best. They should improve their work starting from their leaders and leading bodies. Therefore, those leaders should intensify their study and practice in order to become real experts.

Successful publicity and theoretical work requires joint efforts by the whole Party. Party committees at all levels should take political and leading responsibilities. They should redouble their efforts to study and address major issues, and to coordinate and guide major strategic campaigns. They should steadily upgrade their leadership skills. With a grand publicity blueprint, we should mobilize as many departments as possible in all walks of life and link publicity and theoretical work more closely to administrative, industrial and social governance in all areas.

Notes

[1] Huan Kuan: *On Salt and Iron (Yan Tie Lun)*, an important work for the study of the history of economics and thought during the Western Han Dynasty (206 BC-AD 25). The author (dates unknown) was a court minister of that dynasty.

Strong Ethical Support for the Realization
of the Chinese Dream*

September 26, 2013

Paragons of morality are important banners for building public ethics. We need to carry out campaigns to publicize such paragons of morality and let people learn from them, foster the true, the good and the beautiful, and spread positive energy. We should inspire the people to esteem virtue, perform good deeds and emulate virtuous people. Moreover, we should encourage the whole of society to cultivate morality by practicing virtue and to exert a positive influence through ethical behavior. In this way, we will marshal strong spiritual and ethical support for realizing the Chinese Dream of national renewal.

Inner strength is infinite, as is moral strength. Chinese civilization has a long history stretching back to antiquity; it gave birth to the precious character of the Chinese nation and cultivated the Chinese people's pursuit of noble values. The pursuit of constant self-improvement and embracing the world through virtue have been the stimuli behind the Chinese nation's ceaseless self-regeneration, and today this pursuit is still a powerful motivation for us to carry out reform and opening up, and for socialist modernization.

To meet the requirements of the central authorities, local governments and departments have long worked hard to promote public morality, advocated traditional Chinese virtues and fostered the new trends of the times. Consequently, ethical models have emerged in large numbers. National ethical models are outstanding representatives of these people. Some of you have hearts of gold and are always

---

* Main points of the speech when meeting the fourth group of nominees and winners of national ethical model awards.

ready to help others; some act bravely for a just cause without considering personal safety; some are honest and trustworthy, and keep to the right way; some work diligently at their posts dedicating their lives to serving the public; and some treat the elderly and their relatives with filial respect. With noble characters, you have warmed and touched the hearts of our people, and have set good examples for the whole of society.

A great era calls for a great spirit, and a worthy cause demands role models to take the lead. Now the people of China are working hard for the Chinese Dream. In line with the requirement to cultivate and practice the core socialist values raised at the Party's 18th National Congress, we should pay close attention to advocating socialist morals, intensify education in public morality, professional ethics, family virtues and individual integrity, promote basic moral standards such as patriotism, dedication to work, integrity and friendliness, and cultivate social trends of recognizing honor and disgrace, practicing integrity, encouraging dedication and promoting harmony.

Now I'd like to introduce Gong Quanzhen, a national ethical model. She is the widow of General Gan Zuchang, a veteran Red Army officer from Jiangxi Province and a founding general of the People's Republic. In 1957 Gan voluntarily resigned his post to be a farmer, and Gong Quanzhen returned with him to the countryside in Jiangxi. Half a century later, Gong still maintains the spirit of hard work and plain living. For this, she was elected a national ethical model, and is present at this meeting. I feel gratified and want to express my greatest respects to her. We must carry forward the spirit of hard work and plain living generation after generation.

Enhance China's Cultural Soft Power[*]

December 30, 2013

The strengthening of our cultural soft power is decisive for China to reach the Two Centenary Goals and realize the Chinese Dream of rejuvenation of the Chinese nation.

We should carry forward advanced socialist culture, further the reform of the cultural system, develop and enrich socialist culture, inspire the whole nation to engage in cultural creation, beef up the growth of cultural enterprises, enrich the people's cultural life, ignite their inspiration, strengthen our cultural power and competitiveness, and reach the goal of building China into a socialist cultural power.

To strengthen our cultural soft power, we should reinforce the cornerstone of our national cultural soft power. We should adhere to a development path of socialist culture featuring Chinese character-istics, intensify the study of and education in the core socialist value system, carry forward the national spirit and the spirit of the times, encourage people to have their ideals and beliefs, establish prosper-ous cultural undertakings, and speed up the growth of cultural enter-prises.

To reinforce the foundation for domestic cultural progress, one of the major tasks is to enhance ideological and moral education, and build up social morality by starting with every individual. We should carry forward and foster the traditional morality long cultivated and developed by our ancestors.

Under the guidance of Marxist and socialist ethics, we should make the past serve the present and put forth new ideas on the basis

---

[*] Main points of the speech at the 12th group study session of the Political Bureau of the 18th CPC Central Committee which Xi presided over.

of eliminating the false and retaining the true for the creative transformation and progress of traditional Chinese ethics, so as to lead the people on the way to yearning for and aspiring to life-long learning, respecting and obeying moral standards, so that every one of the 1.3 billion Chinese citizens can be part of a team to disseminate Chinese morality and culture.

To strengthen our cultural soft power, we should disseminate the values of modern China. Modern Chinese values are also those of socialism with Chinese characteristics, representing advanced Chinese culture. China has blazed a successful socialist path featuring Chinese characteristics. Facts prove that our path and system, theoretical and social, are successful. More work should be done to refine and explain our ideas, and extend the platform for overseas publicity, so as to make our culture known through international communication and dissemination.

We should relate the Chinese Dream to modern Chinese values during our dissemination and explanation. The Chinese Dream is a dream cherished and aspired to by the Chinese people and nation, a dream of building China into a well-off society in an all-round way and rejuvenating the Chinese nation, a dream for everyone to make his own dream come true, a dream that the whole nation strives for, and a dream to show the world China's commitment to making a greater contribution to the peace and development of mankind.

To strengthen our cultural soft power, we should showcase the unique charm of Chinese culture.

During its 5,000-year history, the Chinese nation has created a brilliant and profound culture. We should disseminate the most fundamental Chinese culture in a popular way to attract more people to participate in it, matching modern culture and society. We should popularize our cultural spirit across countries as well as across time and space, with contemporary values and the eternal charm of Chinese culture. We should tell the rest of the world about the new achievements of modern Chinese culture, which feature both excellent tradition and modern spirit, both national and international.

To this end, efforts should be made to sort out traditional cultural resources and bring back to life relics sleeping in closed palaces, legacies of the vast land of China and records in ancient books. We should convince the people with reason and morality, improve cultural communication with other countries and intensify our system of cultural and educational exchanges, blaze new trails, and use various means, such as mass media, group dissemination and interpersonal communication.

To build a beautiful image of our country, we should display the Chinese civilization of a long history and unity of diversified ethnic groups with varying cultures; an Oriental power with honest and capable political administrations, developed economy, thriving culture, stable society, unified people and splendid landscapes; a responsible great power that is committed to peaceful development, common growth, international fairness and justice, and contributions to mankind; and a socialist power opening its door wider to the outside world, full of hope, vigor and vitality.

To strengthen our cultural soft power, we should intensify our international right to a voice, enhance our capability of international communication and spare no efforts in establishing a system for international discourse to tell, in the right way, the true story of our country and make our voices heard through giving full play to the emerging media and enhancing our creativity, influence and public trust.

We should disseminate the glorious history and excellent culture of the Chinese nation and people. We should also enhance education in patriotism, collectivism and socialism with the help of all possible means, such as classroom teaching, theoretical research, historical study, films and television programs, and literary works, and help our people build up and persist in a correct concept of history, national viewpoint, state outlook and cultural perspective, so as to fortify the will of the Chinese people, who should be prouder of being Chinese.

Cultivate and Disseminate
the Core Socialist Values*

February 24, 2014

We must take cultivating and disseminating the core socialist values as a fundamental project for integrating the people's mindset and reinforcing our social foundations. We should inherit and carry forward the fine traditional Chinese culture and virtues, disseminate the core socialist values and educate the people extensively, guide and encourage the people to act according to them, to respect and follow moral standards, to pursue lofty moral ideals, and to reinforce the ideological and moral foundation of socialism with Chinese characteristics.

Core values, a fundamental factor for the texture and orientation of a culture, are the soul of cultural soft power and a key to building a nation's cultural soft power. In essence, cultural soft power depends on the vitality, cohesion and appeal of the core values of a nation. Therefore, cultivating and disseminating the core values and effectively integrating the people's mindset is an important means of ensuring that the social system operates in a normal manner and that the social order is effectively maintained. It is also a major aspect of a nation's governing system and capacity.

Facts prove that to successfully build a set of core values with strong appeal is connected with a country's social harmony and stability, as well as its long-term peace and order.

To cultivate and disseminate the core socialist values we must take traditional Chinese culture as the base. All concrete core values are deeply rooted. So, to renounce such values is tantamount to severing

* Main points of the speech at the 13th group study session of the Political Bureau of the 18th CPC Central Committee which Xi presided over.

our cultural lifeline. The extensive, profound and outstanding traditional Chinese culture is the foundation for us to stand firm upon in the global mingling and clashing of cultures.

The long-developed Chinese culture embraces our deepest intellectual pursuits. It is an icon of the unique Chinese nation, and has ensured the lineage, development and growth of the Chinese nation. Traditional Chinese virtues are the essence of Chinese culture, and embody rich ethical and moral resources. Only by etching these values in our minds can we forge ahead, and only by carrying forward what our ancestors have left us can we learn to be more creative.

With regard to values, perceptions and ethics handed down for generations, we should make the past serve the present, discard the dross and keep the essential, eliminate the false and retain the true, and put forth new ideas. That is to say, we should treat and inherit them with a critical approach, and cultivate and educate the people with the Chinese cultural legacy.

We need to explain clearly the historical origin, evolution and basic tendency of the outstanding traditional Chinese culture and its uniqueness, perceptions and distinctive features, so as to enhance confidence in Chinese culture and values.

We should work hard to absorb the philosophical and moral essence of traditional Chinese culture, foster and disseminate our national character with patriotism at the core and at the call of the times, highlighted by reform and innovation, and identify and explicate their essential features of benevolence, people-orientation, integrity, righteousness, concordance and common ground.

We should properly handle the relationship between inheritance and innovation, with the focus on transforming and developing the fine traditional Chinese culture in a creative way.

We should make the core values the people's pursuit and conscious actions through education, publicity, cultural edification, habitual development and institutional guarantee.

A fine example has boundless power. All Party members and officials must take the lead in studying and spreading the core socialist values, influence and encourage other people to follow their exemplary behavior and noble personalities.

We should spread the socialist values among children and students, ensuring their inclusion in textbooks and lectures so as to let everyone be aware of them.

Like spring drizzle falling without a sound, we should disseminate the core socialist values in a gentle and lively way by making use of all kinds of cultural forms. We should inform the people by means of fine literary works and artistic images what is the true, the good and the beautiful, what is the false, the evil and the ugly, and what should be praised and encouraged, and what should be opposed and repudiated.

The core socialist values can hardly be effective unless they are put into practice, for only then may the people understand and observe them. What we advocate must be in line with what the people need in their daily life in a manner as detailed and practical as possible. We must uphold the core socialist values when strengthening rules and regulations in all sectors, formulating codes of conduct for students and other citizens in both urban and rural areas so as to turn the core socialist values into basic guidelines for the people's daily life and work.

We should create some forms of ceremonies and conduct various memorial and celebration events to disseminate mainstream values and enhance the people's sense of identity and of belonging.

Efforts should be made to integrate the requirements of the core socialist values into various activities concerning intellectual and cultural progress, so as to attract more people to participate in such activities, upgrade their moral outlook and foster civic virtues in society for family happiness, extending care to others and contributing more to society. We should make use of every opportunity to make this happen, anytime and anywhere.

We should give full play to our policies concerning the economy, politics, culture and society to better serve the cultivation of the core socialist values. Laws and regulations should act as a driving force for the spread of the core values. Moreover, all social administrative agencies should make it their responsibility to advocate the core socialist values and reflect them in their routine work so that all activities conforming with the core values are encouraged and those running counter to the core values are rebuffed.

Young People Should Practice
the Core Socialist Values[*]

May 4, 2014

Dear students, teachers and friends,

Today, as we celebrate China's Youth Day[1] I'm glad to be here with you, honoring the 95th anniversary of the May 4th Movement[2]. First of all, I'd like to extend, on behalf of the Party Central Committee, my festival greetings to the teachers, staff and students at Peking University and young people of all ethnic groups across the country. Also, I want to express my deepest respects to those who work in the fields of education and youth work throughout the country!

This is my fifth visit to Peking University since I started to serve on the Party Central Committee, and each time I am here I find something new that impresses me. My feelings soar whenever I walk on this campus full of vigor and vitality, and I can't help but sigh: The current generation of college students is just adorable, trustworthy and reliable, and you are bound to have a bright future.

The May 4th Movement gave founding to the May 4th spirit of patriotism, progress, democracy and science, kicking off the New Democratic Revolution in China, promoting the dissemination of Marxism in the country and laying the groundwork for the founding of the CPC.

Since the May 4th Movement, under the leadership of the Party, generations of highly motivated young men and women have written

---

* Speech at the seminar with teachers and students of Peking University.

inspiring chapters in the struggles to save the country and rejuvenate the Chinese nation, with the motto "Devoting my youth to creating a family of youth, a country of youth, a nation of youth, a mankind of youth, a planet of youth and a universe of youth."[3]

Peking University was the base of the New Culture Movement[4] as well as a cradle of the May 4th Movement, witnessing this glorious period in modern history. For a long time, teachers and students here have shared a common destiny with the country and the people, and advanced with the times and society, making remarkable contributions to our country's revolution, construction and reform in all respects.

The Two Centenary Goals were put forward at the 18th CPC National Congress. As I have said before, we have never been so close as now to reaching the goal of the great renewal of the Chinese nation, and we are more confident and more capable than ever of fulfiling this goal.

Nevertheless, "A thing is yet to be done until it is done,"[5] as an old saying goes. The closer we approach the goal the more we should redouble our efforts. We can afford no slackening. More importantly, we should encourage more young people to join the great cause of making the dream come true.

The river of time flows nonstop day and night, and things change as the seasons change. Every generation of young people is offered the opportunities of the era for drawing a picture of life and creating history. Young people, the most sensitive weatherglass of an era, are entrusted with the responsibilities of the times and share the glory of their days.

Today, we are here to honor the May 4th Movement. The best way for us to have the May 4th spirit display widely is to join the team of builders, pioneers and dedicators, and together with the people of all ethnic groups shoulder our historic responsibilities with firm beliefs, high morality, a wealth of knowledge and competent skills.

Students and teachers,

University is a place not just for academic studies but for seeking truth. Today, I'd like to take this opportunity to share with you my insights into the core socialist values.

I was inspired by the spirit of the May 4th Movement, which embodies the values the Chinese people and nation have pursued in modern history. Today, we should still adhere to and carry out these core values, highlighted by patriotism, progress, democracy and science. Young people, as well as everyone else in the country, should uphold and carry out these core values.

Looking at human history and social development, we find that the most lasting and profound power for a nation and country is the core values acknowledged by all. Core values carry the spiritual aspiration of a nation and country, and represent the standard for judging right and wrong.

An ancient proverb goes, "The way to great learning is to manifest bright virtue and to treat the people as one's own family, thereby arriving at supreme goodness."[6] Core values are in fact individual virtues, as well as public, social and national virtues. A country cannot prosper without virtues, nor can anyone succeed without virtues. Without shared core values, a nation and country will be at a loss to know what is right and what is wrong, and its people will have no code of conduct to follow, the result being that the nation and country can never progress. It has commonly occurred in our history, and still happens across the globe.

China is a big country with 1.3 billion people and 56 ethnic groups. Upon the recognition of the values with the "greatest common denominator" by the people of all ethnic groups, they work with one heart and one mind to strive in unity. This concerns our nation's future and destiny, as well as our people's happiness and well-being.

Every era has its spirit, and likewise its values. In ancient China our ancestors developed core values highlighted by "propriety, righteousness, honesty and a sense of shame – the four anchors of our moral foundation, and a question of life and death for the country."[7] This was our ancestors' understanding of their core values.

What are the core values for our people and country today? This is both a theoretical and a practical question. We should eventually agree upon this after sorting out opinions and understandings from all walks of life. The core socialist values that we should cultivate and practice are prosperity, democracy, civility, harmony, freedom, equality, justice, the rule of law, patriotism, dedication, integrity and friendship.

The values of prosperity, democracy, civility and harmony are for the country; those of freedom, equality, justice and the rule of law for the society; and those of patriotism, dedication, integrity and friendship for citizens. They explain what sort of country and society we are striving for, and what kind of citizens we are cultivating.

Since ancient times the Chinese people have developed their country through studying the nature of things to acquire knowledge, correcting thoughts with sincerity, cultivating the moral self, managing the family, governing the state and safeguarding peace under Heaven. As we see it today, the principles of "studying the nature of things, correcting thoughts with sincerity and cultivating the moral self" are for individuals; the principle of "managing the family" is for the society; and those of "governing the state and safeguarding peace under Heaven" are for the country.

What we put forward for the core socialist values is a combination of requirements for the country, society and citizens, which represent the nature of socialism, carry forward the fine traditional Chinese culture, draw on the best of world civilization and reflect the spirit of the times.

Prosperity, democracy, civility, harmony, freedom, equality, justice, the rule of law, patriotism, dedication, integrity and friendship are all ideas that inherit the essence of the outstanding traditional Chinese culture, embody the ideals and faith formed by modern Chinese people through unremitting and painstaking efforts, and reflect the wishes and vision of every Chinese citizen.

We should foster the core socialist values throughout society. The people should join hands and work persistently to make China richer and stronger, more democratic, more harmonious and more beautiful, so that our country can be confident enough to stand proudly among all other nations.

Since the Opium War of the 1840s the Chinese people have long cherished a dream of realizing a great national rejuvenation and building China into a strong, democratic and harmonious modern socialist country – the highest and most fundamental interests of the nation. And that's what our 1.3 billion people are striving for.

China used to be a world economic power. However, it missed its chance in the wake of the Industrial Revolution and the consequent dramatic changes, and thus was left behind and suffered humiliation under foreign invasion. Things got worse especially after the Opium War, when the nation was plagued by poverty and weakness, allowing others to trample upon and manipulate us. We must not let this tragic history repeat itself.

The construction of a strong, democratic and harmonious modern socialist country is our goal and responsibility – for the nation, for our forefathers and for our future generations. Therefore, we should maintain our willpower, intensify our faith, and walk unswervingly along the road towards our destination.

China has stood up. It will never again tolerate being bullied by any nation. Yet it will never follow in the footsteps of the big powers, which seek hegemony once they grow strong. Our country is following a path of peaceful development.

Why are we so confident? Because we have developed and become stronger. China has won worldwide respect with its century-long efforts. Its prestige keeps rising, and its influence keeps expanding. Today's China forms a sharp contrast to China in the 19th century when the country was humiliated, its sovereignty was infringed upon, and its people were bullied by foreigners.

Chinese civilization has formed a unique value system over several millennia. The brilliant traditional Chinese culture is the essence of the nation and has deep roots in the Chinese people's mentality, influencing their way of thinking and behavior unconsciously.

Today, we advocate and carry forward the core socialist values through absorbing the rich nourishment of Chinese culture, so as to invigorate its vitality and broaden its influence.

Here are some quotations from ancient classics that I'd like to share with you today:

"The people are the foundation of a state,"[8]

"The harmony of Nature and man,"[9]

"Harmony without uniformity,"[10]

"As Heaven changes through movement, a gentleman makes unremitting efforts to perfect himself,"[11]

"When the Great Way prevailed, a public spirit ruled all under Heaven,"[12]

"Everyone is responsible for his country's rise or fall,"[13]

"Govern the country with virtue and educate the people with culture,"

"A gentleman has a good knowledge of righteousness,"[14]

"A gentleman is broad-minded,"[15]

"A gentleman takes morality as his bedrock,"[16]

"Be true in word and resolute in deed,"[17]

"If a man does not keep his word, what is he good for?"[18]

"A man of high moral quality will never feel lonely,"[19]

"The benevolent man loves others,"[20]

"Do things for the good of others,"[21]

"Don't do unto others what you don't want others to do unto you,"[22]

"Care for each other and help one another,"[23]

"Respect others' elders as one respects one's own, and care for others' children as one cares for one's own,"[24]

"Help the poor and assist those in difficulty,"

"Care less about quantity and more about quality."[25]

These thoughts and ideas all displayed and still demonstrate distinctive national features, and have the indelible values of the times. We have updated them in keeping abreast of the times, while carrying them forward in an unbroken line.

As Chinese, we should always keep our own unique inner-world spirit, uphold values that we practice every day without noticing. The core socialist values we advocate today represent the inheritance and upgrading of outstanding traditional Chinese culture.

Values appear and develop in the process of human beings getting to know and shape nature and society. Core values vary in different nations and countries due to different natural conditions and courses of development. The core values of a nation and country are closely related to its history and culture, as well as to what its people are striving for and to the present issues it needs to resolve.

There are no two leaves exactly alike on earth. A nation, or people of a country, must know who they are, where they came from and where they are heading. Keep on going when you have made your choice.

On December 26 last year, I said at the meeting commemorating the 120th birthday of Mao Zedong:

Boasting a vast land of 9.6 million sq km, a rich cultural heritage and a strong bond among the 1.3 billion Chinese people, we are resolved to go our own way. We have a big stage to display our advantages on, a long and rich history to draw benefit from, and a powerful impetus to push us ahead. We Chinese people – every single one of us – should draw confidence from this.

We should modestly learn from the best of other civilizations, but never forget our own origin. We must not blindly copy the development models of other countries nor accept their dictation.

What I mean here is that we should enhance our confidence in the path we have chosen, in the theories we have devised and in the system we have established to reach our goal of development and make the Chinese Dream come true. "In the face of all blows, not bending low, it still stands fast. Whether from east, west, south or north the wind doth blast."[26] Our confidence is supported by our core values.

Why am I talking about the core socialist values with you young people? Because your value orientation will decide the values of the whole of society in the years to come. Besides, young people are at the time of life when they form and establish their values. It is therefore very important to offer some guidance. That reminds me of something that happens in our daily life. When we button up our coat, we may inadvertently put the first button in the wrong button hole, and that will result in all the other buttons being put in the wrong holes. That's why we say that young people should "button right" in the early days of their life. "A deep well is dug starting with a shallow pit."[27] Every young person should learn about the core socialist values starting right now, take them as his basic rules and disseminate them throughout society.

When young people adopt the core socialist values they should emphasize the following points:

First, work diligently to acquire true knowledge. Knowledge is an important cornerstone for the cultivation of the core values. The great philosophers of ancient Greece believed that knowledge was a virtue. Our ancestors also asserted, "One cannot enhance one's ability and wisdom if one does not work hard; neither can one succeed without ambition."[28]

A person enjoys only once the youthful days at college, so you should cherish them. To acquire knowledge, one has to study diligently, intensively and persistently. Lu Xun[29] once said, "Who said I'm a genius? I spent all my time working when others were sipping coffee."[30] In college days, "Young we were, schoolmates, at life's full flowering."[31] One can totally throw oneself into seeking knowledge without any distractions, learning from teachers, exchanging views with classmates and rummaging through piles of books. So there is no reason not to study hard. Work hard, acquire more knowledge and turn what you have learned into your own views and ideas. I hope that you will not only concentrate on book knowledge but also care about the people, the country and the world, and assume your responsibility for society.

Second, cultivate morality and virtue, and pay attention to them in practice. "Virtue is the root."[32] Mr Cai Yuanpei[33] believed, "He who is strong physically and talented but has no virtue will end up on the side of vice."[34] Virtues are fundamental for both individuals and society. What is most important is to cultivate morality. This explains why we select those who are both talented and morally cultivated for our work, with morality as priority. One can be placed in the right position only if one recognizes virtue, follows social ethics and restricts personal desires.

When talking about cultivating morality, one needs to have high ambitions as well as pragmatic plans. To devote oneself to one's country and serve one's people, this is the great virtue with which one is able to accomplish the great cause. In the meantime, one needs to start to do small things well and be self-disciplined even in small matters. "Learning from fine things that may appear and correcting any mistakes that may occur,"[35] one needs to cultivate public and personal virtues, learn to work, to be thrifty, to be grateful, to help others, to be modest, to be tolerant, to examine oneself and to exercise self-restraint.

Third, learn to tell right from wrong and make correct decisions. As our ancestors believed, "Reading without thinking makes one muddled; thinking without reading makes one flighty."[36] Knowing what is right or wrong, what is the correct direction and what is the proper way to follow, one is bound to reap the reward of one's work.

Facing a complex and fast-changing world, an information era with the surge of various schools of thought, a multifaceted society of genuine and false ideas, and the pressure associated with one's academic pursuit, relationships and employment, you may feel somewhat confused, hesitant or frustrated. This is a normal experience everybody will go through. The key is to learn to think about and analyze situations before making decisions in order to arrive at correct decisions. You should be sturdy, confident and self-reliant. You must form a correct world outlook, view of life and values, then you will see – crystal-clear – the true nature of society and have a better understanding of your life's experience, and be able to tell what is right and what is wrong, what is primary and what is secondary, what is true and what is false, what is good and what is evil, and what is beautiful and what is ugly before making judgments and decisions. As a Tang verse goes, "Gold glitters only after countless washings and sievings."[37]

Fourth, be honest and sincere; do solid work and be an upright person. The correct way needs to be pursued in practice, while morality requires no empty talk. One should be more pragmatic. Knowledge and action should go hand in hand, and the core values should be turned into moral pursuits as well as a drive to make people engage in conscious action. *The Book of Rites*[38] says, "Learn extensively, inquire earnestly, think profoundly, discriminate clearly and practice sincerely."[39]

　Some people believe that "sages are mediocre people who work hard, while mediocre people are sages who refuse to work hard." With more opportunities, young people should make their steps steady, lay a solid foundation and make unremitting efforts. It is no good for study or running a business if one works intermittently, or chops and changes. "Difficult things are done starting from easy ones; a great undertaking begins with minor work."[40]

No matter what you opt to do, success always favors hard workers. Young people should take a difficult environment as a challenge or test. "Little strokes fell great oaks." Success awaits those who work doggedly and unyieldingly, and those who are never daunted by repeated setbacks.

The cultivation of the core values can't be done overnight. It requires efforts from the easy to the difficult, from close-up to faraway until it becomes a faith and idea that we follow conscientiously. When things are smooth, you may be confident; when there are frustrations, you may have doubts and waver. In all circumstances we should always uphold the core socialist values which have been formed and developed here in our country, make contributions to the great cause in the modern era and fulfill our lifetime expectations.

Students and teachers,

The Party Central Committee has decided to build world-class colleges and universities – a strategic policy that we should follow without hesitation. To make them world-class, they must feature Chinese characteristics. It won't do to copy others mechanically, because we always believe that "the more national the more international."

In this world there is only one Harvard University, University of Oxford, Stanford University, Massachusetts Institute of Technology and University of Cambridge; likewise, there is only one Peking University, Tsinghua University, Zhejiang University, Fudan University and Nanjing University in China. We should draw on the world's best experience in running institutions of higher learning, follow the rules of education, and establish more excellent colleges and universities on Chinese soil.

Lu Xun asserted, "Peking University is always innovative and plays a pioneering role in reforming movements, leading China along an upward path towards a better future."[41]

The decision on advancing the reform in an all-round way was made at the Third Plenary Session of the 18th CPC Central Committee, defining the demands for the further reform of higher education in China. What we must do now is to turn this blueprint into reality.

Institutions of higher learning should take the lead in educational reform throughout the country, centering on the fundamental tasks of building virtues and morality, and moving faster in establishing an educational system and mechanism that is full of vigor and vitality, efficient, more open and favoring educational development in a balanced and coordinated way. I do hope that Peking University can realize its long-cherished dream as soon as possible of advancing into the ranks of world-class universities through painstaking efforts, reform and innovation.

Teachers are entrusted with the noblest mission in this world. Mr Mei Yiqi[42] opined that the key to the success of a university lies in having a lot of highly accomplished gurus rather than imposing buildings.[43] What he meant by "highly-accomplished gurus," as I see it, are people most knowledgeable in their academic fields and who are also virtuous. Always bearing in mind their responsibilities, teachers should be ready to serve as human ladders, inspiring the souls of the students whom they are teaching with the help of their personal charisma and scholarly attainments.

Party committees and governments at all levels should pay closer attention to colleges and universities, show more concern for the students and erect a platform for them to dream upon and make their dreams come true. We should accelerate the reform in an all-round way, create a fair and just social environment, promote social mobility and inspire the vigor and creativity of young people. We should improve the system of employment and business startups so as to assist graduates at the beginning of their life-long careers. Leading officials at all levels should keep in communication with the students, make friends with them and listen to what they have to say.

Today, the majority of college students are around the age of 20; and they will be under the age of 30 by 2020, when we complete the building of a moderately prosperous society in all respects. They will be around 60 by the mid-21st century, when we basically realize our country's modernization. That is to say, you will participate in the cause of reaching the Two Centenary Goals along with myriads of other young people.

I believe that life is meaningless for anyone without faith, without dreams, without concerted endeavors and without contributions. I hope that you can create your own wonderful life while making the Chinese Dream come true since you have never been given a platform as spacious as this or as promising as this.

I believe that young Chinese people today are more than capable of undertaking the historic mission entrusted to them by the Party and the people, and will go on to write a brilliant chapter worthy of our times in their efforts to take advantage of their youthful vigor, explore life and contribute to society!

Notes

[1] The year 1939 saw the nomination of China's Youth Day on May 4th by the Northwestern Youth Association of National Salvation in the Shaanxi-Gansu-Ningxia Border Region to carry forward and foster the glorious revolutionary tradition of the Chinese young people since the May 4th Movement in 1919. In December 1949 the Government Administration Council – the predecessor of China's State Council – of the Central People's Government officially named it China's Youth Day.

[2] The May 4th Movement, which started in Beijing on May 4, 1919, was a patriotic movement of the Chinese people against imperialism and feudalism. Soon af-

ter the end of World War I, victorious nations, including Britain, the United States, France, Japan, and Italy held the Paris Peace Conference, awarding Germany's rights in Shandong Province to Japan. China was one of the victorious nations, but the Chinese Beiyang (Warlord) Government was about to sign the treaty. On the afternoon of May 4, 1919, over 3,000 students of Peking University and other schools protested against the treaty and the compromise of the Beiyang Government, provoking a quick response throughout the country. By June 3 the movement turned out to be a patriotic movement against imperialism and feudalism, with participants from the working class, urban petite-bourgeoisie and national bourgeoisie. It also sparked off the New Culture Movement against feudal Chinese culture. Bolstered by the founding of the journal *Youth* (later known as *New Youth*) in 1915, the New Culture Movement called for Mr Science and Mr Democracy by replacing old moral standards and old literature with the new. The May 4th Movement marked the end of the Old Democratic Revolution and the start of the New Democratic Revolution in China, thereby opening a brand-new chapter of revolution in Chinese history.

[3] Li Dazhao: *Youth*. Li Dazhao (1889-1927) was a pioneer in acquiring and disseminating Marxism and one of the founders of the CPC.

[4] See note 2, p. 196.

[5] See note 2, p. 60.

[6] *The Great Learning (Da Xue)*.

[7] *Guan Zi*.

[8] *The Book of History (Shang Shu)*.

[9] An ancient Chinese philosophical viewpoint, from the Idea of God's Will of the Western Zhou Dynasty (1046-771 BC), which believed that Heaven and Man were closely related.

[10] *The Analects of Confucius (Lun Yu)*.

[11] *The Book of Changes (Yi Jing)*, also known as the *I Ching*, one of the Confucian classics. The book was used as a work for the divination of natural and social changes through the calculation of the Eight Trigrams representing Heaven, Earth, Thunder, Wind, Water, Fire, Mountain and Lake, believing that the interactions of the *yin* and *yang* give birth to everything in the universe and advocating simple yet dialectical viewpoints, such as "Changes derive from the mutual acceleration of the hard and soft."

[12] *The Book of Rites (Li Ji)*.

[13] Gu Yanwu: *Records of Daily Knowledge (Ri Zhi Lu)*. Gu Yanwu (1613-1682) was a thinker and historian in the late Ming (1368-1644) and early Qing (1644-1911) dynasties.

[14] *The Analects of Confucius (Lun Yu).*

[15] *Ibid.*

[16] *Ibid.*

[17] *Ibid.*

[18] *Ibid.*

[19] *Ibid.*

[20] *The Mencius (Meng Zi),* one of the Confucian classics compiled by Mencius and his disciples. The book is a collection of anecdotes and conversations of the Confucian thinker and philosopher Mencius during the Warring States Period (475-221 BC). It is one of the "Four Classics of Confucianism," the other three being *The Great Learning, The Doctrine of the Mean* and *The Analects of Confucius.*

[21] *Ibid.*

[22] *The Analects of Confucius (Lun Yu).*

[23] *The Mencius (Meng Zi).*

[24] *Ibid.*

[25] See note 4, p. 111.

[26] See note 2, p. 26.

[27] Liu Zhou: *Liu Zi.* Liu Zhou (514-565) was a man of letters of the State of Northern Qi during the Northern and Southern Dynasties (386-589).

[28] Zhuge Liang: *Advice to My Son.* Zhuge Liang (181-234), also known as Kong Ming, was a legendary prime minister and statesman of the Shu Kingdom during the Three Kingdoms Period (220-280).

[29] Lu Xun (1881-1936) was a litterateur, thinker and revolutionary as well as one of the founders of modern Chinese literature.

[30] "Postscripts of Selected Works of Lu Xun," *Selected Works of Lu Xun,* Vol. 20, Chinese ed., People's Literature Publishing House, Beijing, 1973, p. 663.

[31] Mao Zedong: "Changsha," *Mao Zedong Poems,* Eng. ed., Foreign Languages Press, Beijing, 1998, p. 5.

[32] *The Great Learning (Da Xue).*

[33] Cai Yuanpei (1868-1940) was a democratic revolutionary, educator and scientist. He served as president of Peking University from 1916 to 1927.

[34] Cai Yuanpei: "Speech at the Patriotic Girls School," *Complete Works of Cai Yuanpei,* Vol. 3, Chinese ed., Zhonghua Book Company, Beijing, 1984, p. 8.

[35] *The Book of Changes (Yi Jing).*

[36] *The Analects of Confucius (Lun Yu).*

[37] Liu Yuxi: *Nine Poems (Jiu Shou).* Liu Yuxi (772-842) was a man of letters and philosopher of the Tang Dynasty (618-907).

[38] *The Book of Rites (Li Ji),* one of the Confucian classics, is an important work

for the study of ancient China's social forms, laws and regulations, and traditional Confucian canon, covering the realms of society, politics, moral principles, philosophy and religion.

[39] *The Doctrine of the Mean (Zhong Yong)*, one of the Confucian classics, used to be a part of *The Book of Rites*. Published as an independent book during the Song Dynasty (960-1279), it became one of the "Four Classics of Confucianism," the other three being *The Great Learning, The Analects of Confucius* and *The Mencius*.

[40] *Lao Zi* or *Dao De Jing*. This is an important philosophical work from ancient China, which proposed the thought of the "Tao" and advocated the ideas of "governing by doing nothing" and "going along with Nature."

[41] Lu Xun: "Peking University in My Eyes," *Complete Works of Lu Xun*, Vol. 3, Chinese ed., People's Literature Publishing House, Beijing, 1973, p. 155.

[42] Mei Yiqi (1889-1962) served as the president of Tsinghua University from 1931 to 1948.

[43] This is an idea for running schools initiated by Mei Yiqi in his inaugural speech on accepting the presidency of Tsinghua University on December 2, 1931.

Foster and Practice Core Socialist Values from Childhood[*]

May 30, 2014

Dear students, teachers and friends,

Good morning! We're happy to be here today to attend your Young Pioneers[1] event and initiation ceremony for new Young Pioneers. International Children's Day is just around the corner. Here I wish you and children of all ethnic groups in China a happy festival!

Attaching great importance to moral cultivation, Minzu Primary School of Haidian District has organized many activities and achieved good results. Just now I listened to some thought-provoking speeches from you students, teachers and parents. You all talked about the need to strengthen moral education and to guide children to foster and practice core socialist values from childhood. This is great! I have the same idea. And I want to discuss this issue with you.

The cultural progress of a nation and the development of a country require continuous efforts of generations and various driving forces. Among these forces, core values are the deepest and most everlasting. The Chinese nation boasts a long history and splendid culture of over 5,000 years, and our civilization has developed in an unbroken line from ancient to modern times. How could our nation survive and develop over this long course of history? One important reason is that our nation has a moral pursuit and ethos that have been carried on for generations. The written Chinese characters we now use are not basically different from the oracle bone inscriptions of the Shang Dynasty (c. 1600-1046 BC), and the brilliant insights of

---

* Speech at a discussion held at the Minzu Primary School of Haidian District in Beijing.

Lao Zi[2], Confucius[3], Mencius[4], Zhuang Zi[5], and other ancient sages have been passed down to us today. Our civilization has developed for several thousand years without interruption. This is a unique achievement in world history.

Today, our nation is set to make further progress. We must take stock of the current conditions and carry on our national spirit and culture, especially our traditional virtues.

The core socialist values we now uphold are prosperity, democracy, civility, harmony, freedom, equality, justice, the rule of law, patriotism, dedication, integrity and friendship. These values embody the thoughts of the ancient sages, the aspirations of public-spirited people, the ideals of the revolutionary martyrs and the expectations of ordinary people. All Chinese people should act conscientiously to foster and practice these values.

I have stressed this issue on several occasions. In February this year, the Political Bureau of the Party Central Committee held a special group study session on the topic. I made a speech, in which I raised the requirements for the whole of society in this regard. I also talked about this issue when visiting the students of Peking University on Youth Day, May 4, and when meeting leading officials in Shanghai a few days ago. Today, I want to talk about it to you pupils. Because in order for an idea to be established and developed on a long-term basis, we must start by telling our children about it.

Children are the future of our country and the hope of the Chinese nation. As Liang Qichao said in his "Young China"[6]: "If the youth are wise, the country will be wise. If the youth prosper, the country will prosper. If the youth are strong, the country will be strong.... If the youth progress, the country will progress." The new replacing the old is an irresistible law; and the future will always be created by today's children. Last year, on International Children's Day, I said that every adult grew up from childhood. The realization of our dream is reliant on us, and, more importantly, on you. Children are sensitive and are ready to accept all beautiful things. "Since antiquity, it is from adolescents that heroes emerge." To create a better future for our nation we need to encourage our children to set great goals and shape their characters, and ensure a sound environment for their growth.

How should children foster and practice the core socialist values? They should do so in a different way from adults, a way which conforms to their ages and traits. Here I want to raise four points: remembering the requirements, following role models, starting from childhood and accepting help.

First, remembering the requirements means that children need to learn by heart the core socialist values, and always keep these values in mind. You pupils are still studying at school and don't have much social experience; so you may not thoroughly understand the meanings of these values. But you will acquire more knowledge and experience as you grow up, and thus gain a better understanding of them, as long as you bear them in mind. In this process, you need to think about the requirements and acquire a better understanding in your studies and life. Through the ages, most people with great achievements have been strict with themselves since childhood.

Second, following role models means that children need to learn from heroes and advanced figures, and to cultivate good characters through study. There are many young heroes in our history and in the revolution, construction and reform drive of our people under the leadership of the Party. You may have heard some of their names from films such as *Red Children*, *Zhang Ga the Soldier Boy*, *The Feathered Letter*, *Little Hero Soldier* and *Young Heroic Sisters of the Mongolian Grassland*. Now we have more exemplary children. I know that some students in your school have won the title of "the most beautiful children." Besides, there are many other role models from all professions whose examples we should follow. For example, astronauts, Olympic champions, scientists, model workers, young volunteers, and many other people who are ready to help others or to take on a just cause, and who are honest, trustworthy, filial, or dedicated to their work. The power of role models is infinite. You should take them as examples in pursuing virtues. Confucius said, "When we see men of virtue, we should think of equaling them; when we see men of a contrary character, we should examine ourselves."[7]

Third, starting from childhood means that children need to start with themselves, and make every possible effort to cultivate good morality. "A young idler, an old beggar."[8] And "a journey of one thousand miles begins with the first step." Everyone's life consists of small matters. Starting with small virtues, you can nurture great virtues. Being young, you may not be able to do as many things for our society as adults do. But you can start from minor things. You can ask yourself every day: Do I love my country? Do I love my school? Do I study hard? Do I care about my classmates? Do I respect my teachers? Do I honor my parents? Do I conform to social morality? Do I admire good people and good deeds? Do I feel angry at bad people and bad things? The more you think, the more you will urge yourself to act; the more you act, the more virtues you will acquire. I heard that some students like to compete with each other in food, clothes or parents' jobs, and some even take pride in having cars to take them to school and then back home. Such competition makes them stray from the correct path. You should never vie with each other in these matters. "A hard life breeds great talents, whereas an easy life is not the way to cultivate great men." "Work hard when young, and you will have a future; time flies, and you should not slacken your efforts."[9] However, you can compete with each other as to who is more ambitious, who works harder, who loves work more, who loves physical training more or who is more caring.

Fourth, accepting help means that children need to accept both suggestions and criticisms, and grow up in a good environment where you correct your mistakes and make yourself a better person. No one is flawless. We make progress by overcoming shortcomings and correcting mistakes. As the saying goes, "A jade uncut will not be a useful vessel; a man without learning will not know the way."[10] At your age, you children are establishing a world view, an outlook on life and values, and you need help. Don't complain that parents talk too much, that teachers are too strict, or that classmates are overreaching. Think about whether they are right, or if they are doing so for your good. If they are, you should accept their admonitions. You may not do well in all aspects. It doesn't matter. As long as you see where you have fallen down and are willing to improve, you are making progress. Sometimes you may not know where you are going wrong, but your parents, teachers and classmates may point it out. Then you are also making progress if you correct what you have done wrong. Of course, good medicine tastes bitter, and good advice is harsh to the ear. We should be strict with ourselves, and make a habit of modestly accepting criticism and help. A bright future awaits you, as long as you take a correct path from childhood, practice what you learn and do your best.

Families, schools, organizations of the Young Pioneers of China, and our society as a whole should all take the responsibility of promoting core socialist values among children.

The family is the first classroom, and a parent is the child's first teacher. Parents should always set a good example for their children, and guide them with correct actions, ideas and methods. Parents should teach children to appreciate the true, the good and the beautiful, and to keep away from the false, the bad and the ugly in everyday life. Parents should observe children closely for any change in idea or action, and educate and guide them when needed.

Schools should attach greater importance to moral education, and work hard to enhance the school spirit and teachers' professional ethics. Teachers should take into consideration children's personalities and traits, and patiently impart knowledge and cultivate virtues. Schools should ensure that their activities are good for the students' physical and mental health, and will exert a favorable influence on their characters. Schools should also ensure that all students receive sincere care and help, making the seeds of core socialist values take root and grow in their hearts.

The Chinese Young Pioneers need to launch educational campaigns and activities to better serve students in fostering and practicing core socialist values, and unite, educate and guide children through these activities. Meanwhile, our society needs to understand, respect, care about and offer help to children, provide a favorable environment for them, and oppose and prevent violations of their rights and damage to their physical or mental health.

The waves behind drive on those before, and the younger generation will excel the previous one. I believe that children of this generation will have great goals and beautiful dreams, love study, work and our country, and conscientiously foster and practice core socialist values from childhood. I believe you have made yourselves ready to realize the Chinese Dream, guided by your flag of the star and torch[11].

Notes

[1] The Young Pioneers of China is a national organization for children run by the Communist Youth League, an organization of young adults, that is under the CPC. It was named the Youth and Children of China Movement when it was founded on October 13, 1949 by the Communist Youth League, and was given its present name on August 21, 1953.

[2] Lao Zi (dates unknown), also known as Li Dan and Li Er, was a philosopher and the founder of philosophical Taoism in the Spring and Autumn Period (770-476 BC). His ideas include: "The Tao follows Nature," "existence and non-existence give birth to each other," and "governance by doing nothing." It was said that he wrote *Lao Zi* or *Dao De Jing*.

[3] Confucius (551-479 BC), also known as Kong Qiu and Zhongni, was a philosopher, educator, statesman and the founder of Confucianism in late Spring and Autumn Period (770-476 BC). He created a school of thought with benevolence (*ren*) as the core. He devoted himself to education and compiled numerous ancient classics. His main ideas and doctrines were recorded in *The Analects of Confucius*. From the Han Dynasty (206 BC-AD 220), Confucianism became the mainstream of traditional Chinese culture for over 2,000 years, and Confucius was respected as a sage by China's feudal rulers.

[4] Mencius (c. 372-289 BC), also known as Meng Ke and Ziyu, was a philosopher and educator in mid Warring States Period (475-221 BC). He believed that "man is an integral part of Nature," put forth a theory that man is born good, and summarized moral rules as four virtues: benevolence, justice, propriety and wisdom. He carried forward and developed the idea of benevolence and the rule of virtue propounded by Confucius, and raised a new idea that "the people are more important than the ruler." He was the most famous Confucian after Confucius, or secondary sage. He wrote *The Mencius* (*Meng Zi*).

[5] Zhuang Zi (369-286 BC) was a Taoist philosopher of the Warring States Period. He carried forward Lao Zi's thought, and believed that Taoism was the highest principle of the world. His philosophy embodies the goal that "Heaven, Earth and I were produced together, and all things and I are one."

[6] "Young China" was an essay written by Liang Qichao (1873-1929), a thinker and scholar, and one of the leaders of the Hundred Days' Reform (or 1898 Reform) in late Qing Dynasty.

[7] *The Analects of Confucius (Lun Yu)*.

[8] *Collected Yuefu Songs and Ballads (Yue Fu Shi Ji)*. This is a collection of songs and ballads dating from the remote past to the Five Dynasties period, compiled by Guo Maoqian (1041-1099) of the Song Dynasty.

[9] Du Xunhe: *For Nephews at School*. Du Xunhe (846-904) was a poet of the Tang Dynasty (618-907).

[10] *Three-character Classic (San Zi Jing)*, a textbook for elementary education in ancient China. It was said to have been written by Wang Yinglin (1223-1296) or Ou Shizi (1234-1324) in the Song Dynasty (960-1279), and was supplemented in the Ming (1368-1644) and Qing (1644-1911) dynasties. Written in triplets of characters for easy memorization, the book focuses on moral education.

[11] The flag of the Young Pioneers of China is composed of a five-pointed star and a torch, the former symbolizing the leadership of the CPC and the latter symbolizing brightness. The red flag symbolizes the success of the revolution.

Social Undertakings

Eliminate Poverty and Accelerate Development in Impoverished Areas[*]

December 29 and 30, 2012

It is the essential requirement of socialism to eradicate poverty, improve the people's livelihood and achieve common prosperity. We should pay close attention to people in straitened circumstances, and extend care to them with respect and love. We should do our best to solve their problems and keep their needs and sufferings in mind, and bring the solicitude and concern of the Party and the government to the people in the impoverished areas.

The old revolutionary base areas and the people there made an enormous contribution to the victory of the Chinese revolution, which will never be forgotten by the Party and the people. Since the reform and opening-up policy was introduced over 30 years ago, the people's overall living conditions have been substantially improved. However, China is still in the primary stage of socialism, so the number of people living in poverty is still quite large. With regard to completing the building of a moderately prosperous society in all respects, the hardest and most arduous tasks lie in the rural areas and the poverty-stricken regions in particular. We cannot say we have realized a moderately prosperous society if the rural areas, especially the backward parts of the countryside, are left behind. The central leadership has always attached great importance to development-oriented poverty alleviation. Party committees and governments at all levels should strengthen their sense of responsibility and mission in development-oriented poverty alleviation. To free them from destitution so that

---

* Main points of the speech during an inspection of poverty-alleviation and development work in Fuping County, Hebei Province.

they can live a better life as soon as possible, we must work diligently and effectively to map out plans, allocate funds, set targets, work out detailed measures, and carry out evaluations in this respect.

As we often say, "With confidence, even barren clay can be turned into gold." Party committees and governments at all levels should make it a priority to help people in difficulties, especially those in the old revolutionary base areas and poverty-stricken areas, to break away from poverty and achieve prosperity. To this end, we will make full use of local advantages, improve plans, and provide specific and targeted guidance. When formulating policies concerning poverty alleviation, more considerations should be given to the old revolutionary bases and the impoverished areas. At the same time, we should bolster our confidence, find the correct method, and make strenuous efforts to facilitate development in those areas. Leading officials at all levels should keep people living in deprivation in mind, help them in good time and work for them diligently.

The rural areas long for development and the farmers demand a better life. The key to their prosperity lies with the Party committees at the primary level. You local officials work in the forefront, face poor conditions, and toil all year round. It's not easy for you. I would like to express my sincere gratitude to you all. We should work together with one heart to put the Party's policies into full practice, and make every effort to ensure a better life for our fellow-countrymen in the rural areas.

Better and Fairer Education
for the 1.3 Billion Chinese People[*]

September 25, 2013

Education is the foundation of national development in the long run. It is the fundamental way for mankind to pass on culture and knowledge, raise new generations and create a better life.

China will continue to support this initiative led by the UN. With 260 million students and 15 million teachers, the task for China to develop education is an arduous one. China will resolutely implement the strategy of reinvigorating the country through science and education, and will always give priority to education. China will increase its investment in education, promote universal and life-long education, and build itself into a society in which people enjoy learning. Moreover, the country will work hard to ensure that every child has the opportunity to go to school, and enable its 1.3 billion people to enjoy a better and fairer education, so that they can acquire the ability to develop themselves, contribute to society and help others. In addition, China will strengthen educational exchanges with other countries, open its educational field wider to the outside world, and actively support the development of education in developing countries. We are determined to work with peoples of all other countries towards a brighter future.

---

[*] Main points of the video message for the first anniversary of the UN Global Education First Initiative.

Accelerate the Development
of Housing Security and Supply[*]

October 29, 2013

Accelerating housing supply is important for meeting the people's basic need for housing and ensuring that all of them have access to housing. It is a requirement for social fairness and justice as well as an important measure for the people to share the fruits of reform and development. Party committees and governments at all levels should exercise better leadership to ensure that all the relevant objectives, tasks, policies and measures are implemented, and regard housing security and supply as a project of good governance that can stand the test of practice, time and the people's expectations.

Housing is an issue related not only to the people's livelihood but also the development of our country. It concerns the people's immediate interests, determines whether they can live and work in contentment, and affects the country's overall economic and social development, as well as social harmony and stability. The Party and government have always attached great importance to the housing issue. Thanks to protracted efforts, great achievements have been made in China's housing industry. However, we must realize that we cannot solve our housing problems overnight as there is still a large number of people having difficulty getting decent housing, a general inadequate supply of basic housing, and an inappropriate and unbalanced allocation of housing resources. Many people lack their own dwelling, so we must be more resolved and make greater efforts to address all the problems standing in the way of housing supply.

---

* Main points of the speech at the tenth group study session of the Political Bureau of the 18th CPC Central Committee which Xi presided over.

In the matter of housing security and supply, we must properly handle the relationship between public services provided by the government and services provided by the market, between the economic and social functions of housing supply, between needs and possibilities, and between the need to provide housing security and the need to avoid total welfare dependence. We must carry out market-oriented reforms in order to fully enliven the market and meet the multilevel needs for housing. However, there are always people who have housing difficulties due to labor skill mismatch, being out of a job or low income, so the government must step in to provide them with basic housing.

As conditions stand in China, we in general should build a housing supply system for the government to provide basic housing security and for the market to satisfy multilevel housing demands. We should review and sum up our experience in housing reform and development, learn from other countries in solving their housing problems, study the rules of housing supply, emphasize top-level design, and speed up the establishment of a uniform, standardized, mature and stable housing supply system. While making every effort to increase the housing supply, we must also do our best to satisfy the people's demands for better housing, establish a sound system of housing standards so that houses are economical, affordable, eco-friendly, energy-conserving and safe, and advocate a housing consumption mode fitting China's conditions.

According to the 12th Five-year Plan[1] (2011-2015), the number of basic-need housing units built and houses in run-down areas rebuilt will be 36 million, and by 2015 the basic-need housing coverage will hit around 20 percent. This is a commitment made by the government to the people, and we should do whatever we can to fulfill this promise. We should focus on the development of public-rental housing, build low-rent housing more quickly, and accelerate the rebuilding of houses in all the run-down areas. In carrying out this project, we must do our best according to our abilities, and endeavor to meet the people's basic need for housing. A residence is home to a family, so its quality and safety are essential. We must improve the planning, accompanying facilities and design of housing to meet the basic need.

We should improve supporting policies for housing, give full play to the supportive, guiding and leading roles of such policies, and maximize the enthusiasm and initiative of all sectors. We should improve the land policy, give priority to ensuring that land is used to enhance the people's wellbeing, develop a balanced land supply plan, increase residential land supply, and give priority to allocating land for constructing basic-need housing. We should improve our fiscal policy and use more public funds to build such housing. We should adopt policies and measures to encourage enterprises and other institutions to build and manage public-rental housing. We should also actively explore systems and mechanisms for non-profit organizations to build and manage basic-need housing, so that all sides involved can join forces in this endeavor.

Building basic-need housing is a great endeavor that benefits both the country and the people, but to accomplish this task and ensure that those in need get housing we must strengthen management, and establish procedures for entry, use and exit of such housing, so as to ensure that people have fair access to public resources. We must make sure that basic-need housing is fairly allocated, and that the people who are entitled to it get it. We must stop illegal acquisition of basic-need housing, and block institutional loopholes in this regard. Those who acquire basic-need housing illegally must be punished in accordance with laws and regulations.

Notes

[1] The 12th Five-year Plan refers to the 12th Five-year Plan for National Economic and Social Development of the People's Republic of China.

Always Put People's Lives First[*]

November 24, 2013

This accident has sounded an alarm for us once more. We must maintain constant vigilance against workplace accidents, pay close attention to this problem, and guarantee without fail workplace safety, otherwise accidents will cause irreversible damage to the country and the people. We must establish a sound workplace safety responsibility system, highlight the key responsibilities of enterprises, enhance workplace safety inspections, apply lessons learned to analogous situations, and strengthen workplace safety.

This heart-rending accident has caused grave loss of lives and severe damage to property. Now, through the joint efforts of the relevant departments under the State Council, Shandong provincial committee of the CPC and Shandong provincial people's government, Qingdao municipal committee of the CPC and Qingdao municipal people's government, we have achieved preliminary results. Next, we should direct all our attention to treating the injured, making proper arrangements for the funerals of the deceased, consoling their families, and seeing to bringing the people's life back to normal. We should conduct a prompt investigation into the accident and hold those involved accountable in accordance with the law.

Party committees, governments and officials at all levels should be keenly aware of the importance of safety issues, and always put people's lives first. All regions, government departments, and enterprises should be relentless in applying the highest standards of workplace safety, stringently supervise workplace safety when pursuing

* Main points of the speech in the Huangdao Economic and Technological Development Zone of Qingdao when assessing the relief effort following an oil pipeline leak explosion.

investment and implementing projects, increase the weighting of workplace safety in performance indicators, and follow the approach of "one vote against meaning veto"[1] for ensuring workplace safety and guarding against the risk of major work-related accidents.

The responsibility of ensuring workplace safety is paramount. To reinforce the workplace safety responsibility system, senior Party and government officials should be personally involved. We must make sure that responsibility for workplace safety is assigned to relevant government departments and officials. Officials in charge of industrial sectors and officials responsible for businesses must ensure workplace safety. We should strengthen supervision and inspection concerning workplace safety, strictly implement the assessment, reward and punishment system, and constantly promote workplace safety.

Every enterprise must fulfill its principal responsibility for workplace safety with absolute dedication, and guarantee funding, training, basic management measures, and emergency rescue provisions to ensure workplace safety. Central-government-owned enterprises should take the lead and set a good example in this regard. Governments at all levels should perform their due responsibilities in places within their jurisdiction, and exercise strict supervision over workplace safety in full accordance with laws and regulations.

To ensure workplace safety, we should forestall any possible work-related risk. We should continue with large-scale workplace safety inspections that cover all workplaces, defuse all risks with zero tolerance, strictly enforce laws and regulations, and ensure substantial results. In conducting inspections we should neither give prior written or verbal notice, nor listen to second-hand reports, nor accept escort or reception. Instead, we should go directly to the front line and conduct confidential investigations, especially in terms of concealed risks like underground oil pipelines. We should intensify our efforts in addressing potential safety risks, establishing an inspection accountability system for workplace safety in which whoever conducts the inspection must take full responsibility by signing his name on the inspection report, making no accommodations, leaving no place unchecked, and not going through formalities. We must see actual results.

We should see to it that when an accident occurs in one factory, every other factory learns the hard lesson; when a potential risk is identified in one locality, the whole country goes on the alert. All regions and industries should learn their lesson from workplace accidents, enhance workplace safety accountability and oversight, and take preventive measures against any work-related accident.

Winter has already come. At the turn of the year, there is a greater risk of accidents. I hope that you all enhance your awareness of your weighty responsibility to the Party and the people, remain vigilant against potential accidents, conscientious and meticulous in ensuring workplace safety, resolute in preventing major and serious accidents, and steadfast in improving workplace safety across the whole country.

Notes

[1] A decision cannot be passed at a meeting if one attendee casts a vote against no matter how many votes are in favor. – *Tr.*

Build China into a Cyberpower*

February 27, 2014

Cyber security and information technology application are major strategic issues concerning the security and development of the country, and the work and life of the people. We should, based on both the international and domestic situations, make overall plans, coordinate all related parties, promote innovative development, and work hard to build China into a cyberpower.

In the world today the IT revolution is making rapid advances, exerting a profound influence on politics, economy, culture, society and the military in all countries. IT application and economic globalization stimulate each other. The Internet has already been integrated into all aspects of social life worldwide, even going so far as to change the mode of production and way of life. China is going along with and being profoundly influenced by this trend. China has made remarkable achievements in the development of the Internet and IT application. Numerous households in China now have access to the Internet, and China ranks first in the number of netizens in the world. However, we should also be aware that China lags behind in cyber innovation; the gaps in Internet use between regions and between urban and rural areas within China are still wide, and there is a profound gap in per capita bandwidth between China and the advanced level of the world. All in all, the bottlenecks constricting China's Internet development are still prominent.

Cyber security and IT application are closely interconnected with many other fields in any country. We should be fully aware of where

---

* Main points of the speech at the first meeting of the Central Leading Group for Cyberspace Affairs.

218

we stand and what we should do. We must understand that it is vital for us to act right now. We must make plans accordingly and carry them out as the conditions permit. Cyber security and IT application are as important to China as wings are to a bird. We must, therefore, make coordinated plans for both, and implement them in a unified way. To promote cyber security and IT application, we should balance security and development, and ensure that the two proceed in tandem and stimulate each other to secure long-term development.

It is a long-term task to ensure that online public opinion is healthy and sound. We should innovate and improve online publicity, and use Internet communication rules to advocate things wholesome and positive, and disseminate and put into practice the core socialist values. We should properly handle timing, extent and efficiency so as to make our cyberspace wholesome and clean.

Online information knows no national boundaries. The flow of information assists that of technology, capital and talent. Information resources have become important factors of production and social wealth. The amount of information a country possesses has become a major indicator of its soft power and competitiveness. The development level of a country's IT and information and communications technology industry decides the level of its IT application. We should enhance the innovation of core technology and improve core technology infrastructure, and become better able to collect, process, disseminate and utilize information and ensure information security, in order to better benefit the people's wellbeing.

Without ensuring cyber security, we cannot safeguard national security; without promoting IT application, we cannot realize modernization. To build China into a cyberpower, we should have exclusive and powerful information technologies, rich and comprehensive information services and a thriving cyber culture. We should have a good information infrastructure and a strong information economy. We should have high-caliber cyber security and IT application professionals. In addition, we should carry out bilateral and multilateral Internet exchanges and cooperation with other countries. The strategy for building China into a cyberpower should be carried out at the same time as we work to accomplish the Two Centenary Goals. We should keep making progress in making the Internet infrastructure basically universal, improving our innovation capacity, developing the information economy, and ensuring cyber security.

We should formulate comprehensive research and development strategies for information and cyber technology, and make great efforts to turn research findings into practical applications. We should promulgate policies to support the development of enterprises, and encourage them to make technological innovations and become the main developers of the IT industry.

We should lose no time in formulating plans for improving the laws and regulations on managing Internet information and protecting the key information infrastructure. We should supervise cyberspace in accordance with the law to safeguard our citizens' legitimate rights and interests.

To build China into a cyberpower we should pool all our resources of talent and train them to become a powerful force with political integrity, top-flight expertise and fine conduct. "It is easy to muster a 1,000-man army, but hard to find a capable general."[1] We should train globally renowned scientists, leading Internet sci-tech figures, outstanding engineers and high-level innovation teams.

The Central Leading Group for Cyberspace Affairs should provide centralized leadership, coordinate major issues concerning cyber security and IT application in all fields, formulate and implement development strategies, overall planning and major policies on cyber security and IT application, and enhance security guarantees in this regard.

Notes

[1] Ma Zhiyuan: *Autumn in Han Palace* (*Han Gong Qiu*). Ma Zhiyuan (c. 1250- c. 1324) was a playwright in the Yuan Dynasty (1279-1368).

A Holistic View of National Security[*]

April 15, 2014

We need to acquire an accurate understanding of new developments and trends of the situation of national security, adhere to a holistic view and develop national security with Chinese characteristics.

In running the Party and the country, one of our basic principles is to remain keenly alert to potential dangers and on guard against adversity in times of peace. To secure its leadership role and unite the country in upholding and developing socialism with Chinese characteristics, our Party should make national security its top priority.

The Third Plenary Session of the Party's 18th Central Committee decided to establish the National Security Commission (NSC). This is a pressing requirement for modernizing the national governance system and enhancing our governance capacity, and for achieving long-term political stability. This will provide a strong guarantee for building a moderately prosperous society in all respects, and for fulfilling the Chinese Dream of the rejuvenation of the Chinese nation. The aim of the establishment of the commission is to better handle new developments and new tasks in the realm of national security, and build a national security system which is centralized, integrated, highly efficient, and authoritative, so as to improve leadership over the work of national security.

At present, the national security issues facing China encompass far more subjects, extend over a greater range and cover a longer time scale than at any time in the country's history. Internally and externally, the factors at play are more complex than ever before. Therefore,

* Main points of the speech at the first meeting of the National Security Commission.

we must maintain a holistic view of national security, take the people's security as our ultimate goal, achieve political security as our fundamental task, regard economic security as our foundation, with military, cultural and public security as means of guarantee, and promote international security so as to establish a national security system with Chinese characteristics.

To implement a holistic view of national security, we should attach equal importance to internal and external security – promoting development, reform and stability and building China into a safe country domestically, while seeking peace, cooperation and mutual benefits and building a harmonious world internationally. Homeland security and the people's security are equally important. We must follow the principle of people first, insist that everything done for national security is for the sake of the people, should rely on the people, and gain the support of the people. We must pay close attention to both traditional and non-traditional security, and build a national security system that integrates such elements as political, homeland, military, economic, cultural, social, science and technology, information, ecological, resource and nuclear security. We should pay close attention to both development and security. The former is the foundation of the latter while the latter is a precondition for the former. A wealthy country may build a strong army, and a strong army is able to safeguard the country. While paying close attention to our own security, we must also pay attention to the common security of the world, and contribute our effort to turning the world into a secure place for all nations. We should urge all parties to work hard for the goals of mutual benefit and common security.

The NSC should abide by the principles of centralized leadership, scientific planning, exercising power in both centralized and separated ways, coordinated actions, and high performance and efficiency. It should focus its efforts, follow the key guidelines, and vigorously implement the overall strategy of China's national security.

Safeguard National Security and Social Stability*

April 25, 2014

At a time when we are confronted with new situations and challenges, successfully safeguarding national security and social stability is particularly important for furthering the reform, achieving the Two Centenary Goals and realizing the Chinese Dream of the rejuvenation of the Chinese nation. All regions and government agencies should perform their functions and duties, assume their responsibilities, fully cooperate with each other, and work together to maintain national security and social stability.

Since the reform and opening-up policy was adopted in 1978 our Party has paid close attention to correctly balancing reform, development and stability, and made safeguarding national security and social stability a basic task of the Party and the central government. We have maintained overall social stability in China, thereby providing a favorable environment for reform, opening up and socialist modernization. "One should be mindful of possible danger in times of peace, downfall in times of survival, and chaos in times of stability."[1]

However, we should be aware that in our efforts to safeguard national security and social stability in these new circumstances we are confronted with increasing threats and challenges. And, more importantly, these threats and challenges are interlocked and can be mutually activated. We must remain clear-minded, stay true to our principles, effectively avert, manage and respond to risks to our national security, and take up, cope with and resolve challenges to our social stability.

---

* Main points of the speech at the 14th group study session of the Political Bureau of the 18th CPC Central Committee which Xi presided over.

All regions and government agencies should implement China's holistic view of national security, and acquire an accurate understanding of the new characteristics and trends of our national security. We should attach equal importance to external and internal security, homeland security and the people's security, traditional and non-traditional security, development and security, our own security and the common security of the world, and carry out to the full all our work related to national security. We should promote national security education among all the Chinese people and enhance their awareness in this regard.

Countering terrorism has a direct bearing on national security, the people's immediate interests, and reform, development and stability. The battle against terrorism safeguards national unity, social stability and the people's wellbeing. We must take decisive measures in deterring terrorism and keep up the pressure to thwart terrorism. We should work out a sound anti-terrorism work pattern, improve our anti-terrorism work system and build up our anti-terrorism strength. We should enlist both professional forces and the public in the fight against terrorism, get the general public to carry out different forms of activities against terrorism, build an impregnable anti-terrorism network, and ensure that terrorists are hunted down like rats. We should also let patriotic religious personages play a role, enhance positive guidance for religious believers, meet the latter's normal religious needs, and effectively resist the infiltration of religious extremism.

Terrorism denies basic human rights, tramples on humanitarian justice and challenges the shared norms of human civilization. It is not an issue of ethnicity, nor an issue of religion. Terrorists are the common enemy of people of all ethnic groups. We should firmly trust and rely on the officials and the general public of all ethnic groups, and unite with them in safeguarding ethnic unity and social stability.

We should increase our efforts to combat separatist activities in the new circumstances, promote ethnic unity, ensure that all ethnic groups work together for common prosperity and development, enhance publicity for and education in ethnic unity, consolidate the theoretical foundation of ethnic unity, and maximize our efforts to unite with the people of all ethnic groups. We should enhance the building of community-level Party organizations and governments, and carry out educational work thoroughly and meticulously among the people. We should acquire a correct understanding of the Party's policies regarding ethnic and religious affairs, promptly and properly resolve all conflicts and disputes undermining ethnic unity, and contain and crack down on separatist, infiltration and sabotage activities by domestic or foreign hostile forces on the pretext of ethnic issues.

To safeguard national security we must maintain social harmony and stability, prevent and resolve social conflicts, and improve our institutions, mechanisms, policies and practical endeavors to make this happen. We should make China's development more comprehensive, coordinated and sustainable, work harder to ensure and improve the people's wellbeing, and tackle social conflicts at the source. We should make promoting social fairness, justice and the people's wellbeing our ultimate goal, and increase our efforts in balancing the interests of all sectors, so that all the people can increasingly share in the fruits of development in a fairer way. We should implement and improve the institutions and mechanisms for protecting the legitimate rights and interests of the people, and the mechanism for assessing potential risks, so as to reduce and prevent conflicts of interest. We should comprehensively promote law-based governance, and better safeguard the people's lawful rights and interests. We should encourage all the people to resolve all social conflicts through legal procedures and by legal means, and ensure that people do things in accordance with the law, examine the law provisions in case of conflict, and use laws to solve problems and conflicts.

Notes

[1] *The Book of Changes (Yi Jing).*

Ecological Progress

A Better Environment for a Beautiful China*

April 2, 2013

We need to strengthen publicity and education and carry out new activities to get more people to plant trees. We will protect forests in accordance with the law, persistently carry out this campaign and make it more effective. This will create a better environment for completing the building of a moderately prosperous society in all respects and realizing the Chinese Dream of national rejuvenation.

Our tree-planting campaign was launched more than 30 years ago. It has boosted the recovery and development of China's forest resources, and increased public awareness of the importance of tree planting and environmental protection. However, we must recognize the fact that China is still an ecologically vulnerable country with a scarcity of forest resources, and faces a long-term and arduous mission of afforestation and ecological improvement.

Forests are the mainstay and an important resource for the land ecosystem. They are also an important ecological safeguard for the survival and development of mankind. It is hard to imagine what would happen to the earth and human beings without forests. Our Party raised a requirement to build a beautiful China at its 18th National Congress. The whole of society should enhance its ecological awareness and strengthen environmental protection in accordance with this requirement, so as to build China into a country with a good environment.

---

* Main points of the speech at a voluntary tree-planting activity in Beijing.

Usher in a New Era of Ecological Progress*

May 24, 2013

Our efforts for ecological conservation and environmental protection will benefit future generations. We must be aware that it is a pressing and difficult task to protect the environment and control pollution, and that it is important and necessary to advance ecological progress. We must take a responsible attitude towards our people and future generations, be resolute in controlling environmental pollution, strive to usher in a new era of ecological progress and improve the environment for our people to live and work in.

Ecological progress is of vital importance to the future of the nation and the wellbeing of its people. The 18th National Congress of the CPC listed ecological progress along with economic, political, cultural and social progress as the five goals in the overall plan for the cause of Chinese socialism, vowing to promote ecological progress to build a beautiful China and achieve lasting and sustainable development of the Chinese nation.

To promote ecological progress, we must comprehensively implement the guiding principles of the Party's 18th National Congress, and take Deng Xiaoping Theory, the important thought of the Three Represents and the Scientific Outlook on Development as our guide. We must raise awareness of the need to respect, protect, and accommodate ourselves to nature, follow the basic state policy of resource conservation and environmental protection, and give high priority to conserving resources, protecting the environment and promoting its natural restoration. We must dedicate ourselves to raising our ecological

---

* Main points of the speech at the sixth group study session of the Political Bureau of the 18th CPC Central Committee which Xi presided over.

awareness, enhancing relevant systems, safeguarding ecological security, and improving the environment. We must preserve our geographical space and streamline our industrial structure, our mode of production, and our way of life in the interest of resource conservation and environmental protection.

We must strike a balance between economic growth and environmental protection, and bear in mind that protecting the environment equates to protecting productivity and that improving the environment also equates to developing productivity. We will be more conscientious in promoting green, circular, and low-carbon development. We will never again seek economic growth at the cost of the environment.

It is through land use that ecological progress can be advanced. Maintaining a balance between population, resources and the environment, and promoting economic, social and ecological efficiency, we will determine an overall plan for developing our land, and allot space to production, to daily life, and to ecological development as appropriate, in order to leave more space for nature's self-restoration. We will accelerate the work of functional zoning, follow the functional definitions of different areas where development must be optimized, prioritized, restricted, or forbidden, and delimit and strictly enforce ecological red lines. We will work out appropriate plans for urbanization, agricultural development and ecological security to safeguard national and regional ecological security, and improve services for ecological conservation. We must fully understand the importance of enforcing ecological red lines. Any violations regarding environmental protection will be punished.

Resource conservation is a fundamental way to protect the environment. We will conserve resources and use them efficiently, bring about a fundamental change in the way resources are utilized, increase conservation efforts in all respects, and drastically reduce the consumption of energy, water and land resources per unit of GDP. We will vigorously develop a circular economy to reduce waste and resource consumption, re-use resources, and recycle waste in the process of production, distribution and consumption.

We will launch major projects to restore the ecosystem, and increase our capacity for producing eco-friendly products. A sound ecological environment is the basic foundation for the sustainable development of humanity and society. The public are greatly concerned about the environment. So we should place emphasis on serious environmental problems that pose health hazards to the people, and take a holistic approach to intensifying the prevention and control of water, air and soil pollution, with the focus on water pollution in key river basins and regions, and on air pollution in key industrial sectors and areas.

We must have the strictest possible institutions and legislation in place in order to guarantee ecological progress. To do this, we should first of all improve the evaluation norms for economic and social development to include resource consumption, environmental damage, ecological benefits and other indicators that can be used to assess ecological improvement, and use them to direct and shape our ecological work. We will establish an accountability system, and call to account officials whose ill-judged decisions have caused serious ecological damage.

We will increase publicity and education on the need to promote ecological progress, raise public awareness of the need to conserve resources and protect the environment, and foster a social atmosphere of cherishing our environment.

Leave to Our Future Generations Blue Skies, Green Fields and Clean Water*

July 18, 2013

On behalf of the Chinese government and people, and in my own name, I would like to extend congratulations on the opening of the Eco Forum Annual Global Conference Guiyang 2013, and a warm welcome to heads of state and government, United Nations officials, experts, scholars, business leaders and all other distinguished guests at this conference.

"Building Eco Civilization: Green Transformation and Transition – Green Industry, Green Urbanization and Green Consumption-led Sustainable Development" is the theme of this conference. It reflects the shared interest of the international community in promoting ecological progress. I am convinced that the achievements made by the participants at this conference will make a useful contribution to protecting the global environment.

Ushering in a new era of ecological progress and building a beautiful China is an important element of the Chinese Dream. China will respect and protect nature, and accommodate itself to nature's needs. It will remain committed to the basic state policy of conserving resources and protecting the environment. It will promote green, circular and low-carbon development, and promote ecological progress in every aspect of its effort to achieve economic, political, cultural and social progress. China will also develop a resource-efficient and environmentally friendly geographical layout, industrial structure, mode of production and way of life, and leave to our future generations a

---

* Letter of congratulations to the Eco Forum Annual Global Conference Guiyang 2013.

working and living environment of blue skies, green fields and clean water.

Protecting the environment, addressing climate change and securing energy and resources is a common challenge for the whole world. China will continue to assume its due international obligations, carry out in-depth exchanges and cooperation with all other countries in promoting ecological progress, and work with them to promote the sharing of best practices, and make the earth an environmentally sound homeland.

I wish the conference every success.

Xi Jinping
President of the People's Republic of China

National Defense

Build Up Our National Defense and Armed Forces*

November 16, 2012

The leading body of the Central Military Commission and the senior officers in the army shoulder major historical responsibilities in building up our national defense and armed forces. We must remain clear-headed, cherish the achievements of past generations, draw upon the precious experiences we have accumulated, and value the progress that is already being made. We must serve the Party and the people whole-heartedly and further strengthen our national defense and armed forces.

Studying and applying the guiding principles of the Party's 18th National Congress must be our number one political task, and we must do it well. In line with the requirements of the Party Central Committee and the Central Military Commission, a campaign should be launched promptly in the armed forces to study and apply these principles. We should continue to study the Scientific Outlook on Development, and use it to guide our work. We should study the Party's guiding thoughts concerning the building of national defense and armed forces, taking the Scientific Outlook on Development as the guiding principle in this respect, and fully understand the features and laws of the building of national defense and armed forces in the new environment. We should summarize the valuable experience gained by Chairman Hu Jintao in building our national defense and armed forces, maintain the principles he developed, and continue to implement his policies and strategic decisions.

---

* Main points of the speech at an enlarged meeting of the Central Military Commission.

We must uphold the Party's leadership of the armed forces. This is central to the nature and mission of the armed forces, the future of socialism, the enduring stability of the Party, and the lasting peace of our country. It is fundamental to the existence and development of the armed forces. In our efforts to strengthen our armed forces we must treat theoretical and political education as our first priority, so that the Party's leadership of them will take firm root in the minds of our officers and soldiers, and the whole armed forces will follow without hesitation the commands of the Party Central Committee and the Central Military Commission at all times and under all conditions. We must strengthen the leadership of the Party over the armed forces in the aspects of theoretical and political education, and political and organizational affairs. We will apply political convictions as a measure when reviewing and appointing officers to ensure that our weaponry is always in the hands of those who are reliable and loyal to the Party. We must strictly enforce discipline on those who commit errors in political or organizational affairs, safeguard the authority of the Central Committee and the Central Military Commission, and ensure the smooth implementation of their military orders.

We must be able to fulfill a complete range of military tasks. The whole of the armed forces must have an in-depth understanding of the important role it has in the broad picture of China's national security and development strategies. It must put national sovereignty and security before any other consideration. Being "action ready" must be its major task, and it must comprehensively enhance its deterrence and combat capacity in the information age. The whole of the armed forces must attach strategic importance to military training, and keep raising its "real combat" capacity.

In line with the principle of comprehensive development we must continue to modernize and standardize our forces, and strengthen their revolutionary spirit. We will take a holistic approach to all work related to political and military matters, logistics and equipment, in order to upgrade the overall capacity of our forces. In a new environment, we must promote innovation and development of our military strategy, use our strategy to guide our tasks in strengthening our forces, and base our policies on a military strategy of active defense.

We will thoroughly apply the Party's guidelines on the development of national defense and the armed forces, promote such development in a balanced and coordinated manner, and strive to make real progress in transforming the mode of increasing combat effectiveness. We will press forward with the transformation of our military affairs and build a system of modern military forces with Chinese characteristics.

We must carry on the glorious traditions of our military. These traditions have been developed under the leadership of Mao Zedong, Deng Xiaoping, Jiang Zemin and Hu Jintao, and we will continue to apply them as we strive to modernize our national defense and armed forces. We will educate our officers and soldiers to intensify their ability to respond to adversity and crisis, so that their commitment will remain firm, their work determined, their morale high and their discipline unwavering. Our officers and soldiers will maintain an indomitable revolutionary spirit and be dauntless in combat. We will make every effort to combat corruption and promote integrity in the armed forces. Senior officers must take a clear-cut stand against corruption, and set an example in abiding by the code of honest conduct.

With the firm leadership of the Party Central Committee and Central Military Commission, with the strong support of the people, and with the concerted efforts of all our armed forces, we will succeed in our determined campaign to forge an ever-stronger national defense and armed forces.

Build Strong National Defense and Powerful Military Forces[*]

December 8 and 10, 2012

China's military forces must unite in upholding socialism with Chinese characteristics, and take Deng Xiaoping Theory, the important thought of the Three Represents, and the Scientific Outlook on Development as their guiding principles. The Party's 18th National Congress produced a series of guidelines and defined a set of strategic measures on national defense and the development of China's military forces. These must be thoroughly and rigorously implemented. China's military must never lose sight of the fact that following the Party's command is its core duty, to fight and win is its fundamental role, and to run the army strictly and in accordance with the law is key to achieving these aims. We must build a modern and standardized military dedicated to our revolutionary goals.

In our efforts to strengthen our armed forces we must treat theoretical and political education as our first priority, and ensure that our work is always done in accordance with the right political principles. We will educate our officers and soldiers in the theories of socialism with Chinese characteristics and foster their core values as contemporary revolutionary service personnel[1]. We will ensure that they follow the Party's commands, fulfill their missions without fail, and maintain the great traditions of our armed forces. To reinforce their theoretical and political education, our forces' first responsibility is and will remain the task of studying, disseminating, and applying the guiding principles of the 18th National Congress. We must integrate study

* Main points of the speech during his inspection visit to the Guangzhou Military Command.

with practice, and implement these guiding principles in our actions.

We will enhance our combat readiness through full-scale combat simulation exercises, and reinforce the belief that as soldiers our mission is to fight, and as officers our mission is to lead our men to victory. We must train our troops strictly and provide rigid criteria for real combat, modernize our armed forces, and enhance their capacity to fulfill diverse military tasks. The armed forces must be capable of winning regional engagements in the information age. We must follow to the letter such military practices as strictly observing discipline, executing every order, and acting in unison. The rank and file must be the focus of our work.

Achieving the great renewal of the Chinese nation has become the dream of the Chinese people in modern times. This great dream we have is to make our country strong. To the military, the dream is to make our forces strong. To achieve these aims we must strive both to enrich the country and build a strong national defense and powerful military. The armed forces must never falter in upholding the Party's absolute leadership, and all service persons must be well-disciplined, so as to ensure that the armed forces are secure and stable.

The heroic armed forces of the people will carry on its great traditions, build on past merits, so as to forge ahead to fulfill the historical responsibilities they shoulder.

Notes

[1] The core values of the armed forces are: loyalty to the Party, love for the people, devotion to the country, dedication to the mission, and respect for honor.

Build People's Armed Forces That Follow the Party's Commands, Are Able to Win Battles and Have Fine Conduct*

March 11, 2013

Our armed forces must thoroughly implement the guiding principles of the 18th CPC National Congress, uphold socialism with Chinese characteristics, follow the guidance of Deng Xiaoping Theory, the important thought of the Three Represents and the Scientific Outlook on Development. We must firmly follow the Party's goal of military development under the new circumstances and, build revolutionary, modernized and standardized people's armed forces that faithfully follow the Party's commands, are able to win battles and have fine conduct.

Building such forces is the Party's goal for developing the military under the new circumstances. It is essential for the military to follow the Party's commands, which determines the political orientation of military development. It is vital for the military to be capable of fighting to win, which is the basic function of the military as well as the fundamental objective of its development. To have fine conduct ensures that the military demonstrates its nature, aspiration and character. Our armed forces must understand this goal, bear it in mind in their efforts to promote military development, reform and preparedness, and bring national defense and military development to a new level.

---

* Main points of the speech at the plenary meeting of the People's Liberation Army delegation during the First Session of the 12th National People's Congress.

We must ensure the absolute leadership of the Party over the military that follows the commands of the Party and serves the people. It must be loyal, pure and reliable, and all its actions must be under the command of the Party Central Committee and the Central Military Commission. We must focus on the key task of building strong military forces which are able to fight to win, make sure that soldiers are capable of fighting, officers of commanding, and troops well trained. We must uphold combat capacity as the sole and fundamental standard for military development. We should promote our military development and preparedness to meet the needs of war, being ready to fight at all times and in all conditions. Having a fine work style is the unique feature and political advantage of our military. We must step up efforts to improve our work style, ensure good conduct in every aspect of military development and management, stay realistic, pragmatic and results-oriented, and reinforce the basic principle of running the military strictly and in accordance with the law. In doing this, we will maintain our long-established image as the armed forces of the people.

We should coordinate the development of our economy and defense capabilities, and combine efforts to make the country prosperous and the military strong. We should further the great integration of military and civilian development, and work to achieve in-depth integration of the use of infrastructure and other key facilities based on demands and led by the government. At the same time, we should manage the military budget well and use it properly by working hard, practicing economy, and opposing extravagance and waste, so as to put the funds to their best use. We should carry on the fine tradition of the military supporting the government and cherishing the people while the government and the people respect the troops and provide preferential treatment to their families. We should ensure that the military and local people work together to promote material advance, and cultural and ethical progress, as well as social harmony. To show concern for and support the development of national defense and the military, Party committees and governments at all levels should enhance education in national defense knowledge and popular awareness so that the whole of society will have common understandings and joint initiatives in caring for, loving, developing and safeguarding national defense.

"One Country, Two Systems"

Hong Kong, Macao and the Chinese Mainland Are Closely Linked by Destiny[*]

December 20, 2012, March 18, 2013 and December 18, 2013

I

Since the new government of the Hong Kong Special Administrative Region (HKSAR) took office, Mr Leung Chun-ying and his team, both enterprising and pragmatic, have made many achievements. The central government affirms their efforts and will continue to support the HKSAR government in its administration in accordance with the law.

People are concerned whether the policies and principles of the central government towards Hong Kong and Macao will change after the election of the new central leadership. I would like to take this opportunity to reiterate that the central government will continue to implement the policy of "one country, two systems"[1] and handle things in strict conformity with the Basic Law; there will be no change in our resolve to support the chief executive and the HKSAR government in their administration in accordance with the law and the performance of their duties; nor will there be any change in our policy of supporting the Hong Kong and Macao special administrative regions in developing their economies, improving their people's wellbeing, and promoting democracy and harmony. The fundamental policies and principles on handling Hong Kong and Macao affairs expounded at the 18th CPC National Congress are in line with the

---

* Main points of talks with Leung Chun-ying, chief executive of the Hong Kong Special Administrative Region, and Fernando Chui Sai On, chief executive of the Macao Special Administrative Region.

policies and principles the central government has long adopted for the two regions. The key lies in a comprehensive and accurate understanding and implementation of the "one country, two systems" principle, and respect for and maintenance of the authority of the Basic Law.

China's development is good, and splendid prospects have been unfolding before us, featuring the completion of the building of a moderately prosperous society in all respects and the achievement of the rejuvenation of the Chinese nation. As I have said, achieving the rejuvenation of the Chinese nation has been the greatest dream of the Chinese people since the advent of modern times. I believe that people in Hong Kong also hold this dream dearly. I also believe that Hong Kong people, who have a deep sense of national respect and pride, will surely make their contribution along with the people of the rest of the country to achieving the rejuvenation of the Chinese nation.

(Main points of the talk with Leung Chun-ying,
chief executive of the HKSAR, December 20, 2012)

II

Today is the 13th anniversary of Macao's return to the motherland. First of all I wish to convey through Mr Fernando Chui Sai On my cordial greetings to and best wishes for Macao's people. The general situation in Macao is good. Fernando Chui Sai On, the government of the Macao Special Administrative Region (MSAR) and people of all walks of life in Macao have been working together to maintain the prosperity, stability and development of Macao, and the central government affirms the efforts made by Fernando Chui Sai On and the MSAR government.

The central government will, as always, implement the "one country, two systems" principle, the policy of "Macao people governing Macao" with a high degree of autonomy and the Basic Law of the MSAR, support the chief executive and the MSAR government in their administration in accordance with the law and the performance of their duties, and support the MSAR in developing its economy, improving its people's wellbeing, and promoting democracy and harmony. We are fully confident of the future of our country and the Chinese nation, and we firmly believe that progress will be made in all social undertakings in Macao.

(Main points of the talk with Fernando Chui Sai On,
chief executive of the MSAR, December 20, 2012)

III

Hong Kong, Macao and the Chinese mainland are closely linked by destiny. To realize the Chinese Dream – the rejuvenation of the Chinese nation – Hong Kong, Macao and the Chinese mainland must pool and share our strength, and seek common development. Moreover, the people of Hong Kong, Macao and the Chinese mainland must help each other to make progress.

Leung Chun-ying has put forward the administrative idea of "seeking change while preserving stability," which has been accepted by the citizens of Hong Kong. Now the key question lies in its implementation. It is not only a responsibility of the chief executive and the HKSAR government, but a mission relying on the joint efforts of people of all walks of life in Hong Kong. When everybody adds wood to the fire, the flames rise high. We hope that people of all walks of life in Hong Kong will unite closely to support the chief executive and the HKSAR government in administration in accordance with the law and jointly create a brighter future for Hong Kong.

Macao is experiencing a relatively good time in its history, but its future development faces challenges too. We hope that the MSAR government and people of all walks of life will be keenly aware of potential problems, take advantage of favorable timing and conditions, and study and solve major problems that may hinder Macao's progress, so as to lay a solid foundation for the future development of Macao.

(Main points of the talk with Leung Chun-ying,
chief executive of the HKSAR, and Fernando Chui Sai On,
chief executive of the MSAR, March 18, 2013)

IV

Implementing the administrative principles of "seeking change while preserving stability" and "people's wellbeing first," you and the HKSAR government have focused on the resolution of major problems in economic and social development, and achieved initial results. The central government fully affirms your efforts.

The Third Plenary Session of the 18th CPC Central Committee made an overall plan on driving reform to a deeper level, which is a major strategic plan concerning China's development. According to the plan, the mainland will let the market play a decisive role in resource allocation and give better play to the government's functions, which will be conducive to the expansion of the mainland's openness to and cooperation with Hong Kong, Macao and Taiwan, further exchanges and cooperation between the mainland and Hong Kong, and more opportunities and scope for Hong Kong's development.

The central government has been consistent and clear-cut in its stance towards universal suffrage when it comes to electing the Hong Kong chief executive in 2017. We hope that people of all walks of life in Hong Kong will build a consensus through down-to-earth consultations in accordance with the Basic Law and decisions of the Standing Committee of the NPC, and lay a good foundation for the universal suffrage for the election of the chief executive.

(Main points of the talk with Leung Chun-ying, chief executive of HKSAR, December 18, 2013)

V

Macao is maintaining a good development trend, its economy is on a steady rise, its society is harmonious and stable, and its people live and work in peace and contentment. The central government fully affirms the efforts you and the MSAR government have made. At present, Macao should think of potential problems in times of peace and make a long-term plan. This requires the MSAR government and people of all walks of life in Macao to make continuous efforts to find out how to remain both pragmatic and innovative on the basis of Macao's rapid economic development over the past few years, how to solve problems emerging in the process of development, how to explore ways for the appropriately diversified development of Macao and how to realize sustainable progress for it.

The Third Plenary Session of the 18th CPC Central Committee made an overall plan on driving reform to a deeper level, which is a major strategic plan concerning China's development. Robust positive energy has been gathered in all sectors across China to comprehensively advance reform further, and the people of all ethnic groups in the country are working diligently in unity for the realization of the Two Centenary Goals and the Chinese Dream of the rejuvenation of the Chinese nation. The destiny of Macao is closely linked with that of the mainland, and Macao will advance in tandem and make progress together with the mainland in their development.

(Main points of the talk with Fernando Chui Sai On,
chief executive of the MSAR, December 18, 2013)

Notes

[1] "One country, two systems" is a concept put forward by the CPC and the Chinese government for realizing China's reunification and solving the Taiwan, Hong Kong and Macao issues. The framework of the concept is: Under the premise of national reunification, the mainland keeps practicing socialism, while Taiwan, Hong Kong and Macao retain their original capitalist system and ways of life for a long time while enjoying a high degree of autonomy. China resumed sovereignty over Hong Kong and Macao in 1997 and 1999, respectively, in accordance with this concept.

Create a Better Future
for the Chinese Nation Hand in Hand[*]

April 8 and October 6, 2013

I

The Chinese mainland is strong in its resolution and clear in its policies and principles for peaceful development on both sides of the Taiwan Straits. We will maintain the continuity of our fundamental strategy towards Taiwan, continue to implement effective policies, and keep moving our relations forward so as to bring benefits to the people on both sides. The Chinese people on both sides of the Taiwan Straits should strengthen solidarity and cooperation, and jointly work towards realizing the Chinese Dream, a great renewal of the Chinese nation.

Comprehensive, direct and two-way links, namely the "three direct links"[1] have been realized between the mainland and Taiwan. The signing and implementation of the Economic Cooperation Framework Agreement (ECFA), in particular, initiated a new stage for developing cross-Straits economic relations. "Those who are clear about the trend of the times will stand in the van, and those who can take advantage of the trend of the times are bound to succeed." For the Chinese people on both sides of the Straits, it is important to be aware of and seize the opportunities history has afforded us, follow the trend of the times, work hand in hand to promote peaceful cross-Straits relations, and bring about a better future for the Chinese nation.

---

[*] Main points of talks with Vincent Siew, honorary chairman of the Cross-Straits Common Market Foundation of Taiwan, and his delegation.

First, we hope that cross-Straits economic cooperation can be boosted by the people on both sides of the Straits through the concept of "one family." All of us, whether from the mainland or Taiwan, are members of the Chinese nation, and both economies are that of the Chinese nation. Giving more consideration to the needs and interests of our Taiwan compatriots, we will offer the same treatment to Taiwan enterprises as to mainland enterprises in the fields of investment and economic cooperation sooner rather than later, and provide greater scope for enhancing cross-Straits economic cooperation.

Second, we hope that both sides will further pursue high-level economic dialogues and coordination, and raise our economic cooperation to a new level. It is essential to give better play to the role of the Economic Cooperation Committee (ECC) within the ECFA, enhance communication on our situations, policies and development plans, and strengthen foresight and coordination in economic cooperation. We must speed up the expansion of industrial cooperation, increase two-way investment, deepen cooperation in financial services and explore new ways of cooperation.

Third, we hope that both sides can accelerate the negotiation of subsequent agreements following the signing of the ECFA, and improve our rules in respect of economic cooperation. The mainland and Taiwan should sign a service trade agreement as soon as possible, and strive to complete consultations on such topics as cargo trade and dispute settlements by the end of the year. The two sides can discuss appropriate and workable measures to realize common economic growth and link the processes of regional economic cooperation of both sides, which will invigorate cross-Straits economic cooperation.

Fourth, we hope that people on both sides of the Taiwan Straits will jointly work towards achieving the rejuvenation of the Chinese nation. Every achievement made by the mainland or Taiwan can make all Chinese people proud. Our joint efforts for promoting peaceful cross-Straits relations are contributions towards achieving the great renewal of the Chinese nation. We will surely overcome all difficulties and remove all barriers on the way as we move ahead, and make new progress in the peaceful development of cross-Straits relations as long as we always keep the interests of the entire Chinese nation in mind.

(April 8, 2013)

II

Both sides of the Straits should keep to the correct path of peaceful development of cross-Straits relations, advocate the idea that we are one family, strengthen exchanges and cooperation, and together promote the rejuvenation of the Chinese nation.

We must cherish historic opportunities and maintain the positive momentum of peaceful development of cross-Straits relations. The people on both sides of the Straits long for greater progress in their relations, so both sides should comply with the aspirations of the people, seize the opportunities and make new achievements in such relations.

We must increase political trust between the mainland and Taiwan, and reinforce the common political foundation of the two sides, which are critical for maintaining the peaceful development of cross-Straits relations. Sooner or later we will have to resolve the political disputes that have long existed in cross-Straits relations rather than leave them to later generations. We have stated several times that we would like to hold consultations on an equal footing with Taiwan on cross-Straits political issues within the framework of "one China," and make fair and reasonable arrangements. The heads of responsible departments from both sides can meet and exchange views on matters concerning cross-Straits relations.

Both economies are parts of the overall economy of the Chinese nation. In the new era of the Asia Pacific economic development, the two sides can better meet challenges through enhanced cooperation. We must improve the systems of cross-Straits economic cooperation while attaching more importance to promoting industrial cooperation.

(October 6, 2013)

Notes

[1] The "three direct links" are direct links in transportation, postal matters and trade across the Taiwan Straits.

Handle Cross-Straits Relations in the Overall Interests of the Chinese Nation[*]

June 13, 2013

Over the past five years, thanks to the concerted efforts of the two parties, two sides and people from both sides of the Taiwan Straits, we have opened a right path and made important progress in the peaceful development of cross-Straits relations. Under the new circumstances, the CPC Central Committee will continue to follow its established policies and commit itself to consolidating and pushing forward the trend of peaceful development of cross-Straits relations and bringing benefits to the people and the Chinese nation as a whole. I hope both parties and both sides will continue to enhance mutual trust, maintain constructive interaction and steadily promote the comprehensive development of cross-Straits relations, strengthen the foundations for peaceful development, unite with all the people on the two sides of the Straits and work collaboratively towards the great renewal of the Chinese nation.

At present, cross-Straits relations are at a new starting point, and we are all facing important opportunities. We should carefully sum up our experience, have a clear understanding of the changing situation and make responses accordingly, resolutely follow the path of peaceful development of cross-Straits relations, consolidate and further develop our political, economic, cultural and social foundations, and bring about fresh achievements in cross-Straits relations.

First, we must firmly handle cross-Straits relations in the overall interests of the Chinese nation. We are committed to safeguarding the

---

[*] Main points of the talk with Wu Po-hsiung, honorary chairman of the Kuomintang of China, and his delegation.

fundamental interests of the Chinese nation and the common interests of all sons and daughters of China, including our Taiwan compatriots. In addressing the general picture of cross-Straits relations in the overall interests of the Chinese nation, the most important and most fundamental thing to do is to maintain China's sovereignty and territorial integrity. Although the mainland and Taiwan are yet to be reunited, they belong to one and same China, which is an indivisible whole. The Kuomintang and the CPC have every reason to uphold the one-China stance and work together to maintain the one-China framework. I hope both parties will, displaying a responsible attitude for history and the people, put the overall interests of the Chinese nation above all else, keep in mind the overall picture of the peaceful development of cross-Straits relations and move those relations steadily forward in the right direction.

Second, we must handle cross-Straits relations on the basis of a clear understanding of the trend of history. The great renewal of the Chinese nation has never been closer thanks to the tireless efforts of all the sons and daughters of China. We should view from the high ground the great trend of history with changing times and the rise of the Chinese nation, and realize that the peaceful development of cross-Straits relations has become part and parcel of China's great renewal. We should break away from outdated perceptions, and identify this renewal as the common goal. This has become a prevailing trend of development in cross-Straits relations. We should determine our own road map for continued progress in accordance with this. Both parties should take national renewal and the people's wellbeing as their bounden duty, promote unity and cooperation among compatriots as belonging to the same family, pool the wisdom and strength of the Chinese people on both sides of the Straits, and work to heal the historical trauma through working together towards national renewal, thus writing a shining page in China's journey towards prosperity.

Third, we must strengthen mutual trust and constructive interactions, seek common ground while reserving differences, and devote ourselves to pragmatic progress. The key to increasing mutual trust lies in reaching a clearer common understanding of an identical stance on the principal issue of upholding and consolidating the one-China framework. Constructive interactions mean enhanced communication, consultations on an equal basis, meeting each other halfway, mutual release of goodwill, efforts to cherish the hard-won peaceful development of cross-Straits relations, and the solving of outstanding problems in a fair and reasonable way. Seeking common ground while reserving differences demands that both sides give full play to their political wisdom, reach and expand a consensus for enhancing cross-Straits relations, and properly handle and control their differences in the spirit of sharing and mutual assistance, as passengers in the same boat. Pragmatic progress requires that the two sides adopt a down-to-earth approach, proceed from reality and go for steady and incremental progress, never shrinking from difficulties, never being thrown off balance by interruptions, and being on guard against retrogression. As cross-Straits relations have entered a new phase of consolidation and deepening, it is all the more necessary for the two sides to keep a positive and enterprising spirit, and to face and overcome difficulties on the road to progress with greater courage and determination. I hope the two sides will work together to make even greater achievements in cross-Straits relations, while expanding steadily the scope of peaceful development of such relations.

Fourth, we must firmly promote the comprehensive development of cross-Straits relations. Above all, we must work hard to keep cross-Straits relations stable. Forces and activities for "Taiwan independence" remain a real threat to the peace of the Taiwan Straits. It is therefore incumbent upon us to oppose and contain any rhetoric or move for "Taiwan independence" without any compromise. On the basis of overall stability in the Straits, there can be a broad scope for cross-Straits exchanges and cooperation in various fields. The two sides should take more positive steps to stimulate their economic, scientific, technological, cultural and educational cooperation, provide greater policy support, and offer still more convenient facilities, so as to expand the scope and texture of cooperation, and thereby generate even greater benefits. We must endeavor to enhance the wellbeing of the people on both sides of the Straits. All of them are entitled to the fruits of the peaceful development of cross-Straits relations. We should help them, while working to expand their common interests and promoting Chinese culture, cultivate a deeper sense of cross-Straits community of common destiny, strengthen their national pride and reaffirm their common commitment to China's rejuvenation.

Together Fulfill the Chinese Dream
of National Rejuvenation*

February 18, 2014

Distinguished Honorary Chairman Lien Chan and Madame Lien,
Dear friends from all walks of life in Taiwan,

Good afternoon! I am delighted to meet Chairman Lien and other friends, old and new, right after the Spring Festival. You are the first Taiwanese guests I have met since the beginning of this year, the Year of the Horse. First of all, I would like to extend my warm welcome to you. I wish you all a happy New Year and every success!

Chairman Lien and I have met several times, and we are old friends now. He has deep feelings for our motherland, and has long been an advocate of cross-Straits relations and has done a great deal for the rejuvenation of the Chinese nation. I greatly appreciate his dedication.

A whole year's work depends on a good start in the spring. Last year, Chairman Lien and other friends also paid us a visit at the beginning of spring, setting a favorable course for the development of cross-Straits relations in the year. Progress in our relationship has been of great benefit to the people of both sides, as well as offering further potential for development. This year, we hope that both sides can work together on the basis that we are one family, seize every opportunity that presents itself, and make a concerted effort to make further progress in the peaceful development of cross-Straits relations

---

* Speech delivered when receiving Lien Chan, honorary chairman of the Kuomintang of China, and his delegation.

and bring more benefits to the people on both sides of the Taiwan Straits.

Thank you, Chairman Lien, for the good points you have just raised on the subject of cross-Straits relations, which are very enlightening to me. You are representatives of all circles in Taiwan; and I would like to have a heart-to-heart talk with you.

Due to history and present circumstances, there are many thorny problems for the moment between our two sides, but this will pass, for we are both doing our best to solve them, and to ensure that they do not adversely affect our relationship, our cooperation, or our exchanges. Meanwhile, the people on both sides of the Straits are one family with shared blood, culture, bonds, and aspirations, all of which serve as an important force for promoting our mutual understanding and common progress.

First, we are one family, and no one can ever cut the veins that connect us. I am impressed by our compatriots in Taiwan for their worship of the ancestors, their love for the homeland, and their honesty, frankness, diligence and hard work. The closeness between us is rooted in our blood, our history and culture. We all believe that Chinese on both sides of the Taiwan Straits are members of one Chinese nation, and we all inherit and pass on Chinese culture. During the 50 years when Taiwan was occupied by the Japanese aggressors,[1] our fellow Taiwanese maintained a strong sense of national consciousness and deep feelings for Chinese culture, regarding themselves first and foremost as members of the Chinese nation. Such consciousness and feelings are inherent and natural, and can never be erased.

Looking back on the history of Taiwan and that of cross-Straits relations, I have come to a clear understanding that no matter what trials and hardships Taiwan has experienced, and no matter what vicissitudes cross-Straits relations have been through, the hearts of the people on both sides of the Straits remain in accord with each other, and the people on both sides always show concern for and help each other. It is a simple truth that blood is thicker than water. All Taiwanese are our kinsmen, including the descendants of those who crossed the dangerous "Black Ditch"[2] hundreds of years ago to seek a new life in Taiwan, and those who migrated to Taiwan a few decades ago. We share origins and ancestors, and we are one close family. To strengthen these ties has been our common aspiration, and no force on earth can sever the bond between us.

Second, people on both sides of the Straits share the same destiny, and there is no knot that cannot be unraveled. Despite the Straits that separate us geographically, we share the same destiny. A great Chinese nation will be a blessing for all Chinese, while a weak and divided one will be disastrous. After experiencing so many twists and turns in modern times, we all have a deep understanding of this.

A hundred and twenty years ago China was a weak country, and the Japanese aggressors took advantage of this to occupy Taiwan. This was a traumatic experience for all Chinese people on both sides of the Straits. In the bitter years when Taiwan was under Japanese occupation, countless Taiwanese compatriots shed their blood, and many laid down their lives, proving they were inseparable members of the extended family of the Chinese nation. For more than six decades now, although the two sides have yet to be reunited, we belong to one country and the same nation – a fact that has never changed, nor will ever change in the future. The blood of the Chinese nation flows in every one of us, and ours is forever the soul of the Chinese nation.

Due to their historical suffering and the distinct social environment in which they have lived, the people of Taiwan have their own mindset. They bear particular historical scars, they are eager to be masters of their own destiny, they cherish their established social systems and way of life, and they wish to live a stable and happy life. Putting ourselves in their place, we can fully understand their feelings.

We identify with our compatriots in Taiwan in terms of their historical trauma, for it is a shared trauma of all sons and daughters of the Chinese nation. With the advent of the new era, it has become a common goal cherished by each one of us on both sides of the Straits to become a dignified Chinese and a helmsman of his own destiny.

Family affection heals trauma, and sincerity leads to realistic solutions to problems. We have no lack of patience, and have confidence aplenty. Family affection cannot only heal wounds, relieve pain, and unlock hearts, but help achieve mutual affinity. We respect the social system and the way of life chosen by the people of Taiwan, and would also like them to be first in sharing the opportunities brought by the mainland's development. None of us can choose our history, but we can all seize the moment and create a better future.

Third, the people on both sides of the Straits should join our efforts in promoting peaceful cross-Straits relations. Over the past five years or more, we have together chosen the path of peaceful development in cross-Straits relations. As a result we have broken new ground, to the benefit of all concerned. Facts have proved that this is the right path, leading to peace, common development, national rejuvenation and mutual benefit. The two sides should eliminate all obstacles, and advance along this path firmly, step by step, and with full confidence.

The current peaceful development of cross-Straits relations is beneficial to both sides, and no one wants to reverse such a favorable trend. For this reason, the two sides must consolidate and hold fast to our common foundation of the "1992 Consensus"[3] and our opposition to "Taiwan independence," and be fully aware of the importance of maintaining the one-China framework. Such a foundation is the anchor for cross-Straits relations. Only when our vessel is at anchor will we be able to "sit tight on the fishing boat despite the rising wind and surging waves." As long as a solid foundation is maintained, the prospects for cross-Straits relations will continue to grow brighter. If the foundation is jeopardized, the relations will go back to turbulence and instability. Only recently, a consensus was reached at a meeting of the heads of departments in charge of cross-Straits affairs from both sides which is conducive to the all-round development of cross-Straits relations.

As far as any significant political differences between the mainland and Taiwan are concerned, we are willing to conduct consultations with the people of Taiwan, based on equality within the one-China framework, and come to reasonable arrangements. We are ready to communicate with the people of Taiwan on any and every subject. Not every problem has an ideal solution, but where there is communication, there is hope, and, as a saying goes, "Faith can move mountains." I believe that the people of China on both sides of the Straits have the wisdom to find the right approach to the problems between us.

"When everybody adds wood to the fire, the flames rise high." We invite more of our compatriots in Taiwan to work together with us. Let us make a concerted effort, work out effective methods, and pool all of our wisdom and strength so as to consolidate and expand the peaceful development of cross-Straits relations, transform this goal into an irresistible historic trend, and bring the benefits to the general public in Taiwan, and in particular to those at the grassroots. We will welcome people from Taiwan and treat them equally and without discrimination, regardless of whatever stance they might previously have taken, to boost the peaceful development of cross-Straits relations.

Fourth, the people of the two sides should work hand in hand towards the Chinese Dream, the rejuvenation of the Chinese nation. These were the long-cherished wishes of Dr Sun Yat-sen[4]: to achieve the rejuvenation of the Chinese nation, to realize the greatness and prosperity of China, and to ensure the happiness of the Chinese people. These have also been the long-cherished wishes of all CPC members and all the Chinese people since the advent of modern times. The Chinese Dream is a vivid expression of this wish.

Just as Chairman Lien has said, the Chinese Dream is closely related to Taiwan's future. It is a dream shared by both sides of the Straits that can only be realized through joint effort. As a saying goes, "If brothers are of the same mind, their edge can cut through metal."[5] The people of both sides of the Straits, regardless of their parties, social strata, religions, or localities, should support each other in achieving national rejuvenation and the Chinese Dream as quickly as possible.

We treat the people of Taiwan in all sincerity, and we are open to advice from all sides. We will do our best to deal properly with any matter concerning the wellbeing of our compatriots in Taiwan, the peaceful development of cross-Straits relations, and the overall interests of the Chinese nation. We will do our best to ensure that the people of Taiwan benefit from the peaceful development of cross-Straits relations, and to ensure that all Chinese people live a better life.

Enjoy your stay here! Thank you!

Notes

[1] In 1895, China was defeated in the Sino-Japanese War, and was forced to sign the Treaty of Shimonoseki, ceding to Japan Taiwan and the Penghu Islands, which were returned to China after Japan's unconditional surrender in 1945 at the end of World War II.

[2] This refers to the Taiwan Straits. Early immigrants to Taiwan from the mainland of China mostly chose to cross the Straits via the Penghu water area, where sea currents were swift and shipwrecks frequent. Since the sea water looked dark, and the journey was perilous, the immigrants called this area the "Black Ditch."

[3] The "1992 Consensus" refers to an oral agreement reached at a November 1992 meeting between the Association for Relations Across the Taiwan Straits (ARATS) and the Straits Exchange Foundation (SEF). The meeting discussed how to express the one-China principle in negotiations on general affairs, and agreed that both sides would follow the one-China principle, each with its respective interpretation.

[4] Sun Yat-sen (1866-1925), also known as Sun Wen and Sun Zhongshan, was revered as a great national hero, a patriot, and a forerunner of the Chinese democratic revolution. He put forward the political philosophy known as the "Three Principles of the People" – nationalism, democracy and the people's livelihood. He was the first to call for the revival of the Chinese nation, and under his leadership, the rule of absolute monarchy that had lasted for thousands of years in China was finally ended by the Revolution of 1911. Later, with the help of the CPC, the Communist Party of the Soviet Union and Vladimir Lenin, Sun Yat-sen reorganized the Kuomintang, adopted the "New Three Principles of the People" – which consisted of "alliance with the Soviets, alliance with the Communist Party of China and helping the farmers and workers" – established cooperation between the Kuomintang and the Communists, and advanced the anti-imperialist and anti-feudal democratic revolution in China.

[5] *The Book of Changes* (*Yi Jing*), also known as *I Ching*.

Take On the Task of
Expanding Cross-Straits Relations and
Achieving National Rejuvenation[*]

May 7, 2014

The peaceful development of cross-Straits relations is a choice made by the people on both sides of the Taiwan Straits in accordance with the historical trend. As long as we stick to the idea that we are one family, put ourselves in each other's shoes and treat one another with all sincerity, there are no hard feelings which cannot be removed and no difficulties which cannot be overcome between us.

The overall situation of the peaceful development of cross-Straits relations is stable and can stand the test of any storm. In general, our relations have been improving over the decades, which is a reflection of the trend of history, despite the occasional ups and downs. Peaceful development is the common aspiration of the people on both sides of the Straits, and it brings benefits to both sides. We will not change our policies or measures for promoting peaceful cross-Straits relations, abandon the pragmatic measures of promoting cross-Straits exchanges, cooperation and mutually beneficial results, dampen our enthusiasm for uniting with our Taiwan compatriots in making progress, or waver in our opposition to any scheme of "Taiwan independence." We sincerely hope that our Taiwan compatriots can enjoy a peaceful and happy life in a stable society with sustainable economic growth and improved wellbeing.

Developing peaceful cross-Straits relations is a long-term and arduous task that calls for deeper mutual trust between the two sides.

---

* Main points of the talk with James Soong Chu-yu, chairman of Taiwan's People First Party, and his delegation.

Mutual trust leads to solutions to many difficult problems. We must create the conditions for expanding contacts in various fields among people from all walks of life on both sides of the Straits, increase face-to-face and heart-to-heart communication, enhance mutual understanding and close the psychological gap between the two sides.

The prospects for peaceful development of cross-Straits relations are broad and promising, and continuous efforts need to be made to expand them. Bringing the comprehensive reform to a higher level and opening wider to the outside world by the mainland will give a strong momentum and favorable conditions for cross-Straits economic cooperation. Economic integration is conducive to mutual benefits, so it should not be disturbed at any time or in any circumstances. We will try to gain an in-depth knowledge of the real needs of ordinary, especially grassroots, Taiwan people, and take positive and effective measures to take care of disadvantaged groups, so that more Taiwan compatriots can benefit from cross-Straits economic exchanges and cooperation.

The younger generation is entrusted with the future of cross-Straits relations. We must work out more measures and create more opportunities for them so that they can have more contacts and communication, perceive the trend of peaceful development of cross-Straits relations and that of the great renewal of the Chinese nation, so as to enable them to assume the responsibilities of expanding cross-Straits relations and achieving the rejuvenation of the Chinese nation in the future.

We hope that the People First Party will adhere to the "one China" stand, continue its opposition to any scheme of "Taiwan independence," firmly maintain the overall situation of peaceful development of cross Straits relations, and promote the overall interests of the Chinese nation together with people from all walks of life in Taiwan.

Peaceful Development

Strengthen the Foundation for
Pursuing Peaceful Development[*]

January 28, 2013

To pursue peaceful development in keeping with the development trend of the times and China's fundamental interests is a strategic choice made by our Party. We should, under the guidance of Deng Xiaoping Theory, the important thought of the Three Represents and the Scientific Outlook on Development, enhance our strategic thinking and confidence, and better balance China's overall domestic and international interests. We should pursue mutually beneficial development featuring openness and cooperation, develop China by securing a peaceful international environment and, at the same time, uphold and promote world peace through our own development. We should continuously improve China's overall national strength, make sure that the people share the benefits of peaceful development, and consolidate the material and social foundations for pursuing peaceful development.

The Chinese nation loves peace. To abolish war and achieve peace has been the most pressing and profound aspiration of the Chinese people since the advent of modern times. Pursuing peaceful development is what the fine traditional Chinese culture calls for, and it is a natural choice made by the Chinese people who have suffered so much in modern times. With the agonizing sufferings inflicted by war etched in our memory, we Chinese cherish peace and stability. What we abhor is turbulence, what we want is stability and what we hope to see is world peace.

---

* Main points of the speech at the third group study session of the Political Bureau of the 18th CPC Central Committee which Xi presided over.

Our pursuit of peaceful development was not an easy-going process. Rather, this pursuit was made possible thanks to the CPC's arduous quest and endeavors since the founding of the PRC in 1949 and, in particular, to the introduction of the reform and opening-up initiative in 1978. Our Party has always upheld peace and never wavered in this commitment. Over the years, we have put forward and adhered to the Five Principles of Peaceful Coexistence, and adopted and followed an independent foreign policy of peace. And we have made a solemn pledge to the whole world that we will never seek hegemony or commit any act of expansion, and that China is and will remain a staunch force for upholding world peace. We remain true to these commitments and we remain firm in honoring them.

The CPC put forward at its 18th National Congress the Two Centenary Goals. We have also put forward the goal of achieving the Chinese Dream – the rejuvenation of the Chinese nation. To realize these goals, we need a peaceful international environment. Neither China nor the rest of the world can develop without peace, nor can they enjoy lasting peace without development. We must seize the opportunity and run our own affairs well so as to make our country stronger and more prosperous, and our people lead a better life. This will enable us to pursue peaceful development by relying on our growing strength.

"The tide of history is mighty. Those who follow it will prosper, while those who resist it will perish." Looking back on history, we can see that those who launched aggression or sought expansion by force all ended in failure. This is a law of history. A prosperous and stable world provides China with opportunities, and China's development also offers an opportunity for the world as a whole. Whether we will succeed in our pursuit of peaceful development to a large extent hinges on whether we can turn opportunities in the rest of the world into China's opportunities and China's opportunities into those for the rest of the world so that China and other countries can engage in sound interactions and make mutually beneficial progress. We must act in keeping with China's national conditions and stick to our own path. At the same time, we should acquire a global vision. In this way, we can both promote China's domestic development and open the country wider to the outside world and advance both China's development and the development of the world as a whole, as well as the interests of both the Chinese people and other peoples. In this way, we can continuously expand mutually beneficial cooperation with other countries, be actively involved in international affairs, address global challenges together with other countries, and contribute our share to global development.

While pursuing peaceful development, we will never sacrifice our legitimate rights and interests or China's core interests. No foreign country should expect China to trade off its core interests or swallow bitter fruit that undermines China's sovereignty, security or development interests. China is pursuing peaceful development, and so are other countries. This is the sure way for all the countries in the world to seek common development and peaceful coexistence. We should let the world learn more about China's strategy of pursuing peaceful development and let the international community view China's development for what it is and treat it accordingly. China will never seek development at the expense of any other country's interests, nor will it shift its problems onto others. We will actively pursue peaceful and common development, uphold the multilateral trading system and participate in global economic governance.

Work Together for
Mutually Beneficial Cooperation[*]

June 19, 2013 and May 19, 2014

I

As well as its many important missions, the United Nations (UN) carries the expectations of the peoples of all countries. The world is undergoing dramatic and complex changes, and it requires the joint efforts of all UN member states to address global issues and challenges. The UN should grasp the theme of peace and development, uphold fairness and justice, and speak and act justly. The time of the zero-sum mentality is past, so we should work together for mutually beneficial cooperation instead. The UN should contribute to this.

China has set forth the Two Centenary Goals as a grand blueprint for its future development. China needs the UN and the UN needs China. China values the UN and will support it.

China's permanent membership of the UN Security Council entails not only power but also responsibility that it is ready to shoulder. China will continue to work for the peaceful resolution of international disputes and support the UN in achieving its Millennium Development Goals. China is willing to work with all parties in addressing climate change and other problems, and to do whatever it can for world peace and human progress.

(June 19, 2013)

---

* Main points of talks with Ban Ki-moon, secretary-general of the UN.

II

The year 2015 will mark the 70th anniversary of victory in the World Anti-Fascist War (1941-1945) and the victory of the Chinese People's War of Resistance Against Japanese Aggression[1] (1937-1945). It will also mark the 70th anniversary of the founding of the UN. The world community should avail itself of this important opportunity to reiterate its commitment to multilateralism, safeguard the principles set forth in the UN Charter and commit itself to strengthening the role of the UN.

The world community should make concerted efforts to promote world peace and development.

First, seeking political solutions is the right path to address the seemingly endless sequence of international flashpoints. "Just when you press the gourd into the water, there floats the gourd ladle."[2] These issues must be tackled properly and reasonably. Exerting pressure won't work, and external military intervention will make things worse. Both the UN and the rest of the international community should adhere to political solutions to all conflicts.

Second, the world community should adhere to the goal of common development. The UN should play its political and coordinating role, and exploit its moral advantage. It should formulate its post-2015 Development Agenda with poverty alleviation at its core to achieve sustainable growth. China wishes every success for the UN Climate Summit in September.

Third, the UN should play a leading role in international affairs. Regarding the fight against terrorism, the UN should play a bigger role by promoting clear-cut criteria of right and wrong so as to advance the fight against terrorism of all forms. It should also serve as the main channel in protecting cyber security, advocate rules, sovereignty and transparency in this regard, respect the concerns of different countries over information safety, and achieve common management. China will continue to firmly support the UN.

(May 19, 2014)

Notes

[1] The War of Resistance Against Japanese Aggression refers to a war against Japan's imperialist invasion that lasted from the September 18th Incident in 1931 until September 1945. Through the advocacy of the Communist Party of China, the war was waged under the banner of the Chinese united front against Japanese aggression, and involved KMT-CPC cooperation. It was an important battlefield during World War II and one of the major theaters in the East. The war was the first complete victory achieved by the Chinese people against foreign aggression since the Opium Wars in the mid-19th century. It also made a significant contribution to overall victory in World War II (known in China as the World Anti-Fascist War).

[2] A traditional Chinese saying that means "tackling one problem only to find another emerging." – *Tr.*

Follow a Sensible, Coordinated and Balanced Approach to Nuclear Security[*]

March 24, 2014

Your Excellency Prime Minister Mark Rutte,

Dear colleagues,

Today, we are meeting here at The Hague for an important discussion on ways to enhance nuclear security. First of all, I wish to express heartfelt thanks to Prime Minister Rutte and the Dutch government for the active efforts and considerate arrangements they have made for this summit.

During the 20th century, the discovery of the atom and the subsequent development and utilization of nuclear energy gave new impetus to the progress of humanity and greatly enhanced our ability to understand and shape the world. Yet the development of nuclear energy has its associated risks and challenges. To make better use of nuclear energy and achieve greater progress, mankind must be able to respond to various nuclear security challenges and ensure the safety of nuclear materials and facilities.

Dear colleagues,

Enhancing nuclear security is a never-ending process. As long as we continue to tap nuclear energy, we must maintain our efforts in enhancing nuclear security. From Washington DC in 2010 to Seoul in 2012 and to The Hague today, the Nuclear Security Summit (NSS) has the great responsibility of building international consensus in this regard and deepening nuclear security efforts. We must take a sensible,

---

* Speech at the Nuclear Security Summit in The Hague, the Netherlands.

coordinated and balanced approach to nuclear security and keep it on the track of sound and sustainable development.

First, we should place equal emphasis on development and security, and develop nuclear energy on the premise of security. The peaceful use of nuclear energy is important for ensuring energy security and tackling climate change. Like Prometheus who gave fire to humanity, the peaceful use of nuclear energy has sparked a flame of hope and opened up a bright future for mankind. But without effective safeguards for nuclear safety and without an adequate response to the potential security risks of nuclear materials and facilities, such a bright future will be overshadowed by dark clouds or even by nuclear disaster. Therefore, we must strictly abide by the principle of making safety the top priority if we are to keep the flame of hope for nuclear energy development burning.

We must follow the approach of enhancing security for the sake of development and promoting development by upholding security, and bring the goals of development and security in alignment with each other. We must convince the governments and nuclear power companies of all countries that developing nuclear energy at the expense of security can neither be sustainable nor bring real development. Only by adopting credible steps and safeguards can we keep risks under effective control and develop nuclear energy in a sustainable way.

Second, we should place equal emphasis on rights and obligations, and push forward the international nuclear security process on the basis of respecting the rights and interests of all countries. Nothing can be accomplished without norms and standards. All countries should earnestly fulfill their obligations under international legal instruments relating to nuclear security, fully implement the relevant UN Security Council resolutions, consolidate and strengthen the existing legal framework governing nuclear security, and provide institutional support and universally accepted guidelines for international efforts to enhance nuclear security. China hopes that more countries will consider ratifying the Convention on the Physical Protection of

Nuclear Material and its amendment, and the International Convention for the Suppression of Acts of Nuclear Terrorism.

Countries differ in national conditions and in the status of their nuclear power development, and the nuclear security challenges they face also vary from one to another. As the saying goes, you need different keys to open different locks. While stressing the importance of countries honoring their international obligations, we should respect their right to adopt nuclear security policies and measures best suited to their specific conditions as well as their right to protect sensitive nuclear security information. We should adopt a fair and pragmatic attitude, and advance the international nuclear security process in an active yet prudent manner.

Third, we should place equal emphasis on independent and collaborative efforts, and seek universal nuclear security through mutually beneficial cooperation. Nuclear security is first and foremost a national goal, and the primary responsibility must be borne by national governments. They must understand and fulfill their responsibilities, develop a stronger awareness of nuclear security, foster a nuclear security culture, strengthen institutions, and enhance technological capacity. This is the responsible thing to do not only for their own sake but also for the good of the world as a whole.

Nuclear security is also a global endeavor. The amount of water a barrel can hold is determined by its shortest stave. The loss of nuclear material in one country can be a threat to the whole world. A concerted, global effort is therefore required to achieve universal nuclear security. We must bring more countries into the international nuclear security process and try to turn it into a global undertaking, so that all will contribute to and benefit from it. We should strengthen exchanges to learn from each other and share experiences, and improve coordination between the relevant multilateral mechanisms and initiatives. Although the starting line may be different for different countries, we should make sure that no one falls behind in this common endeavor.

Fourth, we should place equal emphasis on treating symptoms and addressing causes, and advance the nuclear security endeavor in all respects with the goal of removing the associated risks at the root. The issue of nuclear security has many dimensions, from exercising sound and effective management to developing advanced and secure nuclear energy technologies and to dealing with nuclear terrorism and nuclear proliferation. To eliminate the potential risks of nuclear security and nuclear proliferation in a direct and effective way, we must improve relevant policies and measures, develop modern, low-risk nuclear energy technologies, maintain balanced supply and demand of nuclear materials, strengthen non-proliferation efforts and export control, and step up international cooperation against nuclear terrorism.

But more importantly, we must tackle the root causes. We need to foster a peaceful and stable international environment, encourage harmonious and friendly relations between countries, and conduct exchanges among different civilizations in an amicable and open-minded manner. This is the only way to tackle the root causes of nuclear terrorism and nuclear proliferation, and to achieve lasting security and development of nuclear energy.

Dear colleagues,

China gives top priority to nuclear security in the peaceful use of nuclear energy, and manages nuclear materials and facilities in accordance with the highest standards. China has maintained a good record of nuclear security in the past 50 years and more.

According to Dutch philosopher Erasmus, prevention is better than cure. The horrific nuclear accidents of the past few years have rung the alarm bell for all of us, and we must do whatever we can to prevent a recurrence of past tragedies.

As a precautionary step, China has tightened nuclear security measures across the board. We have made great efforts to improve our technology and emergency response, and conducted comprehensive security checks on nuclear facilities across the country to make sure that all nuclear materials and facilities are placed under effective safeguards. We have adopted and implemented a medium- and long-term program on nuclear security and improved the relevant legal framework, and we are in the process of drafting national regulations with a view to putting our nuclear security endeavors on an institutional and legal footing.

China is actively promoting international cooperation on nuclear security, beginning with the Center of Excellence on Nuclear Security, a joint project between China and the United States. Construction of the Center is well under way. It will contribute to technical exchanges and cooperation on nuclear security in the region and beyond. China has also launched a number of cooperation projects with Russia and Kazakhstan to combat illicit trafficking of nuclear materials. China supports the efforts to reduce to a minimum the use of highly-enriched uranium (HEU) when economically and technologically feasible, and is helping Ghana convert an HEU-fueled research reactor to one using low-enrichment uranium within the IAEA framework. China has also made contributions to the IAEA Nuclear Security Fund, and helped enhance the nuclear security capability of Asia Pacific countries through hosting training sessions and a variety of other ways.

Dear colleagues,

Where light inches forward, darkness retreats. The more we do to enhance nuclear security, the fewer opportunities we will offer to terrorists. To achieve lasting nuclear security, China will continue its efforts in the following areas:

First, China will stay firmly committed to strengthening its own nuclear security capability. We will continue to enhance the government's regulatory capacity, increase investments in relevant technological development and human resources, and foster and develop a nuclear security culture.

Second, China will stay firmly committed to building an international nuclear security system. We will work with other countries to build an international nuclear security system featuring fairness and mutually beneficial cooperation, and encourage countries to share the fruits of the peaceful use of nuclear energy.

Third, China will stay firmly committed to supporting international cooperation on nuclear security. We stand ready to share technology, experience, resources and platforms to promote regional and international nuclear security cooperation. China supports the IAEA's leading role and encourages it to help developing countries build their nuclear security capacity. China will continue to take an active part in nuclear security activities, and invite the IAEA to conduct an International Physical Protection Advisory Service.

Fourth, China will stay firmly committed to upholding regional and global peace and stability. We will continue to pursue peaceful development and mutually beneficial cooperation, handle differences and disputes through equality-based dialogue and friendly consultations, and work with all other countries to remove the root causes of nuclear terrorism and nuclear proliferation.

Dear colleagues,

To strengthen nuclear security is our shared commitment and common responsibility. Let us work together so that the people of the whole world will have more confidence in lasting nuclear security and the benefits nuclear energy brings them.

Thank you!

Exchanges and Mutual Learning
Make Civilizations Richer and More Colorful*

March 27, 2014

Civilizations become richer and more colorful through exchanges and mutual learning, which form an important driver for human progress and global peace and development.

To promote exchanges and mutual learning among civilizations we must adopt a correct approach with some important principles. They, in my view, contain the following:

First, civilizations come in different colors, and such diversity has made exchanges and mutual learning among civilizations relevant and valuable. Just as the sunlight has seven colors, our world is a place of dazzling colors. A civilization is the collective memory of a country or a nation. Throughout history, mankind has created and developed many colorful civilizations, from the earliest days of primitive hunting to the period of agriculture, and from booming industrial revolution to the information society. Together, they present a magnificent genetic map of the exciting march of human civilizations.

"A single flower does not make spring, while one hundred flowers in full blossom bring spring to the garden." If there were only one kind of flower in the world, people would find it boring no matter how beautiful it was. Be it Chinese civilization or other civilizations in the world, they are all fruits of human progress.

I have visited the Louvre Museum in France and the Palace Museum in China, both of which house millions of art treasures. They are attractive because they present the richness of diverse civilizations. Exchanges and mutual learning among civilizations must

* Part of the speech at the UNESCO Headquarters.

not be built on the exclusive praise or belittling of one particular civilization. As early as over 2,000 years ago, the Chinese people came to recognize that "it is natural for things to be different."[1] Greater exchanges and mutual learning among civilizations can further enrich the colors of various civilizations and the cultural life of people and open up still greater alternatives in the future.

Second, civilizations are equal, and such equality has made exchanges and mutual learning among civilizations possible. All human civilizations are equal in value, and they all have their respective strengths and weaknesses. No civilization is perfect on the planet. Nor is it devoid of merit. No single civilization can be judged superior to another.

I have visited many places in the world. What interested me most during the trips was to learn about differing civilizations across the five continents, what makes them different and unique, how their people think about the world and life and what they hold dear. I have visited Chichen Itza, a window on the ancient Maya civilization, and the Central Asian city of Samarkand, an icon of the ancient Islamic civilization. It is my keenly felt conviction that an attitude of equality and modesty is required if one wants to truly understand various civilizations. Taking a condescending attitude towards a civilization cannot help anyone to appreciate its essence, and may risk antagonizing it. Both history and reality show that pride and prejudice are the biggest obstacles to exchanges and mutual learning among civilizations.

Third, civilizations are inclusive, and such inclusiveness has given exchanges and mutual learning among civilizations the impetus to move forward. The ocean is vast because it refuses no rivers. All civilizations are crystallizations of mankind's diligence and wisdom. Every civilization is unique. Copying other civilizations blindly or mechanically is like cutting one's toes to fit one's shoes – impossible and highly detrimental. All achievements of civilizations deserve our respect and must be cherished.

History proves that only by interacting with and learning from others can a civilization enjoy full vitality. If all civilizations are inclusive, the so-called "clash of civilizations" can be avoided and the harmony of civilizations will become reality; as a Chinese saying goes, "Radish or cabbage, each to his own delight."

Having gone through over 5,000 years of vicissitudes, the Chinese civilization has always kept to its original root. As an icon, it contains the most profound pursuits of the Chinese nation and provides it with abundant nourishment for existence and development. Deriving from Chinese soil, it has come to its present form through constant exchanges with and learning from other civilizations.

In the 2nd century BC, China started the Silk Road[2] leading to the Western Regions. In 138 BC and 119 BC, Envoy Zhang Qian[3] of the Han Dynasty (206 BC-AD 220) made two trips to those regions, disseminating Chinese culture and bringing into China grapes, alfalfa, pomegranates, flax, sesame and other products.

During the Western Han Dynasty (206 BC-AD 25), China's merchant fleets sailed as far as India and Sri Lanka where they traded China's silk for colored glaze, pearls and other products.

The Tang Dynasty (618-907) saw dynamic interactions between China and other countries. Historical records reveal that China exchanged envoys with more than 70 countries, and Chang'an, the capital of Tang, bustled with envoys, merchants and students from other countries. Exchanges of such a magnitude helped spread Chinese culture to the rest of the world and introduce other cultures and products to China.

During the early 15th century, Zheng He[4], a famous navigator of the Ming Dynasty (1368-1644), made seven expeditions to the Western Seas, reaching many Southeast Asian countries and even Kenya on the eastern coast of Africa, leaving behind many stories of friendly exchanges between China and countries along the route.

During the late Ming and early Qing (1644-1911) dynasties, the Chinese people began to access modern science and technology through the introduction of European knowledge in the realms of astronomy, medicine, mathematics, geometry and geography, which helped broaden the horizon of Chinese people. Thereafter, exchanges and mutual learning between Chinese civilization and other civilizations became more frequent. Naturally, there were conflicts, frictions, bewilderment and denial, but the more dominant features of the period were learning, digestion, integration and innovation.

Buddhism originated in ancient India. After it was brought to China, the religion went through an extended period of integrated development with the indigenous Confucianism and Taoism, and finally became Buddhism with Chinese features, thus greatly impacting the religious beliefs, philosophy, literature, art, etiquette and customs of China. Xuan Zang[5], an eminent monk of the Tang Dynasty, who endured untold sufferings as he went on a pilgrimage to ancient India for Buddhist scriptures, gave full expression to the determination and fortitude of the Chinese people to learn from other cultures. I am sure you have heard of the Chinese mythological classical novel *Journey to the West*[6] based on his stories.

The Chinese people enriched Buddhism and developed some special Buddhist thoughts in the light of Chinese culture, and helped it spread from China to Japan, Korea, Southeast Asia and beyond.

Over the last 2,000 years religions such as Buddhism, Islam and Christianity have been introduced into China, nurturing the country's music, painting and literature. China's freehand oil painting, for instance, is an innovative combination of its own traditional painting and Western oil painting, and the works by Xu Beihong[7] and other master painters have been widely acclaimed. China's Four Great Inventions – papermaking, gunpowder, printing and the compass, brought drastic changes to the whole world, including the European Renaissance. Its philosophy, literature, medicine, silk, porcelain and tea have been shared by the West and become part of its people's life. The book *Travels of Marco Polo* provoked widespread interest in China.

I think some of you might be familiar with the terracotta warriors and horses[8] of the Qin Dynasty (221-207 BC), one of the eight wonders in the world. After his visit to the site, President Chirac of France remarked that a visit to Egypt would not be complete without seeing the pyramids, and that a visit to China would not be complete without seeing the terracotta warriors and horses.

In 1987 this national treasure was listed as one of UNESCO's World Cultural Heritage Sites. Many Chinese legacies are ranked as World Cultural Heritage Sites, and World Intangible Cultural Heritage Sites and are listed on the Memory of the World Register. Here, I'd like to express my heartfelt thanks to UNESCO for its contribution to the preservation and dissemination of Chinese civilization.

Today, we live in a world with different cultures, ethnic groups, skin colors, religions and social systems, and all people on the planet have become members of an intimate community of shared future.

The Chinese people have long come to appreciate the concept of "harmony without uniformity."[9] Zuoqiu Ming[10], a Chinese historian who lived 2,500 years ago, recorded a few lines by Yan Zi[11], prime minister of the State of Qi during the Spring and Autumn Period (770-476 BC) in *Zuo's Chronicles* (*Zuo Zhuan*)[12]: "Harmony is like cooking thick soup. You need water, fire, vinegar, meat sauce, salt and plum to go with the fish or meat. It is the same with music. Only by combining the texture, length, rhythm, mood, tone, pitch and style adequately and executing them properly can you produce an excellent melody. Who can tolerate soup with nothing but water in it? Who can tolerate the same tone played again and again with one instrument?"

On the planet, there are more than 200 countries and regions inhabited by over 2,500 ethnic groups with a multitude of religions. Can we imagine a world with only one lifestyle, one language, one kind of music and one style of costume?

Victor Hugo once said that there was a prospect greater than the sea – the sky; there was a prospect greater than the sky – the human soul. Indeed, we need a mind that is broader than the sky as we approach different civilizations, which serve as water, moistening everything silently. We should encourage different civilizations to respect each other and live in harmony, so as to turn exchanges and mutual learning between civilizations into a bridge promoting friendship between peoples around the world, an engine driving human society, and a bond cementing world peace. We should draw wisdom and nourishment and seek spiritual support and psychological consolation from various civilizations, and work together to face down the challenges around the globe.

In 1987, 20 exquisite pieces of colored glaze were brought to light from an underground tomb of Famen Temple in Shaanxi, China. They proved to be Byzantine and Islamic relics brought to China during the Tang Dynasty. Marveling at these exotic relics, I was struck by the thought that we should appreciate their cultural significance rather than simply admiring their exquisiteness, and bring their inherent spirit to life instead of merely appreciating the artistic presentation of life in the past.

Notes

[1] *The Mencius (Meng Zi)*.

[2] The Silk Road was a trade thoroughfare on land connecting ancient China with South Asia, Western Asia, Europe and North Africa through Central Asia. The name derives from the bustling trade in silk and silk products from China to the western regions.

[3] Zhang Qian (?-114 BC) was a minister of the Western Han Dynasty. He was dispatched by Emperor Wudi as an envoy to the western regions (a historical name specified in the Han Dynasty that referred to the regions west of Yumen and Yangguan passes) in 138 BC and 119 BC, respectively, to seek alliances among local ethnic groups to fight against the Xiongnu, an aggressive tribe. His travels, as far as Central Asia today, tightened the ties between the central plains and the western regions and contributed remarkably to the opening of the ancient Silk Road.

[4] Zheng He (1371 or 1375-1433 or 1435) was a navigator of the Ming Dynasty. He began his service at the imperial court in the early Ming Dynasty and was later promoted to be the Grand Director (*Taijian*) of the Directorate of Palace Servants. He eventually served as chief envoy during his seven grand sea voyages between 1405 and 1433 when he traveled to more than 30 countries and regions in Asia and Africa, including Southeast Asian countries, the Indian Ocean and the Red Sea, as well as the East Coast of Africa and Mecca – the sacred place for Islamic pilgrimages (Zheng He was a Muslim.). His expeditions were dubbed Treasure Voyages, which greatly boosted the economic and cultural exchanges between China and other Asian and African countries.

[5] Xuan Zang (600 or 602-664), also known as Tang Seng, was an eminent monk of the Tang Dynasty, translator of Buddhist scriptures, and co-founder of the Vijnaptimatrata (Consciousness-only) School. He requested to take Buddhist orders at the age of 13, after which time he learned from many masters who confused him with different ideas, causing him a dream of journey to India – the western regions. His dream came true in 629 (or 627) when he headed to India for the study of Buddhist sutras. After his return to Chang'an, capital of the Tang Dynasty, Xuan Zang committed himself to translating 75 Buddhist scriptures in 1,335 volumes and writing a book, *Great Tang Records on the Western Regions* (*Da Tang Xi Yu Ji*).

[6] *Journey to the West* (*Xi You Ji*) is a mythical novel attributed to Wu Cheng'en (c. 1500-c. 1582), a novelist of the Ming Dynasty. It recounts the legendary pilgrimage of the Tang Dynasty monk Tang Seng (Xuan Zang), who traveled to the western regions (India) to obtain sacred texts (sutras) with his three disciples, Sun Wukong (Monkey King), Zhu Bajie (Pig of the Eight Prohibitions), and Sha Wujing (Friar Sand), and returned after many trials and much suffering subduing demons and monsters. It is dubbed one of the four great classical novels of Chinese literature, the other three being *Three Kingdoms*, *Outlaws of the Marsh* and *A Dream of Red Mansions*.

[7] Xu Beihong (1895-1953) was a master painter and fine arts educator.

[8] Terracotta warriors and horses of the Qin Dynasty (221-207 BC) were archaeological discoveries from the mausoleum of Emperor Yingzheng (259-210 BC), or the First Emperor of Qin – the first to unify feudal China. They were listed as one of UNESCO's World Cultural Heritage Sites in 1987.

[9] See note 10, p. 197.

[10] Zuoqiu Ming (556-451 BC) was a historian in the State of Lu during the Spring and Autumn Period.

[11] Yan Zi (?-500 BC), also known as Yan Ying, was a prime minister of the State of Qi during the Spring and Autumn Period.

[12] *Zuo's Chronicles* (*Zuo Zhuan*), also known as *Zuo's Commentary on the Spring and Autumn Annals*, is believed to have been written by Zuoqiu Ming. Acclaimed as one of the Chinese Confucian classics, it is one of the three "commentaries" on the *Spring and Autumn Annals*, along with *Gongyang's Commentary on the Spring and Autumn Annals* (*Gong Yang Zhuan*) and *Guliang's Commentary on the Spring and Autumn Annals* (*Gu Liang Zhuan*).

China's Commitment to Peaceful Development*

March 28, 2014

Mutual understanding is the foundation of state-to-state relations. Deeper mutual understanding will cement and broaden the foundation of our exchanges and cooperation.

Thanks to over 30 years of rapid growth through reform and opening up, China's GDP now ranks second in the world. As China continues to grow, some people start to worry. Some take a dark view of China and assume that it will inevitably become a threat as it develops further. They even portray China as being the terrifying Mephisto who will someday suck the soul of the world. Such absurdity couldn't be more ridiculous, yet some people, regrettably, never tire of preaching it. This shows that prejudice is indeed hard to overcome.

A review of human history shows that what keeps people apart are not mountains, rivers or oceans, but lack of mutual understanding. As Gottfried Wilhelm Leibniz once observed, only the sharing of our talents will light the lamp of wisdom.

Let me take this opportunity to share with you China's reform and development, focusing on its commitment to peaceful development. I hope this will help your understanding of our country.

Long ago, China made the solemn declaration to the world that it is committed to pursuing peaceful development. It has developed itself by upholding world peace and maintained world peace through development. Pursuing peaceful development is China's response to international concern about the direction it is taking. Moreover, it demonstrates the Chinese people's confidence in and commitment to achieving its development goals. Such confidence and commitment is

* Part of the speech at the Körber Foundation, Berlin, Germany.

rooted in the rich heritage of Chinese civilization, in our understanding of conditions for achieving its goals, and in our keen appreciation of the general trend of global development.

The Chinese nation is a peace-loving nation. And the most profound pursuit of a nation has its origin in the national character formed through generations. The Chinese nation, with 5,000 years of civilization, has always cherished peace. The pursuit of peace, amity and harmony is an integral part of the Chinese character which runs deep in the blood of the Chinese people. This can be evidenced by axioms from ancient China such as: "A warlike state, however big it may be, will eventually perish"[1]; "peace is of paramount importance"; "seek harmony without uniformity"[2]; "replace weapons of war with gifts of jade and silk"; "bring prosperity to the nation and security to the people"; "foster friendship with neighbors"; and "achieve universal peace." These axioms have been passed down from generation to generation. China was long one of the most powerful countries in the world. Yet it never engaged in colonialism or aggression. The pursuit of peaceful development represents the peace-loving cultural tradition of the Chinese nation over the past centuries, a tradition that we have inherited and carried forward.

China has set the following goals for its future development: By 2020, it will double its 2010 GDP and per capita income of urban and rural residents and realize a moderately prosperous society in all respects; and by the mid-21st century, it will have turned itself into a modern socialist country, prosperous, strong, democratic, culturally advanced and harmonious. We refer to this goal as the Chinese Dream of the great renewal of the Chinese nation. We will accelerate China's overall prosperity and raise the happiness index for our 1.3 billion Chinese people as long as we are on the right path. Yet, it will not be easy to make this happen for every individual. Consider the difference between eight people sharing one meal and 80 or even 800 people sharing the same meal. No matter how big the meal is, the individual share differs dramatically for diners different in number. We are keenly aware that China will remain the world's largest developing country for a long time and that to improve life for its 1.3 billion people calls for strenuous efforts. Two things will enable China to focus on development: a harmonious and stable domestic environment and a peaceful and stable international environment.

History is the best teacher. It faithfully records the journey that every country has gone through and offers guidance for its future development. In the 100 years from the Opium War in 1840 to the founding of the People's Republic in 1949, China was ravaged by wars, turmoil and foreign aggression. To the average Chinese, it was a period of ordeal too bitter to recall. The war of aggression against China waged by Japanese militarism alone inflicted over 35 million Chinese military and civilian casualties. These atrocities remain fresh in our memory. We Chinese have long held the belief expressed in the maxim "Don't do unto others what you don't want others to do unto you."[3] China needs peace as much as human beings need air and plants need sunshine. Only by pursuing peaceful development and working together with all other countries to uphold world peace can China realize its goal and make greater contributions to the world as a whole.

Dr Sun Yat-sen, the pioneer of China's democratic revolution, had this to say: "The trend of the world is surging forward. Those who follow the trend will prosper, whilst those who go against it will perish." History shows that a country, for its prosperity, must recognize and follow the underlying trend of the changing world. Otherwise, it will be abandoned by history. What is the trend of today's world? The answer is unequivocal. It is the trend of peace, development, cooperation and mutually beneficial progress. China does not subscribe to the outdated logic that a country will invariably seek hegemony when it grows strong. Are colonialism and hegemonism viable today? Absolutely not. They can inevitably lead to a dead end, and those who stick to this beaten track will only hit a stone wall. Peaceful development is the only alternative. That is why China is committed to peaceful development.

Facts speak louder than words. Over the past few decades China has consistently followed an independent foreign policy of peace and made it crystal clear that China's foreign policy is aimed at maintaining world peace and promoting common development. China has stated on numerous occasions that it opposes hegemonism and power politics in all forms, does not interfere in the internal affairs of other countries, and will never seek hegemony or expansion. This is our guiding principle for China's political system, and for each step we take. Moreover, China will firmly uphold its sovereignty, security and development interests. No country should expect China to swallow any bitter fruit that undermines its sovereignty, security or development interests.

In short, China's pursuit of peaceful development is not an act of expediency, still less diplomatic rhetoric. Rather, it is the conclusion drawn from an objective assessment of China's history, its present and future. It showcases confidence in thinking and readiness for practice. As peaceful development benefits both China and the world as a whole, we cannot think of any reason why we should not pursue this approach that has proven so effective.

Notes

[1] *The Methods of Sima (Si Ma Fa)*, also known as *The Marshal's Art of War*, is an ancient Chinese book on the art of war and was used as a basic textbook for marshal art training during the Song Dynasty (960-1279).

[2] See note 10, p. 197.

[3] See note 22, p. 198.

New Model of
Major-Country Relations

Follow the Trend of the Times and Promote Global Peace and Development[*]

March 23, 2013

Distinguished Mr Anatoly Vasilyevich Torkunov, Rector of the
  Moscow State Institute of International Relations,
The Honorable Olga Golodets, Deputy Prime Minister of the
  Russian Federation,
Dear faculty members and students,

I am very pleased to come to the beautiful Moscow State Institute of International Relations today and meet so many faculty members and students here.

The Moscow State Institute of International Relations is a prestigious school of world renown, boasting an outstanding faculty and distinguished alumni. I wish to express my warm congratulations on the remarkable successes you have achieved in various fields.

Russia is a friendly neighbor to China. My current visit to Russia is the first leg of my first overseas trip since becoming China's president. It is also my second visit to your beautiful and richly endowed country in three years. Yesterday, I had fruitful talks with President Putin, and together we attended the launch of the Tourism Year of China in Russia.

The month of March marks the return of spring, a season of sowing and great renewal. As a popular Chinese saying goes, "he who hopes for a good year starts planning in spring." China and Russia, having taken advantage of this season to plough and hoe not only for our bilateral relations but also for peace and development in the

* Speech at the Moscow State Institute of International Relations, Moscow, Russia.

world, will surely reap a bumper harvest to the benefit of our two peoples and those of other countries.

Dear faculty members and students,

The Institute of International Relations, as an institution of higher learning specialized in the study of international issues, pays close attention to the international landscape and can appreciate especially keenly the enormous changes the world has gone through over the past decades. Indeed, we live in a time of kaleidoscopic changes that make the world constantly different.

It is a world where peace, development, cooperation and mutual benefit have become the trend of the times. The old colonial system has long since disintegrated, and confrontations between blocs as during the Cold War have long gone. No country or group of countries can dominate world affairs single-handedly.

It is a world where emerging markets and developing countries in large numbers have embarked on the track of fast development. Billions of people are moving towards modernization at an accelerating pace. Multiple growth engines have emerged in regions across the world. And the international balance of power continues to evolve in a direction favorable for peace and development.

It is a world where countries are linked with and dependent on one another at a level never seen before. Mankind, by living in the same global village in the same era where history and reality meet, has increasingly emerged as a community of shared future in which everyone has in himself a little bit of others.

And it is a world where mankind is beset with numerous difficulties and challenges. They range from the continued underlying impact of the international financial crisis, an apparent upsurge of all kinds of protectionism, incessant regional flashpoints, rising hegemonism, power politics and neo-interventionism, to a web of conventional and non-conventional security threats, such as the arms race, terrorism and cyber security. Upholding world peace and promoting common development remain a long and uphill battle.

We hope that the world will become a better place. We have every reason to believe that it will. At the same time, we are soberly aware that while the future is bright, the path leading to it can be tortuous. Chernyshevsky once wrote, "The path of history is not paved like Nevsky Prospekt; it runs across fields, either dusty or muddy, and cuts across swamps or forest thickets." Yet as shown by humanity's progress, history always moves forward according to its own laws despite twists and turns, and no force can hold back its rolling wheels.

The tide of the world is surging forward. Those who submit to it will prosper and those who resist it will perish. Keeping up with the times, one cannot live in the 21st century while thinking in the old fashion, lingering in the age of colonial expansion or with the zero-sum mentality of the Cold War.

In the face of the profoundly changed international landscape and the objective need for the world to rally together like passengers in the same boat, all countries should join hands in building a new model of international relations featuring cooperation and mutual benefit, and all peoples should work together to safeguard world peace and promote common development.

We stand for the sharing of dignity by all countries and peoples in the world. All countries, irrespective of size, strength and wealth, are equal. The right of the people to independently choose their development paths should be respected, interference in the internal affairs of other countries opposed, and international fairness and justice maintained. Only the wearer of the shoes knows if they fit or not. Only the people can best tell if the development path they have chosen for their country suits or not.

We stand for the sharing of the fruits of development by all countries and peoples. Every country, while pursuing its own development, should actively facilitate the common development of all countries. There cannot be sustainable development in the world when some countries are getting richer and richer while others languish in prolonged poverty and backwardness. Only when all countries achieve common development can there be better worldwide development.

Such practices as beggar-my-neighbor, shifting crises onto others and feathering one's nest at the expense of others are both immoral and unsustainable.

We stand for the sharing of security by all countries and peoples. Countries should make concerted efforts to properly address the issues and challenges they face. As challenges often take on global dimensions, there is all the more need for countries to take them on cooperatively, turning pressure into motivation and crises into opportunities. Confronted with complex threats to international security, fighting alone or fighting with a blind faith in the use of force will not get one anywhere. The only solution lies in cooperative, collective and common security.

As the trends of world multipolarity and economic globalization grow and those of upholding cultural diversity and applying information technology in social life continue to make progress, mankind has never been better blessed with opportunities for taking strides towards peace and development. And mutually beneficial cooperation provides the only practical way to achieving such a goal.

The destiny of the world must be left in the hands of the peoples of all countries. Matters that fall within the sovereign rights of a country should be managed only by the government and people of that country. And affairs of the world should be addressed by the governments and peoples of all countries through consultation. Herein lies the democratic principle for the handling of international affairs which should be universally observed.

Dear faculty members and students,

Last November, the CPC held its 18th National Congress. According to the blueprint it mapped out for the country's development in the near future, China will double its 2010 GDP and per capita income for both urban and rural residents by 2020, complete the building of a moderately prosperous society in all respects when the Party celebrates its centenary in 2021, and turn itself into a modern socialist country that is prosperous, strong, democratic, culturally advanced and harmonious when the PRC marks its centenary in 2049.

At the same time, we are soberly aware that, as a large developing country with over 1.3 billion people, China will encounter still greater and more testing challenges on the road to progress, which calls for continuous and strenuous efforts on our part if the goals as identified are to be reached.

The great renewal of the Chinese nation has become the grandest dream of the Chinese people in modern times. We call it the Chinese Dream, with prosperity for the country, renewal for the nation and happiness for the people as its fundamental elements. China has always been a peace-loving nation. But it was subjected to a century of untold sufferings as a result of repeated foreign aggression and domestic turmoil. We know too well the value of peace, and the need to build the country and improve the people's wellbeing in a peaceful environment. China is committed to the path of peaceful development, dedicating itself to open, cooperative and mutually beneficial development, while calling on all countries to follow this path. China always pursues a defense policy that is defensive in nature, not engaging in any arms race nor posing a military threat to any country. By growing stronger through development, China will bring more opportunities, rather than threats, to the rest of the world. The Chinese Dream which we cherish will not only serve the Chinese people but benefit people throughout the world.

It is heartening to see that, each as the other's largest neighbor, China and Russia enjoy a high complementarity in development strategy. Russia has set the goal of reaching or approaching the level of the developed countries by 2020 in terms of per capita GDP and is accelerating its advance in material development. We sincerely wish you success in achieving your goals as soon as possible. A strong and prosperous Russia is in the interests of China, and conducive to peace and stability in the Asia Pacific and the world at large.

The relationship between China and Russia is one of the most important bilateral relationships in the world. It is also the best relationship between major countries. A strong and high-performance relationship like this not only serves the interests of our two countries but also provides an important safeguard for maintaining the international strategic balance as well as peace and stability in the world. With our consistent efforts over the past 20 years and more, we have established a comprehensive strategic partnership of coordination, and a relationship that fully accommodates each other's interests and concerns, and delivers tangible benefits to the two peoples. We have resolved historical boundary issues once and for all and signed the Treaty of Good-neighborliness and Friendly Cooperation Between the People's Republic of China and the Russian Federation, thus laying a solid foundation for the long-term growth of China-Russia relations.

At present, both China and Russia are at a crucial stage of national renewal, as their relations have entered a new period characterized by provision of vital mutual development opportunities and serving as primary mutual cooperation partners. To ensure continued growth of China-Russia relations, we need to work still harder in the following areas:

First, stay firmly committed to building a forward-looking relationship. That China and Russia should live in everlasting amity and never be enemies is the shared aspiration of the two peoples. We need to stand tall and look far, working on our bilateral relations with a holistic approach. President Putin once said, "Russia needs a prosperous and stable China, and China needs a strong and successful Russia." I could not agree more. By achieving common development, we will give ever broader space to our comprehensive strategic partnership of coordination and provide positive energy to the international order and global systems in their movement towards greater fairness and rationality. China and Russia will forever be good neighbors, good friends and good partners, taking concrete actions to firmly support each other on respective core interests, on respective development and renewal, on following the development paths suited to our national conditions and on success in our affairs and endeavors.

Second, stay firmly committed to cultivating a cooperative and mutually beneficial relationship. China and Russia differ in realities and national conditions. By engaging in close cooperation and drawing on each other's strengths to make up for respective shortcomings, we can show to the world that one plus one can be greater than two. Last year, our two-way trade reached US$ 88.2 billion-worth and there were 3.3 million visits exchanged between our peoples. These figures give full expression to the enormous potential and broad prospects of China-Russia relations. Bilateral cooperation in energy has advanced steadily. The China-Russia oil and gas pipelines have long since replaced the "Ten Thousand *Li* Tea Route"[1] of the 17th century as the new "arteries of the century" connecting the two countries. Right now, we are looking actively to bridge the development strategies of our respective countries and regions in an effort to create still more converging interests and growth areas in bilateral cooperation. We will expand the scope of bilateral cooperation from the energy and resources sector to investment, infrastructure, hi-tech, finance and other areas, and from trade in goods to joint R&D and joint production so as to elevate the result-oriented cooperation between the two countries.

Third, stay firmly committed to cementing the friendship between the two peoples. Amity between peoples holds the key to relations between countries. It is the people's deep friendship that drives state-to-state relations forward. Here, I want to share a couple of stories about the mutual support and mutual help between our peoples. During the War of Resistance Against Japanese Aggression, Captain Gregory Kurishenko of the air force of the Soviet Union came to China and fought side by side with the Chinese people. He once said, "I feel the Chinese people's sufferings as if I were feeling the sufferings of my own motherland." He died heroically on Chinese soil. The Chinese people never forget this hero. An ordinary Chinese mother and her son have kept vigil at his tomb for more than half a century. In 2004, China invited some of the children traumatized in the Beslan school hostage incident[2] to China for rehabilitation treatment. The children received meticulous care. The head doctor from the Russian side said to the Chinese side, "Your doctors have given our children such great help, and they will always remember you." When Wenchuan was hit by a devastating earthquake in 2008[3] Russia raced against time to extend a helping hand, and invited the children from disaster areas to Russia's Far East for rehabilitation. Three years ago, I saw with my own eyes at the Ocean Children's Center in Vladivostok the loving care Russian teachers showered on our children. As we Chinese often say, love knows no borders. These Chinese children have learned for themselves the love, friendship and kindness of the Russian people. There are many more touching stories like these, and together they keep the tree of our friendship nourished, strong and evergreen.

Russia and China each has a time-honored history and splendid culture, and cultural exchanges between us play an irreplaceable role in advancing the friendship between the two peoples. Ancient Chinese philosophers such as Confucius and Lao Zi are well known in Russia while Russian culture left a deep mark on the older generations of Chinese revolutionaries. Even people of my age have read many Russian classic masterpieces. In my youth, I read the works of such Russian literary giants as Pushkin, Lermontov, Turgenev, Dostoyevsky, Tolstoy and Chekhov, and savored the powerful charm of Russian literature. It is no wonder that cultural exchanges between China and Russia enjoy fertile ground.

The youth are the future of a country and the future of the world. They also hold in their hands the future of China-Russia friendship. During this visit of mine, President Putin and I jointly announced that China and Russia would host the Year of Youth Friendship and Exchanges in 2014 and 2015, respectively. On the Chinese side, we will invite a delegation of Russian university students, including students of the Moscow State Institute of International Relations, to China. I see in you some of the best and brightest of the young generation in Russia. I hope that more and more young people from both countries will take over the baton of China-Russia friendship by actively involving themselves in the cause of friendship.

Dear faculty members and students,

As a Russian proverb goes, "Big ships sail far." We also have lines of an ancient poem which read, "Forging ahead like a gigantic ship breaking through strong winds and heavy waves, I'll set my towering sail to cross the sea which raves."[4] I am convinced that with the joint efforts of the governments and peoples of our two countries, China-Russia relations will continue to press ahead, overcoming difficulties, bringing greater benefits to the two peoples, and making ever-greater contributions to global peace and development.

Thank you.

Notes

[1] The "Ten Thousand *Li* Tea Route" was a tea trade route stretching 13,000 km through more than 200 cities. Opened by Shanxi businessmen from the late Ming Dynasty (1368-1644) to the early Qing Dynasty (1644-1911), it started from Meicun Village at the foot of the Wuyi Mountain in Fujian Province in Southeast China, reached Kyakhta in Russia and from there to St. Petersburg. It was an important route for international trade, enjoying equal fame with the Silk Road.

[2] It refers to a terrorist attack at School Number One in the town of Beslan, North Ossetia (an autonomous republic in the North Caucasus region) of the Russian Federation on September 1, 2004, resulting in more than 300 deaths.

[3] The earthquake, registering 8.0 on the Richter scale, occurred at 14:28:04 China Standard Time on May 12, 2008 in Wenchuan County, Sichuan Province. The epicenter (06:08:01 UTC) was located 38° southwest of and 11 km away from Yingxiu Town. As of September 25, 2008, official figures stated that 69,227 were confirmed dead, 374,643 injured and 17,923 missing. The direct economic loss in the hardest-hit areas reached RMB 845.1 billion.

[4] See note 3, p. 39.

Build a New Model of Major-Country Relationship Between China and the United States[*]

June 7, 2013

President Obama and I have just had our first meeting. We had a candid and in-depth exchange of views on our respective domestic and foreign policies, on building a new model of major-country relationship between China and the United States, and on major international and regional issues of mutual concern. We have reached a consensus on many important issues.

I told President Obama explicitly that China will unswervingly follow the path of peaceful development, further its reform and opening up, strive to realize the Chinese Dream of the rejuvenation of the Chinese nation, and promote the noble cause of peace and development of mankind.

The Chinese Dream is about making our country prosperous and strong, revitalizing the nation and bringing a happy life to its people. It is a dream of peace, development, cooperation and mutual benefit. It has many things in common with all the beautiful dreams, including the American Dream, of people all over the world.

President Obama and I both maintain that China and the US should and can build a new model of relationship different from the historical clashes and confrontations between major powers, given the rapid economic globalization and the need for all countries in the world to work together. We both agreed to make joint efforts to build a new model of major-country relationship, respect each other, cooperate and seek mutual interests, and bring benefits to our people and the people of the world at large. The world community also expects

* Main points of the speech when meeting the press with US President Barack Obama.

a continuously improved and expanded China-US relationship. Good China-US cooperation will serve as an anchor for global stability and a booster for world peace.

The two sides agreed to enhance dialogues and communication at all levels, and constantly increase mutual trust and understanding. President Obama and I will keep in close touch with each other through exchanges of visits, meetings, telephone conversations and letters. I have extended an invitation to President Obama to visit China at a suitable time for a new round of meetings and realize an exchange of visits as soon as possible. The two sides will act in close coordination to make sure that the new round of China-US strategic and economic dialogues, and high-level consultations on cultural and people-to-people exchanges will achieve positive results. The Chinese defense minister and foreign minister will visit the US on invitation.

The two sides also agreed to enhance cooperation in a wide range of areas such as economy, trade, energy, environment, and culture and humanities, as well as cooperation among different regions, so as to expand the converging interests between the two countries in an all-round way. We will improve and develop bilateral military relations, and build a new model of China-US military relationship. We will strengthen coordination concerning macro-economic policies, expand cooperation in the process of our economic development, and promote robust, sustainable and balanced economic growth in the Asia Pacific region and the world at large.

Where there is a will there is a way. I am confident about the new model of major-country relationship between China and the US. First, both sides have the political will to build such a relationship. Second, bilateral cooperation between the two countries over the past more than 40 years has laid a solid foundation for our future cooperation. Third, the two sides have established more than 90 mechanisms for high-level dialogues on strategy, economy, culture and humanities, which serve as guarantee mechanisms for the building of the new model of major-country relationship. Fourth, sister provinces and states, and sister cities totaling more than 220 pairs have been established between the two sides; nearly 190,000 Chinese students are studying in the US and more than 20,000 US students are studying in China – a good public opinion foundation for the building of the new model of relationship. Fifth, there is broad scope for future bilateral cooperation.

The building of a new model of major-country relationship between China and the US is unprecedented, but it will be faithfully carried out by the two sides. China and the US should work together to push forward the new model of major-country relationship by increasing dialogues, promoting mutual trust, expanding cooperation and controlling disputes.

Both the Chinese and American nations are great nations, and both peoples are great peoples. I believe that, with determination, confidence, patience and wisdom, the two sides will accomplish our goals as long as we keep the overall situation in mind while starting with the daily routine and making constant progress.

China has been a victim of computer hacker attacks. As a defender of cyber security, China has the same concerns as the US in this field. The two sides have decided through consultations to establish a cyber security working team within the framework of China-US strategic and security dialogues, and to start to work on the issue as soon as possible. The two sides should eschew mistrust and engage in cooperation so as to make cyber security a new bright spot in China-US cooperation.

Build a Bridge of Friendship and Cooperation Across the Eurasian Continent*

April 1, 2014

China and Europe may seem far apart geographically, but we are living in the same era and on the same earth. I feel that we are as close to each other as neighbors. Both China and Europe are in a crucial stage of development, and are facing unprecedented opportunities and challenges. I hope to work with our European friends to build a bridge of friendship and cooperation across the Eurasian continent. For that we actually need to build four bridges – for the peace, growth, reform and progress of civilization – so that the China-EU comprehensive strategic partnership will take on even greater global significance.

– We need to build a bridge of peace and stability, linking the two strong forces of China and the EU. Together, China and the EU make up one tenth of the total area of the earth, and represent one fourth of the world's population. Together we hold three permanent seats on the United Nations Security Council. We all need peace, multilateralism and dialogue, instead of war, unilateralism and confrontation. We need to enhance communication and coordination on global issues, and play a key role in safeguarding world peace and stability. Culture can spread, and so can peaceful development. China stands ready to work with the EU to let the sunlight of peace drive away the shadow of war, and the bonfire of prosperity warm up the global economy in the cold early spring, and enable all mankind to embark on the path of peaceful development and mutually beneficial cooperation.

– We need to build a bridge of growth and prosperity linking the two big markets of China and Europe. China and the EU are the two

* Part of the speech at the College of Europe in Bruges, Belgium.

most important economies in the world, accounting for one third of the global economy. We must uphold open markets, speed up negotiations on investment agreements, proactively explore the possibility of a free trade area, and strive to achieve the ambitious goal of bringing bilateral trade to US$1 trillion-worth by 2020. We should also look to combine China-EU cooperation with the initiative of developing the Silk Road Economic Belt, so as to integrate the markets of Asia and Europe, energize the people, businesses, capital and technologies of Asia and Europe, and make China and the EU the twin engines for global economic growth.

– We need to build a bridge of reform and progress, linking the reform process in China and the EU. Both China and the EU are pursuing reforms that are unprecedented in human history, and both are sailing uncharted waters. We should enhance dialogue and cooperation on macro economy, public policy, regional development, rural development, social welfare and other fields. We need to respect each other's paths of reform, draw upon each other's reform experience, and promote world development and progress through our reform efforts.

– We need to build a bridge of common cultural prosperity linking the two major civilizations of China and Europe. China represents in an important way Eastern civilization, while Europe is the birthplace of Western civilization. The Chinese people are fond of tea, and Belgians love beer. To me, the moderate tea drinker and passionate beer lover represent two ways of understanding life and knowing the world, and I find them equally rewarding. When good friends get together, they may want to drink to their hearts' content to show their friendship. They may also choose to sit down quietly and drink tea while chatting about their lives. In China we value our ideal of "harmony without uniformity."[1] And here in the EU people stress the need to be "united in diversity." Let us work together for all flowers of human civilization to blossom together.

In the face of all changes in the international landscape, China has always supported European integration and a bigger role in international affairs for a united, stable and prosperous EU. China will soon release its second EU policy paper to reiterate the great importance it places on the EU and on its relations with the EU. Last year, China and the EU jointly formulated the Strategic Agenda 2020 for China-EU Cooperation, setting out a host of ambitious goals in nearly a hundred fields. The two sides should work in concert to turn the blueprint into reality at an early date, and strive for greater progress in China-EU relations in the coming decade.

Notes

[1] See note 10, p. 197.

Neighborhood Diplomacy

Work Together to
Build the Silk Road Economic Belt*

September 7, 2013

More than 2,100 years ago during the Han Dynasty (206 BC-AD 220), a Chinese envoy named Zhang Qian was twice sent to Central Asia on missions of peace and friendship. His journeys opened the door to friendly contacts between China and Central Asian countries, and started the Silk Road linking the East and West, Asia and Europe.

Shaanxi, my home province, is right at the starting point of the ancient Silk Road. Today, as I stand here and look back at history, I seem to hear the camel bells echoing in the mountains and see the wisps of smoke rising from the desert, and this gives me a specially good feeling.

Kazakhstan, located on the ancient Silk Road, has made an important contribution to the exchanges between the Eastern and Western civilizations and the interactions and cooperation between various nations and cultures. This land has borne witness to a steady stream of envoys, caravans, travelers, scholars and artisans traveling between the East and the West. The exchanges and mutual learning thus made possible the progress of human civilization.

The ancient city of Almaty is also on the ancient Silk Road. In Almaty, there is a Xian Xinghai[1] Boulevard, which got its name from a true story. After the outbreak of the Great Patriotic War in 1941, Xian, a renowned Chinese composer, found his way to Almaty. By then, he was worn down by poverty and illness and had no one to turn to. Fortunately, the Kazakh composer Bakhitzhan Baykadamov took care of Xian and provided him with the comfort of a home.

* Part of the speech at Nazarbayev University, Astana, Kazakhstan.

It was in Almaty that Xian composed his famous works: *Liberation of the Nation, Sacred War* and *Red All over the River.* He also wrote the symphony *Amangeldy* based on the exploits of the Kazakh national hero. These works served as a rallying call to fight Fascism and proved immensely popular with the local people.

Throughout the millennia, the peoples of various countries along the ancient Silk Road have written a chapter of friendship that has been passed on to this very day. More than 2,000 years of exchanges demonstrate that on the basis of unity, mutual trust, equality, inclusiveness, mutual learning and mutually beneficial cooperation, countries of different races, beliefs and cultural backgrounds are fully able to share peace and development. This is the valuable inspiration we have drawn from the ancient Silk Road.

Over the past 20 years, the relations between China and Eurasian countries have grown rapidly, and the ancient Silk Road has gained new vitality. In a new way, it is lifting the mutually beneficial cooperation between China and Eurasian countries to a fresh height.

A neighbor is better than a distant relative. China and Central Asian countries are close and friendly neighbors. China values its friendship and cooperation with these countries, and takes improving these relations as a foreign policy priority.

China's relations with the Central Asian countries now face a golden opportunity of growth. We hope to work with these countries to strengthen trust, friendship and cooperation, and promote common development and prosperity to the benefit of all our peoples.

– We should pass on our friendship from generation to generation and remain good neighbors living in harmony. China is committed to peaceful development and an independent foreign policy of peace. We respect the development paths and domestic and foreign policies pursued independently by the people of every country. We will never interfere in the internal affairs of Central Asian countries. We do not seek to dominate regional affairs or establish any sphere of influence. We stand ready to enhance consultation and coordination with Russia and all Central Asian countries to sustain harmony in our region.

– We should firmly support and trust each other and be sincere and good friends. Rendering each other firm support on major issues concerning core interests such as sovereignty, territorial integrity, security and stability underlies China's strategic partnership with the Central Asian countries. We will reinforce trust and cooperation with the Central Asian countries bilaterally and within the framework of the Shanghai Cooperation Organization (SCO)[2] to combat the "three forces" of terrorism, separatism and extremism as well as drug trafficking and organized transnational crimes, and this will create a favorable environment for promoting economic development and improving the wellbeing of the people in this region.

– We should vigorously enhance practical cooperation and be good partners of mutually beneficial cooperation. Both China and the Central Asian countries are at a crucial stage of development, and we face unprecedented opportunities and challenges. We have all set medium- to long-term development goals based on our national conditions. Our strategic goals are the same – to ensure sustainable and stable economic development, build a prosperous and strong nation and achieve national revitalization. Therefore, we need to enhance practical cooperation across the board, use our good political relations, geographical proximity and economic complementarities to boost sustainable growth, and build a community of shared interests and mutual benefit.

– We should expand regional cooperation with a more open mind and broader vision, and achieve joint progress. Global economic integration is accelerating, and regional cooperation is booming. The Eurasian region has a number of regional cooperation organizations. The members and observers of the Eurasian Economic Community (EAEC) and the SCO are from Eurasia, South Asia and West Asia. By intensifying cooperation between the SCO and the EAEC, we will create further space for development.

To forge closer economic ties, deepen cooperation and expand development space in the Eurasian region, we should take an innovative approach and jointly build an economic belt along the Silk Road. This will be a great undertaking benefitting the people of all countries along the routes. To turn this vision into reality, we may start in specific areas and connect them over time to cover the whole region.

First, we need to step up policy consultation. Countries should have full discussions on development strategies and policies, adopt plans and measures for advancing regional cooperation through consultation in the spirit of seeking common ground while setting aside differences, and give the policy and legal "green light" to regional economic integration.

Second, we need to improve road connections. The SCO is working on an agreement on transport facilitation. Its early signing and implementation will open up a major transport route connecting the Pacific and the Baltic. On this basis, we can actively discuss the best way to improve cross-border transport infrastructure and work towards a transport network connecting East Asia, West Asia and South Asia to facilitate economic development and travel in the region.

Third, we need to promote unimpeded trade. The envisaged economic belt along the Silk Road is inhabited by nearly three billion people and it represents the biggest market in the world, with enormous, unparalleled potential for trade and investment cooperation between the countries involved. We should discuss a proper arrangement for trade and investment facilitation, remove trade barriers, reduce trade and investment costs, increase the speed and raise the quality of regional economic flows and achieve mutually beneficial progress in the region.

Fourth, we need to enhance monetary circulation. China and Russia already have sound cooperation on settling trade in local currencies, and have made good progress and yielded rich experience in this respect. This good practice can be shared with others in the region. If our region can realize local currency convertibility and settlement under the current and capital accounts, it will significantly lower circulation cost, increase our ability to fend off financial risks, and make our region more competitive internationally.

Fifth, we need to increase understanding between our peoples. Friendship between peoples is the key to good relations between states. To pursue productive cooperation in the above-mentioned areas, we need the support of our peoples. We should encourage more friendly exchanges between our peoples to enhance mutual understanding and traditional friendship, and build strong public support and a solid social foundation for regional cooperation.

Notes

[1] Xian Xinghai (1905-1945) was a Chinese musician.

[2] The Shanghai Cooperation Organization (SCO) is a permanent intergovernmental international organization established on June 15, 2001, in Shanghai (China) by six countries – China, Russia, Kazakhstan, Kyrgyzstan, Tajikistan and Uzbekistan. Its prototype was the Shanghai Five Mechanism. The main goals of the SCO are strengthening mutual confidence and good neighborly relations among the member countries; promoting effective cooperation in politics, trade and economy, science and technology, and culture as well as education, energy, transportation, tourism, environmental protection and other fields; making joint efforts to maintain and ensure peace, security and stability in the region; and moving towards the establishment of a new, democratic, just and rational political and economic international order. The heads of state meet once every year, and the heads of government meet at fixed time, alternatively in each of the member states.

Work Together to Build a
21st-Century Maritime Silk Road*

October 3, 2013

China and the ASEAN countries are close neighbors sharing kinship. This year marks the tenth anniversary of the China-ASEAN strategic partnership, and our relationship is at a new historical starting point.

China places great importance on Indonesia's standing and influence in ASEAN. We wish to work with Indonesia and other ASEAN countries to ensure that China and ASEAN are good neighbors, good friends and good partners who share prosperity and security and stick together through thick and thin. Through our joint efforts, we can build a close China-ASEAN community of shared future so as to bring more benefits to both China and ASEAN and to the people in the region.

To achieve this goal, we should take the following steps:

First, build trust and good-neighborly ties. Trust is the very foundation of both interpersonal and state-to-state relations. China is committed to forging a relationship with the ASEAN countries featuring sincerity, friendship, and enhanced mutual political and strategic trust.

There is no one-size-fits-all development model in the world or an unchanging development path. Both the Chinese people and the people of the ASEAN countries have embraced change and innovation with an open mind, and searched and found, in a pioneering and enterprising spirit, development paths in keeping with their specific national conditions that conform to the trend of the times. These

* Part of the speech at the People's Representative Council of Indonesia.

efforts have opened up a broad prospect for their economic and social development.

We should each respect the other's right to independently choose social system and development path as well as the right to explore and pursue new ways of economic and social development, and improve its people's lives. We should have full confidence in each other's strategic choice, support each other on issues of major concern, and never deviate from the general goal of China-ASEAN strategic cooperation.

China is ready to discuss with the ASEAN countries the conclusion of a treaty of good-neighborliness, friendship and cooperation in a joint effort to build good-neighborly relations. China will continue to support ASEAN in enhancing its strength, building the ASEAN community, and playing a central role in regional cooperation.

Second, work for mutually beneficial cooperation. As a Chinese saying goes, "The interests to be considered should be the interests of all."[1] China is ready to open its door wider to the ASEAN countries on the basis of equality and mutual benefit and enable the latter to gain more from China's development. China is prepared to upgrade the China-ASEAN Free Trade Area and increase two-way trade to US$1 trillion-worth by 2020.

China is committed to enhancing its connections with the ASEAN countries. China proposes the establishment of an Asian infrastructure investment bank to support the ASEAN countries and other developing countries in our region to strengthen links in infrastructural development.

Southeast Asia has since ancient times been an important hub along the ancient Maritime Silk Road. China will strengthen maritime cooperation with the ASEAN countries, and the China-ASEAN Maritime Cooperation Fund set up by the Chinese government should be used to develop maritime partnership in a joint effort to build the Maritime Silk Road of the 21st century. China is ready to expand its practical cooperation with the ASEAN countries across the board to meet each other's needs and complement each other's strengths. This will enable us to jointly seize opportunities and meet challenges in the interest of common development and prosperity.

Third, stand together and assist each other. China and the ASEAN countries are intimate partners, and we share the responsibility for regional peace and stability. In the past, the people of China and the ASEAN countries stood together in the fight to take our destiny back into our own hands. In recent years, our peoples have stood side by side and forged strong synergy in responding to the Asian financial crisis and the international financial crisis, and in responding to the Indian Ocean tsunami and China's Wenchuan earthquake.

We should cast away the Cold War mentality, champion the new thinking of comprehensive security, common security and cooperative security, and jointly uphold peace and stability in our region. We should have deeper cooperation in disaster prevention and relief, cyber security, combating cross-border crimes and joint law enforcement to create a more peaceful, tranquil and amicable home for the people of the region.

China is ready to work with the ASEAN countries to improve the China-ASEAN defense ministers' meeting mechanism and hold regular dialogues on regional security issues.

With regard to differences and disputes between China and some Southeast Asian countries on territorial sovereignty and maritime rights and interests, peaceful solutions should be sought, and differences and disputes should be properly handled through equality-based dialogue and friendly consultation in the overall interests of bilateral ties and regional stability.

Fourth, enhance mutual understanding and friendship. As a Chinese saying goes, "A tall tree grows from a small seedling; and the building of a nine-story tower starts with the first shovel of earth."[2] To ensure that the tree of China-ASEAN friendship remains evergreen, the soil of social support for our relations should be fertile. Last year saw 15 million people traveling between China and the ASEAN countries, and there are over 1,000 flights between the two sides each week now. Increased interactions have nurtured a deeper bond between us and made our people feel ever-closer to each other.

We should encourage more friendly exchanges between the young people, think tanks, parliaments, NGOs and civil organizations of the two sides, which will generate further intellectual support for the growth of China-ASEAN relations and help increase the mutual understanding and friendship between our peoples. China is ready to send more volunteers to the ASEAN countries to support their development in the cultural, educational, health and medical fields. China proposes to designate 2014 as the year of China-ASEAN cultural exchanges. China will provide the ASEAN countries with 15,000 government scholarships in the coming three to five years.

Fifth, be open and inclusive. The sea is vast because it is fed by all rivers. In the long course of human history, the people of China and the ASEAN countries have created splendid and great civilizations renowned throughout the world. Ours is a diversified region where various civilizations have assimilated and interacted with one another, and this has provided an important cultural foundation for the people of China and the ASEAN countries to gain from each other's experience.

We should draw on the experience gained by other regions in development, and welcome countries outside the region to play a constructive role in promoting development and stability in the region. The outside countries, on their part, should respect the diversity of our region and do their part to facilitate its development and stability. The China-ASEAN community of shared future is closely linked with the ASEAN community and the East Asian community. The two sides need to give full rein to our respective strength to enhance diversity, harmony, inclusiveness and common progress in our region for the benefit of both our people and the people outside the region.

An increasingly cohesive China-ASEAN community of shared future conforms to the trend of the times of seeking peace, development, cooperation and mutual benefit and meets the common interests of the people of Asia and the rest of the world. This gives it a broad space and huge potential for growth.

Notes

[1] A scroll hand-written by Yu Yu-jen (1879-1964), an educator, scholar, calligrapher and politician as well as one of the founders of the Kuomintang of China. It was a gift to Chiang Ching-kuo (1910-1988), former chairman of the Kuomintang of China.

[2] *Lao Zi* or *Dao De Jing*.

Diplomacy with Neighboring Countries Characterized by Friendship, Sincerity, Reciprocity and Inclusiveness*

October 24, 2013

Good diplomacy with neighboring countries is a requirement for realizing the Two Centenary Goals, and the Chinese Dream of the rejuvenation of the Chinese nation. We need to work harder to promote our diplomacy with neighboring countries, strive for a sound regional environment for our development, apply our own development for the benefit of neighboring countries, and achieve common development with them.

Following the founding of the PRC in 1949, the Party's first generation of collective central leadership under Comrade Mao Zedong, the second generation under Comrade Deng Xiaoping, the third generation under Comrade Jiang Zemin, and the CPC Central Committee with Comrade Hu Jintao as general secretary, all attached high importance to diplomacy with neighboring countries. They developed important strategic ideas and guiding policies, created a sound environment, and laid a solid foundation for future diplomatic work. After the 18th National Congress, committed to ensuring continuity and stability in China's foreign policy, the CPC Central Committee defined, planned, and carried out a series of major diplomatic initiatives, paying particular attention to neighboring countries which are important to our development and diplomatic strategy.

Regions around our borders are strategically significant to our country in terms of geography, the environment, and relationships.

---

* Main points of the speech at a seminar on the work of neighborhood diplomacy.

When dealing with neighboring countries and related issues, we need a multi-dimensional perspective that extends beyond the immediate confines of time and space. Reviewing the situation, we can see that great changes have taken place in the general environment and in relationships with our neighbors. Our economic and trade ties with neighboring countries are closer, with unprecedented levels of exchange between them and us. Current circumstances demand that we keep pace with the times and be ever more active in blueprinting diplomatic strategies and undertaking diplomatic work with our neighbors.

China and its neighbors are full of vigor and vitality, and show obvious strengths in development and high potential. The region is stable on the whole, and most of our neighbors maintain an amicable relationship geared towards mutual benefit and cooperation with China. We must appreciate the situation to the full, devise appropriate strategies, and plan carefully, to perform better in our diplomatic exchanges with our neighbors.

China's diplomacy in this area is driven by and must serve the Two Centenary Goals and our national rejuvenation. To achieve these strategic aims, we must create and cement friendly relations and further mutually beneficial cooperation with neighboring countries, maintain and make the best use of the strategic opportunities we now enjoy, and safeguard China's state sovereignty, national security, and development interests. Together we must strive to build more amicable political relationships and closer economic ties, to further security cooperation and to encourage more cultural and people-to-people exchanges with neighboring countries.

China's basic policy of diplomacy with neighboring countries is to treat them as friends and partners, to make them feel secure and to support their development. This policy is characterized by friendship, sincerity, reciprocity and inclusiveness. Friendship is a consistent principle of China's diplomacy with its neighbors. In adherence to this principle, we need to help neighbors in times of crisis, treat them as equals, visit them frequently, and take actions that will win us support and friendship.

In response, we hope that neighboring countries will be well inclined towards us, and we hope that China will have a stronger affinity with them, and that our appeal and our influence will grow. We must treat neighbors with sincerity and cultivate them as friends and partners. We should cooperate with our neighbors on the basis of reciprocity, create a closer network of common interests, and better integrate China's interests with theirs, so that they can benefit from China's development and China can benefit and gain support from theirs. We should advocate inclusiveness, stressing that there is enough room in the Asia Pacific region for all countries to develop, and promoting regional cooperation with an open mind and enthusiasm. We must embrace and practice these ideas, so that they will become the shared beliefs and norms of conduct for the whole region.

As circumstances evolve, diplomacy with neighboring countries requires us to analyze and deal with issues strategically, improve our capabilities in planning and implementation, and promote every aspect of this diplomacy. We must also do everything possible to safeguard peace and stability in the region. The path of peaceful development is the Party's strategic choice, in line with the times and aligned with the fundamental interests of the country. A major aim of this diplomacy is peace and stability in the region.

We must make every effort to achieve mutually beneficial reciprocity. We have to make overall plans for the use of our resources in the areas of economy, trade, science and technology, and finance. We must take advantage of our comparative strengths, accurately identify strategic points of convergence for mutually beneficial cooperation with neighbors, and take an active part in regional economic cooperation. We should work with our neighbors to speed up connection of infrastructure between China and our neighboring countries, and establish a Silk Road Economic Belt and a Maritime Silk Road geared towards the demands of the 21st century. We should accelerate the pace of implementation of the strategy of free trade zones with our neighboring countries as the base, expand cooperation in trade and investment, and create a new pattern of regional economic integration.

We need to further advance regional financial cooperation, prepare for and establish an Asian Infrastructure Investment Bank, and improve the regional financial security network. We should open the border areas more quickly and reinforce reciprocal cooperation between the border areas of China and neighboring countries.

We must make efforts to promote regional security cooperation, which is needed by both China and our neighboring countries. A new outlook on security is required that features mutual trust and reciprocity, based on equality and cooperation. We must develop a comprehensive security strategy with neighboring countries, actively participate in regional and sub-regional security initiatives, push forward cooperation and enhance mutual trust.

We must strengthen publicity work, public diplomacy, people-to-people and cultural exchanges with neighboring countries, and consolidate and expand the social and public basis for the long-term development of our relationships with them. Diplomatic relations rely on the bonds between peoples. We should promote exchanges in all respects, including tourism, science, education and regional cooperation, to make friends in a broad range of sectors. We should clearly present our domestic and foreign policies to the outside world, explain China in an acceptable way, speak out and make ourselves heard, interpret the Chinese Dream from the perspective of our neighbors and their aspirations for a better life and regional prosperity, and let a sense of common future take root.

Policies and strategies are the lifelines of the Party, and of our diplomatic work as well. To do good diplomatic work, we must keep our eye on the situation both at home and abroad. Our domestic focus is to realize the Two Centenary Goals and the Chinese Dream; our international objectives are to strive for favorable external conditions for China's reform, development and stability, to safeguard state sovereignty, security and development interests, and to maintain world peace and stability, and promote common development. We should seek common ground and find converging interests, stick to the sound values of justice and benefit, hold to principles that we can act upon, cherish friendship and righteousness, and offer any assistance to developing countries that is within our means. For best results we need to promote reform and innovation in diplomatic work and strengthen the planning of our diplomatic activities. To achieve greater progress we should build a general framework to coordinate diplomatic work, weigh every relevant factor, and give full play to every department involved.

Diplomatic work with neighboring countries is arduous and demanding. Those charged with this responsibility must have a sense of mission and urgency. They must bear in mind the purpose of this work, improve their competence and working practices, devote themselves to the task, be bold in assuming responsibilities and making innovations, and engage in this work with drive and enthusiasm.

Cooperation with
Developing Countries

Be Trustworthy Friends and
Sincere Partners Forever[*]

March 25, 2013

Your Excellency President Jakaya Mrisho Kikwete,
Ladies and gentlemen,
Dear friends,

Habari[1]! *Habari*! It both gives me great pleasure and fills me with warmth to meet so many friends here at the Julius Nyerere International Convention Center.

This is my first visit to Africa as the Chinese president but my sixth visit to the African continent. The moment I set foot on this beautiful land, I was overwhelmed by the friendship of the Tanzanian people towards the Chinese people. The government and people of Tanzania held a special and grand welcoming ceremony for me. It shows not only the importance you accord to me and my delegation, but also the profound traditional friendship between the two countries and two peoples.

Let me begin by extending, on behalf of the Chinese government and people and in my own name, warm greetings and best wishes to all the friends present today and to the brotherly people of Tanzania and across Africa. I also wish to thank you, President Kikwete, and the Tanzanian government for your warm hospitality.

Tanzania is a cradle of mankind. The Tanzanian people have a glorious tradition, and you have made a substantial contribution to the victory of the African people's struggles for independence and their fights against apartheid.

* Speech at the Julius Nyerere International Convention Center in Dar es Salaam, Tanzania.

Under the leadership of President Kikwete, Tanzania has maintained political stability, made big strides in development, and played an important role in African and international affairs. The Chinese people rejoice at what you have achieved and sincerely wish the brotherly people of Tanzania new and still greater success.

When I visit Africa, I am always struck by two things. One is its continuous progress. Each time I come to Africa, I am deeply impressed by new progress in development, which is most encouraging. The other is the warmth of the African people. The goodwill of the African people towards the Chinese people is as warm and unforgettable as the sunshine in Africa.

As an African saying goes, "A river runs deep because of its source." The friendly exchanges between China and Africa date back a long time. In the 1950s and 60s, the first-generation leaders of the PRC – Mao Zedong, Zhou Enlai[2] and others – and African statesmen of the older generation ushered China-Africa relations into a new era. Since then, the Chinese and African peoples have supported and cooperated with each other in our respective endeavors to fight against colonialism and imperialism and win independence and liberation, and in the pursuit of development and national renewal. A fraternal bond of shared future has been forged between us.

Today, thanks to the concerted efforts of both sides, China-Africa relations are on a fast track of all-round development. We have set up the Forum on China-Africa Cooperation[3] and established a new type of strategic partnership. Our cooperation in various fields has delivered many gains. In 2012, China-Africa trade approached US$200 billion-worth. Over 1.5 million mutual visits were made between the two sides. China's cumulative direct investment in Africa topped US$15 billion. This year marks the 50th anniversary of the dispatch of Chinese medical teams to Africa. In the past five decades, 18,000 Chinese medical personnel have worked in Africa, providing medical care and treatment to 250 million local patients.

The African people, on their part, have given full support and selfless help to the Chinese people. When the 2008 Beijing Olympic torch relay came to Dar es Salaam, the Tanzanian people welcomed the Olympic flame with song and dance, as if celebrating their own festival. This jubilant occasion is etched in the memory of the Chinese people.

In the wake of the devastating earthquake in Wenchuan, African countries rushed to China's assistance. An African country, with a population of fewer than two million and not well-off itself, made a generous donation of two million Euros to the quake area – about one Euro per person! This outpouring of compassion warmed our hearts.

In regional and international affairs, China and Africa have stepped up coordination and collaboration, and successfully upheld the common interests of developing countries. Friendship and cooperation between the Chinese and African peoples have become a symbol of China-Africa relations and are well regarded by the international community.

Our joint endeavors and the fruitful results therefrom over the past five decades have laid a solid groundwork and provided valuable experience for furthering China-Africa relations.

– A review of this period of history shows that China-Africa relations have not grown to this stage overnight, nor are they a gift from some third party. Rather, they have been nurtured and built, step by step, by our two sides over the years as we met challenges and faced difficulties together. As a Chinese saying goes, "When we drink water from the well, we should not forget those who dug it." We will always honor the memory of all those pioneers who devoted themselves to building China-Africa relations. As we move ahead, we can always draw strength from history.

– A review of this period of history shows that China and Africa have always shared a common destiny. Similar historical experience, common development tasks and shared strategic interests have bound us together. We both view the other's development as our own opportunity, and we both seek to promote mutual development and prosperity through closer cooperation.

– A review of this period of history shows that the defining features of China-Africa relations are sincerity, friendship, mutual respect, equality, mutual benefit and common development. We get along well and treat each other as equals. Neither side seeks to impose its will on the other. China has done its best to help Africa's development. Yet China is always grateful to African countries and peoples for their firm support and selfless help over the years. On issues involving the core interests of either side, we have taken a clear position and given unequivocal support to each other.

– And a review of this period of history shows that if we are to maintain the strong vitality of China-Africa relations, we must keep pace with the times and forge ahead in an innovative and enterprising spirit. Over the past 50 years, at every crucial juncture of China-Africa relations, both sides were able to approach these relations with vision, identify new converging interests and growth areas for cooperation, and bring bilateral relations to new heights. Such an enterprising spirit of "cutting a way through when confronted by mountains and building a bridge when blocked by a river" is crucial for steadily upgrading China-Africa cooperation.

Ladies and gentlemen,

China-Africa relations, enjoying a favorable international and domestic environment as well as popular support, stand at a new historical starting point. Africa, a continent of hope and promise, has become one of the fastest-growing regions in the world and is forging ahead like a galloping African lion. China, on its part, continues to enjoy a sound development momentum. The foundation of China-Africa cooperation is more solid, and our cooperation mechanisms have been further improved. Advancing China-Africa cooperation represents the trend of the times and the will of our peoples.

This is what I want to tell you, my dear friends: In this new era, China-Africa relations have become more important with increasing common interests, instead of less important with fewer common interests. China will intensify, not weaken, its efforts to develop relations with Africa.

First, we will continue to treat our African friends with sincerity. Nothing is more valuable than true friends. The China-Africa traditional friendship is what we cherish dearly. Unity and cooperation with African countries have always been an important foundation of China's foreign policy. This will never change, even should China grow stronger and enjoy a higher international standing. China believes in equality among all countries, big or small, strong or weak, rich or poor. China upholds justice and opposes the practice of the big bullying the small, the strong lording over the weak, and the rich oppressing the poor, just as it opposes interference in others' internal affairs. China and Africa will continue to support each other on issues involving their core interests and major concerns. China will continue to firmly support Africa's just position on regional and international affairs, and uphold the common interests of developing countries. China will continue to firmly support Africa in its endeavors to independently resolve African issues, and make a greater contribution to peace and security in Africa.

There is no one-size-fits-all development model in the world. The diversity of civilizations and development models should be respected by all. China will continue to firmly support African countries in their quest for development paths that suit their national conditions and increase exchanges of experience in governance with African countries. This will enable us to draw on each other's time-honored civilizations and development practices, and better promote the common development and prosperity of China and Africa.

To all Chinese, "harmony in the family leads to success in everything." Africa is a big family of shared destiny. This year marks the 50th anniversary of the founding of the Organization of African Unity – a milestone in the African people's pursuit of greater strength through unity. We sincerely hope that Africa will make bigger strides in seeking strength from unity and achieve new success in peace and development, and we will firmly support Africa in this endeavor.

China is dedicated to developing strong ties with Africa. We also hope to see better relations between other countries and Africa.

Africa belongs to the African people. In promoting relations with Africa, all countries should respect Africa's dignity and independence.

Second, we seek to deliver real outcomes in conducting cooperation with Africa. China both champions and applies mutually beneficial cooperation with Africa. China views its own development as closely connected with that of Africa and the interests of the Chinese people as closely connected with those of the African people. China shares development opportunities with Africa. China sincerely hopes to see faster development in Africa and a better life for the African people. While pursuing its own development, China has provided support and assistance to African friends to the best of our ability. In recent years, in particular, China has increased assistance to and cooperation with Africa. We will honor every commitment we have made to Africa in both letter and spirit.

China will continue to expand investment and financing cooperation with Africa, follow through on the commitment of providing a US$20 billion credit line to Africa from 2013 to 2015, implement the partnership on transnational and trans-regional infrastructural development, enhance mutually beneficial cooperation in agriculture and manufacturing, and help Africa exploit its wealth of resources, and achieve independent and sustainable development.

As the saying goes, "It is more helpful to teach people how to fish than to just give them fish." China will actively implement the "African Talent Program," train 30,000 African professionals in various areas, provide 18,000 government scholarships to Africa between 2013 and 2015, and increase technology transfer and experience sharing with Africa.

As its own economy and strength increase, China will continue to provide due assistance to Africa with no political strings attached.

Third, we will continue to build a close bond of friendship with Africa. The Chinese and African peoples share a natural feeling of affinity towards each other. We Chinese believe that "the pleasure of life lies in having bosom friends." Then how can China and Africa become bosom friends? I believe that in-depth dialogue and concrete action are the way to strike a chord in our hearts.

Our two peoples form the foundation and lifeline of China-Africa relations. Therefore, the growth of our relations should be more people-oriented. In recent years, growing China-Africa relations have brought our peoples closer to each other than ever before. Some African performers have become popular stars in China. *Great Life of a Wife*, a Chinese TV series about how life unfolds in ordinary Chinese families, has become quite a hit in Tanzania.

Let me tell you a story about a young Chinese couple. When they were children, they got to know about Africa from Chinese TV programs and have since been captivated by this continent. Later, they got married and decided to make Tanzania their honeymoon destination. So, on their first Valentine's Day after the wedding, they came here on a visit. They were overwhelmed by the hospitality and friendship of the local people and the magnificent savanna of Serengeti. After the couple returned to China, they posted what they had experienced in Tanzania on their blog, which was visited tens of thousands of times and received several hundred comments. This is what they wrote on their blog, "We have fallen head over heels in love with Africa, and our hearts will forever be with this fascinating land." This story highlights the natural affinity between the Chinese and African peoples. As long as we keep expanding people-to-people exchanges, friendship between our peoples will strike deep roots and flourish.

We will further boost people-to-people and cultural exchanges between China and Africa so as to enhance mutual understanding and perception, and increase public support for China-Africa friendship. To promote China-Africa relations is a cause for the future, an undertaking that calls for unremitting efforts of young people in China and Africa from generation to generation. Both sides should vigorously promote youth exchanges so that China-Africa friendship will be full of vigor and vitality.

Fourth, we will resolve problems that may occur in our cooperation with good faith. China and Africa are both experiencing rapid development and each needs to learn more about the other. China will deal with new developments and new problems confronting our relations with sincerity. We should handle such problems in a spirit of mutual respect and mutually beneficial cooperation.

I am convinced that there will always be more opportunities than challenges and more solutions than difficulties. Together with the African countries, China has taken and will continue to take concrete measures to resolve problems in our economic cooperation and trade, and we will make sure that Africa gains more from its cooperation with China. At the same time, we sincerely hope that African countries will help Chinese enterprises and businessmen in pursuing cooperation in Africa.

Ladies and gentlemen,

Since the founding of the PRC more than 60 years ago, and particularly since the introduction of the reform and opening-up policy more than 30 years ago, the CPC has led the Chinese people in opening a path of socialism with Chinese characteristics. China has made historic progress in its development, becoming the second largest economy in the world. China's comprehensive national strength has grown significantly, and our people's living standards have improved markedly. It only took China, a country of over 1.3 billion people, a few decades to travel a journey that took developed countries several centuries to cover. One can easily imagine how many challenges and difficulties China encountered in these years.

At present, China remains a populous country with a weak economic foundation and uneven development. Our aggregate GDP is quite large. However, when divided by 1.3 billion, China's per capita GDP is only around the 90th place in the world. Some 128 million Chinese are still living below the poverty line set by the United Nations. To provide a decent life for the over 1.3 billion people, we still have a long way to go, and persistent and strenuous efforts are called for. As China continues to develop, its people will surely achieve a better life. However, no matter how strong it may grow, China will always see in Africa a tried and tested friend.

Ladies and gentlemen,

China cannot develop in isolation from the rest of the world or Africa. On their part, both the rest of the world and Africa also need China to seek prosperity and stability. Though there is a broad ocean between us, China and Africa share a strong empathy. We are bound not only by profound traditional friendship and closely-linked interests, but also by the dreams we each have.

More than 1.3 billion Chinese are working hard to realize the Chinese Dream of great national renewal, and more than one billion Africans are striving to realize the African dream of gaining strength through unity and achieving development and rejuvenation. We Chinese and Africans should enhance unity, cooperation, mutual support and assistance so as to fulfill our dreams. We should also work with the international community to realize the global dream of enduring peace and common prosperity, and make a new and even greater contribution to the noble cause of peace and development of mankind.

Asantenisana[4]!

Notes

[1] *Habari*, Swahili, meaning "Hello."

[2] Zhou Enlai (1898-1976) was a Marxist, Chinese proletarian revolutionary, statesman, military strategist and diplomat, as well as one of the major leaders of the Communist Party of China and the People's Republic of China, and co-founder of the Chinese People's Liberation Army.

[3] The Forum on China-Africa Cooperation is a new platform for collective dialogues and cooperation between China and African countries – an effective mechanism to promote South-South cooperation. The First Ministerial Conference was held in October 2000 in Beijing. The Beijing Summit and the Third Ministerial Conference was held in November 2006, also in Beijing, attended by Chinese leaders and 48 heads of state and government and representatives from Africa. The Beijing Summit passed the Declaration of the Beijing Summit of the Forum on China-Africa Cooperation and Forum on China-Africa Cooperation – Beijing Action Plan (2007-2009), confirming a new type of strategic partnership between China and Africa.

[4] *Asantenisana*, Swahili, meaning "Thank you."

Forge a Stronger Partnership Between China and Latin America and the Caribbean[*]

June 5, 2013

Once again, visiting Latin America, a vibrant and promising continent, I am all the more convinced that with its rich natural endowment, this continent is embracing another golden period of development. We believe that a more prosperous Latin America and the Caribbean will benefit both the rest of the world and China.

Our relations with this area have now entered a period of opportunity for rapid growth. We should be visionary in approach, keep abreast of the times, build on traditional friendship, enhance exchanges in all areas, and upgrade cooperation. In so doing, we can forge a stronger partnership of comprehensive cooperation featuring equality, mutual benefit and common development.

Politically, we should treat each other as sincere friends, and continue to show understanding and support for each other on issues involving the core interests and major concerns of both sides.

Economically, we should seize opportunities created by the shift of growth model on both sides, fully tap cooperation potential, create new cooperation modalities, expand converging interests and foster an enduring, stable and mutually beneficial business partnership.

Culturally, we should enhance inter-civilizational dialogue and cultural exchanges. As a Chinese saying goes, "One should value not only one's own culture, but also the cultures of others, and this will contribute to the flourishing of all cultures."[1] I hope we will develop a mutually reinforcing and exemplary relationship of harmony between different civilizations.

---

* Part of the speech at the Senate of Mexico, Mexico City, Mexico.

I hope that we will work together to launch the Forum of China-Latin America and the Caribbean Cooperation at an early date. We should give full rein to our respective strengths, build a strong partnership of comprehensive cooperation, and thus contribute more to stability and prosperity in the Asia Pacific region.

As a Chinese proverb goes, "Just as distance tests a horse's strength, time will show a person's sincerity." The growth of China-Latin America and the Caribbean relations has proved and will continue to prove that ours is an open, inclusive, mutually beneficial and cooperative relationship. We are convinced that a stronger partnership of comprehensive cooperation will boost the development of both sides as well as the peace, stability and prosperity of our respective regions and the world as a whole.

Notes

[1] Fei Xiaotong: *Appreciating Others' Cultures and Human Civilizations*, Chinese ed., Inner Mongolia People's Publishing House, Hohhot, 2009, p. 262. Fei Xiaotong (1910-2005) was a Chinese sociologist, anthropologist and social activist. He served as vice chairman of the Standing Committee of the National People's Congress and vice chairman of the Chinese People's Political Consultative Conference.

Promote the Silk Road Spirit,
Strengthen China-Arab Cooperation*

June 5, 2014

Your Excellency Prime Minister Jaber,
Secretary-General El Araby of the League of Arab States,
Heads of delegations,
Ladies and gentlemen,
Dear friends,

Al Salam aleikum[1]! Good morning! I am very happy today to get together with our Arab friends and discuss the development of the China-Arab States Cooperation Forum (CASCF)[2] and China-Arab relations. Let me begin by extending, on behalf of the Chinese government and our people and in my own name, a warm welcome to all the guests, and let me offer my hearty congratulations on the convening of the sixth ministerial conference of the CASCF!

Arab friends always feel like old friends to me. This is attributable both to the warm and sincere attitude with which we treat each other, and to the long history of exchanges between the Chinese and Arab peoples.

Looking back on the history of exchanges between the Chinese and Arab peoples, we immediately think of the land Silk Road and the maritime spice route. Our ancestors "crossed the desert for months on end on post-horses,"[3] and "sailed the oceans day and night,"[4] putting themselves at the forefront of friendly exchanges between different nations in the ancient world.

---

* Speech at the opening ceremony of the Sixth Ministerial Conference of the China-Arab States Cooperation Forum.

Gan Ying[5], Zheng He, and Ibn Battuta[6] were goodwill envoys for China-Arab exchanges whom we still remember today. It was by way of the Silk Road that China's four great inventions – paper-making, gunpowder, printing, and the compass – were transmitted via the Arab region to Europe, and it was also by way of the Silk Road that the Arabs' astronomy, calendrical system, and medicines were introduced to China, marking an important chapter in the history of exchanges and mutual learning between civilizations.

For hundreds of years the spirit embodied by the Silk Road, namely peace and cooperation, openness and inclusiveness, mutual learning, and mutual benefit, has passed down through the generations. The Chinese and Arab peoples have supported each other in maintaining national dignity and safeguarding state sovereignty, helped each other in exploring development and achieving national rejuvenation, and learned from each other in encouraging people-to-people and cultural exchanges and revitalizing national culture.

We will not forget the promise to support the cause of the Palestinian people that China made to the Arab states – with which we had not yet established diplomatic relations – at the Bandung Conference[7] 60 years ago. Nor will we forget the votes cast over 40 years ago by 13 Arab states, together with our African friends, for the PRC to regain its UN seat. We will not forget the 10,000 Chinese doctors who worked to save lives in the Arab states. Nor will we forget the most generous aid China received from our Arab brothers after the massive Wenchuan earthquake.

Ladies and gentlemen, dear friends,

The next decade will be a crucial period for the development of both China and the Arab states. China has entered a decisive phase in its drive to complete the building of a moderately prosperous society in all respects, and the fulfillment of this goal represents a crucial step towards the Chinese Dream of national rejuvenation. To do so, we have made overall plans for driving our reform to a deeper level. A key focus of this drive is to develop all-round international cooperation within an open economic system of quality and vitality, and to expand our common interests with various countries and regions in pursuit of mutual benefit. The Middle East is in a phase of unprecedented change, and the Arab states are making efforts to seek reform in their own way. The challenge of achieving national renewal calls on us to carry forward the Silk Road spirit, bolster development and cooperation, and constantly reinforce a strategic China-Arab relationship of comprehensive cooperation and common development.

To promote the Silk Road spirit, we need to boost mutual learning between civilizations. There is no such thing as a good or a bad civilization. Rather, different civilizations are enriched through exchange. As a Chinese philosopher said, "The matching of different colors leads to greater beauty, and the combination of different musical instruments creates harmony and peace."[8] China and the Arab states have always viewed each other with an open and inclusive attitude, and engaged in dialogues and exchanges rather than conflict and confrontation. We have set a good example of harmonious coexistence between countries with different social systems, beliefs, and cultural traditions. China will never falter in its support for the Arab states in safeguarding their national cultural traditions, and will oppose all discrimination and prejudice against any ethnic groups and religions. We should work together to advocate tolerance towards different civilizations, and prevent extremist forces and ideas from creating division between us.

To promote the Silk Road spirit, we need to respect each other's choice of development path. "People don't need to wear the same shoes; they should find what suit their feet. Governments don't have to adopt the same model of governance; they should find what benefits their people."[9] Whether the path of a country is the right one is a matter to be decided by its people. Just as we do not expect all flowers to be violets, we cannot demand that countries with diverse cultural traditions, historical experiences, and contemporary national conditions should adopt the same development mode. That would make for a dull world. The Arab states are making their own efforts to explore their own development paths. We are willing to share our experience of governance with our Arab friends, so that each can draw on the wisdom of the other's time-honored civilization and development mode.

To promote the Silk Road spirit, we need to focus on mutually beneficial cooperation. What China pursues is common development, which means we are aiming for a better life for the Chinese people and for the peoples of other countries. In the next five years, China's imports will surpass US$10 trillion-worth, and our outward FDI will surpass US$500 billion. In 2013, China's imports from the Arab states were worth US$140 billion, accounting for only 7 percent of the annual US$2 trillion in imported goods that China plans for the years ahead; and China's outward FDI to the Arab states was US$2.2 billion, accounting for only 2.2 percent of the US$100 billion in annual outward FDI that China plans for the years ahead. These facts represent an indicator of great potential and opportunity. China is happy to connect its own development with the development of the Arab states, and to support them in promoting employment, industrialization and economic growth.

To promote the Silk Road spirit, we need to advocate dialogue and peace. China firmly supports the Middle East peace process and the establishment of an independent State of Palestine, with full sovereignty, based on the 1967 borders, and with East Jerusalem as its capital. We hope the parties involved will take concrete measures to remove obstacles to peace talks and break the stalemate as soon as possible. China respects the reasonable demands of the Syrian people, and supports the early adoption of the Geneva communiqué and the opening of an inclusive political transition, to bring about a political resolution to the Syrian issue. China is deeply concerned about the humanitarian situation in Syria, and will provide a new batch of humanitarian aid to Syrian refugees in Jordan and Lebanon to alleviate their plight. China supports the establishment of a Middle East nuclear-weapon-free zone, and opposes any attempt to change the political landscape of the Middle East. China will play a constructive role in regional affairs, speak up for justice, and work with the Arab states to encourage dialogue as a way to find the greatest common denominator on issues of concern to all parties. We will direct a greater level of diplomatic effort to the proper settlement of regional flashpoints.

Ladies and gentlemen, dear friends,

The Belt and Road, namely the Silk Road Economic Belt and the Maritime Silk Road of the 21st Century, represent paths towards mutual benefit which will bring about closer economic integration among the countries involved, promote development of their infrastructure and institutional innovation, create new economic and employment growth areas, and enhance their capacity to achieve endogenous growth and to protect themselves against risks.

As friends brought together by the Silk Road, China and the Arab states are natural partners in a joint effort to develop the Belt and Road.

To develop the Belt and Road, the two sides need to follow the principles of extensive consultation, joint contribution, and shared benefits. "Extensive consultation" requires that we pool collective wisdom and carry out relevant initiatives through negotiations, so that the interests and concerns of both sides are balanced, and the wisdom and ideas of both sides are reflected. "Joint contribution" requires that we give full play to the strengths and potential of both sides, so that a combination of efforts will lead to sustained progress. As the saying goes, "A tower can be built one stone at a time; a pool can be formed from single drops of water." So we must persist in doing so. "Shared benefits" requires that both peoples benefit equally from the fruits of development, with a view to joining China and the Arab states even more closely through our shared interests and destiny.

To develop the Belt and Road, the two sides need to be both far-sighted and down-to-earth. To be far-sighted, we need to produce the optimum top-level design, identify our orientation and goals, and establish a "1+2+3" cooperation pattern.

"1" refers to cooperation in energy as the core. We will strengthen cooperation in the whole industrial chain of oil and natural gas, safeguard the security of energy transport corridors, and establish mutually beneficial, safe and reliable strategic cooperation in energy based on long-term friendship.

"2" refers to "two wings" – one being infrastructure and the other being trade and investment. We will strengthen cooperation on major development programs and landmark projects for public wellbeing, and devise relevant institutional mechanisms to facilitate bilateral trade and investment. China will encourage its enterprises to import more non-oil products from the Arab states and optimize its trade structure, in a bid to increase the bilateral trade volume from last year's US$240 billion-worth to US$600 billion-worth in the decade ahead. China will also encourage its enterprises to invest in energy, petrochemicals, agriculture, manufacturing, and services in the Arab states, aiming to increase China's investment in the non-financial sector in the Arab states from last year's US$10 billion to over US$60 billion in the following decade.

"3" refers to using three advanced technologies – nuclear energy, space satellites and new energy – as breakthrough levers in an effort to raise the level of pragmatic China-Arab cooperation. The two sides may discuss the establishment of technology transfer centers, jointly develop training centers in the Arab states for the peaceful use of nuclear energy, and launch programs to introduce China's BeiDou Navigation Satellite System to the Arab states.

To be down-to-earth, we need to aim for quick successes. As an Arab proverb goes, "Words proved by action are the most powerful." We need to step up negotiations on programs on which consensus has already been reached and for which the foundations have been laid – programs such as the Free Trade Area between China and the Cooperation Council for the Arab States of the Gulf, the China-United Arab Emirates Joint Investment Fund, and the Arab states' participation in the preparations for the Asian Infrastructure Investment Bank. These programs must be launched as soon as the conditions are ripe. The sooner we have substantial results to show from the development of the Belt and Road Initiative, the easier it will be to keep the various parties motivated and set examples for other programs.

The two sides need to rely on and enhance the traditional friendship between China and the Arab states. The fostering of friendship between the peoples of the two sides represents a key foundation and an important element of the Belt and Road Initiative. I hereby declare that China and the Arab states have decided to designate 2014 and 2015 as Years of China-Arab Friendship and to hold a series of friendly exchange events. We are also willing to enhance cultural exchanges by hosting arts festivals, to encourage more students to engage in social exchanges with the other side such as study, and to strengthen cooperation in tourism, aviation, journalism, and publishing. In the next three years China will train another 6,000 Arab people in various skills to be applied in the Arab states. We will share our experiences of development and poverty alleviation with the Arab states, and introduce those of our advanced technologies that are suited to their needs. In the next decade, China will organize mutual visits and exchanges by 10,000 Chinese and Arab artists, promote and support dedicated cooperation between 200 Chinese and Arab cultural institutions, and invite and support 500 Arab cultural and artistic personages to study in China.

Ladies and gentlemen, dear friends,

The establishment of the CASCF was a strategic step taken for the long-term development of China-Arab relations. After 10 years, the Forum has become an effective means by which we are able to enrich the strategic content of China-Arab relations and promote pragmatic cooperation between the two sides. Our joint efforts to develop the Belt and Road Initiative represent a new opportunity and a new starting point for upgrading the Forum. Only by seizing this opportunity will we be able to maintain our current progress while ensuring sustainable development in the future; and only by starting from this new point will we be able to broaden our prospects and give further impetus to development. In one sentence, the Forum needs to serve as the basis of and support for further development between the two sides.

We should take the Forum as a lever to enhance communication on policy. Instead of sidestepping the differences and problems between us, we need to treat each other in a frank and honest way, communicate with each other with regard to our respective foreign policies and development strategies, enhance political trust, and facilitate coordination strategies, with a view to providing policy support for our cooperation.

We should take the Forum as a lever to extend cooperation in a pragmatic fashion. The development initiatives of both sides are mutually complementary. We need to promote the sharing of resources on both sides, and talk and cooperate with each other with the greatest possible frankness and sincerity. Instead of trying to achieve headline-grabbing successes, collective cooperation should aim for measures that lay the foundations for long-term development.

We should take the Forum as a lever to forge ahead with innovation. Innovation constitutes the lifeblood of the Forum. The two sides need to adopt new ideas, new measures, and new mechanisms in a bid to resolve the difficulties that we encounter in pragmatic cooperation, and clear practical bottlenecks and unlock potential for cooperation through a spirit of reform and innovation.

Ladies and gentlemen, dear friends,

The rapid development of China-Arab relations has created a close link in the future of the peoples of both sides. In Zhejiang Province where I used to work, there is a Jordanian businessman named Muhamad who runs a genuine Arabian restaurant in Yiwu City, where a lot of Arab business people gather. Through bringing genuine Arabian cuisine to Yiwu, he has achieved business success in this prosperous Chinese city, and has gone on to marry a Chinese girl and settle down in China. Integrating his own goals with the Chinese dream of happiness, this young Arab man has built a marvelous life for himself through his perseverance – he embodies a perfect combination of the Chinese Dream and the Arab Dream.

Both the Chinese and the Arab nations have created splendid civilizations, and both have experienced setbacks amidst the changing times of modern history. Therefore, national rejuvenation has become the goal of both sides. Let us work shoulder to shoulder to promote the Silk Road spirit, strengthen China-Arab cooperation, realize the Chinese Dream and Arab revitalization, and strive for the lofty cause of peace and development for humankind!

Shukran[10]! Thank you!

Notes

[1] *Al Salam aleikum,* Arabic, meaning "Hello."

[2] Consisting of China and the 22 member states of the League of Arab States, the China-Arab States Cooperation Forum was established on January 30, 2004, aiming at strengthening the dialogue and cooperation between China and the Arab states to promote peace and development.

[3] Fan Ye: *The Book of Eastern Han (Hou Han Shu).* Fan Ye (398-445) was a historian of the Northern and Southern Dynasties.

[4] *Records of the Manifestation of the Goddess' Power (Tian Fei Ling Ying Zhi Ji),* commonly known as the "Inscription by Zheng He," records the seven voyages by Zheng He to the western ocean (Indian Ocean). See note 4, p. 288.

[5] Gan Ying (dates unknown) was an envoy of the Eastern Han Dynasty. Being sent to the Roman Empire in 97, Gan Ying traveled to as far as the Persian Gulf before returning. Although he did not reach Rome, his mission served to enhance China's knowledge of Central Asian countries.

[6] Ibn Battuta (1304-1377) was a Moroccan explorer.

[7] The Bandung Conference was a meeting of India, Indonesia, Burma (Myanmar), Ceylon (Sri Lanka), Pakistan, China, and 23 other Asian and African countries, which took place during April 18-24, 1955, in Bandung, Indonesia.

[8] Feng Youlan: "Inscription on the Monument of National Southwestern Associated University," *Complete Works of Sansongtang (San Song Tang Quan Ji),* Vol. 14, Chinese ed., Henan People's Publishing House, Zhengzhou, 2000, p. 154. Feng Youlan (1895-1990) was a Chinese philosopher and historian of philosophy.

[9] Wei Yuan: *Treatise on Scholarship and Politics (Mo Gu).* Wei Yuan (1794-1857) was a thinker, Confucian classicist, historian, and poet of the Qing Dynasty.

[10] *Shukran,* Arabic, meaning "Thank you."

Holding talks with Russian President Vladimir Putin in the Kremlin, Moscow, Russia, March 22, 2013.

Speaking at the Julius Nyerere International Convention Center in Dar es Salaam, Tanzania, March 25, 2013.

*Attending the Fifth BRICS Summit in Durban, South Africa,
March 27, 2013.*

With state leaders and heads of international organizations, at the Boao Forum for Asia Annual Conference 2013, held in Hainan Province, April 7, 2013.

Visiting a farming family with his wife, Peng Liyuan, during a state visit to Costa Rica, June 3, 2013.

Meeting with US President Barack Obama at Sunnylands, California, USA, June 7, 2013.

Attending the Eighth G20 Summit in St. Petersburg, Russia, September 6, 2013.

Taking part in the 13th SCO Summit in Bishkek, Kyrgyzstan, September 13, 2013.

Attending the 21st APEC Economic Leaders' Meeting, Bali, Indonesia, October 8, 2013.

At a state banquet with his wife, Peng Liyuan, in their honor given by King Willem-Alexander of the Netherlands at the Royal Palace in Amsterdam, March 22, 2014.

At the inauguration ceremony, with his wife, Peng Liyuan, of the Center for the Promotion of China-Lyons Relations and the Museum of History of Universite Franco-Chinoise, during his visit to the original site of the university, Lyons, France, March 26, 2014.

Hosting a welcoming banquet on behalf of the Chinese government and people at the Shanghai International Conference Center for guests attending the Fourth Summit of the Conference on Interaction and Confidence-Building Measures in Asia, May 20, 2014.

Multilateral Relations

Work Hand in Hand for Common Development[*]

March 27, 2013

Your Excellency President Jacob Zuma,
Your Excellency President Dilma Rousseff,
Your Excellency President Vladimir Putin,
Your Excellency Prime Minister Manmohan Singh,
Ladies and gentlemen,

It gives me great pleasure to come back to South Africa, the Rainbow Nation, after my last visit more than two years ago. I am deeply impressed by the warm hospitality of the South African people and their strong support for BRICS cooperation. I wish to extend my heartfelt thanks to you, President Zuma, and the South African government for the thoughtful arrangements you have made for the meeting.

As an old Chinese saying goes, "Nothing, not even mountains and seas, can separate people with common goals and ideals."[1] The five countries from four continents are gathering here for the great goal of fostering partnership for common development and the noble cause of promoting democracy in international relations, and advancing the peace and development of mankind. To pursue peace, development and mutually beneficial cooperation is our common aspiration and responsibility.

We should firmly uphold international fairness and justice, and world peace and stability. The world today is not peaceful, continually facing new global threats and challenges. The BRICS countries love and cherish peace, and we share the aspiration of lasting peace in the

* A keynote speech at the Fifth BRICS Leaders Meeting, Durban, South Africa.

world, a peaceful and stable social environment for all countries and a decent life for all peoples.

No matter how international situations may unfold, we should stay committed to pursuing peaceful development and mutually beneficial cooperation. What we need is peace and cooperation, not war and confrontation. While pursuing our own interests, we should also accommodate the legitimate concerns of other countries.

No matter how the international setup may evolve, we should stay committed to the principles of equality, democracy and inclusiveness. We should respect the right of all countries to independently choose their social systems and development paths and the diversity of civilizations. Countries, irrespective of their size, strength and level of development, are all equal members of the international community; the internal affairs of a country should be handled by its own people, and international affairs should be managed by all countries through consultation.

No matter how the reform of the global governance system may proceed, we should take an active and constructive part in the process of making the international order truly just and equitable, and thus provide institutional safeguards for world peace and stability.

We should vigorously promote a global development partnership and work for the common prosperity of all countries. A single tree does not make a forest. In this era of continuing economic globalization, we BRICS countries should not just seek our own development, but also work for the common development of all countries.

We should run our own affairs well by expanding our economy and improving the people's lives, and create new sources of growth for the world economy. We should encourage all countries to strengthen coordination of macro-economic policies, reform the international monetary and financial systems, promote, liberalize, and facilitate trade and investment, and bolster the momentum of global economic growth.

We should work together on setting the international development agenda, make full use of the productivity and material resources accumulated by mankind, achieve the UN Millennium Development Goals, narrow the North-South gap in development, and make global development more balanced. The theme of today's meeting, "Partnership for Development, Integration and Industrialization," is not only the development goal of the BRICS countries, but also an important area of cooperation between the BRICS countries and the African countries.

We should forge a strong bond among the BRICS countries through building this partnership, advance our cooperation in economy and trade, finance, infrastructure, personnel interflow and other fields, and move towards the goal of integrated markets, multi-tiered financial, network, land, air and sea links, and greater cultural exchanges.

We should jointly support Africa's pursuit of stronger growth, accelerated integration, and industrialization, and help Africa become a new growth pole in the world economy.

We should reinforce mutually beneficial cooperation and outcomes. We still have a long way to go before we can deliver a decent life to the three billion people of our countries and fully meet their aspirations for a better life. To accomplish this task, we should rely first and foremost on our own efforts, but we also need closer cooperation among the BRICS countries.

We should continue to enhance political trust among our five countries and friendship among our peoples, do more to share experiences in governance, and jointly promote industrialization, IT application, urbanization and agricultural modernization. We should follow the law governing development, foster new ideas and meet difficulties head on in pursuing development. We should continue to step up coordination and cooperation under the frameworks of the United Nations, the G20 and international economic and financial institutions to uphold our common interests.

We should translate our political consensus into concrete actions, actively pursue such initiatives as a BRICS development bank and contingent reserve arrangement, accelerate practical cooperation in all fields, consolidate the economic and social foundation of cooperation, and present a positive image of the BRICS countries pursuing both domestic development and international cooperation.

It is only five years since the BRICS mechanism was launched, and it is still at its initial stage of development. We should run our own affairs well, strengthen the cooperative partnership among BRICS countries and improve institutional building for BRICS cooperation. Our cause will surely thrive as long as we keep firm confidence in our own development paths and in cooperation among the BRICS countries, do not flinch from facing risks and are not misled by any distraction.

Dear colleagues,

I know you all have a keen interest in China's future development. Looking ahead, China will work towards two goals: First, we will double China's 2010 GDP and per capita income of urban and rural residents by 2020 and bring about a moderately prosperous society in all respects that benefits our population of more than one billion. Second, we will build China into a modern socialist country that is prosperous, strong, democratic, culturally advanced and harmonious by 2049, when we mark the centenary of the founding of the People's Republic of China.

To achieve these two goals, we will continue to make development our top priority and economic growth our central task, and promote economic and social development. We will put the people's interests first, strive for all-round progress in the economic, political, cultural, social and ecological fields, coordinate all aspects of our modernization drive, and make China a beautiful country.

Our development endeavor is an open one, as we will remain committed to the basic state policy of opening to the outside world and the mutually beneficial strategy of opening up and further liberalize our economy.

Our development endeavor is a cooperative one, as we will work for common development, carry out economic and technological cooperation with all other countries on the basis of equality and mutual benefit, and promote our own development and the common development of all countries through cooperation.

To achieve these two goals, we need a sound external environment. China will continue to pursue an independent foreign policy of peace and align the interests of the Chinese people with those of the peoples of all other countries. We will work with other countries to strengthen macro-economic policy coordination, oppose protectionism, improve global economic governance and boost global growth.

Dear colleagues,

Enhancing cooperation with other BRICS countries has always been a diplomatic priority for China. Our country will continue to strengthen cooperation with the other BRICS countries, improve the structure, and make it more productive. The result will be more robust growth for all concerned. This will deliver real gains to people of all countries and make a greater contribution to world peace and development.

Thank you!

Notes

[1] Ge Hong: *The Master Who Embraces Simplicity (Bao Pu Zi)*. Ge Hong (c. 281-341), also known as Bao Pu Zi, was a minor official during the Eastern Jin Dynasty (317-420). He was best known for his interest in Taoism, alchemy and techniques of longevity. Composed of two volumes, the Inner Chapter and the Outer Chapter, *The Master Who Embraces Simplicity* recounts the author's pursuit of life through maintaining health with Taoism and governing the country with Confucianism.

A Better Future for Asia and the World[*]

April 7, 2013

Your Excellencies, Heads of State and Government, Speakers of
  Parliament, Heads of International Organizations, Ministers,
Members of the Board of Directors of the Boao Forum for Asia,
Distinguished guests,
Ladies and gentlemen,
Dear friends,

In this balmy season of clear skies and warm, coconut-scented
breezes, I am so glad to meet all of you at the Boao Forum for
Asia Annual Conference 2013 here in Hainan, a picturesque island
embraced by the vast ocean.

Let me begin by extending, on behalf of the Chinese government
and people and also in my own name, a heartfelt welcome to you and
warm congratulations on the opening of the Annual Conference of
the Boao Forum.

In the 12 years since its founding, the Boao Forum for Asia
has become an important forum with growing global influence. In
Chinese culture, 12 years form a zodiacal cycle[1]. In this sense, the
Boao Forum has reached a new starting point, and I hope it will scale
even greater heights.

The theme of the current annual conference, "Asia Seeking Development for All: Restructuring, Responsibility and Cooperation," is a
highly relevant one. I hope you will engage in in-depth discussions on
promoting development in Asia and beyond, thus contributing, with
your vision and commitment, to peace, stability and prosperity in Asia
and the world at large.

* A keynote speech at the Boao Forum for Asia Annual Conference 2013.

The world today is going through profound and complex changes. Countries have become increasingly inter-connected and inter-dependent. Several billion people in a large number of developing countries are embracing modernization. The trend of the times – peace, development, cooperation and mutual benefit – is gaining momentum.

On the other hand, our world is far from peaceful. Development remains a major challenge; the global economy has entered a period of profound readjustment, and recovery remains elusive. The international financial sector is fraught with risks, protectionism in various forms is on the rise, countries still face many difficulties in adjusting their economic structure, and the global governance mechanisms call for improvement. It remains an uphill battle for all countries to achieve common development.

Asia is one of the most dynamic and most promising regions in the world, and its development is closely connected with that of other continents. Asian countries have energetically explored development paths suited to their national conditions and greatly boosted global development through their own. Working side by side with the rest of the world in a time of difficulty to tackle the international financial crisis, Asia has emerged as a major engine driving world economic recovery and growth. In recent years, Asia has contributed more than 50 percent of global growth, instilling much-needed confidence into the rest of the world. What is more, Asia's cooperation with other groupings at regional and sub-regional levels has great vitality and promising prospects.

But we should also be keenly aware that Asia still faces many difficulties and challenges in boosting both its own development and joint development with other regions. The road ahead is neither smooth nor straight.

Asia needs to transform and upgrade its development model in keeping with the trend of the times. Sustainable development is still of paramount importance to Asia, because this holds the key to solving major problems and difficulties. It is important that we should shift the growth model, adjust the economic structure, make development more cost-effective and improve the quality of life.

We should make concerted efforts to resolve major difficulties to ensure stability in Asia, which now faces new challenges, as new flashpoints keep emerging, and both traditional and non-traditional security threats exist. Asian countries should increase mutual trust and work together to ensure durable peace and stability in our region.

We need to build on past success and promote cooperation in Asia. There are many mechanisms and initiatives for enhancing cooperation in Asia, and a lot of ideas are being explored by various parties. What we need to do is to enhance mutual understanding, build consensus and enrich cooperation so as to strike a balance among the interests of the various stakeholders and build mechanisms that bring benefits to us all.

Ladies and gentlemen,

Dear friends,

Mankind has only one earth, and it is home to all countries. Common development – the very foundation of sustainable development – meets the long-term and fundamental interests of all the people in the world. As members of the same global village, we should foster a sense of community of shared future, follow the trend of the times, keep to the right direction, stick together in time of difficulty and ensure that development in Asia and the rest of the world reaches new heights.

First, we should boldly break new ground and create an irresistible impetus for common development.

Over the years, many countries and regions have developed good practices in maintaining stability and promoting growth. We should continue such practices. However, nothing in the world remains constant, and, as a Chinese saying goes, "A wise man changes his way as circumstances change; a knowledgeable person alters his means as times evolve."[2] We should abandon our outdated mindsets, break away from the old confines that fetter development, and unleash all potentials for development. We should redouble our efforts to shift the growth model and adjust the economic structure, raise the quality of development and improve the quality of life. We should steadily reform the international economic and financial systems, improve global governance mechanisms, and ensure sound and stable global economic growth. Asia, with its long-standing capacity for adjusting to change, should ride on the waves of the times, and make changes in Asia and the development of the world reinforce and benefit each other.

Second, we should work together to uphold peace so as to provide a secure environment for common development.

Peace is the ever-lasting wish of our people. Peace, like air and sunshine, is hardly noticed when people enjoy it. But none of us can live without it. Without peace, development is out of the question. Countries, big or small, strong or weak, rich or poor, should all contribute their share to maintaining and enhancing peace.

Rather than undermining each other's efforts, we should complement each other and work for joint progress. The international community should champion the vision of comprehensive, common and cooperative security so as to turn our global village into one big platform for common development rather than an arena where gladiators fight each other. No one should be allowed to cause chaos in any region or even the whole world for selfish gains.

With growing interaction among countries, problems are inevitable. What is important is that countries should resolve differences through dialogue, consultation and peaceful negotiation in the broader interest of a sound growth of their relations.

Third, we should boost cooperation as an effective vehicle for enhancing common development.

As we often say in China, a single flower does not make spring, while one hundred flowers in full blossom bring spring to the garden. All countries are closely linked and share converging interests. They should both pool and share their strength. While pursuing its own interests, a country should respect the legitimate concerns of others. In pursuing its own development, a country should promote the common development of all. We should enhance South-South cooperation and North-South dialogue, promote balanced development of the developing and developed countries, and consolidate the foundation for sustaining stable growth of the global economy. We need to work harder to create and upgrade cooperation, deliver more development dividends to our people, and contribute more to global growth.

Fourth, we should remain open and inclusive to broaden the scope for enhancing common development.

The ocean is vast because it is fed by hundreds of rivers. We should respect the right of a country to independently choose its social system and development path, ease distrust and misgivings, and turn the diversity of our world and differences among countries into dynamism and momentum. We should keep an open mind, draw upon development practices of other continents, share development resources and promote regional cooperation.

During the first decade and more of the new century, trade within Asia has increased from US$800 billion-worth to US$3 trillion-worth, and Asia's trade with other regions has grown from US$1.5 trillion-worth to US$4.8 trillion-worth. This demonstrates that cooperation in Asia is open and goes hand in hand with Asia's cooperation with other regions, and that everyone has gained from such cooperation.

Asia should welcome non-Asian countries to play a constructive role in ensuring stability and development of the region. Likewise, non-Asian countries should respect Asia's diversity and its long-standing tradition of cooperation. This will create a dynamic environment in which Asia and other regions enjoy mutually reinforcing progress.

Ladies and gentlemen,

Dear friends,

China is an important member of the Asian family and the global family. China cannot develop itself in isolation from the rest of Asia and the world. On their part, the rest of Asia and the world cannot enjoy prosperity and stability without China.

Last November, the CPC held its 18th National Congress, which designed the blueprint for China's development in the years to come. The main goals we set for China are as follows:

By 2020, China's GDP and per capita income for urban and rural residents will double the 2010 figures, and the building of a moderately prosperous society in all respects will be accomplished. By the mid-21st century, China will be turned into a modern, prosperous, strong, democratic, culturally advanced and harmonious socialist country; and the Chinese Dream – the renewal of the Chinese nation, will be realized. Looking ahead, we are full of confidence in China's future.

Still, we are aware that China remains the world's largest developing country, and it faces many difficulties and challenges. We need to make relentless efforts in the years ahead to deliver a better life to all our people. We are absolutely committed to reform and opening up, and we will concentrate on the major task of shifting the growth model, focus on running our own affairs well and endeavor to advance the drive towards socialist modernization.

As a Chinese proverb goes, "Neighbors wish each other well, just as loved ones do to each other." China will continue to promote friendship and partnership with its neighbors, strengthen friendly ties, intensify mutually beneficial cooperation and ensure that its development will bring even greater gains to its neighbors.

China will contribute more to development and prosperity in both Asia and the world. Since the beginning of the new century, China's trade with its neighbors has grown from US$100 billion-worth to US$1.3 trillion-worth, making China the largest trading partner, the biggest export market and a major source of investment for many of these countries.

China's interests have never been so closely connected with those of the rest of Asia and the world as a whole in both scope and depth. Going forward, China will maintain its robust growth momentum. Its domestic demand, particularly consumption-driven demand, will continue to grow, and its outbound investment will increase substantially. It is projected that in the next five years, China's imports will reach some US$10 trillion-worth, and its outbound investment will reach US$500 billion-worth. In addition, over 400 million outbound trips will be made by Chinese tourists.

The faster China grows, the more development opportunities it will create for the rest of Asia and the world.

We are firm in our resolve to uphold peace and stability in Asia and the world. We Chinese deeply cherish peace, as we know too well the agonies inflicted upon us by war and turbulence. China will continue to develop by securing a peaceful international environment, and at the same time, it will uphold and promote world peace through its own development. China will continue to properly handle differences and disputes with relevant countries. On the basis of defending its sovereignty, security and territorial integrity, China will maintain good relations with its neighbors and overall peace and stability in our region. China will continue to play a constructive role in addressing regional and global flashpoints, encourage dialogue and talks for peace, and work hard to solve all issues properly through dialogue and negotiation.

China will energetically promote regional cooperation in Asia and around the world. It will enhance communication with its neighbors, explore the building of a regional financing platform, and advance economic integration within the region, thus increasing its competitiveness. China will take an active part in Asia's regional cooperation process and promote regional and sub-regional cooperation with non-Asian regions and countries.

China will continue to champion and promote trade and investment liberalization and facilitation, step up two-way investment with other countries and boost cooperation in new priority areas. China firmly supports Asia's opening up and cooperation with other regions for their common development. China is committed to narrowing the North-South gap and supports other developing countries in their efforts to enhance their capacity for self-development.

Ladies and gentlemen,

Dear friends,

Promoting good neighborliness is a time-honored tradition of China. To enhance peaceful development and mutually beneficial cooperation in Asia and the world is a race that has one starting point after another and knows no finishing line. We in China are ready to join hands with friends from across the world in a concerted effort to create a bright future for both Asia and the world, and to deliver real gains to both the peoples of Asia and those of the rest of the world.

Finally, I wish the Boao Forum for Asia Annual Conference 2013 every success!

Notes

[1] *Shengxiao*, the Chinese zodiac – a 12-year cycle. Each year is related to an animal – rat, ox, tiger, rabbit, dragon, snake, horse, ram, monkey, rooster, dog and pig.

[2] See note 1, p. 175.

Jointly Maintain and
Develop an Open World Economy[*]

September 5, 2013

Your Excellency President Putin,
Dear colleagues,

It is a great pleasure to meet you here in beautiful St. Petersburg, and to discuss together measures to promote world economic growth and employment. First, I would like to extend my heartfelt thanks to President Putin and the Russian government for your proactive efforts and considerate arrangements in making this summit possible!

At present, the world economy is gradually recovering, and the situation continues to develop in a good direction. At the same time, the negative impact of the international financial crisis lingers on, and there is still a long way to go for global economic recovery.

The situation decides our tasks, and our actions determine their effectiveness. We should take a long-term view, strive to shape a world economy in which all countries enjoy development and innovation, growth linkage and integration of interests, and firmly maintain and develop an open world economy.

– Innovative development is necessary for the sustainable growth of the world economy. Growth driven by stimulating policies and large-scale and direct government intervention in the economy can only treat the symptoms but not the disease, while growth at the cost of high energy consumption and environmental pollution is even less sustainable. Countries should improve the quality and efficiency

---

* Speech on the world economic situation at the first-stage meeting of the G20 Leaders Summit.

of economic growth and avoid simply measuring development by the GDP growth rate. They should invigorate markets and enhance economic competitiveness through active structural reform.

– Interactive growth is necessary for the sturdy growth of the world economy. A vibrant world economy depends on the joint growth of all countries, which should be aware of the commonality of their destinies, and gain a really clear understanding of the linkage effect, that is, "benefit to one means benefit to all, whereas harm to one means harm to all." We should cooperate while competing, and achieve mutually beneficial results through cooperation. We should take into consideration the interests of other countries when pursuing our own national interests, and take into consideration the development of other countries when seeking our own development. Mutual help between different countries in solving salient problems is the objective requirement of world economic development. Every country should be able to create a linkage between its own development and that of other countries, and to bring to each other positive instead of negative spillover effects.

– Convergence of interests is necessary for the balanced growth of the world economy. Balanced growth is not a zero-sum game that transfers growth from one country to another, but a growth entailing shared welfare. Countries should give full play to their comparative advantages, work together to optimize global resource allocation, improve the layout of global industry, build a global value chain that shares interests equally, and foster a big global market that benefits all parties, so as to achieve mutually beneficial development.

To shape a world economy of this kind, all G20 members need to build a closer economic partnership, and to shoulder their due responsibilities.

First, they need to adopt responsible macro-economic policies. The major economies should take care of their own matters and ensure that their own economies are sound. This is our basic responsibility. We should improve the macro-economic policy coordination mechanism, and strengthen communication and coordination.

Macro- and micro-economic policies and social policies must be integrated. All countries should support economic policies with social ones, and create favorable conditions for the implementation of macro and micro-economic policies. The decision of the G20 Finance Ministers and Central Bank Governors' Meeting and G20 Labor and Employment Ministers' Meeting to strengthen coordination between economic and employment policies is correct, and we should stick to it firmly.

In this regard, China adopts its economic policies not only for the good of its own economy, but for the good of the world economy as well. China's economic fundamentals are good. In the first half of this year its GDP grew by 7.6 percent. Nonetheless, China also faces such problems as high local government debt and excessive capacity in some industries. These problems are controllable, and we are taking measures to address them.

We have realized that to solve the root problems in our long-term economic development we must firmly streamline our economic structure, even if we have to slow down the growth rate a bit. Any undertaking needs comprehensive and far-sighted thinking. A development model resembling killing a goose to get its golden eggs or draining the pond to catch the fish cannot be sustainable.

China's economy is highly integrated with the world economy. A China that enjoys more stable, higher-quality and more sustainable growth is conducive to the long-term economic growth of the world as a whole. China has the conditions and ability to achieve sustainable and healthy economic development, and produce more positive spill-over effects for the world economy.

Second, we must safeguard and develop an open world economy. "A single flower does not make spring while one hundred flowers in full blossom bring spring to the garden." Countries will grow if their economies are open, and conversely decline if their economies are closed. We must follow the tide of the times, oppose all forms of protectionism, and make good use of international and domestic markets and resources.

We should maintain a free, open and non-discriminatory multilateral trading system. We should avoid making exclusive trade standards, rules and systems, so as to prevent the segregation of the global market and the disintegration of trade systems. We should improve the global investment rules, guide the rational flow of global development capital and use development resources more effectively.

Third, we must improve global economic governance, and make it fairer and more just. The G20 is an important platform for developed and developing countries to engage in consultations on international economic affairs. We should build the G20 into an important force for stabilizing the world economy, weave an international financial safety net and improve global economic governance.

We should continue the reform of international financial institutions. The relevant countries should further push forward the implementation of the plan for reforming the management of the International Monetary Fund and for making a new sharing formula that reflects the weight of the economic aggregate of the different countries in the world economy, and continue to strengthen oversight concerning the international financial market, so that the financial system will depend on, serve and promote the development of the real economy in a sound way. The relevant countries should build a stable and risk-resistant international monetary system, reform the basket of currencies for Special Drawing Rights, strengthen the connections between international and regional financial cooperation mechanisms, and build a "firewall" against financial risks.

China supports the strengthening of multilateral cooperation against tax evasion, and is keen to contribute its share towards international tax governance.

I would like to stress that, in order to promote the sustainable and healthy development of its economy and society, China will resolutely carry its reform forward. We are conducting overall research into comprehensively continuing the reform to a deeper level, so as to streamline the structures in the economic, political, cultural, social and ecological sectors through overall planning, further release and develop social productivity, and give full play to the creativity of the whole of our society.

China will build a stronger market system, streamline the structures in the fields of macro-economic regulation and control, taxation, finance, investment, administration and other fields, and give full play to the basic role of the market in resource allocation.

China will further the reform of the marketization of interest and exchange rates, to increase the flexibility of the Renminbi exchange rate, and gradually make the Renminbi capital account convertible.

China will adhere to the opening-up strategy of mutual benefit, continue to streamline the structures of investment and trade, improve relevant laws and regulations, create a legal environment of fair operations for foreign companies in China, and resolve trade disputes with relevant countries through consultations.

Dear colleagues,

As long as we work together and build a closer partnership, the G20 will enjoy more stable, better and further development, and the people of all countries will have more confidence in the world economy and in our future life.

Thank you!

Carry Forward the "Shanghai Spirit" and Promote Common Development[*]

September 13, 2013

Your Excellency President Almazbek Atambayev,
Dear colleagues,

It gives me great pleasure to attend the Bishkek Summit of the Shanghai Cooperation Organization. I would like to thank Kyrgyzstan, the SCO Presidency, for your meticulous preparations and thoughtful arrangements for the success of this summit. China commends Kyrgyzstan for your enormous and effective efforts over the past year for the SCO's development.

In light of the latest developments in the international and regional situation and in response to the common aspirations of member states for stability, growth and better lives for their peoples, this summit has focused on the implementation of the Treaty of Long-term Good-neighborliness, Friendship and Cooperation. It will ratify the Plan of Action of the Treaty and map out the blueprint for the development of the SCO in the next five years. These efforts will offer broader prospects for the organization.

Just as the SCO enjoys precious opportunities for development, it also faces severe challenges. The "three forces" of terrorism, separatism and extremism all pose threats to the security and stability of this region as do drug trafficking and transnational organized crime. The international financial crisis has caused varying degrees of economic difficulties for countries in this region, leaving them in a period of adjustment and recovery.

* Speech at the 13th meeting of the Council of Heads of Member States of the Shanghai Cooperation Organization in Bishkek.

Challenges such as these are more than any one country can handle alone. We must therefore enhance cooperation and unite to become stronger. And in this regard, I would like to suggest that we do the following.

First, we should carry forward the "Shanghai Spirit."[1] To implement the "Shanghai Spirit," we should build up trust among member states and conduct mutually beneficial cooperation based on equality, consultation, mutual understanding and mutual accommodation. This conforms to the trend of peace and development of the times and accords with the interests and aspirations of the people of the member states.

We should implement the Treaty of Long-term Good-neighborliness, Friendship and Cooperation with real actions and promote cooperation wholeheartedly in all fields within the SCO framework, so that member states will become good neighbors living in harmony, good friends pulling together in troubled waters and good partners sharing weal and woe.

Second, we should jointly safeguard regional security and stability. A secure and stable environment is a prerequisite for mutually beneficial cooperation, and common development and prosperity. We should implement the Shanghai Convention on Combating Terrorism, Separatism and Extremism and the Program of Cooperation, improve the system of law enforcement and security cooperation of the SCO, entrust the regional counter-terrorism structure with responsibility for anti-narcotics operations, and on this basis establish a center for comprehensive responses to security threats and challenges.

The relevant authorities within the member states should also open up a channel for routine communication, and explore ways to act and work together to combat terrorism, separatism and extremism so as to create a sound working and living environment for the peoples of this region.

Afghanistan is an observer of the SCO, and its situation is closely related to regional security and stability. The SCO should support it in national reconciliation, help it realize peace and stability as soon as possible, and safeguard regional security.

Third, we should focus on practical cooperation. This is the material basis and main driver for the SCO's development. All the six member states and the five observers are located along the routes of the ancient Silk Road. As such, we are all duty-bound to carry forward the Silk Road spirit by taking the following steps:

Number one, open up new transport and logistics routes. The member states could move speedily to sign the Agreement on the Facilitation of International Road Transport. Once signed, the agreement would be open for wide observer participation on a voluntary basis so that the participating countries could build unimpeded transport corridors connecting the Baltic with the Pacific and connecting Central Asia with both the Indian Ocean and the Persian Gulf.

Number two, explore a trade and investment facilitation agreement. Extensive trade and investment cooperation with full consideration for the interests and concerns of all parties would allow us to thoroughly unlock the potential for cooperation among member states and achieve mutual complementarity in the interest of our common development and prosperity.

Number three, step up cooperation in the financial sector. We should establish an SCO development bank which would provide funding guarantees and serve as a settlement platform for the organization's infrastructure development and collaborative economic and trade projects. In the meantime, the SCO should set up a special account to ensure funding for project studies, exchanges and training within its framework. We should make full use of the inter-bank consortium to intensify exchanges and cooperation between financial institutions of the countries in this region.

Number four, establish an energy club. This would help us coordinate energy cooperation within the SCO framework, secure stable supply and demand, ensure energy security, and, on top of these, encourage extensive cooperation in such areas as energy efficiency and new energy sources.

Number five, put in place a cooperation mechanism for food security. We should enhance cooperation in agricultural production, agrotrade and food safety to ensure greater food security.

Last but not least, we should intensify people-to-people and cultural exchanges to build strong public support and a social foundation for the SCO's future development. We should promote cooperation in a wide range of areas such as culture, education, film and TV, health, sports and tourism.

At the Beijing Summit, China announced a ten-year program of 30,000 government scholarships for the other member states. We are ready to work closely with the other member states to maximize the benefit of this program.

China will also establish a China-SCO base for international judicial exchanges, cooperation and training at Shanghai University of Political Science and Law. We would like to make it a platform for training judicial professionals for other member states.

Traditional medicine is a new area of cooperation. China stands ready to join hands with other member states in building medical institutions specializing in traditional Chinese medicine to make full use of such resources for the benefit of the people of our member states.

China has taken the lead in establishing an SCO Committee on Good-neighborliness, Friendship and Cooperation in line with a consensus among the parties concerned. We hope that all fellow member states and observer countries will establish similar organizations for the purpose of enhancing mutual understanding and traditional friendship among our peoples.

The Bishkek Declaration clarifies the stand of member states on the Syrian issue. Here I would like to reiterate that China pays close attention to the Syrian situation, supports the international community's drive for a cease-fire and peace talks, and calls on both sides of the Syrian conflict to work out a political solution to the crisis. China supports Russia's proposal that Syria surrender its chemical weapons to international control for their eventual destruction. China is ready to enhance communication and coordination with related parties through the UN Security Council, and will continue its unremitting efforts in facilitating a political settlement.

Thank you!

Notes

[1] The "Shanghai Spirit" was formally proposed in the Declaration on the Establishment of the Shanghai Cooperation Organization (SCO). On June 15, 2001, the heads of state of China, Kazakhstan, Kyrgyzstan, Russia, Tajikistan and Uzbekistan met in Shanghai, declaring the founding of the Shanghai Cooperation Organization and publishing the Declaration. In the Declaration the "Shanghai Spirit," whose essence is mutual trust, mutual benefit, equality, cooperation, respect for diverse civilizations and pursuit of common development, was established as the norm for relations among SCO member states.

Work Together for a Better Asia Pacific*

October 7, 2013

Distinguished Chairman Wishnu Wardhana,

Ladies and gentlemen,

Dear friends,

It is a great pleasure for me to have the opportunity to join you, distinguished representatives of the Asia Pacific business community, in this island paradise.

Bali is not only a world-renowned tourist attraction, but also the birthplace of the Bali Process and the Bali Road Map. And now, hosting the APEC Economic Leaders' Meeting, Bali carries the expectations of Asia Pacific and the rest of the world.

The world economy is still struggling towards recovery, and the Asia Pacific economy, while enjoying positive growth, is confronted with new challenges. People around the world are looking to this year's APEC meeting to give new impetus to regional and global economic growth.

Ladies and gentlemen,

Dear friends,

The world economy is still in the middle of profound readjustment. While there are signs of recovery, there are also problems of fragile foundations, inadequate momentum and uneven pace. Major developed economies are far from resolving their structural problems, making it all the more necessary to strengthen macro-economic policy coordination. Emerging market economies have slowed down, and now face more external risks and challenges. The WTO Doha Round

---

* Speech at the APEC CEO Summit, Bali, Indonesia.

378

negotiations are fraught with difficulty, and trade and investment protectionism is resurfacing in new forms. To achieve a full recovery and healthy growth of the world economy will be a long and tortuous process.

Confronted with these new challenges, both developed and developing economies are looking for new drivers of growth.

Where can we find them? In my opinion, they can only be found through reform, readjustment and innovation. The Asia Pacific region has long been an important engine of world economic growth. To push for a recovery in the sluggish world economy, economies in the Asia Pacific region should have the courage to do what has never been done before and build an open growth mode featuring innovative development, interactive growth and converging interests. Only by so doing can the Asia Pacific economies play a leading role in the recovery of the world economy. A Chinese poem runs, "When one doubts whether there is a way out from the endless mountains and rivers, one suddenly finds a village shaded by soft willows and bright flowers."[1]

This is exactly what China is doing. China's economy grew at a rate of 7.6 percent in the first half of this year. This is, indeed, somewhat lower than the previous growth rate of over 8 percent, which has caused worries about the prospects for the Chinese economy. Some wonder whether there will be a hard landing, whether sustainable, healthy growth is still possible, how China will deal with this situation, and what impact this will have on the Asia Pacific region. Here I wish to share with you some of my observations.

To begin with, I want to emphasize that based on a comprehensive analysis of all factors, I am fully confident about the future of China's economy.

I am confident because first of all China's growth rate is within a reasonable and expected range. From the previous double-digit growth rate to 9.3 percent in 2011, 7.8 percent last year and 7.6 percent in the first six months of this year, the change in pace of growth has on the whole been smooth. In fact, the growth rate of 7.6 percent makes the

Chinese economy the fastest growing among all major economies. The fundamentals of the Chinese economy are good; GDP growth and other major economic indicators are within the expected range. So everything has been going as expected, and nothing has come as a surprise.

The slowdown of the Chinese economy is an intended result of our own regulatory initiatives. This is because, according to a thorough calculation done at the time we set our mid- and long-term development goals to double the 2010 GDP and per capita income by 2020, it is judged that a 7 percent annual growth rate would suffice. Moreover, we have recognized that to ensure long-term economic development China has to press ahead with structural reform, even if this requires some sacrifice of pace. In whatever undertaking, one has to look far and plan wisely to take care of both short- and long-term needs. Killing the goose to get the eggs or draining the pond to catch the fish is no formula for sustainable development.

Second, I am confident because the quality and efficiency of China's economic development are improving steadily. China's economy in the first six months of this year has generally made smooth progress. By "smooth" I mean our economic growth has been within a reasonable range, and by "progress" I mean the shift of our growth mode has picked up pace. China is moving from over-reliance on investment and export in the past to increased dependence on domestic demand, especially on consumption. The economic figures for the first half of this year show an increasingly visible role of structural adjustment in boosting growth. Domestic demand has contributed 7.5 percentage points to the GDP growth, with 3.4 percentage points coming from consumption. We no longer take the GDP growth rate as the sole criterion for success; instead, we are focusing more on improving the quality and efficiency of growth. This has proved a responsible approach for both China and the rest of the world.

Third, I am confident because China has a strong domestic driving force for growth. This force is increasing and will continue to get stronger. The ongoing process of a new type of urbanization will create space for hundreds of millions of Chinese to move from villages to cities in pursuit of a better life. The improvement of education in China will bring about a modern, professional workforce of higher caliber, broader vision and better skills. China's vigorous implementation of the innovation-driven development strategy will more closely link science and technology with economic growth, and foster innovation and emerging industries. The continued expansion of domestic demand and consumer market in China will unlock considerable potential for growth. And, above all, China is committed to putting people first and making development benefits accessible to more people across the country. All these will translate into a strong homegrown force for our economic advance.

Fourth, I am confident because the Asia Pacific region enjoys sound development prospects. Thanks to the concerted efforts of all its economies, the Asia Pacific region boasts a high level of free movement of capital, information and people, and an increasingly clear division of labor. A substantial Asia Pacific market is emerging. The new scientific and industrial revolution that is now in the making will add to the existing strength of the region. The Asia Pacific economies are also in a much better position to fend off risks, with more flexible exchange rate schemes, notably larger foreign exchange reserves and various multilateral and bilateral financial arrangements providing institutional protection. China has faith in the development prospects of the Asia Pacific region. Benefiting from overall economic growth in the region, China has achieved its own development. At the same time, China's development has also contributed to regional economic growth. I believe that such interaction will gain even stronger momentum, thus creating more opportunities for the development of the whole region.

I am firmly convinced that the Chinese economy will maintain its sound growth. At the same time, we are soberly aware of potential problems and challenges from falling demand, production overcapacity, local debts and shadow banking, and we are paying close attention to possible impacts from external forces. In this connection, we are taking prudent and proper measures to forestall any potential problems.

Ladies and gentlemen,

Dear friends,

The Chinese economy has entered a new development stage. Its growth mode and structural readjustment are undergoing profound transformation. In this process, there will inevitably be one challenge after another. Efforts to meet these challenges will be accompanied by the throes of readjustment and other troubles in the development process, which will prove to be unavoidable.

Rainbows mostly appear after wind and rain. As someone aptly put it, "No mountain is too high for a man to scale and no road too long for a man to walk." However high the mountain may be or however long the road may seem, we will be able to get there as long as we stay the course and keep moving forward.

If China is to make progress, it must drive all-round reform and opening up to a deeper level. To live up to the new expectations of our people, we must, with firm confidence in reform and opening up, greater political courage and wisdom, and stronger measures to advance reform and opening up, free our minds, unleash and develop social productivity, and unlock and enhance the creative forces of society.

China is drawing up a master plan for the continuation of reform in all respects. Our general approach is to press ahead with reform in the economic, political, cultural, social and ecological fields in a balanced manner, address the challenges cropping up in the course of development, remove institutional obstacles to sustainable and healthy economic growth, and create a new impetus for economic development through reform.

We will improve our basic economic system, strengthen the market system, advance institutional reform in macro regulation, fiscal and tax systems, financial sectors and investment, extend the market-oriented reform of interest rates and the exchange rate, make the RMB exchange rate more flexible, and achieve, over time, the convertibility of the Renminbi under the capital account. We will continue to reform the administration system, transform the functions of the government, streamline government and delegate powers, in order to have a clearly defined relationship between the government and the market and let the market play its basic role in allocating resources to a greater degree and in a wider scope. We will improve the management of science and technology, enhance innovation capability, and build a system for technological innovation which is led by enterprises and guided by the market and which integrates the efforts of enterprises, universities and research institutes. We will ensure and improve standards of living on a priority basis, promote social equity and justice, achieve higher quality employment, further the reform of income distribution, and improve social security and basic public services. We will step up environmental protection and resource conservation to create a good working and living environment for our people and respond to global climate change.

We will follow a more proactive opening-up strategy, improve the open economy which is mutually beneficial, diversified, balanced, secure and efficient, encourage coastal, inland and border areas to draw on each other's strengths in opening up, develop open areas that take the lead in global economic cooperation and competition, and establish pilot open areas that drive regional development. We will continue to attach equal importance to export and import, and promote balance in foreign trade. We will attract foreign investment and encourage companies to "go global" at the same time, and enhance international investment cooperation. We will promote investment- and trade-related institutional reforms, and improve relevant legislation to create a legal environment in which foreign companies in China can operate in a fair manner. We will make overall planning for bilateral, multilateral, regional and sub-regional opening up and cooperation, accelerate the implementation of the FTA strategy, and promote communication and exchanges with our neighboring countries.

We are aware that the reform is a profound revolution that involves adjustment of major interests and improvement of systems and institutions in various fields. China's reform is sailing in uncharted waters with tough challenges. The problems we face in the current phase of reform are especially difficult. It is extremely important that we press ahead without letting up. If we hesitate and become indecisive, we will not be able to make breakthroughs, and all our previous gains may be lost.

China is a big country. We cannot afford any drastic mistake on issues of fundamental importance, as damage from such mistakes will be beyond remedy. Our position is that we must be both bold enough to explore and advance, and prudent in carefully planning our actions. We will stick to the right direction and press ahead with reform and opening up. We will have the courage to crack the "hard nuts," navigate the uncharted waters and take on the deep-rooted problems that have piled up over the years. We must not stop our pursuit of reform and opening up – not for one moment.

Ladies and gentlemen,

Dear friends,

The nations of the Asia Pacific region are a big family, and China is one of the members. China cannot develop in isolation from the Asia Pacific region while the Asia Pacific region cannot prosper without China. Sustainable and healthy development of the Chinese economy will bring greater opportunities to the development of the region.

China will firmly uphold regional peace and stability, and help cement the foundations for a mutually beneficial situation in the Asia Pacific region. I want to repeat what I noted at the Boao Forum for Asia and other events this year: "Peace, like air and sunshine, is hardly noticed when people are enjoying it. But none of us can live without it." Without peace, development is out of the question, like water without a source and a tree without roots. We Chinese often say, "A family in harmony prospers." As a member of the Asia Pacific family, China is ready to live in amity with other family members, which help each other. We hope that all members of the Asia Pacific family will cherish the peace and stability we now enjoy, which has not come easily, and will work together for a harmonious Asia Pacific of enduring peace and common prosperity.

China will work energetically to boost regional development and prosperity, and broaden opportunities for mutual benefit in the Asia Pacific region. China is the biggest trading partner, largest export market and a major source of investment for many Asia Pacific region economies. In 2012 China accounted for more than 50 percent of Asia's economic growth. By the end of the same year China had approved more than 760,000 foreign commercial investments, and attracted around US$1.3 trillion in foreign direct investment. China has signed 12 free trade agreements with 20 countries and regions, with six more under negotiation. Most of China's free trade partners are APEC members. In the coming five years, China will import over US$10 trillion-worth of goods, invest over US$500 billion overseas and send over 400 million tourists abroad. China's growing domestic demand, particularly consumption and investment demand, will offer foreign investors more opportunities for cooperation.

China will commit itself to building a cross-Pacific regional cooperation framework that benefits all parties. The vast Pacific is free of natural barriers, and we should not erect any man-made ones. We should let APEC lead and coordinate our actions, and uphold the approach of openness, inclusiveness and mutual benefit. We should enhance coordination on macro-economic policies and regional free trade arrangements, promote regional integration, and avoid the Spaghetti Bowl effect, so as to build closer partnerships across the Pacific and jointly pursue long-term development of Asia Pacific.

Ladies and gentlemen,

Dear friends,

"Boundless is the ocean where we sail with the wind."[2] Like a vast ocean, the Asia Pacific region offers enough space for us to make progress together. Each and every APEC member has a stake in the future development of this region.

China has high hopes for this year's APEC Economic Leaders' Meeting. We stand ready to work with our partners in the region to build a beautiful Asia Pacific that leads the world, benefits all parties, and ensures the wellbeing of future generations. With this in mind,

I would like to share with you my vision for the Asia Pacific region in four aspects.

First, an Asia Pacific region that seeks common development. The Asia Pacific economies have close ties and shared interests. We should draw upon our respective strengths, optimize the allocation of economic resources, improve the industrial layout, and build an Asia Pacific value chain and a large-scale Asia Pacific market where benefits are shared by all. The developed economies should provide stronger support and assistance to the developing ones, while the latter should for their part work hard to catch up. Only by narrowing the development gap can we all rise with the tide of development in this region.

Second, an Asia Pacific region that stays committed to open development. The end of World War II was followed by an economic boom of more than 25 years in 13 economies around the world. One common feature of the economies was their opening-up policy. We should follow the trend of the times, uphold a multilateral trading system that is free, open and non-discriminatory, and oppose all forms of protectionism. We should work together in building an open economy and a framework for regional cooperation, and, in an open and inclusive spirit, build the Asia Pacific region into a free trade area.

Third, an Asia Pacific region that promotes innovation-driven development. Growth will be unsustainable if it is solely driven by fiscal stimulus measures and unconventional monetary policies, and will be too costly if it is based on excessive consumption of resources and achieved at the expense of the environment. We need innovation in both theory and practice of development. We should abandon outdated mindsets, break away from old confines, and pursue green, circular and low-carbon development. We should continue to improve our capability in innovation so as to foster emerging industries, explore new forces for growth, and enhance core competitiveness.

Fourth, an Asia Pacific region that pursues interactive growth. The Asia Pacific economies are interdependent, with shared interests and a common future. The success or failure of one may ultimately lead to the success or failure of all. In this chain of dynamic interactions, one economy's development will have a knock-on effect on other econo-mies. We should strengthen the sense of community and of common future, contribute to others' development with our own, tap fully into our respective strengths through coordination and interaction, pass on positive energy, and achieve sound interactions and coordinated devel-opment among all the Asia Pacific economies.

At present, the Asian countries, especially emerging markets and developing countries, are in great need of infrastructure. Particularly in the face of such severe challenges as mounting downward pressure and financial volatility, it is necessary for us to mobilize more funds for infrastructural development to maintain sustained and steady economic growth and promote economic integration in the region. To this end, we propose to establish an Asian infrastructure invest-ment bank to help fund the infrastructural development of ASEAN countries and other developing countries in the region. This proposed bank would work together with the existing multilateral development banks in and outside the region to fuel the sustainable and steady growth of the Asian economy.

Ladies and gentlemen,

Dear friends,

The business community is a major force for the development of economy and trade as well as an integral part of APEC cooperation. China places great importance on the role of the business commu-nity. We are ready to hear your views and suggestions, and facilitate your deeper and more rapid engagement, especially that of SMEs and micro businesses, in economic development and regional cooperation.

Last August China's business community established an APEC China Business Council. This provides an institutional guarantee for the business sector's further involvement in formulating economic and trade rules of the Asia Pacific region, and demonstrates the readi-ness of China's business community to undertake more international responsibilities.

More friends, more opportunities. Many of you present here are old friends of the Chinese people who have participated in all

China's reform and opening-up endeavors. We will never forget our old friends, and we will be most happy to make new ones. China welcomes and encourages businesses from all economies, APEC members in particular, to invest and do business in China and take an active part in China's reform and opening up. The more friends we have, the more China's reform and opening up will thrive and prosper.

I hope friends from the business community will make full use of APEC as a platform to make your voices heard on how to improve trade and investment environment in the Asia Pacific region, and, with your strength in market information, technology incubation and innovative capability, put forward strategic and progressive suggestions for promoting trade and investment liberalization and facilitation, deepening regional economic integration and the future development of APEC.

Ladies and gentlemen,

Dear friends,

China will host the 2014 APEC Economic Leaders' Meeting and the related events. Taking this opportunity and focusing on the future of APEC, we will seek to build closer partnerships, further pragmatic cooperation, and enhance the leading role of APEC in shaping the long-term development vision of the Asia Pacific region.

I hope that all of you, friends from the Asia Pacific business community, will meet in Beijing then for discussions and witness another important moment in the development of the Asia Pacific region.

Thank you!

Notes

[1] Lu You: *Visiting a Mountain Village*. Lu You (1125-1210) was a poet of the Southern Song Dynasty (1127-1279).

[2] Shang Yan: *Farewell to a Korean Hermit Returning Home*. Shang Yan (date unknown) was a poet of the Tang Dynasty (618-907).

New Approach for Asian Security Cooperation[*]

May 21, 2014

Distinguished guests,
Dear colleagues,
Ladies and gentlemen,
Dear friends,

I would like to thank Foreign Minister Ahmet Davutoglu, Special Representative of the Turkish President, for his address. China has assumed the chairmanship of the Conference on Interaction and Confidence-Building Measures in Asia (CICA), so please allow me to take this opportunity to express heartfelt thanks to all sides, in particular Kazakhstan, the initiator of the CICA, and Turkey, the previous chair of the CICA, for your trust and support.

Now, let me make some observations on behalf of the People's Republic of China.

The summit today has brought together leaders and representatives from 47 countries and international organizations, including CICA member states, observers and invited guests of the Shanghai Summit. Under the theme "Enhancing Dialogue, Trust and Coordination for a New Asia of Peace, Stability and Cooperation," we will discuss the important subject of security cooperation, explore policies for long-term peace and stability, and jointly promote development and prosperity. As such, this summit is of great importance to security in Asia and the world at large, and will have far-reaching consequences.

---

[*] Speech at the Fourth Summit of the Conference on Interaction and Confidence-Building Measures in Asia.

Asia today is home to 67 percent of the world's population, and accounts for one third of the global economy. It is a place where diverse civilizations and nations meet and interact. Peace and development in Asia are closely connected with the future of mankind, and Asia's stability and revival are a blessing to the peace and development of the rest of the world.

Asia today, though facing risks and challenges, is still the most dynamic and promising region in the world. Peace, development and mutually beneficial cooperation are the main trend in the region, and countries in the region generally prefer policies that address differences and disputes through consultation and negotiation. Asia enjoys a rising status in the international strategic landscape, and plays an increasingly important role in promoting a multi-polar world and democracy in international relations. Such a healthy situation in the region has not come easily and ought to be doubly cherished.

Asia today is engaged in vibrant cooperation in the economic field. Cooperation in the security field is making progress despite difficulties, and various cooperation mechanisms are becoming more dynamic. Asia has come to a crucial stage in security cooperation at which we need to build on past achievements and strive for new progress.

As a Chinese saying goes, "A wise man changes his way as circumstances change; a knowledgeable person alters his means as times evolve."[1] We need to keep pace with changing circumstances and evolving times. One cannot live in the 21st century with the outdated thinking of the era of the Cold War and zero-sum game. We believe that it is necessary to advocate common, comprehensive, cooperative and sustainable security in Asia. We need to innovate our security concept, establish a new regional security cooperation architecture, and jointly build a road towards security in Asia that is shared by and of benefit to all.

Common security means respecting and ensuring the security of each and every country. Asia is a region of great diversity. The countries there differ in size, wealth and strength. They vary in historical and cultural traditions as well as social systems, and have different security interests and aspirations. However, we are all part of the same Asian family. With our interests and security so closely intertwined, we will sink or swim together, and we are increasingly becoming a community of shared future.

Security must be universal. We cannot have the security of just one or a few countries while leaving the rest insecure, in no way can we accept the so-called absolute security of one at the expense of the security of others. Otherwise, just as a Kazakh proverb aptly puts it, "One who tries to blow out another's oil lamp will get his beard singed."

Security must be equal. Every country has the equal right to participate in the security affairs of the region as well as the responsibility for upholding regional security. No country should attempt to dominate regional security affairs or infringe upon the legitimate rights and interests of other countries.

Security must be inclusive. We should turn Asia's diversity and the differences among Asian countries into a vital driving force for regional security cooperation. We should abide by the basic norms governing international relations such as respecting sovereignty, independence and territorial integrity and non-interference in internal affairs, respect the social systems and development paths chosen by individual countries, and fully respect and accommodate the legitimate security concerns of all parties. To buttress and entrench a military alliance targeted at a third party is not conducive to common security.

Comprehensive security means upholding security in both traditional and non-traditional fields. Asia's security challenges are extremely complicated, and include a range of flashpoints and sensitive issues, as well as ethnic and religious problems. The challenges brought by terrorism, transnational crime, environmental safety, cyber security, energy security, and major natural disasters are clearly on the rise. Traditional and non-traditional security threats are interwoven. Security is a growing issue in both scope and implication.

We should take full account of the historical background and reality of Asia's security issues, adopt a multi-pronged and holistic approach, and enhance regional security governance in a coordinated way. While tackling the immediate security challenges facing the region we should also make plans for addressing potential security threats, and avoid a fragmented and palliative approach that only treats the symptoms.

We should have zero tolerance for terrorism, separatism and extremism, strengthen international and regional cooperation, and step up the fight against these three forces, so as to bring peace and happiness to the people of this region.

Cooperative security means promoting the security of both individual countries and the region as a whole through dialogue and cooperation. As the proverb goes, "Strength does not come from the muscles in the arms, but from the unison of the heart." We should engage in sincere and in-depth dialogue and communication to increase strategic mutual trust, reduce mutual misgivings, seek common ground while resolving differences, and live in harmony with each other. We should bear in mind the common security interests of all countries, and start with low-sensitivity areas to build the awareness of meeting security challenges through cooperation. We should expand the scope and means of cooperation and promote peace and security through cooperation. We should stay committed to resolving disputes through peaceful means, stand against the arbitrary use or threat of force, oppose the provocation and escalation of tensions for self-interest, and eschew the practice of shifting trouble onto neighbors and seeking gain at the expense of others.

In the final analysis, let the people of Asia run the affairs of Asia, solve the problems of Asia and uphold the security of Asia. The people of Asia have the capability and wisdom to achieve peace and stability in the region through enhanced cooperation.

Asia is open to the world. While enhancing our own cooperation with each other, countries in Asia must also firmly commit ourselves to cooperation with countries in other continents, other regions and international organizations. We welcome all parties to play a positive and constructive role in promoting Asia's security and cooperation, and work together to achieve mutually beneficial outcomes for all.

Sustainable security means that we need to focus on both development and security, so that security will be durable. As a Chinese saying goes, "For a tree to grow tall, a strong and solid root is essential; for a river to reach far, an unimpeded source is necessary."[2] Development is the foundation of security, and security the precondition for development. The tree of peace does not grow on barren land, and the fruits of development are not harvested amidst the flames of war. For most Asian countries, development means the greatest security and the master key to regional security issues.

To build an Asian security stronghold that can stand the test of any gale we need to focus on development, zealously improve people's lives and narrow the wealth gap so as to cement the foundation of security. We need to advance the process of common development and regional integration, foster sound interaction between regional economic cooperation and security cooperation for synchronized progress, and promote sustainable security through sustainable development.

Ladies and gentlemen,

Dear friends,

The CICA is the largest and most representative regional security forum with the largest number of participants. Over the past two decades the CICA has undertaken the responsibility to strengthen mutual trust and coordination and promote Asia's security and stability. It has followed the principle of consensus through consultation and made an important contribution to increasing understanding, seeking common ground and expanding cooperation.

Today more than ever, the Asian people wish for peace and stability, and the need to work together to tackle challenges to security is greater than before.

China proposes that we make the CICA a security dialogue and cooperation platform that covers the whole of Asia and, on that basis, explore the establishment of a regional security cooperation architecture. China believes that it is advisable to increase the frequency of the CICA foreign ministers' meetings and possibly summits as circumstances change, so as to strengthen the political guidance of the CICA and chart a blueprint for its development.

China proposes that we enhance the capacity and the institutions of the CICA, support improving the functions of the CICA secretariat, establish a defense consultation mechanism of member states and a task force for supervising the implementation of confidence-building measures in various areas within the CICA framework, and enhance exchanges and cooperation in counter-terrorism, business, tourism, environmental protection, and cultural and people-to-people exchanges.

China proposes that we put in place a nongovernmental exchange network for various parties through holding CICA nongovernmental forums and other means, so as to lay a solid social foundation for spreading the CICA concept of security, increasing the CICA's influence and promoting regional security governance.

China proposes that we strengthen the inclusiveness and openness of the CICA. We need to step up coordination and cooperation with other relevant organizations in the region, and expand dialogue and communication with other regions and relevant international organizations.

China will fulfill its responsibilities as CICA chairman and work with other parties to further improve the status and role of the CICA so that together we can raise security cooperation to a higher level.

Ladies and gentlemen,

Dear friends,

China is a staunch force for upholding peace in the region and the world as a whole and for promoting common development. The Five Principles of Peaceful Coexistence initiated by China together with India and Myanmar have become basic norms governing state-to-state relations. China remains committed to seeking the peaceful settlement of disputes with other countries over territorial sovereignty and maritime rights and interests. China has completely resolved, through friendly consultations, land boundary issues with 12 of its 14 neighboring countries. As an active participant in regional security cooperation, China, jointly with other relevant countries, initiated the Shanghai

Cooperation Organization and proposed the concept of mutual trust, mutual benefit, equality and coordination. China supports ASEAN, the SAARC and the LAS in playing a positive role in regional affairs. China and Russia jointly proposed an Asia Pacific security and cooperation initiative, which has played an important role in strengthening and maintaining peace and stability in the Asia Pacific region. China works to push forward the Six-Party Talks Concerning the Korean Peninsula, and supports peace and reconstruction in Afghanistan, making unremitting efforts in solving international and regional flashpoint issues through dialogue and negotiation. China joined forces with countries in the region and the wider international community to tackle the Asian financial crisis and the international financial crisis, making its due contribution to promoting regional and global economic growth.

China is firmly committed to the path of peaceful development and the mutually beneficial strategy of opening up. It seeks to develop friendly relations and cooperation with other countries on the basis of the Five Principles of Peaceful Coexistence. China's peaceful development begins here in Asia, finds its support in Asia and delivers tangible benefits to Asia.

"Neighbors wish each other well, just as family members do." China always pursues friendship and partnership with its neighbors, seeks to bring amity, security and common prosperity, and works hard to ensure that its development brings benefits to all other countries in Asia. China will work with other countries to speed up the development of a Silk Road Economic Belt and a 21st-century Maritime Silk Road, and hopes that the Asian Infrastructure Investment Bank can be launched at an early date. China will be more involved in the regional cooperation process, and play its part to ensure that development and security in Asia facilitate each other and are mutually reinforcing.

As the saying goes, "Readiness to converge with others makes a mountain high and a river mighty."[3] As a strong champion of the Asian security concept, China also works to put such a security concept into practice. China will take solid steps to strengthen security dialogues and cooperation with other parties, and jointly explore the formulation of a code of conduct for regional security and an Asian security partnership program, making Asian countries good partners who trust one another and cooperate on an equal footing.

China is ready to introduce mechanisms for regular exchange and cooperation with countries in the region to jointly combat the three forces of terrorism, separatism and extremism. China is ready to discuss with other countries in the region the creation of an Asian forum for security cooperation in law enforcement and an Asian security emergency response center, to enhance security cooperation in law enforcement and better respond to major security emergencies. China calls for exchanges and mutual learning among different civilizations and religions through various means, such as conferences for dialogues among Asian civilizations, so that we will be able to draw on each other's experiences and achieve common progress.

Ladies and gentlemen,

Dear friends,

The Chinese people, in their pursuit of the Chinese Dream of great national renewal, stand ready to support and help all other peoples in Asia to realize their own great dreams. Let us work together to realize the Asian dream of lasting peace and common development, and make a greater contribution to advancing the noble cause of peace and development of mankind.

Thank you!

Notes

[1] See note 1, p. 175.

[2] Wei Zheng: *Ten Suggestions to the Emperor*. Wei Zheng (580-643) was a statesman of the Tang Dynasty.

[3] Liu Yuxi: *Inscription on the Stele by the Sacred Way to the Tomb of Wang Ling, Former Imperial Censor of the Tang Dynasty*.

Close Ties with the People

Strictly Enforce Diligence and Thrift,
Oppose Extravagance and Waste[*]

January 17 and February 22, 2013

I

Reports reveal a shocking waste of food. All officials and the public have responded strongly to various sources of wasted food, particularly recreational activities using public funds. It is hurtful to see such severe problems when we all know that more than 100 million rural residents, tens of millions of urban residents and many other people in our country are still plagued by poverty.

We must do something to stop such waste as quickly as possible! We must disseminate our thoughts and intensify our guidance, promote our splendid national tradition of diligence and thrift, and regard frugality as honor and waste as disgrace. The strict enforcement of diligence and thrift must become the common practice of the whole society. All must oppose extravagance and waste.

Party, government and military organs at all levels, institutions, people's organizations and state-owned enterprises as well as leaders and officials at all levels must set an example in strictly obeying the rules for official receptions, and in implementing all measures concerning thrift so as to completely eradicate waste in any activity that is paid with public funds.

Moreover, operational measures that are targeted and instructive should be established, so that thrift is encouraged and waste is punished.

(Comments by Xi Jinping on "Netizens Urging the
Elimination of Waste at the Dinner Table,"
a report submitted by Xinhua News Agency, January 17, 2013)

---

[*] Separate comments on relevant reports by Xinhua News Agency and the *People's Daily*.

II

The Central Committee's call for strict enforcement of diligence and thrift and opposition to extravagance and waste has won widespread acclaim from officials and the public. There should now be a follow-up campaign to ensure that no one simply goes through the motions or follows the rules as a temporary measure, like a passing gust of wind. We must do everything possible, and we must see things through from beginning to end. Nothing can be accomplished unless we take a serious, pragmatic and consistent approach.

For some time now we have solicited advice from people of all walks of life, much of which has been constructive. We must sort through these ideas and put them into practice, sum up the lessons we learn, and draw on experience from both at home and abroad.

Our next major step is to focus on improving the system with regard to official receptions, financial budgets and audits, assessment and accountability, and supervision. To do this we need to refine an overall mechanism that is dynamic, and that provides for rigid institutional constraints, strict systematic execution, strong supervision and examination, and severe sanctions, so that all misbehavior and violation of the rules and regulations relating to recreational activities paid from public funds is reduced to a minimum.

(Comments by Xi Jinping on "Analysis and Suggestions
from Experts and Scholars on Restricting Recreational Activities
Using Public Funds," and some other reports submitted
by the People's Daily, *February 22, 2013)*

The Mass Line: Fundamental to the CPC*

June 18, 2013

The mass line is the life of our Party and the fundamental approach to the Party's work. Launching a program of mass line education and practice is a significant decision taken by the Party to supervise its own conduct and enforce strict discipline. It is an important measure to respond to public demand, to strengthen the Party as a Marxist party that learns, innovates and serves the people, and to advance socialism with Chinese characteristics. It has far-reaching significance for the Party to maintain its progressive nature and integrity, consolidate its governing base and status, and complete the building of a moderately prosperous society in all respects.

First, the program of mass line education and practice is an essential requirement for the Party to realize the objectives set by the 18th CPC National Congress. The Congress proposed to complete the building of a moderately prosperous society in all respects when the CPC celebrates its centenary in 2021, and turn China into a modern socialist country that is prosperous, strong, democratic, culturally advanced and harmonious when the PRC marks its centennial in 2049. After the Congress the CPC Central Committee proposed the Chinese Dream of the rejuvenation of the Chinese nation. To realize the Chinese Dream and the objectives set by the Congress, all Party members must follow the fine tradition of the Party.

What does this mean? It means respecting the Party's long-held traditions of linking theory with practice, maintaining close ties with the people, engaging in criticism and self-criticism, cultivating tenacity

---

* Part of the speech at the conference of the Program of Mass Line Education and Practice held by the CPC Central Committee.

in work, pursuing the truth and being pragmatic. All through the Party's long period of revolution, construction and reform, the Party has always demanded that all its members maintain its fine tradition, and this is what has underpinned one victory after another for the Party and the people.

We must be cognizant, especially during this new era of reform and opening up, that the Party will be exposed to unprecedented risks and challenges as China drives reform and opening up to a deeper level. The task of improving the Party's conduct will never be more important or urgent. Not for one moment should we be lax or suspend our efforts in this regard.

"In the present period of historical change, when problems have piled up and a thousand things wait to be done, it is crucial for us to strengthen the leadership of the Party and correct its work style,"[1] said Deng Xiaoping at the initial launch of reform and opening up. The second generation of the Party leadership headed by Deng Xiaoping, the third generation of the Party leadership headed by Jiang Zemin, and the CPC Central Committee with Hu Jintao as general secretary all made it one of their top priorities to improve the Party's conduct, and carried out a succession of programs to this end – the Party Consolidation[2], the "Three Emphases" Education[3], the Education to Maintain the Pioneering Role of the Party Members[4], and the in-depth study of the Scientific Outlook on Development[5].

The Party has always emphasized that Party conduct has a direct impact on its image, on its prospects of winning or losing public support, and on the very survival or extinction of the Party and the state. Maintaining close ties with the people is essential to improving the Party's conduct. Losing contact with the people would pose the gravest threat to the Party.

Since the Third Plenary Session of the 11th CPC Central Committee in 1978, the Party has reestablished the guiding principles of freeing the mind and seeking truth from facts, attaching more importance to the Party's conduct, and maintaining close ties with the people. The whole Party has burnished its image and improved its conduct, guaranteeing the smooth progress of reform and opening up and the drive for socialist modernization.

As has been the case throughout the Party's history, its close ties with the people are the embodiment of its nature and purpose, the hallmark that distinguishes the CPC from other political parties, and an important factor enabling the CPC to grow strong. The fate of the Party's undertakings relies on whether it can maintain its ties with the people.

Our Party comes from the people, is rooted in the people, and serves the people. Without popular support, none of the Party's achievements or aspirations would be possible. We must always keep close ties with the people, so that the Party can continue to respond to the challenges of governance, reform and opening up, and the market economy, as well as the external environment. Under no circumstances will we ever forsake our commitment to sharing weal and woe with the people. We will never forget the Party's purpose of serving the people wholeheartedly. We will never forgo the historical materialist viewpoint which regards the people as the true heroes. The Party will always serve the public, and govern for the benefit of the people.

In this new era, in order to realize the Chinese Dream and the objectives set by the 18th CPC National Congress, we must remain close to the people, rely on them, and fully mobilize their initiative, enthusiasm and creativity. We have launched the campaign of mass line education and practice with the aim of reminding all Party members that their fundamental purpose is to serve the people wholeheartedly, unite the people through the Party's fine tradition, and work hard with them to realize the objectives set by the Congress and the Chinese Dream.

Second, launching the program of mass line education and practice is an essential requirement for the Party to maintain its progressive nature and its integrity, and consolidate its governing base and status. This is an issue, fundamental to the Party and its future development.

As we have so often repeated, the Party's pioneering role and its role of governance do not remain unchanged once acquired. Even if you had played a pioneering role in the past, there is no guarantee that you will always do so; the fact that you are playing the role now does not mean that you will be progressive forever. Just because you possessed it in the past does not mean that you will own it forever. This is the conclusion of our analysis based on dialectical and historical materialism.

How can we maintain the Party's progressive nature and its integrity, and consolidate its governing role and status? The key is to keep to the Party's mass line and maintain close ties with the people.

As an old Chinese saying goes, "Those who win the people's hearts win the country, and those who lose the people's hearts lose the country." Likewise, the people's support is the most solid foundation for the Party's governance. Winning or losing public support is vital to the Party's survival or extinction. The Party must dedicate its soul and mind to the people, share their weal and woe, and rely on them to continue to make progress. Only then "steadfastly we stand our ground"[6] against "ominous storms that threaten to engulf us."[7]

We have launched the program of mass line education and practice so that the values of honesty, serving the people and remaining down-to-earth can take root in the hearts and actions of all Party members. In this way we can consolidate the Party's governing status, increase the Party's creativity, cohesiveness and professional capabilities, maintain its progressive nature and its integrity, and consolidate its position through broad, profound and reliable public support.

Third, launching the program of mass line education and practice is essential if we are to address the people's pressing concerns. In general, Party organizations, members and officials are practicing the Party's mass line well at present. Party members and officials have set a good example, dedicating themselves to reform, development and stability. They have maintained good relations with the people and won their approval and support. Most of them have done a good job, for which we must give them full credit.

Nevertheless, we must realize that as the world, the country, and the Party undergo profound changes, the perils of mental laxity, mediocrity, isolation from the people, passivity and corruption have become increasingly serious. Many Party officials are losing touch with the people, and some problems are very serious, especially the Four Malfeasances of going through the motions, excessive bureaucracy, self-indulgence, and extravagance.

Going through the motions means doing things for form's sake – the separation of action from knowledge, neglecting what is truly effective, hiding behind piles of documents, and immersing oneself in meetings, the pursuit of vanity and a resort to falsehood.

Some Party officials stop studying Party theory or learning information which they need in performing their duties, while others content themselves with the most superficial understanding, which they can use as window-dressing instead of applying it in real work. They have no intention of studying, nor have they the ability to put what they do know into practice. Some use the requirements for documents and meetings simply as a pretext for generating further documents and meetings; some love to put on a show and seek the limelight; in some places the priority is to highlight leaders' speeches in newspapers and on TV, while neglecting practical work; some have no interest in achieving actual results or solving genuine problems – their only aim is to ingratiate themselves with their superiors, generate headlines or decorate their work reports…one ceremony after another, one summary after another, one award after another. We call this Krikun[8] style.

For some officials, a "grassroots survey" is no more than a comfortable ride in a car, a hurried glance through the window, an affable wave to the cameras, and a casual glance at events outside, rather than a proper investigation into shadows, nooks and crannies. Some turn a blind eye to fake reports, data and models, or even go out of their way to gloss over the truth with lies. No wonder people say that paperwork keeps officials well clear of real life, and a mountain of formalism detaches policies from their implementation.

Excessive bureaucracy means departure from reality, losing touch with the people, arrogance, indifference to facts, conceit, and inflated egos. Some Party officials do not understand or concern themselves with reality. They are reluctant to go to areas experiencing harsh conditions, or help grassroots organizations and people solve problems; they prefer to having nothing to do with them lest there should be more trouble. Their duties are a game to them – they pass the buck or muddle through. Some Party officials, heedless of the people's wishes and the circumstances that apply in their locality, make casual decisions and empty promises. They blindly launch expensive projects, walk away when they fail, and leave behind an unresolved mess; some curry favor with their superiors, and rudely order their subordinates around. People in need of their services find them difficult to access, hard to talk to and impossible to get them to act. They even demand bribes before doing things that are part of their duties, and abuse their power; some follow plans and directions from their superiors without trying to understand them properly. Some implement the decisions of superiors to a superficial degree, while others awkwardly imitate – doing things according to the old way or following others without considering the particular circumstances that apply to them. Some are "empire-builders," high-handed and arbitrary in their approach, intolerant of any alternative view. They reject criticism and offers of help, and refuse to listen to different voices.

The main features of self-indulgence are mental laxity, resting on one's laurels, vanity, coveting pleasure, pursuing ostentation, and seeking to keep oneself amused. Some Party officials have become demoralized, and their faith has been shaken. Their philosophy of life is to indulge themselves in pleasure-seeking – "drinking your fill as long as you have wine to drink"[9] and "seizing the moments of contentment in life and making the most of them."[10] Some have abandoned their ideals in favor of material comforts, vulgar amusements, revelry, drinking, and a life of luxury. Some take on easy tasks and shirk hard work because they have no taste for hardship and effort. They lack motivation and new goals because they are happy with the *status quo*, satisfied with their limited knowledge and understanding, and content with their past achievements. They idle through the day flipping through newspapers, drinking tea and chatting, their gaze wandering abstractedly because they have no purpose.

Extravagance means waste, squandering resources, expensive building programs, endless festivals and ceremonies, a luxurious and dissolute lifestyle, and abuse of power that can extend to actual corruption. Some Party officials spend hundreds of millions of Renminbi on construction of a luxury office building that occupies acres of land and contains facilities for feasting, drinking and amusement. Some are devotees of festivals and ceremonies, sometimes squandering millions of Renminbi or more on a single event. It is the blood and sweat of the people they are tossing away! For some who seek comfort and pleasure their homes can never be too many nor too grand, their cars can never be too luxurious, their banquets can never be too exquisite, and the brands of clothes they wear can never be too famous. Their excesses show disdain for the rules; they take things for granted and always want more. Some demand excessive receptions, stay at expensive hotels, eat all sorts of delicacies, drink fine wines and then take bribes. Some hold membership cards and consumption cards of great value, and indulge themselves in luxury clubs, high-end sports complexes, free travel at home and abroad, and even foreign casinos, where they spend money like water. Some even glory in their misconduct, moral corruption and dissolute lifestyle, instead of feeling shame.

I give these examples to warn all Party members. If we allow these problems to spread like weeds, the consequences will be disastrous, and the tragedy of *Farewell My Concubine*[11], which Mao Zedong used as a metaphor for losing power, may come true. Some of our colleagues have become accustomed to such problems, and take them for granted. This is even more dangerous. As a saying goes, "Stay in a fish market long enough, and one will get used to the stink."[12]

We should keep in mind the ancient warning that "self-indulgence and extravagance lead to decline and demise,"[13] and launch full-scale

examinations, overhauls and clean-ups to eliminate defects and misconduct from the Party, and address the people's most pressing concerns.

Notes

[1] Deng Xiaoping: "Uphold the Four Cardinal Principles," *Selected Works of Deng Xiaoping*, Vol. II, Eng. ed., Foreign Languages Press, Beijing, 1994, pp. 185-186.

[2] "Party Consolidation" refers to the overhaul of the Party's working practices and organization. The program, which lasted from the winter of 1983 to 1987, aimed to unify the Party members' mindset, rectify the Party's work practices, reinforce discipline, and cleanse its organization.

[3] The "Three Emphases" Education refers to the education program in Party spirit and work practices for Party and government leaders above county level. The program, conducted from November 1998 to December 2000, emphasized theoretical study, political awareness, and being honest and upright.

[4] Education to Maintain the Pioneering Role of Party Members refers to the Party-wide program focused on the important thought of the Three Represents. From January 2005 to June 2006 over 70 million Party members and more than 3.5 million grassroots Party organizations participated in the education program.

[5] All Party members took part in the program of in-depth study and implementation of the Scientific Outlook on Development, during the period from September 2008 to February 2010. The program was themed on the Scientific Outlook on Development, with focus on educating Party and government leaders above county level.

[6] Mao Zedong: "Jinggang Mountains," *Mao Zedong Poems*, Eng. ed., Foreign Languages Press, Beijing, 1998, p. 9.

[7] Li He: *Ode to the Journey of Yanmen Prefect*. Li He (790-816) was a leading poet of the Tang Dynasty.

[8] Krikun, a journalist in *Frontline* (1942), a drama written by Alexander Korneychuk during the Great Patriotic War of the former Soviet Union. He created news by reporting rumors and making up stories, and his name is often used to describe fabrication and exaggeration in news reporting.

[9] Luo Yin: *For Myself*. Luo Yin (833-919) was a writer of the Tang Dynasty.

[10] Li Bai: *Invitation to Wine*.

[11] One of the final episodes in the life of rebellious warlord Xiang Yu during the late Qin Dynasty (221-206 BC). Xiang, the self-proclaimed "Overlord of Western Chu" could not tolerate different opinions, and his flawed personality finally resulted in his downfall following the siege of Gaixia. Xiang drank his final toasts

with Concubine Yu, and sang lyrics of heroism and lament. Concubine Yu danced for Xiang one last time, took his sword and committed suicide. Xiang broke out of the siege and fled to the banks of the Wujiang River, where he committed suicide by slitting his throat with his sword. *Farewell My Concubine* is a metaphor for final downfall resulting from arbitrary conduct and losing touch with the people.

[12] *The Family Teaching of Confucius (Kong Zi Jia Yu).*

[13] *New Book of the Tang Dynasty (Xin Tang Shu).*

The Guiding Thoughts and Goals for the Program of Mass Line Education and Practice*

June 18, 2013

The Party Central Committee has stipulated the guiding thoughts, goals and tasks, basic principles, methods, and steps for the Party's program of mass line education and practice. To implement the Central Committee's requirements, we must uphold socialism with Chinese characteristics, and fully implement the plans and decisions made at the Party's 18th National Congress. We must follow the guidance of Marxism-Leninism, Mao Zedong Thought, Deng Xiaoping Theory, the important thought of the Three Represents, and the Scientific Outlook on Development, and make every effort to implement the plans and requirements set forth by the Central Committee since the CPC's 18th National Congress.

We must maintain and develop the Party's pioneering role and integrity, and effectively strengthen education for all Party members on the Party's mass line and the Marxist viewpoint on the people, focusing on serving the people and on being down-to-earth, honest and upright in conduct. We should start by implementing the Eight Rules[1] of the Party Central Committee, and strive to solve the most pressing problems. The key lies in the following:

First, focusing on goals and tasks. We have learned from previous education programs within the Party that well-set goals are central to the success of such programs. When we organize these activities we naturally expect them to produce results, and the greater the better. We should also be realistic when making plans. This

---

* Part of the speech at the conference of the Program of Mass Line Education and Practice held by the CPC Central Committee.

education program will last a year, and be conducted in quarterly units, so we cannot expect to resolve all problems inside the Party at one stroke.

Many problems will remain to be addressed through regular work. Here we must consider one question: Ten wounds partially treated or one completely cured – which is better? Based on this consideration, the Party Central Committee has decided that promoting Party conduct should be the first priority, and our efforts should be concentrated on solving problems relating to the Four Malfeasances of going through the motions, excessive bureaucracy, self-indulgence, and extravagance.

Why should we concentrate on these four problems? Because they run contrary to our Party's very nature and purpose, and because they are the problems that the public hates the most. They are of the most pressing concern to the people, and they are at the root of the greatest damage to the relations between the Party and the people and between officials and the people. All the other problems within the Party are related to the Four Malfeasances, or have spun off from them. Once the Four Malfeasances are resolved, there will be a sounder base for treating other problems.

Following the Party's 18th National Congress, the Political Bureau of the Central Committee made improving Party conduct its priority as a result of the same considerations. We should consolidate our previous achievements in improving Party conduct, and expand them through studying and practicing the Party's mass line.

To solve the Four Malfeasances, we must set an accurate focus, locate the "acupoints," and firmly grasp the vitals, and we must not allow ourselves to be distracted. In fighting against going through the motions, we should focus on promoting down-to-earth work, and educate and guide Party members and officials on improving their approach to theoretical study, meetings and official documents, and working practices. They must be prepared to stand firm on cardinal issues of right and wrong and hold to their principles without flinching. They must devote themselves wholeheartedly to their duties, and spare themselves no effort in understanding the true conditions faced by the people, in promoting concrete measures, and in achieving solid results through a down-to-earth approach.

In fighting excessive bureaucracy, we should focus on solving the problems of isolation from the people and failure to protect their interests. Again we should educate Party members and officials, and guide them in working at the grassroots to understand the true conditions faced by the people, in remaining committed to democratic centralism, in learning from the people, in answering to the people, in serving the people, and in accepting oversight by the people. We must be resolute in correcting problems such as perfunctory performance of duties, evading and shirking responsibilities, and infringing upon the people's interests.

In fighting self-indulgence we should focus on overcoming indulgence in pleasure and privileges. Once more we should educate Party members and officials, and guide them in keeping to the "two musts,"[2] in being wholeheartedly devoted to public service and performing their duties with diligence, in upholding political integrity, and in preserving a spirit of high principles and hard work.

In fighting extravagance, we should focus on putting an end to unhealthy practices such as pleasure-seeking, luxury and dissipation. Again we should educate Party members and officials, and guide them in practicing thrift and standing against waste, in leading a simple life, in being strict with their spending, and in doing everything in a no-frills manner.

To put an end to the Four Malfeasances, we must start from reality, identify the main pressing problems, and concentrate on those problems which are most severe or most pressing. We must be precise in identifying our targets, and achieve effective results.

Second, implementing general requirements with diligence. During the Rectification Movement in Yan'an[3], Mao Zedong proposed an intensive campaign to fight against subjectivism, sectarianism, and "eight-legged Party essays."[4] He said that it was not easy to cleanse the Party of these defects, and that patients must be given a heavy dose of stimulus to wake them up and make them sweat before being sent for treatment. Learning from the experience of the Yan'an Rectification Movement, the current requirements for studying and practicing the Party's mass line have been clearly defined: "Examine oneself in the mirror, straighten one's clothes and hat, take a bath, and treat one's disease." It can also be summarized in four phrases: self-purification, self-improvement, self-innovation and self-cultivation. However, it is easier to say than to do.

To "examine oneself in the mirror," Party members should use the Party Constitution as a mirror in which to measure themselves. How do they perform in terms of the Party's discipline, the people's expectations, and their role models, and how can they improve themselves in performance and conduct? They should identify their shortcomings in upholding the Party's principles, promoting healthy working practices, and maintaining integrity and self-discipline. They should recognize how far they have fallen short of these standards, and they should be clear in terms of how they will improve themselves.

A mirror can be used for self-reflection, and it can also be directed towards others. On this occasion it is to be used for Party members themselves. In real life, some people always feel good about themselves, and seldom look in the mirror. Some are only too well aware of their shortcomings, so they are afraid of looking in the mirror. Some like to admire themselves in the best possible light, and so they put on make-up before looking in the mirror. Some take the view that they are perfect; it is others who are disfigured – they only hold up the mirror in front of others. None of these is compatible with Communist principles. Party members and officials should dare to look in the mirror, and do so frequently; in particular they should use the mirror for profound self-examination, to reflect upon even the tiniest flaws. In this way they will be able to see their shortcomings and rectify them.

To "straighten one's clothes and hat" means that one should, after examining oneself in the mirror, and based on the principles of serving the people, being down-to-earth in one's work, and upholding integrity, dare to face one's weaknesses and shortcomings, strictly

observe the Party's discipline, especially its political discipline, start
with themselves in facing up to problems, and take immediate steps
to rectify their conduct. They should take the initiative to renew their
faith in the Party character, review their obligations as Party members,
and stiffen their resolve to observe Party discipline and state laws, so
as to present a positive image as good Communists. It is not enough
to "straighten one's clothes and hat" only once, they need to "examine
themselves three times a day."[5]

It takes courage to face problems and try to solve them, and this
means taking the initiative. "Disasters often result from neglecting the
smallest things; the wise and brave are often trapped by their minor
indulgences."[6] Developing a habit of regularly "straightening one's
clothes and hat" will help prevent small wrongdoings from growing
into big ones, and can also effectively protect against "falling feathers
submerging a boat and an excess load breaking a cart axle."[7]

To "take a bath," Party members should follow the spirit of the
Rectification Movement and engage in criticism and self-criticism
among themselves. They should conduct in-depth analysis of the rea-
sons for their problems, dust off their minds and their actions, and on
the basis of what they find beneath, address both problems in their
way of thinking and in their conduct, so as to maintain the political
integrity of Communists.

We are exposed to dust every day, which is why we need to take
showers regularly. Use some soap, give yourself a scrub with a loo-
fah, and then rinse yourself off – you will feel clean and refreshed.
Similarly, our minds and actions can get dusty too, tainted by political
microbes, so we also need to "take a bath" to rid ourselves of dust and
grime, refresh our body and mind, unclog our pores, and get our me-
tabolism working, so that we carry out our duties earnestly and uphold
personal integrity. Some prefer to cover up the dust in their minds and
actions, and are loath to "take a bath." In such cases, our colleagues
and our Party organizations should provide them with some help.

To "treat one's disease" means the Party believes that it should
learn from past mistakes to avoid future ones, and cure the disease to

save the patient. Our Party draws distinctions between different cases, and prepares different remedies for different diseases. Party members and officials who have problems in conduct are educated and warned, those with serious problems are investigated and punished, and special programs are organized to crack down on serious misconduct and major problems.

When a person is ill, he must visit the doctor for treatment, perhaps even have an operation if the case is serious. If it is an ailment in mind or conduct, it should also be treated as soon as possible. A minor illness can develop into a serious complication if we conceal the ailment and avoid the doctor, and a disease can spread from the skin to internal organs, and eventually become incurable. This is exactly what we mean by "curing an illness is easy at the start, but saving a terminal patient is hard."[8]

Party organizations at all levels should take strong measures to help Party members and officials who have problems in identifying their diseases, and provide remedies according to the symptoms. Those who need to take Traditional Chinese Medicine (TCM) should take TCM, those who need to take Western medicine should take Western medicine, and those who need combined treatment of TCM and Western medicine should be given such treatment. Those who need operations should have operations performed on them. We must effectively ensure that the Party is run with strict discipline.

Third, engaging in criticism and self-criticism following the spirit of the Rectification Movement. Criticism and self-criticism is a good Party tradition, and an effective weapon for enhancing the capacity of Party organizations in their effort to maintain unity and solidarity inside the Party. Why do we need to follow the spirit of the Rectification Movement and engage in criticism and self-criticism? Because various problems afflicting the people inside the Party, especially the Four Malfeasances, are chronic and persistent conditions that need to be addressed with courage. We must dare to lose face in exposing shortcomings and mistakes, dare to take up our hammers and crack the tough nuts, dare to engage in battles, and dare to dig down to the roots and touch the soul. Currently the keen blade of criticism and self-criticism has become dull and rusty in many places, and cannot reach down to the deeper levels of problems and deal with them. Like hitting a person with a feather duster, it causes no pain. In some places self-criticism has morphed into self-praise, and criticism into flattery. In our new program we must work hard on criticism and self-criticism.

We should ensure that Party branch meetings effectively carry out such criticism and self-criticism. Party organizations at all levels should educate Party members and officials in the formula of "unity-criticism-unity," and relieve them of the worries of losing face when criticizing one's self, of suffering from retaliation for criticizing one's superiors, of damaging friendships with colleagues by criticizing persons of equivalent rank, and of losing support by criticizing subordinates.

Party members and officials should not only conduct in-depth analysis and examination of themselves, but also share genuine criticism of each other to touch the mind and soul. Their reddened faces and sweat that so result will bring a host of problems into the open, and show the direction towards rectification. Both criticism and self-criticism should be conducted with respect for facts, with good intentions towards others, and for the public good. There will be no burying of heads in the sand. No one will act either superficially or excessively during criticism sessions, and personal grudges will be avoided. Good advice is jarring to the ear, just as good medicine is bitter to the tongue. In response to criticism, you should correct mistakes if you have made any, and guard against them if you have not. We should never use "criticism" as a weapon against criticism, or fight each other without principle.

The eyes of the people are sharp. They see very clearly and are only too aware of problems with Party members and officials. In conducting our program we must be open to the public, and solicit opinions and suggestions from the people. We must organize orderly public participation at each stage of the process, and allow the people to supervise our actions and air their views. We should avoid "talking to ourselves or singing to ourselves," or working behind closed doors where the air circulates only internally. We should avoid isolating ourselves from the people.

Fourth, leading officials taking the lead. We often hear voices crying out that long-standing problems cannot be solved because they are rooted in the upper levels, although the symptoms appear at the lower levels. The upper level is sick, but the lower level receives the medicine. Indeed, many problems of isolation from the people are apparent in leading bodies, leading groups and leading officials. This program should concentrate on leading bodies, leading groups and leading officials above the county level.

As the saying goes, one must discipline oneself before disciplining others, and one must be a good blacksmith to forge good tools. The Central Committee has decided to start the program from the Political Bureau, aiming at setting a good example. Leading bodies, leading groups and leading officials above the county level must also set good examples.

Leading officials at all levels are the organizers, promoters and supervisors of the program, but they are also participants. They should take part in activities as ordinary Party members and strive for greater achievements in studying and practicing the Party's mass line, and also in bettering their ability to analyze and solve pressing problems.

Whether an official can conduct a precise, in-depth and strict self-assessment is an important gauge for judging his role as a leader in this program. Those who are selfless are fearless.

Officials should put aside their airs and listen carefully to the opinions of their subordinates, of the grassroots organizations, of Party members, and of the ordinary people. They should engage in self-examination by setting themselves as standards and carefully looking for any pressing problems in improving their own conduct. They should look into the conduct of their leading groups, their departments and their regions, conduct in-depth analysis of the root causes of any problems, and decide on the direction for rectification and any concrete measures to be taken.

In examining problems officials must avoid at all costs dealing with problems while avoiding those who are behind the problems, dealing with the problems of others while avoiding their own, and dealing with minor problems while avoiding serious ones. Backed by confidence and resolve, we will boldly engage in criticism and self-criticism, achieve positive results in solving pressing problems, and succeed in making upper levels set the example for lower levels.

Fifth, establishing a long-term mechanism. Maintaining the Party's close ties with the people is a constant topic for study, and problems relating to conduct recur and persist. It is impossible to accomplish the whole task at one stroke, and we cannot promote Party conduct in temporary phases, like a passing gust of wind. Our efforts in this regard must be constant, and we must have long-term plans. As our first measure we should address pressing problems of keen concern to the people, and at the same time we should plan for the future and establish a long-term mechanism for encouraging Party members and officials to serve the people, be down-to-earth in their work, and uphold integrity in office.

After many years of experimentation and practice, we have developed a systematic framework of regulations for implementing the Party's mass line and maintaining close ties with the people. Most of the regulations are effective and are recognized as such by the people, and we should continue to follow them. At the same time, the Party Central Committee has new requirements for the future, and departments and regions will also participate in creating new and fresh experiences.

We should integrate the requirements of the Central Committee, actual needs, and fresh experiences to develop new systems that are appropriate to the current situation, to upgrade the existing systems and to abolish those that are not required. Any newly-developed or improved system must be easy to implement, be coherent with the established laws, and function within the existing legal framework. Attention must be given to formulating supporting measures to match the new systems and make sure that they are precisely targeted and able to guide our work effectively.

Once a system is in place we must all abide by it, and ensure that everyone is equal before it and that no exceptions arise in its application. We must be firm in protecting its authority, and resolute in responding to those who refuse to be bound by it or feign compliance while undermining it. We should let our systems act as rigorous constraints for ensuring that Party members and officials maintain close ties with and serve the people, and that Party members and officials have the individual will to implement the Party's mass line.

Notes

[1] The Eight Rules were proposed by the Political Bureau of the 18th Central Committee of the CPC to cut bureaucracy and maintain close ties with the people. They are summarized as follows: improving inspection and fact-finding trips, streamlining conferences and other activities, reducing documents and briefings, standardizing arrangements for visits abroad, enhancing security procedures, improving news reports, imposing restriction on publishing of writings without authorization, and practicing diligence and frugality.

[2] The "two musts" refer to "our comrades must remain modest and prudent, neither conceited nor rash, in our working practices; and our comrades must remain hardworking despite difficulties in our working practices." They were proposed by Mao Zedong in the Report to the Second Plenary Session of the Seventh Central Committee of the CPC. At the time, the CPC was about to win state power nationwide. Mao cautioned the whole Party on standing the test of exercising governance and against arrogance and complacency, love of pleasure and estrangement from the people that would end the rule of the CPC.

[3] Yan'an Rectification Movement refers to a Marxist education campaign inside the CPC from 1942 to 1945. Its main aims were: to fight against objectivism in order to improve theoretical study; to fight against sectarianism in order to improve Party conduct; and to fight against "eight-legged Party essays" in order to improve writing.

[4] The "eight-legged essay" was a special writing skill tested in the imperial examinations during China's Ming and Qing dynasties. This type of essay was empty in content, focused exclusively on form and mainly involved word play. Each section of the essay had to follow a rigid pattern, and even the number of words used was

predefined. Examinees just wrote essays by following the rules and according to the literal meaning of the topic. The phrase "eight-legged Party essay" refers to empty writing full of revolutionary stock phrases and jargon composed by Party members for speeches or other publicity work.

⁵ *The Analects of Confucius (Lun Yu)*.

⁶ Ouyang Xiu: *New History of the Five Dynasties (Xin Wu Dai Shi)*. Ouyang Xiu (1007-1072) was a statesman and writer of the Northern Song Dynasty.

⁷ Sima Qian: *Records of the Historian (Shi Ji)*.

⁸ Fan Ye: *The Book of the Eastern Han Dynasty (Hou Han Shu)*. Fan Ye (398-445) was a historian during the Northern and Southern Dynasties.

Establish and Promote the Conduct of "Three Stricts and Three Earnests"*

March 9, 2014

Promoting good Party conduct is always high on our agenda. We will fall short of our aims if this program tails off and we become lax in the later stages. Leading officials at all levels should enforce standards of good conduct on themselves and others. Be strict in self-development, the exercise of power and self-discipline; be earnest in making plans, opening up new undertakings and upholding personal integrity.

Being strict in self-development means that leading officials should strengthen their sense of Party awareness, stand firm in support of the ideals and principles of the Party, cultivate integrity, pursue lofty goals, make a point of distancing themselves from vulgar interests, and resist unhealthy practices and evil influences.

Being strict in the exercise of power means that leading officials should exercise power in the interests of the people, exercise power in accordance with rules and regulations, keep power within the confines of systemic checks, and neither seek privileges at any time nor abuse power for personal gain.

Being strict in self-discipline means that leading officials should respect discipline and always be ready to apply the rod to themselves, guard against all temptations when alone, be prudent, engage in diligent self-examination, abide by Party discipline and state laws, and uphold integrity in governance.

---

* Main points of the speech at the deliberation session of the Anhui delegation to the Second Session of the 12th National People's Congress.

Being earnest in making plans means that leading officials should take facts as the basis for work planning, ensure that all ideas, policies and plans are in line with actual conditions, objective laws and scientific principle, and avoid being overly ambitious and divorced from reality.

Being earnest in opening up new undertakings means that leading officials should be down-to-earth in their approach to their duties, be pragmatic and solid in their work, be bold in taking on responsibilities and facing problems, and be adept at solving problems. They should strive to create concrete results that will stand up to being tested by practice, by the people and by time.

Being earnest in upholding personal integrity means that leading officials should remain loyal to the Party, to the organization, to the people, and to their colleagues. They should be honest and truthful, do sound work, be aboveboard, and be just and upright.

We must work to resolve problems with force and tenacity as a hammer drives a nail. We must make sure that we start well and end well, and work wholeheartedly to produce the best possible results so as to achieve the greatest possible success in improving Party conduct.

Combat Corruption

Power Must Be "Caged" by the System[*]

January 22, 2013

All Party members must act in compliance with the plans made at the 18th CPC National Congress, combat and prevent corruption in a more scientific and effective way, and resolutely press ahead with the effort to improve Party conduct, uphold integrity and root out corruption. In the fight against corruption we must adhere to the guidance of Deng Xiaoping Theory, the important thought of the Three Represents and the Scientific Outlook on Development, and follow the principle of addressing both symptoms and root causes, taking an integrated approach, mete out punishment and ensure prevention, with the emphasis on the latter.

We must strengthen our Party if we are to fulfill the goals and tasks set out at its 18th National Congress, including the Two Centenary Goals, and realize the Chinese Dream of the great renewal of the Chinese nation. Improving Party conduct, upholding integrity and combating corruption are important tasks in the course of building the Party. Only if we remain clean and upright in governance and exercise power in a fair way can we win public trust and support.

Over the past 30 years since the reform and opening-up policy was introduced, the Party's second and third central leadership, with Deng Xiaoping and Jiang Zemin as their respective cores, and the Party Central Committee with Hu Jintao as general secretary, consistently attached great importance to the tasks of improving Party conduct, upholding integrity, and combating corruption.

* Main points of the speech at the Second Plenary Session of the 18th CPC Central Commission for Discipline Inspection.

They maintained a clear stand against corruption, adopted effective measures against it, and made remarkable achievements which have played an important role in preserving and developing the Party's advanced nature and purity, and provided a strong guarantee for the Party's leadership in the reform and opening-up effort, and the socialist modernization drive.

Our Party is by and large sound. Yet, we must be fully aware that some areas are still prone to misconduct and corruption, major cases of violation of Party discipline and state laws have had serious adverse effects on society, the fight against corruption remains a serious challenge, and the people are dissatisfied with our work in many areas. Faced with the long-term, complicated and arduous tasks of improving Party conduct, upholding integrity and combating corruption, we must persevere in our anti-corruption effort and always remain vigilant against corruption and degeneracy. The key is to repeatedly stress the fight against corruption and make a long-term commitment. We must solidify our resolve, ensure that all cases of corruption are investigated and prosecuted, and that all instances of graft are rectified, continue to remove the breeding grounds for corruption, and further win public trust by making real progress in the fight against corruption.

Our Party is a Marxist party, the organization of which relies on revolutionary ideals and strict discipline. This has always been our Party's fine tradition and unique advantage. The more complicated the situation and the heavier the tasks facing the Party, the more we need to reinforce discipline and the more we need to safeguard unity within the Party. In this way we can ensure that the whole Party is unified in terms of determination and synchronized in action and progress. To run the Party with strict discipline, we have to first and foremost implement strict political discipline, which in turn starts from observing and safeguarding the Party Constitution. The essence of observing the Party's political discipline is to adhere to the Party's leadership, basic theory, basic line, basic program, basic experience and basic requirements, keep in line with the Party Central Committee, and conscientiously safeguard its authority. All Party members must keep in line with the Party Central Committee ideologically and politically as well as in their actions concerning the Party's basic theories, guidelines, principles and policies, and other matters of overall importance. Party organizations and officials at all levels must develop a holistic view and appropriately handle the relationship between ensuring smooth implementation of the central leadership's orders and policies and conducting work with an innovative spirit based on concrete conditions, making sure that all plans concerning local work and development are based on the prerequisite of implementing the central leadership's guidelines. We must prevent or, if necessary, rectify departmental and local protectionism and parochialism, and never allow local policies to trump central policies, never countenance the sidelining of central decrees or prohibitions, and never engage in perfunctory, selective or compromised enforcement of the central leadership's policy decisions and plans.

Every Party member, especially leading officials, must enhance his understanding of the Party Constitution, observe the Constitution in both words and actions, and maintain in all circumstances a firm political belief, political stance and political orientation. Party organizations at all levels must take the initiative to implement and safeguard the Party's political discipline, and raise Party members' awareness of observing it. Party discipline inspection commissions at all levels must put priority on ensuring compliance with the Party's political discipline, and strengthen supervision and inspection on the implementation of political discipline.

The issue of working style is in no sense a small one. If misconduct is not corrected but allowed to run rampant, it will build an invisible wall between our Party and the people. As a result, our Party will lose its base, lifeblood and strength. Regarding the task of improving our working style, each effort counts, but carrying on and furthering the spirit of hard struggle is of fundamental importance. The task of improving our working style is arduous. The Eight Rules provide us with a starting point and a call for us to improve our work practices. They are not the highest standards nor our ultimate goal, but the first step to improving our working style as well as the basic requirements for Communists. As a saying goes, "He who is good at governing through restriction should first restrict himself then others."[1] Officials at all levels must conduct themselves in an exemplary fashion, take the lead in improving their conduct, and keep their promises. We must practice frugality in all aspects of our work, and resolutely oppose waste, extravagance and self-indulgence. We should vigorously carry out the fine traditions of thrift and hard work of the Chinese nation, and advocate the ideas of taking pride in thrift and shame in waste so that a healthy atmosphere of practicing thrift and opposing waste will become predominant.

All localities and departments must fully implement the relevant regulations on improving Party conduct, and implement these regulations in every aspect and in every link of our work. The people's satisfaction is the standard for measuring progress in changing our way of work. We must extensively solicit public opinions and suggestions, steadily accept public assessment and supervision by the whole of society, and make improvements in areas concerning which people have expressed dissatisfaction. The Central Commission for Discipline Inspection of the Party, the Ministry of Supervision, and Party discipline inspection commissions and supervision agencies at all levels must strengthen inspection and supervision to ensure that Party discipline is implemented, accountability is maintained, and performance is ensured. We should fight corruption with strong determination, follow the spirit of "leaving a mark in the iron tools we clutch and footprints in the stones we tread," persevere in our anti-corruption effort till we achieve final success rather than start off full of sound and fury and then taper off in a whimper. We must let the whole Party and the people oversee power, and demonstrate to the people continuous and real results of Party conduct and the combat of corruption.

The resolute determination in punishing and wiping out corruption demonstrates the strength of our Party, and is a common aspiration of all Party members and the public as well. The Party has shown a firm determination and an unequivocal attitude in strictly investigating and prosecuting serious cases of violation of Party discipline involving Party members and officials, including some high-ranking ones. This is a clear signal to the whole Party and the whole of society that anyone who violates Party discipline and state laws, whoever he is and whatever position he holds, will be fully investigated and severely punished. This is not empty talk. We must not let up one iota in terms of governing the Party with strict discipline.

We should continue to catch "tigers" as well as "flies"[2] when dealing with cases of leading officials in violation of Party discipline and state laws as well as misconduct and corruption problems that directly affect the people's interests. All are equal before the law and Party discipline; whoever is involved in a corruption case must be thoroughly and impartially investigated.

We should continue to build a complete system of combating corruption through both punishment and prevention, strengthen education on combating corruption and upholding integrity, and promote the culture of clean government. We must improve the system of checking and overseeing the exercise of power, reinforce state legislation against corruption, improve intra-party rules, regulations and institutions concerning the fight against corruption and upholding integrity, carry forward reforms in areas prone to corruption, and ensure that government agencies exercise their power in accordance with authorization and procedures. We must enhance checks and supervision over the exercise of power, make sure that power is "caged" by the system, and form a punishment mechanism to deter corruption, a warning mechanism to prevent corruption and a guarantee mechanism to curb corruption. Officials at all levels must bear firmly in mind the fact that nobody is above the law and that all officials must exercise state power to serve the people, be responsible to the people and be supervised by the people. We must strengthen the monitoring of "the first men in command," implement democratic centralism, increase transparency in administration, and ensure that leading officials do not act in a high-handed manner or seek personal gain.

In combating corruption and upholding integrity we must also oppose ideas and practices smacking of privilege. Members of the CPC are at all times ordinary members of the working people. Party members are only entitled to some personal benefits and job-related functions and powers prescribed by laws and policies, and must not seek any personal gain or privilege over and above those. The issue of privilege is not only a major concern in our efforts to improve Party conduct and build a clean government, but also a crucial problem that affects the Party's and the state's capacity to preserve their vitality and vigor. We must adopt effective measures to resolutely oppose and curb ideas and instances of seeking privilege.

We must mobilize the whole Party to improve Party conduct, uphold integrity and combat corruption. Within the scope of their functions and duties, Party committees at all levels should bear total leadership responsibility for improving Party conduct and building a clean government. We must continue to implement and improve the leadership system and working mechanism for combating corruption, give full play to the role of Party discipline inspection commissions, supervision departments, and judiciary and auditing agencies, and work with them in a concerted effort to better improve Party conduct, uphold integrity and combat corruption. We must ensure support for Party discipline inspection commissions and supervision agencies in performing their duties, and show concern and care for people working at these commissions and agencies. We should pay special attention to protecting those who are fully aware of Party spirit and are courageous enough to stick to principle, and create conditions favorable for them to do their jobs. Party discipline inspection commissions and supervision agencies at all levels must also step up their efforts to build a contingent of honest officials, and improve their capacity to carry out their functions and duties, so that they can ensure better inspection and supervision.

Notes

[1] Xun Yue: *History as a Mirror (Shen Jian)*. Xun Yue (148-209) was a philosopher and historian of the Eastern Han Dynasty.

[2] Referring to senior and junior officials guilty of corruption. – *Tr.*

Historical Wisdom Helps Us
Combat Corruption and Uphold Integrity[*]

April 19, 2013

We should not only draw on historical experiences, but also learn from them. We are confronted with a complex and volatile international situation and an arduous task of promoting reform, development and stability. To fulfill the Two Centenary Goals and realize the Chinese Dream of the rejuvenation of the Chinese nation we must ensure that the Party supervises its own conduct and runs itself with strict discipline. We must draw upon the fine culture of clean government in Chinese history, steadily improve the Party's leadership and governance skills, and become better able to combat corruption, prevent degeneracy and ward off risks. We must also ensure that the Party is always the firm leadership core guiding the cause of Chinese socialism.

To improve Party conduct, uphold integrity and combat corruption, we need to continue the successful practices the Party has long accumulated, learn from other countries' beneficial experiences and draw upon the valuable legacy of Chinese history. China's history of combating corruption and its ancient anti-corruption culture offer enlightenment, as do the failures and successes of the past. This historical wisdom can help us do a better job in combating corruption and upholding integrity today.

Through a thorough review of history in China and elsewhere, our Party has realized that improving Party conduct, upholding integrity and combating corruption are vital for the survival of the Party and the state. The key is to remain firmly reliant on the people, main-

---

* Main points of the speech at the fifth group study session of the Political Bureau of the 18th CPC Central Committee which Xi presided over.

tain close ties with them, and never become isolated from them. To achieve this, we must do everything in our power to address corruption and other negative phenomena, see to it that the Party always identifies itself with the people, and shares their concerns and ultimately their destiny.

The CPC Central Committee has called upon us to improve our working practices by opposing the Four Malfeasances. This serves as a focus for combating corruption and upholding integrity, as well as a starting point for consolidating popular support for the Party's governance. All Party members must understand the political importance of this issue, stay alert, strictly adhere to the "two musts," improve our working practices, and crack down on corruption with a strong determination. We must follow the spirit of "leaving a mark in the iron tools we clutch and footprints in the stones we tread," and continue to win popular trust with new victories in the fight against corruption.

We must raise public awareness of the need to combat corruption and uphold integrity, promote a culture of clean government, and combine the rule of law with the rule of virtue. Starting by enhancing political and moral integrity will be of fundamental importance because political integrity is essential for Marxist parties to stay pure, and moral integrity is a fundamental trait for officials to remain clean, honest and upright. We should encourage and guide Party members and officials to adhere to their convictions and ideals, be politically firm as Communists, become morally stronger to pursue clean government, and build up their psychological defenses against corruption and degeneracy. We should improve Party members and officials politically and theoretically, strengthen education in and fostering of the Party spirit, and bolster ethics. We should guide them in studying and applying Marxism-Leninism, Mao Zedong Thought, and the system of theories of socialism with Chinese characteristics, in developing a solid worldview and a healthy outlook on power and career, and in being model practitioners of the socialist maxims of honor and disgrace[1]. Theoretical study and improvement will ensure that Party members and officials are fully committed to their work, and high moral standards will help them to stay clear-minded in exercising state power. In this way, we can also help Party members and officials increase their awareness of the Party's purpose of serving the people wholeheartedly, and always preserve the noble character and political integrity of Communists.

Institutions are of fundamental, overall and long-lasting importance, and are closely related to the stability of the country. The solution to the problem of corruption is to improve the system that checks and oversees the exercise of power, grant oversight powers to the people, and make the exercise of power more transparent and institutionalized. We should prevent and fight corruption more properly and effectively, establish a complete system for preventing and combating corruption, and work harder to ensure the stringent enforcement of anti-corruption laws and discipline. We should analyze typical cases thoroughly, strengthen reform in areas prone to corruption, improve our institutions and systems to reduce loopholes to an absolute minimum, and eliminate any breeding grounds for corruption through further reform.

We must tirelessly combat corruption, and always remain vigilant against it. We should keep it in mind that "Many worms will disintegrate wood, and a big enough crack will lead to the collapse of a wall."[2] We must be tough in cracking down on corruption, and ensure that all cases of corruption are investigated and that all corrupt officials are punished, catching "tigers" as well as "flies" – senior officials as well as junior ones guilty of corruption. In this way, we will effectively protect the legitimate rights and interests of the people and see to it that our officials remain honest and upright, that the government remains clean, and that political integrity is upheld.

Notes

[1] On March 4, 2006, Hu Jintao attended a group meeting of the Fourth Session of the Tenth National Committee of the Chinese People's Political Consultative Conference and held discussions with committee members of the China Democratic League and China Association for Promoting Democracy. At the meeting, he put forth the socialist maxims of honor and disgrace, which consist of the following eight maxims: Loving the motherland is honorable and harming it is disgraceful; serving the people is honorable and ignoring them is disgraceful; respect for science is honorable and ignorance is disgraceful; working hard is honorable and being lazy is disgraceful; working with and helping others is honorable and profiting at their expense is disgraceful; being honest and trustworthy is honorable and sacrificing principles for profit is disgraceful; being law-abiding and disciplined is honorable and violating the law and discipline is disgraceful; living a simple life is honorable and living extravagantly is disgraceful.

[2] *The Book of Lord Shang (Shang Jun Shu)*. This book is a representative Legalist work by Shang Yang and his followers. It is also an important basis for research into the legal philosophy of the Shang Yang School. Shang Yang (c. 390-338 BC) was a statesman, thinker and major representative of the Legalists in the middle period of the Warring States. He initiated a series of reforms in the State of Qin. These reforms, known as the Reforms of Lord Shang, introduced a new feudal system in the State of Qin and made the state prosperous and strong within a short period of time.

Improve Party Conduct, Uphold Integrity
and Combat Corruption*

January 14, 2014

We should adhere to the principle that the Party should supervise its own conduct and run itself with strict discipline, and strengthen the Party's leadership in improving Party conduct, upholding integrity, and combating corruption. We should improve our institutions to better fight against corruption. We must also redouble our efforts in political and theoretical education, reinforce stricter Party discipline, continue to remove the Four Malfeasances be severe in cracking down on corruption, and respond to the demands of the people.

In 2013 the CPC Central Committee made it a priority to improve Party conduct, uphold integrity and combat corruption. In compliance with the decisions and plans made by the Central Committee, the Central Commission for Discipline Inspection has fought firmly against corruption by strengthening Party discipline, especially by reinforcing political discipline, enhancing oversight of enforcement, and improving investigation into and prosecution of corruption cases. Through the concerted efforts of Party committees, governments, discipline inspection commissions and supervisory agencies at all levels, progress has been made in improving Party conduct, ensuring clean government and combating corruption. The campaign started with the Political Bureau of the CPC Central Committee, emphasizing the exemplary role of the Political Bureau. We started to eliminate malpractices and promote integrity by solving pressing problems,

---

* Main points of the speech at the Third Plenary Session of the 18th Central Commission for Discipline Inspection.

and we have made remarkable progress. In resolutely dealing with cases of corruption, we have caught "tigers" as well as "flies," and thus maintained a tough stance against corrupt officials. We have promoted procedure-based exercise of power, strengthened oversight and inspection, and opened up the channels for public complaint and oversight. All of this has been well received by both officials and the general public.

While affirming our achievements, we must also be aware that there are still breeding grounds for corruption. The fight against corruption remains a serious and complex challenge. Instances of misconduct and corruption have had an adverse effect on society, and they must be immediately addressed. The whole Party must realize that the fight against corruption is a long-term, complex, and arduous task. We must be firm in our determination and demonstrate great courage in carrying this campaign through to the end. Just as we would take a heavy dose of medicine to treat a serious disease, we must apply stringent laws to address disorder.

Establishing a sound system of combating corruption through both punishment and prevention represents our national strategy. In 2013 the Central Committee issued the "Work Plan for Establishing a Complete System of Combating Corruption Through Both Punishment and Prevention (2013-2017)." This is the document that guides our strategy. Party committees at all levels must thoroughly implement the demands of this document, which is an important political task throughout our efforts to promote reform, development and stability.

In terms of maintaining the intimate relationship between the Party and the people, we cannot expect to treat this as a one-off campaign and then rest on our laurels. It must be a continuous and relentless effort. Fortunately, we have already got off to a good start, and we can take it forward from here in steps. If we want to develop a healthy Party culture we must first and foremost have firm beliefs, and bear in mind the Party's nature, fundamental goals, and requirements of officials. As officials under the leadership of the Party, we must separate public and personal interests and put public interests above personal interests. Only if we always act for the public good can we be honest and upright in our conduct, and remain clean and prudent in exercising power. Problems of misconduct often involve the handling of private and public interests, and misuse of public funds and state power. Public funds must be used for public purposes, and not one cent should be spent on seeking personal gain. State power must be exercised for the people, and it must never be used as a tool for private benefit. Officials must always bear this in mind, make a clear distinction between public and private interests, devote themselves to serving the public, and practice strict self-discipline.

To fight resolutely against corruption, and prevent the Party from succumbing to decay and degeneration through overlong access to power are two major political tasks that we must work hard on. We must remain resolute in wiping out corruption and show zero tolerance for it. Once a corrupt official is identified, we must conduct a thorough investigation. The important thing is to take measures to prevent and curb corruption in its earliest stage of development, addressing problems of corruption as soon as they are found, in the same way as we treat a disease promptly when it is diagnosed. Any delay in dealing with corruption may lead to more serious problems, and must not be allowed. Every official must bear the following in mind: "Do not try dipping into the public coffers because a thieving hand is bound to get caught,"[1] and "Contemplating good and pursuing it, as if you could not reach it; contemplating evil, and shrinking from it, as you would from thrusting a hand into boiling water."[2] Officials must be in awe of Party discipline and state laws rather than trust to luck in the hope of escaping punishment for corruption.

We must improve Party conduct, uphold integrity and combat corruption through further reform. We must reform the Party's discipline inspection system, improve the system and mechanisms for combating corruption, double the effectiveness of oversight over and restraint on power, and ensure the independence and authority of discipline inspection commissions at all levels. We must improve checks on power, distribute power in a scientific way, and form an effective framework for the exercise of power. We must strengthen oversight with focus on officials, giving particular attention to those first in command and how they exercise their power, and intensify mutual oversight within leadership. We must increase transparency, publicize the procedures through which power is exercised in accordance with the law, and let the people oversee the exercise of power, so as to ensure that it is properly used. In combating corruption, Party committees should be duty-bound, while discipline inspection commissions should take on supervisory responsibilities. They all should strengthen the accountability system to prevent our institutions from becoming a façade. All Party committees, Party discipline inspection commissions, and other relevant departments must fulfill their responsibilities. In adopting reform measures, we should keep in mind the task of combating corruption through both punishment and prevention, synchronize reform measures with the fight against corruption at all stages from preparation to deployment and implementation, so as to close all possible loopholes and ensure the smooth progress of reform.

Our compliance with Party discipline should be unconditional. We must turn our words into actions, and make sure that Party discipline is fully implemented and any violation is investigated. We must not allow our findings to become a dusty document resting on the top shelf. Party organizations at all levels must increase awareness of the need to abide by the Party's political principles, and discipline inspection commissions at all levels must see their priority as safeguarding the Party's political discipline so as to ensure that all Party members align themselves with the CPC Central Committee ideologically and politically as well as in their actions.

The Party draws its strength from its organization and is constantly invigorated by it. In order to reinforce the Party's organizational discipline, we must enhance our Party spirit, which is a matter of taking a firm stance. We Communists, especially leading officials, must be broad-minded and aim high. We must always bear in mind the interests of the Party, the people and the country, conscientiously uphold the Party spirit, and stick to our principles. All Party members must always remember that we are first and foremost CPC members and our primary duties are to work for it, remain loyal to it, and at all times identify ourselves with it. All Party members must always remember that we are part of the organization, and never neglect our duties and responsibilities to the organization. We must trust, rely on, and obey the organization, readily accept organizational arrangements and disciplinary restraints, and safeguard the unity of the Party.

Democratic centralism and the system of intra-Party organization activities are important institutions of the Party and must be fully implemented. Leading bodies and officials at all levels must rigorously follow the reporting system. We must reinforce organizational management of Party members, and guide all Party members and officials in developing a correct attitude towards the Party organization, matching our deeds to our words, speaking the truth, and embracing the Party organization's education and oversight. Party organizations at all levels must fully observe organizational discipline, make no exceptions in this regard, and have the moral fiber to denounce and rectify violations of Party discipline to preserve it as a high-tension line of deterrence.

Policies and plans made by the Party Central Committee should be implemented not only by the Party's organization departments, publicity departments, United Front departments, and judicial, procuratorial and public security bodies, but also by Party organizations in people's congresses, governments, CPPCC committees, people's courts, and people's procuratorates at all levels, as well as by Party organizations in public institutions and people's organizations. All such Party organizations must fulfill their duty in this regard. Party organizations in general must be accountable to Party committees, report their work to Party committees, and perform their work to the full extent of their functions and duties under the leadership of Party committees.

Notes

[1] Chen Yi: "Keep Your Hands in Your Own Pockets," *Selected Poems of Chen Yi*, Chinese ed., People's Literature Publishing House, Beijing, 1977, p.155. Chen Yi (1901-1972) was a Chinese proletarian revolutionary, military commander and political leader, one of the founders and leaders of the People's Liberation Army and one of the marshals of the People's Republic of China.

[2] *The Analects of Confucius (Lun Yu)*.

The CPC Leadership

Follow a Good Blueprint*

February 28, 2013

Confronted with the arduous and heavy tasks of promoting reform, development and stability, leading groups and leading officials at all levels must act in line with the requirements of the Party Central Committee, bear in mind that "empty talk harms the country, while hard work makes it flourish," and work energetically and productively to accomplish concrete deeds that can stand the test of practice, and survive the scrutiny of the people and history. On our immensely large platform of reform, opening up and modernization, all of us are desirous of doing something, even big things, to prove ourselves trustworthy to the Party and the people. Yet, we should also understand that, while doing that, we must maintain proper continuity in governance. An official in charge of a certain area and for a certain duration should act boldly and effectively in work, but he should also ensure consistency and continuity. The 18th CPC National Congress laid down the goal for completing the building of a moderately prosperous society in all respects and furthering reform and opening up, made an overall arrangement for promoting socialism with Chinese characteristics in the new conditions, and put forth clear requirements to make Party building more scientific in an all-round way.

Now it is time for the whole Party and people of the whole country to make concerted and relentless efforts to implement the decisions of the 18th CPC National Congress. Likewise, we must also remain committed to implementing the guidelines, principles and

---

* Part of the speech at the second full assembly of the Second Plenary Session of the 18th CPC Central Committee.

policies formulated since the Third Plenary Session of the 11th Party Central Committee, Deng Xiaoping Theory, the important thought of the Three Represents and the Scientific Outlook on Development, and all the major strategic arrangements made by the Central Committee, which are to be implemented in real earnest. The same is true in treating work at local and departmental levels. We have already got in our hands a good blueprint. What we should do is to follow it through to the end and make it a success. In this regard, we need to have a "nail" spirit. When we use a hammer to drive in a nail, a single knock often may not be enough; we must keep knocking until it is well in place. Then we can proceed to knock the next one, and continue driving in nails till the job is completely done. If we knock here and there without focusing on the nail, we may end up squandering our efforts altogether. There is no use in saying, "I won't get the credit for success." If a blueprint is good, factually based, scientifically sound and well-received by the people we should keep working on it, one administration after another, and the outcome of our work will be real and appreciated and remembered by the people.

Of course, as practice evolves continuously, our thoughts and work should keep up with the changing times, and when we are absolutely sure, we can make adjustments and improvements in good time. Nevertheless, we must not allow a complete unraveling of policies just because a new leadership takes office, nor must we permit a separate agenda with empty fancy slogans flying all over the place just to show so-called achievements. Under most circumstances, a new look or new atmosphere in work is not related to formulating new plans or designing new slogans. Rather, they come about naturally when earnest, down-to-earth efforts are made to turn scientifically sound goals in the good blueprint into reality by taking stock of new conditions, adopting new ideas and employing new measures. Our officials should have a clear understanding of job performance, thinking more about working to lay a solid foundation which is conducive to long-term development and less about competing pointlessly with others, still less about building wasteful, showcase projects to prop up their own image. Let our officials be true and practical, dedicated to work and bold to shoulder their responsibilities, so as to live up to the expectations of history and the people.

Study for a Brighter Future[*]

March 1, 2013

Our Party has always worked to ensure that all its members, especially leading officials, acquire further knowledge. This has proved to be useful for developing the cause of the Party and the people. At every major turning point, when faced with new circumstances and tasks, the Party has called upon its members to study harder. Each time, it has brought about big changes and developments for the cause of the Party and the people. At the very beginning of reform and opening up in 1978, the Party Central Committee stressed that achieving the Four Modernizations – modernization of agriculture, industry, national defense, and science and technology – is a great and profound revolution. We will have to move forward in this revolution by continuously solving new problems. Therefore, all Party members must know how to study and keep updating their knowledge. Compared with the past, we have more to study today, not less, because of the new circumstances and tasks confronting us.

At present, the entire Party must clearly understand and properly handle the new situations and problems arising from the development of the country. This is an important challenge. Some of the problems we face today are old – either problems that we have long failed to solve properly, or old problems with new manifestations, but most of our problems are new. The reason why new and unfamiliar problems keep surfacing is because of the changes in the world, in our country, and in our Party. The best possible way to understand and address the problems, whether they are new or old, long-standing or old ones in

* Main part of the speech at the celebration assembly of the 80th anniversary of the Central Party School and the opening ceremony of its 2013 spring semester.

new form, is to enhance our capabilities through study. In the process of study, we should not only put what we know into practice, but also acquire new practical problem-solving skills.

The various goals and tasks set by the 18th Party National Congress, including adapting ourselves to a complex and volatile international situation, safeguarding overall reform, development and stability and doing good work in all areas, impose new demands on Party members' capabilities. Throughout its history of revolution, construction and reform our Party has encountered numerous difficulties, and what has been achieved in our cause has come from painstaking explorations and hard work. There is simply no possibility that we can advance our cause and achieve our goals without ever encountering any impediment. It can be anticipated that various difficulties, risks and challenges will continue to surface on our way forward. The key lies in our ability to resolve, manage and conquer them.

Generally speaking, in some areas our abilities already meet the demands of the development of the Party and the country, but in others they are inadequate. As the circumstances and challenges we face continue to change, we become less capable of responding to their demands. If we do not improve our professional level at every opportunity, over time we will lose the ability to fulfill the arduous tasks of leadership in reform and opening up, and socialist modernization.

During the Yan'an period, our Party became aware of its dread of incompetence. The Party Central Committee pointed out clearly that our people suffered a dread. It was not an economic or political dread, but a dread of incompetence. The limited bank of abilities accumulated over the years had been depleted with each passing day, and the coffers were empty.

Are we faced with the same problem today? My answer is yes. Many people have the aspiration to do their work well and are full of enthusiasm, but they are lacking in the abilities required to achieve this in changing circumstances. In response to new circumstances and problems, they cling to old patterns of thinking and old practices. The problem stems from ignorance of general trends and new approaches, as well as inadequate knowledge and abilities. They rush headlong into their work and act blindly. As a result, although they are conscientious in their work and spare themselves no effort, they either take the wrong approach or act in a way that defeats their purpose, or even "head south while their chariot is pointing north." In such cases, it is often the case that our people have no alternative when the tried and trusted methods fail, or they dare not adopt sterner measures when soft ones prove inadequate.

In my opinion, this will continue to be the case for a long time to come. Therefore, all members, especially those in positions of leadership at all levels, must have a sense of crisis and constantly improve their professional competence. Only by doing this can we achieve the Two Centenary Goals, and make the Chinese Dream of national rejuvenation come true.

Nobody is born with knowledge. We all have to acquire it through study and practice. In modern times knowledge is becoming outdated at an ever-increasing pace, with a whole range of new knowhow, new information and new states of affairs cascading over us. Academics have noted that up to the 18th century the body of human knowledge doubled within a period of around 90 years. Since the 1990s there has been an exponential acceleration in this process – the body of human knowledge is now estimated to double every three to five years. The amount of knowledge produced by human society over the past 50 years exceeds the aggregate generated over the previous 3,000 years. It is also believed that in the age of the agrarian economy, a few years of study sufficed for one's lifetime, in the age of the industrial economy, one had to study for at least ten years to obtain all the knowledge necessary for one's life, and in this age of the knowledge economy, one has to keep up with the times through life-long study.

If we fail to improve our knowledge in a wide variety of areas, if we do not take the initiative to learn about science and culture, if we are unwilling to conscientiously update our knowledge and improve our knowledge structure, develop the broadest possible perspective and broaden our horizons, we will not improve our professional competence. As a consequence we will not be able to grasp the initiative and prevail. Ultimately, the future will pass us by. Therefore, all Party members, especially leading officials at all levels, must have a sense of urgency and study more.

It is precisely from this strategic perspective that the 18th Party National Congress highlighted the important task of building the Party into a learning, service-oriented, and innovative Marxist governing party. Studying should be placed first because it is a prerequisite fund of knowledge with which we will be able to better serve the people and stay innovative. Since we are all leading officials who shoulder duties and responsibilities entrusted to us by the Party and the people, we have to constantly raise our professional level, enrich our knowledge, dedicate ourselves to our work, and improve all aspects of our performance. Whether or not leading officials improve themselves through study is not only a personal matter, but a big issue concerning the development of the cause of the Party and the country. An ancient scholar expressed it thus, "One may or may not study for the purpose of becoming an official, but officials must be learned to fulfill their duties."[1]

We must study in order to improve our ability to work in a more scientific way, with greater foresight and initiative, and to keep up with the times, follow the law of development, and be innovative in our leadership and policy-making. We must study in order to avoid bewilderment resulting from inadequate knowledge, blindness resulting from insensibility, and chaos resulting from ignorance. We must also study in order to overcome professional deficiencies, the dread of incompetence, and outdated capabilities. Otherwise, we are no better than "the blind man on a blind horse who is in danger of falling into a deep pool at night"[2] – an imprudent and inadvisable course of action, however courageous. This could lead us to failure in work, losing our way and falling behind the times.

The cause of building Chinese socialism is a great and unprecedented undertaking. Therefore, our approach to study should be comprehensive, systematic and exploratory. We should have focus in our study and widen the scope of our knowledge. We should learn both from books and through practice. We should learn from ordinary people, from experts and scholars, and draw upon beneficial experiences of foreign countries as well. We should nourish ourselves with both theoretical and practical knowledge.

First of all, we should study Marxist theory. This is a special requirement that will help us to work well, and also a necessary requirement that will equip leading officials to excel in leadership. Mao Zedong once stated, "Our Party's fighting capacity will be much greater...if there are one hundred or two hundred comrades with a grasp of Marxism-Leninism which is systematic and not fragmentary, genuine and not hollow."[3]

This task still confronts our Party today. We must acquire a true grasp of Marxism-Leninism, Mao Zedong Thought, Deng Xiaoping Theory, the important thought of the Three Represents, and the Scientific Outlook on Development. And we must especially have a good understanding of the Marxist stand, viewpoint and method that permeate all these ideas. This can enable us to remain sharp-eyed and clear-minded and gain a profound understanding of the laws of the development of human society, the laws of building socialism, and the laws of governance by the CPC. This can help us stay firm in our ideals and convictions, adhere to the correct guiding thoughts, and hold to the correct orientation in any complex situation. This can also enable us to lead the people along the correct road and make progress in building Chinese socialism.

Leading officials must study the Party's guidelines, principles and policies, and the country's laws and regulations. An understanding of these is a basic preparation we must make for our work, and it is also a political attainment we must have. Without this body of knowledge, how can we make policy decisions and solve problems? And we may even end up with mistakes in our work.

Leading officials at all levels should study the history of both the Party and the country and remain patriotic and dedicated to them. We should study the development of the Party and the country, draw upon their historical experiences, and understand major events and figures in the history of the Party and the country. History is the best textbook, so studying it will teach us to understand the country and the Party, and open the gates to a bright future.

Leading officials should study economics, politics, history, culture, science and technology, and knowledge of social, military and foreign affairs related to their work. They should become more knowledgeable and more professionally competent. They should learn what they need in their work and study what they do not know, and acquire knowledge that is conducive to good leadership and high performance. In doing so, they will become experts as well as better leaders in their fields.

Leading officials should also study history and culture, especially traditional Chinese culture, to develop wisdom and become more refined. Traditional Chinese culture is both extensive and profound, and to acquire the essence of various thoughts is beneficial to the formation of a correct worldview, outlook on life and sense of values.

Our ancient scholars commented that our aspirations should be as follows: in politics, "being the first to worry about the affairs of the state and the last to enjoy oneself"[4]; as patriots, "not daring to ignore the country's peril no matter how humble one's position"[5] and "doing everything possible to save the country in its peril without regard to personal fortune or misfortune"[6]; on integrity, "never being corrupted by riches and honors, never departing from principle despite poverty or humble origin, and never submitting to force or threat"[7]; on selfless dedication, "dying with a loyal heart shining in the pages of history"[8] and "giving all, till the heart beats its last."[9] These maxims reflect the fine traditions and spirit of the Chinese nation, and we should all keep them alive and have them further developed.

Leading officials should also study literature. They should refine their tastes and develop uplifting interests through appreciation of works of literature and art. Many revolutionaries of the older generation had a profound literary background and were well versed in poetry.

In short, history helps us understand the failures and successes of the past, and learn lessons from the rise and fall of states. Poetry stimulates us, sends our dreams skywards and makes us witty. Integrity improves our judgment and helps us cultivate a sense of honor and disgrace. We should not only study Chinese history and culture, but also open our eyes to the rest of the world and learn about the histories and cultures of other peoples. We should give preference to what is uplifting in these histories and cultures and reject what is base – obtaining enlightenment and employing it for our own use.

Leading officials must direct their studies correctly. If they deviate from the guiding principle of Marxism, they will be studying without a clear aim and may go astray. They might easily become confused when the situation becomes complex, and might fall victim to defective thinking. Departing from the correct orientation, they might not only fail to acquire sound knowledge, but also find themselves deceived and misled by tempting fallacies and ideas that are unrealistic, ridiculous or absurd.

The purpose of study lies in practice. The ultimate goal of leading officials who dedicate greater effort to their studies lies in honing their capability in work and in solving problems. A Chinese saying goes like this, "Empty talk harms the country, while hard work makes it flourish." This demands real efforts in both study and work. We all should bear in mind the historical lessons of Zhao Kuo[10] of the Warring States Period (475-221 BC), who fought all his battles on paper, or the scholars of the Western and Eastern Jin dynasties (265-420) who became ineffective due to spending too much time in useless debates.

Reading and application are both ways of learning, and the latter is more important. Leading officials should adopt the Marxist approach by combining theory with practice. In the course of their studies there should always be questions in mind. We should respect the people as our mentors, learn from work, and work on the basis of learning, making use of what we have learned and applying it to real-life situations. Study and practice should always promote each other. We should disdain empty talk and never be a "Krikun."

A genuine interest in the subject is the best teacher. This concept is reflected in a Chinese saying, "Regarding knowledge, those who are devoted to it learn better than those who are aware of it, and those who enjoy it the most are the best students."[11] Leading officials should pursue study as a quest, a hobby, and an element of a healthy lifestyle, which will make them happy and eager to learn. With a keen interest in study we will be enthusiastic volunteers rather than reluctant conscripts, and study will be a lifelong habit instead of a temporary pastime.

Study and deliberation complement each other, as do study and practice. As another Chinese saying goes, "Reading without thinking makes one muddled; thinking without reading makes one flighty."[12] If you have problems in mind and want to find solutions, you should start studying and study conscientiously. You must "learn extensively, inquire earnestly, think profoundly, discriminate clearly and practice sincerely."[13]

We should be adept at making time for study. I often hear officials say that they would love to study more, but they "just don't have time because of their busy work schedules." This sounds superficially plausible, but it can never be an excuse for slackening in study. In stressing the need to improve our work, the Party Central Committee has suggested that we spend more time thinking and studying, and cut down on meaningless banquets and formalities.

These days, there is a general public grievance that some officials do more partying than studying. "Those in the dark are in no position to light the way for others."[14] This will have an adverse effect on our work, and will ultimately hinder our overall development. If we bury our heads in our work to the detriment of our studies, we run the risk of mental sclerosis and vulgarization. When engaged in study we should be focused and avoid distractions. Our approach should be persistent, and not that of the dilettante. We must gain a true grasp of what we are studying, rather than reading superficially without understanding. Leading officials must place a high priority on learning and study assiduously. As long as we apply ourselves, even half an hour of reading a day, just a few pages, will add up over time.

In summary, study makes progress. To a large extent we Chinese Communists have relied on learning for our achievements, and we will surely continue to do so in the future. If our officials, our Party, our country and our people are to make progress, we must be advocates of learning. We must study, study, then study some more, and we must practice, practice, then practice some more.

Notes

[1] *Xun Zi.*

[2] Liu Yiqing: *New Accounts of Tales of the World (Shi Shuo Xin Yu)*. Liu Yiqing (403-444) was a man of letters during the Southern Dynasties. *New Accounts of Tales of the World* is a literary collection of words and stories of scholar-bureaucrats from the late Han Dynasty (206 BC-AD 220) to the Eastern Jin Dynasty (317-420).

[3] Mao Zedong: "The Role of the Chinese Communist Party in the National War," *Selected Works of Mao Zedong*, Vol. II, Eng. ed., Foreign Languages Press, Beijing, 1975, p. 209.

[4] See note 3, p. 68.

[5] Lu You: *Feelings After Illness.*

[6] Lin Zexu: *Farewell to My Family on My Way to Exile*. Lin Zexu (1785-1850) was a patriot and statesman of the Qing Dynasty who advocated resistance to Western invasion and a ban on the non-medicinal consumption of opium during the Opium War.

[7] *The Mencius (Meng Zi).*

[8] Wen Tianxiang: *Passing Lingdingyang*. Wen Tianxiang (1236-1283) was a minister and writer of the Southern Song Dynasty.

[9] Zhuge Liang: *Second Petition on Taking the Field (Hou Chu Shi Biao).*

[10] Zhao Kuo (?-260 BC), a high-ranking military officer of the State of Zhao during the Warring States Period, was an armchair strategist without any real experience of battle. In 260 BC, he fell into a trap set by Bai Qi, a general of the State of Qin, and found his army surrounded by the enemy in Changping. Zhao Kuo failed to break through the encirclement and was killed. More than 400,000 Zhao soldiers were captured and buried alive.

[11] *The Analects of Confucius (Lun Yu).*

[12] See note 36, p. 198.

[13] See note 39, p. 199.

[14] *The Mencius (Meng Zi).*

"Governing a Big Country Is as Delicate as Frying a Small Fish"*

March 19, 2013

When I meet foreign leaders, one question they often ask in amazement is this: How can one govern such a large country as China? Indeed, it is not easy to govern a country with 1.3 billion people. Just getting to know the situation there can be a really difficult task. As I often say, it takes a good deal of effort to know China, and just visiting a place or two is not really enough. China has 9.6 million square kilometers of land, 56 ethnic groups and a total of 1.3 billion people. Thus, when trying to learn about China, one needs to guard against drawing conclusions based on partial information.

An ancient Chinese proverb says, "Prime ministers must have served as local officials, and great generals must have risen from the ranks."[1] Our mechanism for selecting officials in China also requires work experience at local levels. For instance, I once worked in a rural area as a Party secretary at a production brigade. Later I served in various posts at county, municipal, provincial and central levels. Extensive experience gained from working at local levels can help officials develop a sound attitude towards the people, know what the country is really like and what the people really need, be better versed in various jobs and professions, and become more competent and effective for meeting future requirements for good work performance.

There is a tremendous amount of work to do in meeting the people's daily needs, ensuring the smooth running of society and the normal functioning of the state apparatus, and building and managing

---

* Part of the answers to a joint interview by the press of the BRICS countries.

the governing party. As the people have given me this job, I must always keep them in the highest place in my heart, bearing in mind their deep trust and the heavy responsibilities they have placed on me. In such a big, populous and complicated country as ours, we the leaders must have an in-depth knowledge of the national conditions, and learn what the people think and what they want. We must act self-consciously and with the utmost care "as if we were treading on thin ice or standing on the edge of an abyss."[2] We must cultivate an attitude of "governing a big country is as delicate as frying a small fish,"[3] never slackening our efforts or being negligent in the slightest, and always devoting ourselves to work and the public interest. The people are where we draw our strength. As long as we stand with our people through thick and thin, there will be no difficulty that cannot be overcome and no task that cannot be accomplished.

As for my workload, you can well imagine that working in such a job can hardly leave me any free time. There are so many things crying out to be done. Of course, I try to prioritize my work. "Many hands make light work." We have within the central leadership an effective mechanism featuring both division of labor and coordination. So we go about our respective duties while working in concert to get the job done properly.

Though very busy, most of the time I manage to "snatch a little leisure here and there."[4] Whenever I have time, I spend it with my family.

I have quite a few hobbies, and my most favorite one is reading, which has become my way of life. I am also a sports fan. I like swimming and hiking, and when I was young I enjoyed playing football and volleyball. I wish to congratulate Brazil for hosting the FIFA World Cup again. What makes sports competitions, especially football matches, fascinating is their unpredictability. During the last World Cup we had Paul the Octopus. I wonder if there will be another octopus next year to predict match results. The Brazilian team has the home-ground advantage, and I wish them good luck.

Notes

[1] *Han Fei Zi.* Han Fei (c. 280-233 BC) was the major representative of the Legalist school in the late Warring States Period. His works were collected in the book *Han Fei Zi.*

[2] *The Book of Songs (Shi Jing).*

[3] *Lao Zi (Dao De Jing).*

[4] Li She: *Written on the Wall of the Monks' Quarters in Helin Temple.* Li She (dates unknown) was a poet of the Tang Dynasty (618-907).

Train and Select Good Officials*

June 28, 2013

At present, all Party members and people of all ethnic groups in China are making concerted efforts to complete the building of a moderately prosperous society in all respects and realize the Chinese Dream of national rejuvenation. Confronted with the present complex and unpredictable international situation and arduous domestic tasks of continuing reform and development and maintaining stability, we must "be prepared to carry out a great undertaking with many new historic features." – This is quoted from the political report to the 18th National Congress of the CPC. With its profound connotations, the idea of "new historic features" represents an important conclusion that has been made after thoroughly reviewing and analyzing the development trends both at home and abroad.

To carry out a great undertaking with many new historic features, and to accomplish the goals and tasks set forth at the 18th CPC National Congress, the emphasis should be laid on our Party and our officials. This means we must ensure that the Party is always the core of leadership during the historic process of developing socialism with Chinese characteristics, and we must build a large contingent of high-caliber officials.

Our Party has always attached great importance to the selection and appointment of upright and talented people, and has always regarded the selection and appointment of officials as an issue of crucial and fundamental significance to the cause of the Party and the people. Employing suitable officials represents the key to governance. As our ancestors said, "Exaltation of the virtuous is fundamental to

---

* Part of the speech at the National Conference on Organizational Work.

governance,"[1] and "Employing capable officials represents the top priority of governance."[2]

In recent years, Party committees and organization departments at all levels have implemented the Party policy on personnel management, and have done a good job of selecting and appointing officials. However, there are still some problems which, if not properly resolved, will demoralize both the Party members and the general public.

At present, there are three questions that are of great concern: what a good official is, how to become a good official, and how to use the right officials for the right job. Good answers and appropriate solutions to the three questions will be a proof of good management of personnel.

First, what is a good official? This should be a question with a clear and ready answer, for there are clear requirements specified in the Party Constitution. However, some people are confused when they see misconduct in the selection and appointment of officials, when unqualified officials are selected at some localities, and when unqualified officials are still promoted, even against regulations. This shows that we need to improve our work in the organization departments. If our selection of officials leads only to confusion over the criteria for good officials, it is obvious that those selected will be only bad examples for the public. We must think more about this issue!

Generally speaking, good officials should be of moral integrity and professional competence. However, there were different criteria in different historical periods. During the revolutionary war period, good officials needed to be loyal to the Party, brave and skillful in battle, and unafraid to sacrifice their lives. During the socialist construction period, good officials needed to be politically and professionally competent. In the early years of the reform and opening up, good officials had to uphold the guidelines, principles and policies set forth at the Third Plenary Session of the 11th CPC Central Committee, have professional knowledge and be determined to carry out reforms. At the current stage, we require that good officials be politically reliable, professionally competent and morally upright, and are trusted by the people.

In summary, good officials must be firm in their ideals and convictions, willing to serve the people, diligent in work, ready to take on responsibilities, honest, and upright.

To be firm in their ideals and convictions means that Party officials must cherish the lofty ideal of communism, sincerely believe in Marxism, strive ceaselessly for socialism with Chinese characteristics, and unswervingly uphold the basic theories, guideline, program, experience and requirements of the Party.

To be willing to serve the people means that Party officials must act as servants of the people, be loyal to the people, and serve them wholeheartedly.

To be diligent in work means that Party officials must be dedicated to their work in a down-to-earth, realistic and pragmatic manner, and take solid and tangible measures to make achievements that can prove their worth in practice, survive the scrutiny of the people and stand the test of time.

To be ready to take on responsibilities means that Party officials must adhere to principles with a responsible attitude, and have the courage to take resolute actions in the face of major issues of principle, to tackle difficulties head-on in the face of conflicts, to step forward in the face of crises, to admit their share of mistakes, and to resolutely fight against misconduct.

To be honest and upright means that Party officials must adopt a cautious attitude towards the exercise of power by holding it in respect and keeping it under control in a bid to sustain their political life, and make constant efforts to maintain their political integrity against corruption.

These requirements might be easy to understand, but they are not so easy to fulfill.

They are also important requirements that I have stressed on various occasions for some time now. Here I would like to lay special emphasis on two aspects: ideals and convictions, and readiness to take on responsibilities, which are outstanding issues facing our officials at the current stage.

To be firm in their ideals and convictions is the supreme criterion for good officials. No matter how competent an official is, he cannot be regarded as the sort of good official that we need if he is not firm in his ideals and convictions, does not believe in Marxism nor socialism with Chinese characteristics, is unqualified politically, and cannot weather political storms. Only those who are firm in their ideals and convictions will adopt an unequivocal approach towards major issues of principle, build "diamond-hard bodies" to withstand any corrosion, remain dauntless when facing political storms, firmly resist all kinds of temptations, and act in a reliable and trustworthy manner at any critical moment.

Ideals and convictions refer to people's aspirations. As one of our ancestors said, "Aspirations can reach any place however far it is, even over mountains and seas; and it can break through any defense however tough it is, even as strong as the best armor and shield."[3] This shows how strong and invincible people can be if they have lofty aspirations. During China's revolution, development and reform, innumerable Party members laid down their lives for the cause of the Party and the people. What supported them was the moral strength gained from the utmost importance they attached to their revolutionary ideals.

It should be fully admitted that most of our officials are firm in their ideals and convictions, and are politically reliable. Nevertheless, there are some Party officials who fail to meet these qualifications. Some are skeptical about communism, considering it a fantasy that will never come true; some do not believe in Marxism-Leninism but in ghosts and gods, and seek spiritual solace in feudal superstitions, showing intense interest in fortune-telling, worship of Buddha and "god's advice" for solving their problems; some have little sense of principle, justice, and right and wrong, and perform their duties in a muddle-headed manner; some even yearn for Western social systems and values, losing their confidence in the future of socialism; and others adopt an equivocal attitude towards political provocations against the leadership of the CPC, the path of socialism with Chinese characteristics and other matters of principle, passively avoid relevant arguments without the courage to express their opinions, or even deliberately deliver ambiguous messages. Isn't it a monstrous absurdity that Party officials, especially high-ranking ones, take no position in the face of major issues of principle, political incidents and sensitive issues?

Some say that officials need to "cherish their reputation." This depends on what kind of "reputation" they are cherishing. Is it a "reputation" which will be applauded by people with ulterior motives, or is it a reputation for acting in the interests of the Party and the people? A Party member should only cherish the latter reputation, and it would be calamitous if he were bent on gaining the former!

Why are the Four Malfeasances prevalent nowadays? Why are some officials becoming corrupt, ending up as criminals? In the final analysis, it is because they are not firm in their ideals or convictions. I have often said that ideals and convictions are the moral "marrow" of Communists. To be firm in our ideals and convictions will "harden our bones," while an absence of ideals and convictions or wavering in our ideals and convictions will lead to fatal moral weakness.

Facts have repeatedly proved that the most dangerous moment is when one wavers in or begins to show doubt about one's ideals and convictions. I have long been wondering if we were confronted with a complex situation such as a "color revolution," would all our officials act resolutely to safeguard the leadership of the Party and the socialist system? I believe most Party members and officials are capable of doing so.

During the revolutionary war, whether an official was firm in his ideals and convictions was judged by whether he could risk his life for the cause of the Party and the people, and whether he could charge ahead as soon as the bugle sounded. This was a most direct test. There are still tests of life and death at our current stage of peaceful development, but there is a much smaller number of them.

As a result, it is really difficult to test whether an official is firm in his ideals and convictions. Even X-rays, CT scans and MRIs will not help.

Nevertheless, there are still ways to test our officials. We need to find out whether they have the political determination in the face of major political challenges, bear in mind the fundamental purpose of the Party, perform their duties in an extremely responsible manner, are the first to bear hardships and the last to enjoy comforts, are ready to take on responsibilities in the face of urgent, difficult and dangerous tasks, and resist the temptations of power, money and sex. Such a test cannot be accomplished overnight based on a few tasks that an official fulfills or a few pledges that he makes; it is a process that depends on the official's behavior over a long period, even throughout his life.

It is essential that Party officials uphold principles and readily take on responsibilities. "Avoiding responsibilities is the greatest disgrace for an official." The responsibilities an official takes on demonstrate his breadth of vision, courage and competence. The greater responsibilities one takes on, the greater undertaking one can accomplish.

With the "nice guy" mentality currently prevailing among some officials, it has become commonplace that many officials dare not criticize errors or take on responsibilities, or are unwilling to do so. Some officials keep on good terms with everybody at the expense of principles, for they are afraid of offending people and losing votes, holding a belief in the vulgar philosophy of "more flowers and fewer thorns." They mind nothing but their own business and will do nothing unless their personal interests are affected, being satisfied with muddling along and accomplishing nothing at all. Some officials are not fulfilling their duties properly. They sidestep difficult problems and matters of public concern, argue and pass the buck, and tackle their responsibilities in a perfunctory manner, with their delay turning small problems into big ones and big problems into dreadful troubles. Some officials are smooth characters who handle matters in an overly "clever" manner, pick easy jobs and posts while shirking hard ones, think of nothing but self-preservation in the face of challenges, rush to claim credit for success, and evade responsibility when any problem crops up. What is more frightening is that some of these officials are popular, even getting on well in official circles, gaining more than others while contributing less. How can the cause of the Party and the people proceed if there are a lot of "nice guys," people of "smooth character," those who always "pass the buck to others," or those who waver like "weeds atop the wall"? These problems are extremely dangerous, and major efforts must be made to solve them.

Ultimately, selflessness leads to fearlessness and the courage to take on responsibilities. Selflessness gives us peace of mind. Good officials must attach the utmost importance to their responsibilities, put the principles and cause of the Party and the interests of the people first, take an unequivocal and tough stance when addressing problems, perform their duties in an uncomplaining and diligent manner, and see their efforts through to the final result. "Sturdy grass withstands high winds; true gold stands the test of fire." For the cause of the Party and the people, our officials should be bold enough to think, to carry out initiatives and to take the consequences, serving as the "sturdy grass" and "true gold" of our times.

Of course, being ready to take on responsibilities is for the cause of the Party and the people, not for personal fame. Being arrogant and overbearing is not being courageous to take on responsibilities. During the Spring and Autumn Period, there was a senior official named Zheng Kaofu, who served several dukes of the State of Song. He had a reputation for being highly self-disciplined. He had a motto engraved on a *ding* in his family ancestral temple, which read, "Head down when I was promoted the first time, back hunched when promoted the second time, and waist bent when promoted the third time. No one insults me if I keep close to the wall when walking along the street. What I need only is this vessel to cook porridge in."[4] I am deeply impressed by this story. Our officials are officials of the Party, and their power is granted by the Party and the people. Thus, they should make ever-bolder efforts and show ever-greater determination in their work, and conduct themselves in a modest and prudent manner free from arrogance and rashness.

Second, how can one become a good official? Good officials do not emerge spontaneously. To become a good official, both personal effort and training by Party organizations are necessary. For officials, their personal effort is essential, because this is the decisive internal factor in their personal development.

The commitment to the Party's cause, theoretical conscious-ness and moral standards of an official are not enhanced automati-cally alongside a longer Party standing or a higher post. Rather, the enhancement requires lifelong endeavors. To become a good official, one needs to constantly remold one's subjective world, and strengthen one's commitment to the Party and moral refinement. One needs to stringently comply with the Party Constitution and the require-ments for Party members, "being strict with oneself and lenient with others."[5] Party members must always behave in a proper manner, scrutinize themselves, keep alert to "resist the myriad temptations of the dazzling world," and be honest and hardworking, clean and upright.

Learning is the ladder of progress. Officials need to be good at learning and thinking, conscientiously study Marxist theories, espe-cially the theoretical system of socialism with Chinese characteristics, focus on the standpoints, viewpoints and methods of these theories, and improve their capacity for strategic, innovative, dialectical, and principled thinking, so that they are able to correctly judge contem-porary situations, and remain clear-headed and determined politically. They also need to enrich their knowledge of various subjects, improve their structure of learning, and accumulate experiences, so as to lay a solid foundation for the performance of their duties.

In addition to learning, good officials also need to focus on prac-tice. "Hearing is not as good as seeing, and seeing is not as good as experiencing."[6] Knowledge and experience are like the two wings of an eagle, which can fly high and far only if it wants to see the outside world and braves storms. The harsher the conditions and the more the difficulties, the more an official will be tempered. Officials should go to the grassroots to see the real situation and communicate with the people, and then they will be able to refine themselves and improve their abilities in their part of the work for reform and opening up, stability, and serving the people.

Good officials need to be trained by Party organizations. We need to focus more on the training of officials along with the changes of the circumstances and the development of the cause of the Party and the people. In this training, we must pay more attention to education on commitment to the Party, virtue and morality, awareness about the Party's ultimate goal, and sense of serving the people. We also need to strengthen the training of officials in practical circumstances to facilitate their progress. Training in practical circumstances is not a way to get "gilded," nor is it a routine process before promotion. If this is the case, officials will not devote themselves wholeheartedly to the training and will not keep in close touch with the people. The training will only be a show.

Moreover, we need to enhance supervision of officials' conduct on a regular basis. The exercise of power without supervision will definitely lead to corruption. This is an axiomatic law. It is not an easy process to train an official, so necessary measures should be adopted to better manage and supervise officials to keep them on the alert "as if they were treading on thin ice or standing on the edge of an abyss." Heart-to-heart talks with officials are needed, so that their shortcomings are pointed out in time, and their enthusiasm is encouraged. This is a good tradition that we need to carry on.

Third, how can we ensure officials' good performance? To employ good officials after they are adequately trained is the key. What is the purpose of training if we do not employ good officials or do not let them play their role? Employment of a competent person will attract more competent people, and all the others will take them as examples. The kind of officials we employ is a political weathervane which determines the conduct of our officials and even the conduct of the whole Party.

It must be noted that some localities and departments are not adopting a correct approach to appointing officials. Some opportunistic officials with doubtful integrity and insufficient professional competence get promoted frequently, while those who devote themselves to work and do not build social connections for promotion do not have such chances. This has given rise to strong discontent among officials and the general public. Party committees and organization departments at all levels need to adhere to the principle that the Party should supervise the performance of officials and the correct approach to official appointment, select officials on the basis of both moral integrity and professional competence with priority given to the former, try to select and appoint virtuous and competent people in a timely manner, and place them in suitable posts according to their abilities. Only in this way can good and competent officials be selected and employed.

To employ officials, the most important thing is to know them. If we do not know them thoroughly and accurately we may employ them in an inappropriate way. "Having no idea of a person's weakness and strength, the weak part of the strength or the strong part of the weakness, we have no ground for appointing or even training that person."[7] We cannot judge an official by impression or personal feeling. We must have a good system and methods to evaluate officials, with reflections through various channels, at various levels and from various perspectives.

We need to keep a close watch on officials and observe their approach to major issues, their concern for the people, their moral conduct, their attitude towards fame and fortune, their realm of thought, their ways of handling matters and results, and their work competence. The evaluation and observation of officials are done in day-to-day work, but the best time is at major events and critical moments. "To understand good music only after singing a thousand songs; to find a fine sword only after appreciating a thousand swords."[8] The performance of an official is reflected in his work, and his reputation is gained from the public. So we need to go to the grassroots to hear opinions from the people, and judge an official's moral conduct in "big events" as well as in "small matters."

To employ good officials, we must observe their performance and moral conduct on an overall, long-term and logical basis. Those who are competent, have distinctive personalities, are ready to take on responsibilities, and dare to offend some people for the sake of upholding principles may receive different comments. Party organizations must give them a correct evaluation. It is also difficult to accurately assess the performance of officials. We need to improve the methods and means of assessment. In the performance appraisal of officials, we should pay equal attention to economic growth and the original economic basis, and to both tangible and intangible achievements, and integrate indicators and achievements with regard to the improvement of the people's living standards, social progress and the ecological environment. We must no longer judge the performance of officials merely by GDP growth rates. Some officials tend to make abrupt decisions, start projects without second thoughts, and finally leave a mess behind, but they still get promoted without being held accountable. We cannot let it happen any more. I have said that we need to implement responsibility systems to address such issues, and hold the relevant officials accountable throughout their lifetime. The organization department of the Party Central Committee should see to this immediately.

To employ good officials we need to take a scientific approach and appoint the right person, at the right time and for the right position. Currently, some localities tend to appoint officials according to seniority or for seeking balance rather than in accordance with their merits, suitability or professional abilities. As a result, the appointed officials find it difficult to perform their duties, thus leaving problems unsolved and work unaccomplished.

What kind of official to appoint and what position is suitable for him should be part of the consideration of work requirements. We should not appoint an official simply because there is a post, or take it as a means of reward. "A good horse can run along dangerous paths but cannot plow the fields like an ox; a strong cart can carry heavy loads but cannot cross rivers like a boat." We should have a good sense of acquiring talented people through different channels and by different methods, treat them as treasures, and let them fully display their abilities. Only by so doing will large numbers of good officials emerge to contribute their wisdom and knowledge.

There is a phenomenon that we must notice. To judge an official on his work performance in a locality or a unit, people have their own comments, practice has its proof, and leaders are clear in mind, but the final appointment is often not according to the actual needs, and usually disappoints people. The reason is the selfishness of some leading officials, "relationship-ism" or some "hidden rules" that people dodge behind. Influenced by these unhealthy factors, officials are no longer appointed on their merits but by favoritism or by seeking personal gain. Officials and the public abhor this practice very much, so we should make resolute efforts to change it and make it a clean process.

Notes

[1] See note 8, p. 68.

[2] Sima Guang: *Historical Events Retold as a Mirror for Government (Zi Zhi Tong Jian)*. Sima Guang (1019-1086) was a minister and historian in the Northern Song Dynasty. This monumental work was China's first comprehensive history in the form of a chronicle.

[3] Jin Ying: *A Collection of Maxims (Ge Yan Lian Bi)*.

[4] *Zuo's Chronicles (Zuo Zhuan)*.

[5] *Collection of Ancient Texts (Shang Shu)*.

[6] Liu Xiang: *Garden of Stories (Shuo Yuan)*.

[7] Wei Yuan: *Treatise on Scholarship and Politics (Mo Gu)*.

[8] Liu Xie: *Carving a Dragon with a Literary Mind (Wen Xin Diao Long)*. Liu Xie (c. 465-c. 532) was a literary critic during the Southern Dynasties. *Carving a Dragon with a Literary Mind* is a work on literary theory in ancient China.

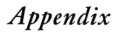

Appendix

Man of the People

Profile of Xi Jinping, General Secretary of the CPC

It was a pleasant early morning on December 8, 2012 in a verdant park known as Lianhuashan (Lotus Flower Mountain) in Shenzhen, in south China's Guangdong Province. The park was not cordoned off to the public. There was no red carpet, nor were there people waving welcoming banners. None of the early risers, doing their usual morning exercises, were expecting to encounter a notable figure.

A middle-aged man in a dark suit and an open-necked white shirt laid a wreath at a statue of the late Chinese leader Deng Xiaoping. Then he circulated among the crowd, engaging in casual conversation.

The visitor was Xi Jinping, elected general secretary of the CPC Central Committee only 24 days previously.

During his visit to Guangdong, Xi called on the entire Party and all of the people of China to continue supporting the path of reform and opening up, and focus on pursuing reform in a more systematic, integrated and coordinated way. He vowed that there would be no slowdown in reform and opening up.

In his first visit outside Beijing as the top CPC leader, Xi went to Guangdong – the wellspring of China's reform and opening up, following the route Deng had taken 20 years earlier, when the country found itself at a crossroads.

Media reports characterized Xi as a leader who has breathed fresh life into the country's politics, committed to reform and opening up, and determined to lead the nation in realizing the Chinese Dream.

Xi, who was elected to his new role at the First Plenary Session of the 18th CPC Central Committee on November 15, 2012, is the first top Party leader to have been born after 1949, the year the People's Republic of China (PRC) was founded.

He now leads the 91-year-old CPC, the world's largest political party with more than 82 million members, as it rules over China, the world's second largest economy.

The whole country and the world beyond are watching Xi with interest and expectations:

– How will he lead the CPC to better serve the people?

– How will he lead China's 1.3 billion people to build a moderately prosperous society in all respects by the centenary of the CPC in 2021? Furthermore, how will he lead the people to achieve the goal of building a modern socialist country that is prosperous, strong, democratic, culturally advanced and harmonious by the centenary of the PRC in 2049?

– How will he lead the country to make its due contribution to world peace and development?

As he met the press on November 15, right after the closing of the first plenum, Xi summed up the CPC's mission as comprising three responsibilities – to the nation, to the people and to the Party.

Advocate of the Chinese Dream

"The people aspire to a decent life – that is what we are fighting for," remarked Xi to the press in his first public speech as CPC general secretary.

Shortly after taking office, Xi and the other six members of the Standing Committee of the Political Bureau of the CPC Central Committee visited the exhibition "The Road to Rejuvenation" at the National Museum of China. The display illustrated the huge challenges China has surmounted on the road to national revival since 1840.

"Nowadays, everyone is talking about the Chinese Dream," he noted. "In my view, realizing the renewal of the Chinese nation is the greatest dream in modern history."

To achieve this goal, Xi has clarified his position on various aspects of the country's development:

– On economic development, Xi opposes blind focus on growth, and upholds the principle of balanced and coordinated development, which seeks sustainability in terms of both resources and the environment.

– On political development, he stresses the idea that all power belongs to the people, and calls for active and steady political reform while keeping to the path of socialism with Chinese characteristics. He also stresses the rule of law and exercising state power in accordance with the Constitution.

– On cultural development, he aspires to develop human talent and foster a Chinese national spirit, especially as typified by the words of the national anthem: "We will use our flesh and blood to build our new Great Wall."

– On social development, he stresses that we must be fully aware of the fact that we are in the primary stage of socialism. We should make continuous efforts to ensure and improve the people's standard of living through economic development. He also supports building a harmonious society and realizing a good life for the people based on hard work, while taking into consideration the country's actual circumstances. He calls for joint efforts from all sectors in building a harmonious society.

– On ecological progress, he emphasizes a national strategy of resource conservation, environmental protection and sustainable development.

From the Loess Plateau in the northwest to the southeast coast of China, from distant localities to the central leadership, Xi has had a well-rounded political career and has developed a deep understanding of the conditions of his country and its people. Xi worked for decades in several localities, including Shanghai and the provinces of Shaanxi, Hebei, Fujian and Zhejiang as a Party or government official, as well as a period spent serving in the army, before he came to Beijing to chair the routine work of the CPC Secretariat.

He was fully aware of the importance of strengthening the Party and regularly emphasized that the Party must discipline itself according to strict standards. Under him, a number of intra-Party rules and regulations were enacted. He has repeatedly stressed that the Party must supervise its own conduct and run itself with strict discipline. At the first group study session of the new Political Bureau, he said, "Worms can only grow in something rotten."[1] "A large number of facts have proved that corruption is now raging; if it is not curbed our Party and country will surely be doomed. We must keep on high alert."

Xi pays great attention to investigation, holding that, "investigation should be carried out throughout the decision-making process." He has also stressed that all officials should go to the grassroots communities and find out what the people think and want, and solve the problems the people are most concerned with.

Beginning in 2008, he served as the head of the leading group in charge of the nationwide study and implementation of the Scientific Outlook on Development within the Party. This 18-month program helped build consensus behind the Scientific Outlook on Development on the part of the whole Party and the country at large, and make the concept a driving force for economic and social development.

He also led a group of people in drafting the 17th CPC Central Committee's report to the 18th CPC National Congress as well as the amendment to the CPC Constitution, both of which were adopted at the congress and have become important guidelines for China's future.

Xi has had a connection with the armed forces since his early days. After graduating from university, he worked at the General Office of the Central Military Commission (CMC) of the CPC for three years, a job that gave him a deep affection for the armed forces.

In the following years he served concurrently as Party chief for military subareas in addition to holding his Party and government titles. In the course of this, he became familiar with grassroots military affairs.

He became CMC vice chairman in 2010 and was named CMC chairman at the First Plenary Session of the 18th CPC Central Committee in November 2012.

Xi is also familiar with issues related to Hong Kong, Macao and Taiwan. His 17-year service in Fujian gave him a deep understanding of Taiwan and enterprises from Taiwan. The first Taiwan chamber of commerce on the mainland was established in Xiamen when he worked in Fujian. He solved many problems for people from Taiwan, and has subsequently been seen as a "good friend" by many of them.

As a member of the central leadership, Xi was in charge of Hong Kong and Macao affairs. He helped work out a number of important policies on the long-term stability and prosperity of the two special administrative regions.

In 2008 and 2009, when Hong Kong and Macao were seriously hit by the international financial crisis, Xi visited both regions to show his support. He encouraged the local people, saying, "There are always more means than difficulties as long as we have a firm resolve." In 2012, when he talked to deputies to the NPC and the Chinese People's Political Consultative Conference (CPPCC) from Hong Kong and Macao at the annual "two sessions,"[2] he quoted a line from a classic: "If brothers are of the same mind, their edge can cut through metal,"[3] to call on the people of Hong Kong and Macao to stick together to strive for a better life.

In 2008 Xi was tasked with heading the preparations for Beijing's much-anticipated 2008 Olympic Games and the subsequent Paralympics, playing a key role in China's hosting of these great events.

Regarding the People as Parents

Xi has expressed his deep regard for the people on many occasions: "The importance of the people in the minds of officials determines the importance of officials in the minds of the people." His love for the people stems from his unique upbringing.

Though son of Xi Zhongxun, a Communist revolutionary and former vice premier, Xi Jinping's youth was not spent in comfort.

Beginning in 1962, when his father was wronged and disgraced, Xi experienced tough times. During the Cultural Revolution he suffered public humiliation and hunger, experienced homelessness and was even held in custody on one occasion.

At the age of 16 he volunteered to live and work in a small village named Liangjiahe in Yanchuan County in northwest China's Shaanxi Province as an "educated youth."

That area, part of the Loess Plateau, was where the Communist revolutionaries, including his father, had risen to found the PRC.

Life there was tough for an urban youth. In the beginning, fleas troubled him so badly he could hardly sleep. In the Shaanxi country-side, he had to do all sorts of hard labor – carrying manure, hauling a coal cart, farming, and building dykes. He was able to walk for 5 km on a mountainous path with two dangling baskets filled with almost 100 kg of wheat on a shoulder-pole. Locals called him "a tough boy."

As time passed, the tough work became easier. Xi grew into a capable and hard-working young man in the eyes of the villagers. Through gaining their trust, he was elected village Party chief.

He led the farmers to reinforce the river bank in the slack season of winter in a bid to prevent erosion, organized a small cooperative of blacksmiths in the village to make farming tools, and built a meth-ane tank for gathering cooking gas, the first in landlocked Shaanxi.

On one occasion he was awarded a motorized tricycle after being named a "model educated youth." However, he exchanged the tricycle for a walking tractor, a flour milling machine, a wheat winnowing machine and a water pump to benefit the villagers.

Although he did not attend school, Xi never stopped reading. He brought a case of books to the village and, as recalled by villagers of Liangjiahe, he was always "reading books as thick as bricks while herd-ing sheep on mountain slopes or under a kerosene lamp at night."

He formed close ties with the villagers during his seven years in the province. After being recommended for enrollment at Tsinghua University in 1975 all the villagers lined up to bid him farewell, and a dozen young men walked more than 30 km to accompany him to the county seat for his trip back to Beijing.

Xi has never forgotten the villagers of his Shaanxi home. Even after he left, he helped the village get access to electric power, build a bridge, and renovate a primary school. When he was Party chief of Fuzhou City he returned to the village, calling on people door to door. He gave some money to senior villagers, and provided schoolchildren with new schoolbags, school supplies and alarm clocks. When a farmer friend got sick, Xi, then a senior provincial official of Fujian, brought him to Fujian at Xi's own expense for better medical treatment.

Years of toiling alongside the villagers allowed him to get to know the countryside and farmers well. Xi has said that the two groups of people who gave him the greatest help in his life were revolutionary veterans and the folk from the Shaanxi village where he once lived.

He arrived at the village as a slightly lost teenager and left as a 22-year-old man determined to do something for the people.

Xi's affection for the common people influenced him in a number of critical decisions. In the 1980s, when many of his contemporaries opted to do business or went to study abroad, Xi gave up a comfortable office job in Beijing and went to work as deputy secretary of the Party committee of the small and poverty-stricken county of Zhengding in north China's Hebei Province. In 1981 the annual per capita income of this county was less than RMB150. At first local people doubted this young man's ability. Xi lived in his office, and had meals at the canteen. He was often seen chatting with people while having a simple meal under a tree. Frequently he rode a bicycle to villages to find out how the farmers fared. Thus he won the local people's trust.

In 1988 he became Party secretary of Ningde Prefecture in southeast China's Fujian Province, one of the poorest parts of the country at that time.

The needs of the people weighed heavy on Xi's heart, and visits to grassroots units were a regular part of his schedule.

During his tenure at Ningde he often traveled for days on mountain roads to reach the farthest corners of the prefecture. The roads were so rough that he had to take breaks on the way to ease the pain in his back. He once walked for nearly five hours on a rugged mountain road to get to a village called Xiadang, which was not accessible by highway. There he received a warm welcome from the villagers, who said that Xi was the highest-ranking official who had ever come to the village.

He also helped thousands of farmers in Ningde renovate dilapidated thatched huts, and built houses for fishermen who used to live on boats.

When working as Party secretary of Fuzhou, capital of Fujian Province, he took the lead in the country in establishing a system for officials to meet petitioners face to face. He introduced the same system in other places where he served later.

At one point he and other senior officials in Fuzhou met with more than 700 petitioners in two days, and solved many of their problems on the spot or set a time limit to find solutions.

Before Chinese New Year in 2005, while working in east China's Zhejiang Province, he visited a coal mine named Changguang, went down nearly 1,000 m underground, then walked more than 1,500 m along a narrow and inclined shaft to visit miners and see their working conditions.

Xi also attaches great importance to communication with the people via news media. He contributed many articles to a popular column of *Zhejiang Daily*, using the pen name Zhe Xin. In his 232 articles, he discussed everyday problems of interest to ordinary people. His writings were very popular and people praised him as "using plain words to discuss big problems."

A mild person, Xi is very tough in disciplining officials and preventing them from acting against the interests of the public. In an investigation into illegal housing construction by officials in Ningde, he grew angry and pounded the table as he asked, "Will we offend a few hundred officials, or will we fail millions of people?" A number of officials in Zhejiang were punished for irregular conduct during his tenure.

Xi is a man of compassion. On each Chinese New Year he sends greetings to his teachers. He provided the only car of the Zhengding Party Committee for the use by war veterans, and built a clinic and a club especially for them. When in Fuzhou, he supported children from poor families to go to school with money from his own pocket.

His work style earned him the nickname "Secretary of the People."

"Officials should love the people in the way they love their parents, work for their benefit and lead them to prosperity," he once said.

Leader with Foresight

Xi regularly shows a strong sense of responsibility towards the future of the nation and has declared his determination to press forward with reform and opening up.

Throughout his political career his foresight and resolve have been apparent, as well as his willingness to sacrifice personal gain and transient fame for a greater cause.

When working in Xiamen, a coastal city in Fujian and one of the special development zones in China, he took charge of drafting the Social and Economic Development Strategy of Xiamen 1985-2000, which laid a solid foundation for the city's urban planning and future economic development. He was put in charge of financial reform, and served as head of an administrative body of the special development zone. Under his leadership, a number of policies and measures to advance the reform and opening up of Xiamen were enacted. Xi was active in enabling Xiamen to be listed as a "city specifically designated in the state plan," which was approved and benefited the city long after he had left the province.

When working in Zhengding, Hebei Province, he saw a potential business opportunity when he learned that the crew of *A Dream of Red Mansions*, a popular classic novel-turned-TV drama, was looking for a filming location.

He proposed building in Zhengding a large residential compound, known as the "Rong Mansion," that featured in the novel. The compound, which was used for TV shooting, later became a tourist attraction. Tourist income from the Rong Mansion exceeded RMB10 million the year it was completed, more than paying back the initial investment. The site has been used as the set for more than 170 movies and TV dramas, with up to 1.3 million tourists every year.

In Fuzhou, after intense deliberation, he and his colleagues devised the Fuzhou Three-, Eight-, and Twenty-year Development Strategy. All the main targets set by the strategy were achieved on time, and a number of enterprises that were set up or brought to Fuzhou when Xi served there remain industry leaders today, playing a significant role in the city's development over the past two decades.

Working as Fujian governor, he was the first in the country to launch a campaign to crack down on food wastage and ensure food security.

In 1999 he took the lead in putting forward the idea of improving IT infrastructure and introducing information technology to help the public. In 2010 Fujian became the first province in China where all hospitals were linked by computer networks, and digital medical cards were issued to everyone for medical care.

In 2002 Fujian launched the reform of the collective forest property right system, the first of its kind in the country.

Also, during Xi's tenure, Fujian was among the first provinces in China to adopt special policies to restore the ecological balance and protect the environment. This has made Fujian the province with the best water and air quality, as well as the best ecology and environment in the country.

In 2002 Xi was transferred to Zhejiang Province, one of the most economically developed provinces in China. There Xi made extensive fact-finding trips and in 2003 formulated and put into practice the strategy of "making full use of eight advantages and implementing eight major measures,"[4] laying a solid foundation for the province's future development.

He initiated local industrial restructuring, transforming the province's extensive and inefficient growth model, and encouraged leading enterprises from outside the province to invest in Zhejiang.

In addition, he proposed a development mode that would give equal weight to both manufacturing and commerce, a mode particularly suited to the local conditions in Zhejiang. He also supported local companies' efforts to expand overseas, as well as business start-ups by ordinary citizens.

At the same time he encouraged cooperation between Zhejiang and neighboring Shanghai and Jiangsu, in order to tap their potential and build an integrated economic powerhouse.

In 2004, under Xi's leadership, Zhejiang made an attempt to improve community-level democracy. Villages set up special committees to supervise the village Party committees and administrative committees on public affairs, a move that was welcomed by the public.

Village supervision committees, which sprang from the Zhejiang model, were later introduced in an amendment to the Organic Law of Villagers' Committees in 2010 by the NPC Standing Committee, the top Chinese legislature.

Xi called on the people of Zhejiang to rely on themselves in developing the local economy. He was fully aware that the people of Zhejiang were business-minded, and had a proud tradition of running businesses. Given that Zhejiang lacked natural resources, people had to work harder and find opportunities in other places such as Shanghai and Jiangsu. A number of measures taken under Xi's leadership enormously promoted the social and economic development not only in Zhejiang but also the whole area of the Yangtze River Delta[5].

Shanghai was Xi's last local post before he was promoted to the central leadership. Despite a relatively short term in the country's financial hub, he left his mark by promoting the economic integration of the Yangtze River Delta and enhancing Shanghai's leading role in the region.

Xi added "enlightened, sagacious, open-minded and modest" to the official wording of the Shanghai City Motto, which previously had simply read "inclusive and sublime." This was intended to capture the essence of the city. Media in Shanghai noted that these modifications helped better present Shanghai to the rest of the world. The changes also attracted attention from further afield.

Only by Hard Work Can We Get to the Fore

"Empty talk harms the country, while hard work makes it flourish," Xi remarked during his visit to "The Road to Rejuvenation" exhibition in Beijing on the 15th day after being elected as the CPC's new helmsman.

To put "hard work" in place, Xi presided over a meeting of the Political Bureau of the CPC Central Committee that adopted "Eight Rules" to improve the Party's conduct and its ties with the people. The rules include more contact with the public, traveling light with a small entourage, using fewer traffic controls, shortening meetings and speeches, and practicing economy. The new rules have elicited a positive response both at home and abroad.

"Only by hard work can we get to the fore," he once commented. He demands concrete efforts to tackle issues that affect people most. He believes that without hard work the best blueprint will be of no use.

When he served in Zhengding County, Xi said that developing its human resources was the key to poverty reduction and local economic development. He invited professionals to the county and drew up recruitment advertisements for talented people from across the country.

On a winter's day in 1983 he traveled to Shijiazhuang, the provincial seat of Hebei, to invite an expert in medicinal cosmetics to work in Zhengding. Without a full address for the expert, he went from door to door asking for help, and finally found him that evening by shouting his name in the street near his home. Xi and the expert talked until midnight, and the man finally accepted the offer. He later created more than RMB300,000 in revenues for the county in his first year.

That same year Xi decided to publish a document listing nine ways to recruit talented people, something that was rare at the time and became a front-page story in the *Hebei Daily*. He wrote more than 100 letters to experts and scholars, as well as to colleges and research institutions, and paid visits to dozens of experts. Within two years, Zhengding attracted 683 professionals and hired 53 well-known experts as economic counselors.

Together with his colleague Lü Yulan, then deputy Party secretary of Zhengding, and in the face of strong opposition, Xi told superior authorities about the excessive burden faced by the county due to compulsory grain purchases. The issue was eventually resolved and the heavy burden on the local people was lifted.

In Ningde, Xi was also pragmatic and realistic. He pooled resources to encourage cultivation of the large yellow croaker, a local specialty, and thereby greatly increased the income of local fishermen.

He also ordered Party and government offices to be easily accessible to the people. When serving in Fuzhou, he advocated the principle of "special procedures for special issues, and do things right away" to make government agencies more efficient. This principle attracted numerous companies from Taiwan, and helped boost the local economy. In 1992 he took the lead in the country to apply the management mode of foreign-funded enterprises to 12 large and medium-sized state-owned enterprises as a pilot project. He also proposed the compilation of two handbooks on government work, helping local residents and overseas businesspeople in their work and daily life.

In 2000 Xi launched an initiative throughout Fujian to make government agencies more efficient. He proposed changes in government functions and procedures to reduce the amount of documentation that required government approval. By the end of 2001 no less than 606 items had been eliminated – more than 40 percent of the total.

In 2001 Fujian became the first province in China to formulate and implement a policy aimed at making government affairs public. Detailed implementation rules were made to require all counties, cities and districts in the province to make their administrative work transparent. A warning system was established to tighten oversight over all government agencies. In addition, a performance complaint center was set up so that people could voice their criticisms and suggestions.

In August 2002 Xi published an article in a major national newspaper on the "Jinjiang experience," which advocated market-orientated development, stressed the role of local advantages, called for improvement of government services, and emphasized the importance of the private economy in the development of the county. Also in 2002, he published another article publicizing Nanping City's experience of sending officials and technicians to work in villages. This practice was later extended from Nanping throughout the province, enhancing ties between officials and farmers, and helping officials to become more oriented towards grassroots results.

In Zhejiang, Xi stressed provincial development in the fields of public security, the environment, culture, the rule of law and the marine economy.

To achieve these goals he carried out individual case studies and attended to general planning. In order to understand how individual localities were affected by provincial policies he paid five visits to a mountain village called Xiajiang in underdeveloped Chun'an County in southwest Zhejiang in less than two years. Located deep in the mountains, the village is some 60 km from the county seat. During each visit Xi chatted with villagers at their homes and in the fields. On one occasion he inspected the construction of a methane tank. He said that thirty years earlier, when he had lived in a village, he had been an expert in building methane tanks. Xi encouraged villagers to manage the tanks properly and make the village a role model in making use of methane.

He paid special attention to the marine economy. In December 2002 he put forward the objective of building Zhejiang into a province with a strong marine economy, and followed up his general proposal with specific plans and measures to realize this objective. The marine economy in Zhejiang has since developed quickly, with an annual growth of 19.3 percent. By 2005 it accounted for nearly 8 percent of the GDP of Zhejiang.

Xi pushed for the integration of the Ningbo and Zhoushan harbors. In 2006 the joint Ningbo-Zhoushan harbor recorded a cargo throughput of 420 million tons, ranking second in China and among the world's top three.

He also pressed on with the construction of the Hangzhou Bay Bridge, an iconic sea-crossing in China, and at one time the world's longest sea bridge.

In 2003 Xi proposed that rural communities should be managed more like urban communities, and every effort should be made to narrow the urban-rural gap in quality of life.

Zhejiang realized its development targets one after another during Xi's tenure. The province had the highest rating in ecology and the environment among all provincial-level regions in 2005. In 2006 almost 95 percent of the public were satisfied with the province's public security, making Zhejiang one of the safest provinces in the country.

During his service in Zhejiang, the province's GDP exceeded RMB1 trillion in 2004, and its annual per capita GDP exceeded US$3,000 in 2005 and stood at nearly US$4,000 in 2006. The province ranked fourth in sustainable development in 2006, after Shanghai, Beijing and Tianjin.

Furthermore, all the counties and townships in the province that had been officially classified as "poverty-stricken" were raised out of poverty during that period.

In 2007 Xi was appointed secretary of the CPC Shanghai Municipal Committee.

In the first month after his appointment Xi began research projects into standards of living, development, the Shanghai World Expo, and the fight against corruption. Despite difficulties and obstacles in the metropolis, Xi convened the Ninth Shanghai Municipal Congress of the CPC, greatly invigorating local officials, rebuilding Shanghai's image, and setting forth a blueprint for Shanghai for the next five years.

Xi always believes that a county Party chief should visit all the villages in the county, a city Party chief all the towns and townships in the city, and a provincial Party chief all the counties, cities and districts in the province.

He visited all the villages in Zhengding. In Ningde, he visited nine counties during the first three months, and traveled to most of the remaining townships later on. After being transferred to Zhejiang in 2002, he visited all 90 counties in just over a year. During his tenure in Shanghai, he visited all 19 districts and counties in seven months. After he came to work with the central leadership, he visited all the 31 provinces, autonomous regions and municipalities directly under the central government on the mainland.

Man with a World Vision

During a recent meeting with foreign experts working in China, Xi said that China, as a responsible country, will not only manage its own affairs, but also properly handle its relations with the rest of the world, so as to foster a more favorable external environment and make a greater contribution to world peace and development.

"China needs to know more about the rest of the world, and the rest of the world also needs to know more about China," Xi said. Whether working at the local level or with the central leadership, Xi has always valued international exchanges and making foreign friends. He takes every opportunity to meet foreign guests visiting China.

Before Xi came to work with the central leadership he had visited over 60 countries, and met a great number of foreign visitors. In the past five years he has traveled to more than 40 countries and regions across five continents and has had extensive contacts with people of all walks of life. He explains frankly and honestly to foreign friends how the Chinese people view their own country and the outside world, and is willing to listen to them as well. In the eyes of many foreign dignitaries, Xi is a confident, pragmatic, sagacious and good-humored leader.

He often tells foreign visitors that the global community is becoming increasingly integrated, and shares a common destiny. China's continuous rapid development depends on world peace and development. It also provides opportunities for other countries to develop, so together we can achieve mutually beneficial results and share benefits through mutual respect and pragmatic cooperation.

At the World Peace Forum organized by Tsinghua University in July 2012, Xi noted that a country must let others develop while seeking its own development, must let others feel secure while seeking its own security, and must let others live better while aspiring to live better itself. In a meeting with Lee Kuan Yew[6] in Singapore, Xi said that not every strong country would seek hegemony. China would stick to the path of peaceful development, a mutually beneficial strategy and opening up, and the pledge of never seeking hegemony. China would pass its commitment from generation to generation.

Xi's foreign visits have sent out a signal that countries should work together to establish a more equal and balanced global partnership, so as to safeguard the common interests of all of humanity and make the earth a better place.

During his five-day visit to the US in 2012, Xi attended 27 events and engaged in exchanges with President Obama and other US politicians, and the public alike. "As long as both sides grasp the thread of common interests, China and the US can explore a path of new partnership in which major powers live in harmony, engage in positive interaction, and achieve mutually beneficial cooperation." His remarks elicited positive feedback from many in the US.

In a recent meeting with former US President Jimmy Carter, Xi called for more "positive energy" for the China-US partnership.

During his visit to Russia, Xi stressed the importance of developing bilateral relations between the two countries. China's strategic partnership of coordination with Russia has become the closest, most dynamic and most profound between major powers, and developing positive relations with Russia is always a priority for China's foreign affairs. Xi attended the second meeting of the dialogue mechanism between the Chinese and Russian ruling parties and had extensive and in-depth discussions with leaders of various parties in Russia, further strengthening Sino-Russian relations.

Xi highly values relations with developing countries. He once said that we would take consolidating and developing relations with developing countries as the aim and basis of China's foreign policy.

In South Africa, Xi attended the fourth plenary session of the China-South Africa Binational Commission, looking forward, together with the South African side, to a bright future for bilateral cooperation.

In a speech delivered at a seminar marking the 10th anniversary of the Forum on China-Africa Cooperation (FOCAC), Xi underscored China's friendship with Africa, highlighting that "a friend in need is a friend indeed."

In Saudi Arabia, he stated that a more prosperous and open China would bring great development opportunities to the Middle East and the Gulf countries.

In Chile, speaking of the relationship over the next decade, he proposed that China and Latin America should be good partners in the fields of politics, economics, culture and international affairs.

Xi has been pragmatic and efficient on the international stage. In one single day, while attending the celebrations for the 150th anniversary of the unification of Italy, Xi exchanged ideas with leaders from more than 20 countries and international organizations. During his visit to Germany and four other European countries, Xi attended five signing ceremonies for economic and trade agreements and six economic and trade forums, and signed 93 cooperation agreements involving a total of US$7.4 billion.

Xi has also emphasized the role of cultural exchanges in the building of a harmonious world. Addressing attendants at the Frankfurt Book Fair in 2009, he remarked that through exchanges between different cultures, people from different countries had come to know Confucius from China, Goethe from Germany and Shakespeare from Britain. Promoting international cultural exchanges created important momentum for human progress and peaceful development, he said.

During his visit to Russia, he stood side by side with Vladimir Putin in the Kremlin as they launched the "Year of the Chinese Language" in Russia. He said in his address: "Culture is enriched, hearts are joined together, and friendship is deepened through exchanges."

Xi has a talent for drawing wisdom from Chinese culture and presenting ideas clearly in a straightforward and humorous way. During his US visit, he borrowed a line from the theme song of the popular Chinese TV drama *Monkey King* to diffuse the gravity of the bilateral issue. "The road is right under our feet," he said, when describing the "unprecedented" relations between China and the US, presenting the image of a confident and forward-looking Chinese leader.

When facing questions about human rights in China, he is forthright: "There is no best, only better." He takes the view that every country's situation is different, and every path is different. "Whether the shoe fits or not, only the wearer knows."

Amity between peoples is the key to sound relations between states. Xi has said the level of state-to-state friendship depends on relations between their peoples. He once light-heartedly remarked to foreign ministry officials on a diplomatic trip that life lay in motion, and diplomacy lay in activity. In other words, diplomats should travel widely and make more bosom friends.

During his visit to Laos, Xi arranged a special meeting with the late Lao leader Quinim Pholsena's children, who had lived and studied in Beijing. He joined them in recalling their days at Beijing's Bayi School. He said that Pholsena's second son bore the nickname "Chubby Boy." This made everybody laugh.

During his US visit, Xi traveled to Iowa to join a dozen old acquaintances for tea and a chat at a house in an Iowa farm community. Most of the people at the gathering were friends Xi had made during a 1985 visit to Iowa as a member of an agricultural research delegation.

In Russia, he visited a children's center which had taken in Chinese students affected by the devastating Wenchuan earthquake of 2008, and expressed his gratitude to the staff.

He kicked off a game of Gaelic football in Dublin's Croke Park when visiting Ireland and watched an NBA game in the US. The media welcomed such activities as evidence of his cordial image.

"He succeeded in demonstrating not only his personal charisma and bearing, but also the image and charm of China," an overseas media outlet commented.

Son of a Revolutionary Family; a Good Husband

Xi Jinping's father Xi Zhongxun was a Party and state leader. At the age of 21 the senior Xi served as chairman of the government of the Shaanxi-Gansu Border Region, a CPC revolutionary base in the 1930s, and was called by Mao Zedong a "leader of the people."

Xi Zhongxun began to suffer political persecution in 1962, which continued for 16 years. However, he never gave in to adversity but tried his best to help clear the names of others who had been persecuted. Once the Cultural Revolution had come to an end, he served as first secretary of the CPC Guangdong Provincial Committee, at the forefront of China's reform and opening-up initiative, making an important contribution to the establishment of the special economic zones in the province and their rapid development.

Xi's mother Qi Xin, nearly 90 years of age, is also a veteran revolutionary and Party member. A dutiful son, Xi often strolls and chats with his mother, holding her by the hand, and regularly makes time to dine with her.

The Xi family has a tradition of being strict with children and living a simple life. Xi Zhongxun believed that if a senior Party official wanted to discipline others, he should begin first with himself and his family. Xi Jinping and his younger brother used to wear clothes and shoes handed down from their elder sisters. After Xi Jinping became a leading official, his mother called a family meeting to ban the siblings from engaging in any business in the areas where Xi Jinping worked.

Xi Jinping has carried on his family's tradition and has been strict with his own family. Wherever he worked, he told his family not to do business there or do anything in his name, otherwise he "would be ruthless." Whether in Fujian, Zhejiang or Shanghai, he pledged at official meetings that no one was allowed to seek personal benefit through making use of his name, and welcomed supervision in this regard.

Xi married Peng Liyuan, a renowned folk song singer and popular soprano singer of opera. In 1980 Peng caused quite a stir when attending a national art performance in Beijing, representing Shandong Province.

She was the first person in China to obtain a master's degree in national vocal music. She is a representative of contemporary national vocal music and one of the founders of the school of national vocal music.

Her most famous works include *On the Fields of Hope*, *People from My Village*, *We Are Yellow River and Mount Taishan*, and *Rivers and Mountains*. She has won many top awards in national vocal music competitions such as China's Golden Disk Award and the State Audio-Video Award.

She has played leading roles in Chinese national operas such as *The White-haired Girl*, *Grief at Dawn*, *The Party's Daughter*, and *Ode to Heroine Mulan*, among others. She has also won the highest theatrical award in China, the Plum Blossom Prize, and the highest performance art award, the Wenhua Prize.

Peng attributes her accomplishments to the people and said that she should contribute all her talent to the people. Over more than three decades, she has given hundreds of free performances for people from all walks of life across the country. These included performances in impoverished mountain areas, coastal areas, oilfields, mines and barracks, as well as in deserts and on the snowy plateau. She also performed in Wenchuan after the devastating earthquake of 2008, in Beijing's Xiaotangshan after the SARS outbreak in 2003, and in flood-hit Jiujiang in Jiangxi Province in 1998.

To better introduce Chinese national vocal music and national opera to the outside world, Peng was the first to play a solo concert in Singapore in 1993. She has also represented China in performances in more than 50 countries and regions, becoming a world-renowned cultural ambassador for China.

She produced and played the leading role in the opera *Ode to Heroine Mulan*, which was performed at New York City's Lincoln Center for the Performing Arts and at the Vienna State Opera House in Austria.

Peng is currently shifting her focus from performance to education, aiming to train new singers and produce new masterpieces.

Peng is very much devoted to work for the public good. She is a WHO Goodwill Ambassador for Tuberculosis and HIV/AIDS, a national AIDS prevention advocate, and an ambassador both for the prevention of juvenile delinquency and for tobacco control. At a recent World AIDS Day activity, raising awareness about AIDS, she was called "Mama Peng" by AIDS orphans.

Xi and Peng fell in love in 1986, and married the same year. Although they were often separated by work commitments, they have understood and supported each other and continuously shown their devotion to each other.

As a member of the People's Liberation Army, Peng was often tasked with staging performances in remote areas. These tours sometimes kept her on the road for two to three months at a time. Always concerned about his wife, Xi would phone her before bedtime almost every night, no matter how late it was.

On Chinese New Year's Eve, Peng would often perform at the Spring Festival Gala presented by China Central Television. Xi would make dumplings while watching the show and wait for her return to have the family feast.

In the eyes of Peng, Xi is a good husband and a good father. She always shows care and consideration for him. Peng takes every opportunity to be together with her husband, cooking dishes of different styles for him.

To Peng, Xi is both a unique and a very ordinary person. He favors home-made cooking in the Shaanxi and Shandong cuisines, and also enjoys a drink during parties or with friends. He likes swimming, mountaineering, and watching basketball, football and boxing matches. Sometimes he stays up late watching sports on television.

The couple have a daughter, Xi Mingze. Mingze in Chinese connotes "living an honest life and being a useful person to society," which is their expectation for her and also a symbol of their simple family style.

Notes

[1] See note 24, p. 22.

[2] The "two sessions" refer to the annual sessions of the National People's Congress and the National Committee of the Chinese People's Political Consultative Conference.

[3] See note 5, p. 265.

[4] In July 2003 the fourth plenary (enlarged) session of the 11th CPC Zhejiang Provincial Committee proposed to make full use of the province's eight advantages for development and implement eight measures for its future growth.

[5] The Yangtze River Delta is one of China's major economic regions, mainly covering Shanghai and the provinces of Jiangsu and Zhejiang.

[6] Lee Kuan Yew (1923-2015) was founder and first premier (1965-1990) of the Republic of Singapore.

Index

图书在版编目 (CIP) 数据

习近平谈治国理政 . 第一卷 : 英文 / 习近平著 ; 英文翻译组译 . – 2 版 .

– 北京 : 外文出版社 , 2018.1

ISBN 978-7-119-11394-4

I. ①习… II. ①习… ②英… III. ①习近平 – 讲话

– 学习参考资料 – 英文②中国特色社会主义 – 社会主义建设

模式 – 学习参考资料 – 英文 IV. ① D2-0 ② D616

中国版本图书馆 CIP 数据核字 (2018) 第 016679 号

习近平谈治国理政
第 一 卷

© 外文出版社有限责任公司

外文出版社有限责任公司出版发行

（中国北京百万庄大街 24 号）

邮政编码：100037

http://www.flp.com.cn

北京盛通印刷股份有限公司印刷

2014 年 10 月（小 16 开）第 1 版

2018 年 3 月（小 16 开）第 2 版

2018 年 3 月第 2 版第 1 次印刷

2019 年 8 月第 2 版第 6 次印刷

（英文）

ISBN 978-7-119-11394-4

08000（平）